KT-116-538

Tony Geraghty

Who Dares Wins

The Story of the Special Air Service
1950–1982

Fontana/Collins

ACKNOWLEDGEMENTS

Thanks are due to the many friends, including some companions in sport parachuting, who gave unstintingly of their time and energy in helping the writing of this book. In large measure, it is their sweat that I have 'recycled'.

I must also thank all those mentioned in the Bibliography, but I am especially grateful to the following authors and their publishers for permission to quote brief passages: *The Regiments Depart: The British Army, 1945–70,* by G. Blaxland, and *The Special Air Service,* by P. Warner (both published by William Kimber Ltd); *Bunch of Five,* by F. Kitson, and *Last Post: Aden 1964–67,* by J. Paget (both published by Faber & Faber Ltd); *The Hilton Assignment,* by P. Seale and M. McConville (published by Maurice Temple Smith Ltd); *Oman: The Making of the Modern State,* by J. Townsend (published by Croom Helm Ltd); and *Congo Mercenary,* by M. Hoare (published by Robert Hale Ltd).

First published in Great Britain by Arms and Armour Press 1980
First issued in Fontana Paperbacks 1981
Eleventh impression February 1983
Twelfth impression, with additional chapter 10 and revisions, July 1983

Set in V.I.P. Baskerville

Made and printed in Great Britain by
William Collins Sons & Co. Ltd, Glasgow

Who Dares Wins

Tony Geraghty, ex-defence correspondent of the *Sunday Times*, has covered warfare and terrorism in Nigeria, Ulster, Jordan and Holland. He has made a special study of terrorism and with Sir Robert Mark and others is a co-author of *Ten Years of Terrorism*.

Contents

List of Maps

Illustrations

Photographs of Sergeant Hanna, 'Squire' Perkins, Aden and
Dhofar have been supplied from regimental sources; the Embassy
siege photograph by the Press Association (Martin Cleaver).

Introduction

In his textbook on guerrilla warfare, *The War of the Flea*, Robert Taber observes that if there is anything new about such warfare, it is only in its modern political application. He continues: 'The guerrilla is a political insurgent, the conscious agent of revolution: his military role, while vital, is only incidental to his political mission . . . the overthrow of the government and the destruction of the existing . . . system.' There are echoes here of Clausewitz's dictum that war is the continuation of 'political intercourse' by other means. Of course, all armies are political and some are more political than others, but the traditional view, as Clausewitz himself expressed it, is that 'the political element does not sink deep into the details of war. Sentries are not planted, patrols do not make their rounds from political considerations. . . .' One of the characteristics of the Special Air Service Regiment which makes it a unique military force is that it does just that. Like the guerrilla army, the modern SAS uses force sparingly, as a precise cutting tool for political policy, and then only as one weapon among many in the essential business of shaping perceptions: the enemy's and that of the civil population.

The effect of its success in post-war years (see the campaigns of Borneo and Oman) carries with it the danger that it may reinforce the belief of ambitious politicians in a favourite fantasy concerning military matters, namely that armed conflict can be fine-tuned. Not surprisingly, therefore, the SAS is sometimes hoisted by its own success and is pitchforked into a campaign for which it is ill-prepared, such as Northern

1

Ireland, or one which, politically, is already a lost cause, such as Aden. On such occasions, the lament may be sometimes aired in the regimental journal that this or that operation is not in keeping with the SAS role. Precisely what that role is, is also a subject of continuous speculation and controversy among commentators outside military circles, some of them highly partisan, as well as within the Bradbury Lines Barracks and the Special Forces Club. The external critique ranges from the hagiographic style of 1950s Fleet Street journalism to the naive dogmatism of the post-1960s New Left. Each of these extreme views overlooks – or is ignorant of – a second peculiarity of the Regiment: its ability to evolve to meet a given task, even if this means discarding centuries of military tradition.

The romantic beginnings of the SAS during the Second World War have naturally caught the imagination of most writers, with the result that all except the participants tend to overlook the fact that the Regiment was founded on a military heresy. The heresy lies in the deliberate rejection by Colonel David Stirling, whose pencil-written proposal from a hospital bed in Cairo started it all, of the traditional concept of military leadership. In his contribution to *The World History of Paratroopers* several years ago, he explained: 'Strategic operations demand, for the achievement of success, a total exploitation of surprise and of guile. Accordingly, a bedrock principle of the Regiment was its organization into modules or sub-units of four men. Hitherto, battalion strength formations, whether Airborne formations or Commandos, had no basic sub-unit smaller than a section or a troop consisting of an NCO plus eight or ten men and it was the NCO who had to do most of the thinking for what we disrespectfully referred to as "the thundering herd" behind him.

'In the SAS each of the four men was trained to a high general level of proficiency in the whole range of the SAS capability and, additionally, each man was trained to have at least one special expertise according to his aptitude. In carrying out an operation – often in pitch-dark – each SAS man in each module was exercising his own individual perception and judgement at full stretch.'

The number four, as Stirling has explained to the author, was deliberately chosen to avoid the emergence of a leader in the orthodox sense. The implications of this decision have affected regimental thinking ever since. Officers joining the SAS do so only after they have faced a barrage of withering criticism from Other Ranks, and restructured their own thinking about the men with whom they will soldier. The obvious danger, that discipline within the unit will break down, has not only been recognized: it was experienced in some terrifying episodes during the Malayan campaign. But before and after that time, the ruthless selection of soldiers who motivate and, therefore, discipline themselves, has virtually eliminated this risk. A further result has been to foster a unique military democracy within the SAS in which, if he succeeds, a man exchanges his former class and even identity for membership of a caste as binding as any family, and expulsion from which, therefore, becomes the only sanction he really fears.

In the paper cited above, Stirling described the Regiment's philosophy in the following way: 'From the start, the SAS Regiment has had some firmly held tenets from which we never depart. They can be summarized as follows:

1. The unrelenting pursuit of excellence.
2. The maintaining of the highest standards of discipline in all aspects of the daily life of the SAS soldier. . . . We always reckoned that a high standard of self-discipline in each soldier was the only effective foundation for Regimental discipline. . . .
3. The SAS brooks no sense of class and, particularly, not among the wives. This might sound a bit portentous but it epitomizes the SAS philosophy.

'The traditional idea of a crack regiment was one officered by the aristocracy and, indeed, these regiments deservedly won great renown. . . . In the SAS we share with the Brigade of Guards a deep respect for quality but we have an entirely different outlook.

'We believe, as did the ancient Greeks who originated the word "aristocracy", that every man with the right attitude and talents, regardless of birth and riches, has a capacity in his own lifetime of reaching that status in its true sense; in fact, in our SAS context, an individual soldier might prefer to go on serving as an NCO rather than . . . leave the regiment in order to obtain an officer's commission. All ranks in the SAS are of "one company" in which a sense of class is both alien and ludicrous.'

The four-man group has another, intensely domestic, side effect. This is that two couples emerge, sharing their lives for months on end in conditions of isolation. The bond thus created is the kinship of the family. Stokes and Lane, who climbed Everest, survived a night near the summit, and massaged each other in order to survive, despite snow blindness and frostbite, were once asked if they talked much while they climbed together. 'Not much,' was the reply. 'After all this time together we don't have much to say to each other.' The same rapport translates into military action. During one furious firefight in Oman, which began, uncharacteristically, with the SAS having fallen victim to enemy ambush, a veteran of the Regiment continued the domestic quarrel with which the two had started the day. He paused between bursts of gunfire to tell his companion: 'Furthermore, you burnt the bloody dinner last night!'

Out of these peculiar elements – anarchy (in the dictionary sense of 'a harmonious condition of society in which law is abolished as unnecessary'); elitism; meritocracy; insularity – has emerged a very special force indeed: a warrior caste born into a century which regards military virtues as, at best, an anachronism. The caste has succeeded largely because of the use of its skill with non-violent weapons, in preference to, say, indiscriminate bombing by B-52s.

But of course, no one can live up to such standards consistently for a lifetime. Few even achieve them for long, which is why the number of operational SAS soldiers is very small. Another potent reason is the sheer danger of SAS undertakings, in which the intelligent man perceives the imminence of his own expendability. As one regimental veteran explained to the author, 'The reason why few of our people become mercenaries is that after regular operations with the SAS, they've usually had enough to last a lifetime.'

David Stirling, the man who started it all, was a Cambridge-educated Scots Guardsman who joined one of the first Army Commando units in 1940, having been sent down from university. Stirling, 6 feet 5 inches tall and an enthusiastic climber who had explored the Rockies, was ideal Commando material. He joined a unit later known as Layforce, after the name of its leader, Robert Laycock. Layforce was sent to the Middle East with the object of capturing Rhodes; instead, because of conflicting operational demands, it was scattered from Tobruk in Libya, to Syria. One of Stirling's brother officers in this organization was an Oxford graduate and rowing blue, Jock Lewes, of the Welsh Guards. Faced with the disbandment of Layforce, because of its need of ships and equipment which were simply not available, the two men mulled over other ways of hitting Germany's extended supply lines in the Western Desert.

In somewhat enigmatic circumstances, a consignment of fifty parachutes on its way to India fell off the back of a movement order in Alexandria, into the hands of Lewes. Soon afterwards Lewes, Stirling and two others – none of them a trained parachutist – rigged up their own static line system in an ancient Valentia aircraft, using seats in the plane as strong points. The design of the aircraft was such that as the parachute canopies deployed, some of them would certainly snag the tail-plane. This is what happened to Stirling. The accident tore several gores out of the canopy and his sixteen-stone weight increased the acceleration of his descent. He crashed on to rock-hard ground and injured his back so severely that both legs were paralysed for a time.

While he was in hospital, Stirling drafted a long memorandum, laboriously written in pencil, wherein he argued that strategic raids – that is, deep penetration operations behind enemy lines – did not require the ponderous naval back-up of full-blown Commando assaults. He did not dwell on the obvious alternative, penetration across the desert, because this was already being carried out with great skill, for reconnaissance and Intelligence purposes, by the Long Range Desert Group. Instead, Stirling proposed using parachutist saboteurs to inflict a level of damage on enemy airfields equivalent to that of a Commando force twenty times greater.

After two months' medical treatment, Stirling was able to move about on crutches. He decided, notwithstanding this disability, to deliver his plan in person to the Commander-in-Chief, Middle East, General Sir Claude Auchinleck. It was highly improbable that the C-in-C would grant an audience to a mere subaltern; even less likely that the plan would work its way through the out-trays of the courtiers at GHQ Cairo, so Stirling decided to make an unannounced visit.

A high wire fence surrounded the headquarters area. Leaving his crutches on the outside of the fence, Stirling hauled himself painfully over, and dropped into the compound. He then walked gingerly into the main administrative block, barging into various offices and their occupants, before discovering that Auchinleck was out. By now, the internal security staff had been alerted to his presence. Stirling found the deputy C-in-C, Lieutenant-General Neil Ritchie, just before they found him. He lurched into Ritchie's office, saluted the surprised general, and said quietly: 'I think you'd better look at this, sir.' Ritchie scanned the paper and subsequently recalled Stirling for a discussion of the scheme with Auchinleck. Soon afterwards, in his new rank of captain, Stirling was given permission to recruit sixty-six men from the remnants of Layforce Commando.

One of those who ran into Stirling during those early days in Cairo was the brave, debonair Fitzroy Maclean, later to become a brigadier and an MP. As Maclean tells it, Stirling propositioned him with a persuasiveness that recurs throughout the Regiment's history. ' "Why not join the Special Air Service Brigade?" he said. I asked what it was. He explained it was not really a Brigade; it was more like a Platoon. It was only called a Brigade to confuse the enemy. But it was a good thing to be in. . . . We could operate in the desert first of all; then in southern and eastern Europe. Small parties could be dropped there by parachute and then picked up on the coast by submarine. There were endless possibilities. It sounded promising. I said I should be delighted to join.'

What followed is now familiar military history, and is merely summarized here: the disaster of the first parachute operation, unwisely carried out during a vigorous sandstorm in which aircraft were lost and men swept away; followed by collaboration with the Long Range Desert Group to destroy more than 100 Luftwaffe aircraft on the ground within a few weeks, with a unit now only twenty strong. This led, by August 1942, to a re-expansion of the unit with the addition of French paratroops and the provision of specially armed jeeps, and formal regimental status as First SAS Regiment. Before the Desert War was over, the SAS had destroyed nearly 400 German aircraft and great quantities of other war material. Their success elicited a personal order from Adolf Hitler which proclaimed: 'These men are dangerous. They must be hunted down and destroyed at all costs.'

Part of the price the Regiment paid for this success was the capture of Stirling himself near Gabes, in Tunisia. After several attempts to escape, he was put into Colditz prisoner-of-war camp for the rest of the war. There he spent his time drafting a paper in which he proposed using British and American special forces to establish bases in China from which to attack Japan. (After the European war, and before the atomic bomb induced Japanese surrender, he was actively preparing for this operation in Britain.)

By the time Stirling was captured, his brother Bill was commanding a second SAS regiment engaged in raids in Sicily and on the Italian coast. First SAS was now commanded by the former Irish rugby international, 'Paddy' Mayne, one of David Stirling's original desert team, who joined forces with an Army and Royal Marine Commando force to seize the Adriatic port of Termoli in October 1943.

The impact of this operation, at a time when the German Army was holding Rome and looking south, was to switch an entire enemy division away from its chosen operational area. Philip Warner, the official SAS historian, records: 'Mayne was observed to have conducted a minor war single-handed. He was observed to have killed twelve Germans early in the fighting and then, when a truck-load of men – 29 in all – had been killed by a German shell he went off on an expedition of his own. He gave no account of what had occurred, but it was thought that he had exacted some adequate revenge for the incident.'

Another adventurous spirit was Philip Pinckney, whose capacity for converting to instant food anything which crawled, hopped, walked and grew, made him an object of speculation even in the SAS. After taking part in the Sicily operation he was parachuted on to the Brenner Pass, the railway tunnel of which he blew up. After being captured he was handed over to the Gestapo and executed.

In addition to the activity in Sicily – where the Regiment prepared the way for the Allied invasion – and mainland Italy, its related Special Boat Service was engaging in intensive raiding activity throughout the Aegean, Greece and the Adriatic. Those who distinguished themselves included Anders Lassen, the Danish SAS major who won a posthumous VC while in support of a Royal Marine Commando attack on Lake Comacchio a month before the war in Europe ended. From Italy, the two regular SAS regiments were brought back to England in March 1944 and augmented by similar Free French and Belgian squadrons, plus a long-distance communications unit, the combined force becoming 1 SAS Brigade.

In Europe, the SAS resisted attempts by orthodox military planners to use them for short-term, pinprick raids, and it was agreed that they should parachute into occupied France and remain there as training and supply units for the Resistance, and to conduct a sabotage campaign on their own account. Colonel Brian Franks, one of the commanders, explained that 'a small reconnaissance party with wireless was dropped by parachute first – sometimes "blind", sometimes with the aid of flares and torches provided by the French Resistance.

'If the report of the advance party was satisfactory, it was quickly reinforced first numerically and later, if the terrain suited, armoured jeeps were dropped. . . . The bases were resupplied most efficiently by the RAF.' (Soon after D-day there were forty-three such bases spread across France from Brittany to the Vosges.)

'With the bases established, small parties, generally on Stirling's module of four, were dispatched to harass enemy communications in every way open to them. Roads were mined, railway lines blown up and convoys of soft transport were ambushed. Bombing targets were reported to the RAF.

'All SAS troops engaged in France were briefed to arm and train any formed bodies of the French Resistance. In certain areas this was carried out with success, but in others it was found impossible to train them. . . . This applied, too, to the population of many small villages close to SAS bases. The enemy reacted with utter ruthlessness, deporting or shooting the males and burning houses. This unpleasant factor had to be taken into account when planning operations.'

It was not until after the war that the unpleasant fate of SAS prisoners-of-war became fully apparent. Between August and October of 1944, a total of twenty-six of the Regiment were taken prisoner in the Vosges mountains and were last heard of alive in a prison camp about fifty miles from Strasbourg. They were not there when the camp was taken by Allied forces. With the end of the war, in May of the following year, a team of British army investigators made efforts to discover what had happened to them. The team concluded that 'the evidence of torture before death by shooting is conclusive concerning nine of them, and points to most of the others having being treated with the same brutality. . . . One man found dead had been beaten by the Germans until the bones of his back showed. Another was found hanging over a bonfire, and had been burned to death.'

The military impact of the SAS in France was, if anything,

even more formidable than it had been in the Western Desert and Italy. One considered judgement is that the disorganization of German resistance in depth after General Patton's break out of Normandy, and the swift seizure of Paris by the Third Army which followed this, was largely attributable to the combined work of the SAS and the French Maquisards.

The direct SAS assaults were damaging enough in themselves – for example, in the destruction of a train carrying 100,000 gallons of petrol – but it seems plausible to conclude that the pin-pointing of targets on behalf of the RAF bomber force was strategically decisive. As one study of the Normandy invasion recalls, during the months before the landings, 'The strategic bomber forces imperceptibly shifted their attacks from targets deep in occupied Europe to objectives related more closely to the landings. Their intent was to isolate the "Overlord" (invasion plan) lodgement area and to make it difficult, if not impossible, for the Germans to send reinforcements to the landing area; to this end, they destroyed bridges across the Seine, railway yards and other transportation facilities. They also struck coastal defences and other important installations useful to the Germans.' The SAS operated mainly in Central France, concentrating on the transport system, with similar effect.

On 8 September 1944, General F. A. M. Browning, ADC to Montgomery, told the Regiment: 'The operations you have carried out have had more effect in hastening the disintegration of the German Seventh and Fifth Armies than any other single effort in the army. . . . You have done a job of work which . . . no other troops in the world could have done.'

In the Low Countries, Germany and Italy, the SAS regiments were in action until the end of the European war. Mayne won a third bar to his DSO in Schleswig-Holstein only weeks before hostilities ended; returned home to his law practice in Northern Ireland and died in a motor accident in 1955. After a brief operation in Norway to disarm thousands of Wehrmacht soldiers, the wartime regiments were disbanded in October 1945.

This book is concerned with the post-war SAS Regiment, from its inauspicious beginnings in Malaya until the present day. If there is a consistent theme here, it is that the Regiment is a success, though the reader will reach his own judgement about that. The measurement of success in such a context is largely a matter of educated guesswork, rendered difficult by the increasing secrecy surrounding SAS operations during the last fifteen years or so; ameliorated somewhat by the Regiment's characteristic self-criticism.

Some of the achievements are so obvious as to seem trite. First, the Regiment has survived as a permanent corps of the British Army, and the smallest. It is the only one of its kind to have done so. The rest – the Long Range Desert Group, Popski's Private Army, the Army Commando – were all consigned to the history books long ago. Secondly, it has evolved as a uniquely effective arm of counter-revolutionary warfare in an increasingly sensitive political climate, internationally and domestically. In an age when great powers avoid direct conflict, preferring to fight their wars by proxy in 'low intensity' campaigns, it has exercised its strategic option in a new way, by choosing as its battleground the British equivalent of Vietnam – in Malaya, Borneo and Oman – but with a vastly different outcome, proving that one dedicated soldier can achieve results beyond the reach of squadrons of B-52 bombers. In doing so, it has suffered minimal casualties and inflicted on its enemies only sufficient damage to achieve a given result.

Its successes have also profoundly influenced the evolution of post-war British strategy. The pioneering use of the SAS for a few critical months in an obscure campaign in Northern Oman in 1958–9 arrested the idea that nuclear weapons were the answer to all Britain's defence problems, and almost certainly inspired the strategically mobile 'fire brigades' which would influence defence policy for ten years. The full importance of SAS intervention in the Omani Dhofar war in 1970 did not become apparent to the outside world until the Soviet invasion of Afghanistan in 1979 (see Chapter V).

With the encouragement of successive British Governments the Regiment has also perpetuated the rule of undemocratic regimes in various parts of the world, a fact which makes it a natural target for vilification by the political Left in Britain. But then, the Left demonstrates great selectiveness in the exercise of its moral conscience: vigorous criticism, for example, of the British in Aden, followed by silence concerning the imposition on that country of a Marxist military dictatorship after the British had departed.

Interestingly, there seem to be no cases in which the Regiment's highly articulate and intelligent critics have been able to prove that the SAS soldier takes life wantonly. The smears tend to be general in nature, and probably are no more unhelpful to the Regiment than the uncritical praise occasionally handed out by right-wingers. If there are numerous war crimes in the SAS cupboard, no doubt some of them will come to light in the fullness of time, though casual brutality is entirely contrary to the Regiment's post-war tradition of winning friends and influencing people. A description of what happened when British mercenaries went to Angola, published in this work and others, is an interesting counterpoint to SAS techniques, and a gruesome illustration of how not to win a war.

Certainly, this author has revealed what he knows about the SAS, with the deliberate exclusion of some data concerning the SAS role in counter-terrorist campaigns in Britain (where it provides an anti-terrorist unit on three-minute standby) and elsewhere. Some light on these matters has been shed by the participation of Major Alastair Morrison and Sergeant Barry Davies in the rescue of eighty-seven West German hostages from a hijacked airliner at Mogadishu in 1977. They were more than advisers: they led the assault team, to blind and deafen the terrorists with a 'percussion' grenade devised by the SAS. Morrison was not permitted to receive a German decoration, but he was awarded the OBE. It is also well known that in 1972, when it was thought that a saboteur's bomb had been planted aboard the liner *Queen Elizabeth II*, the team that parachuted to join her in mid-Atlantic included an SAS soldier; and that on occasions when aircraft hijackings have taken place in Britain, the assistance of the Regiment has been enlisted, as it was by the Metropolitan Police during the IRA siege at Balcombe Street, London, 1975.

In May 1980, the secretly-formed SAS siege-breaking, anti-terrorist Counter Revolutionary Warfare Team went into action in Britain for the first time, in an operation which was as fragile politically as it was difficult in military terms. Seven years' thought, analysis and rehearsal were tested in eleven scorching minutes at the Iranian Embassy in London. A festering international crisis was resolved, and the SAS, after being political pariahs for years, became heroes overnight.

In this context, it is interesting to note that as recently as 1969 the Defence Ministry's *Land Operations Manual*, in its discussion of counter-revolutionary warfare, still placed the SAS firmly in a colonial and probably rural environment. It remarked: 'SAS squadrons are particularly suited, trained and equipped for counter-revolutionary operations. Small parties may be infiltrated or dropped by parachute, including free fall, to avoid a long approach through enemy dominated areas, in order to carry out any of the following tasks:

a. The collection of information on the location and movement of insurgent forces.

b. The ambush and harassment of insurgents.

c. Infiltration of sabotage, assassination and demolition parties into insurgent held areas.

d. Border surveillance.

e. Limited community relations.

f. Liaison with, and organization, training and control of friendly guerrilla forces operating against the common enemy.'

While the manual also acknowledges the value of the SAS as a collector of military Intelligence, it is not the case, as is popularly believed, that the Regiment is an arm of the Secret Intelligence Service. Informal links exist for a variety of reasons, notably the training which SIS men sometimes require from their military friends. But most SAS men, for whom the comradeship of the four-man patrol or sixteen-man troop is one of the fundamental parameters of life itself, are not suited to the silent, lonely, dissembling life of the espionage agent.

There is another sense in which this short history of the SAS is deficient. This is that it does not seek to be an exhaustive and complete account of the SAS campaigns it describes, still less the sometimes enigmatic 'team jobs' performed by SAS training missions around the world, which are merely touched upon. There have been actions for which gallantry awards have been made which are not described, and which must await a more definitive work than this for inclusion in the historical record. This history is essentially indicative and, to some extent, impressionistic in its approach. This is perhaps appropriate for a military unit as dynamic and secretive as the SAS. The author's first attempt to describe the Regiment's methods of selection and training encountered from someone in a position to know, the criticism – the more crushing because of the gentleness with which it was expressed – that the chapter was perfectly accurate, but ten years out of date.

To offset such deficiencies, the reader will find that the highlights of SAS history are covered, as well as much that is new and perhaps surprising: the first full account of the remarkable action at Mirbat in 1972; the detailed story of the ill-fated Edwards patrol in Aden; an account of Britain's first operational use of free-fall parachuting, of which there was no public knowledge. The reader may also discover that, despite much mythology, the SAS philosophy does not reflect the motto of the pre-war Spanish Foreign Legion, 'Down with intelligence, and long live Death!'

Some of those who participated in the actions concerned may differ, in matters of detail, from the consensus accounts that appear here. The author craves their indulgence, as well as the perspective of military history attributed to the Duke of Wellington: 'You might as well try to write the history of a ball as of a battle.'

It is interesting to speculate about the future of such a unique instrument of government policy. Conspiracy theorists, who foresee in its counter-revolutionary role the sharp end of a military takeover in Britain, will be disappointed. SAS men are simply not interested in political power in that sense: rather, they are profoundly conservative with a small 'c', like most British soldiers. But, more than most, they have come to appreciate the political content of military activity in an age in which a single newspaper article, television programme, or (as in the Blunt affair) a single book, can overturn government policy.

The lessons of regimental history in post-war years are that, first, the SAS hates military idleness and that if there is a conflict in which it can be legitimately involved, it will not wait to be asked, but will volunteer its services and adapt its techniques to meet the case. Secondly, the Regiment retains – most consistently through its Territorial volunteer arms – a role within NATO. That role is still the one originally envisaged by Stirling: the offensive strategic raid in which tiny groups of men live without resupply or the usual logistical support expected by orthodox troops, while creating havoc far behind enemy lines. For many years, the West's reliance upon American nuclear superiority to offset the greater number of Warsaw Pact conventional forces tended to reduce the credibility of such a force. That situation has been profoundly changed during the last five years or so, as a result of the achievement by Soviet Russia of nuclear parity with the West. Consequently, the West has now had to rethink much of its strategy where Continental Europe, Scandinavia and the Mediterranean are concerned. The emphasis is more upon conventional warfare and, where nuclear weapons are concerned, to scale down the level of conflict through the use of more precise missiles with diminished explosive power. Implicit in the new doctrine is a belief in a limited nuclear war, a concept which, in the absence of experience, must be an act of faith.

Many things are unclear about the future shape of a European conflict, but what is abundantly plain is that the smaller the military group, the better its chances of survival as a cohesive unit in an environment where both sides possess a range of firepower of all kinds, conventional as well as nuclear, on a scale unique in human history. The SAS's four-man module is the smallest organic fighting unit since prehistoric times. Its ability to call down artillery, missile and air strikes is now potentially greater than ever before. Thus, military technology as well as strategy is moving its way. But the speed at which that technology is evolving – for example through the use of lasers, communication satellites, the microchip – means that even the SAS will have to work hard to keep up with it. The problem is one affecting all armies. The SAS, through its readiness to experiment and adapt, and its reliance on the judgement and intelligence of the individual, has a better chance than most of coming to terms with high technology. In that sense, it is the shape of things to come.

The SAS's unique preparedness for the South Atlantic conflict in 1982 resulted from the shrewdness of a few key officers who appraised the Regiment as an organic part of a fast-changing world rather than a military statue frozen into a single defensive posture. John Woodhouse's role has been discussed in earlier editions. To his name should be added two others. Peter de la Cour de la Billière, CBE, DSO, MC, joined the SAS as a troop commander in Malaya and retired as Director, SAS, with the rank of brigadier in December, 1982. Dare Newell, OBE, a veteran of SOE in Albania and Force 136 in Japanese-occupied Malaya, is still Regimental Adjutant. De la Billière's questioning mind and sometimes ruthless commitment to the effectiveness of unconventional warfare kept the SAS in step with armed conflict as it evolved in post-war years. Thus the Regiment was capable of handling an embassy siege in London *and* the first military action in Antarctica. Newell played a crucial role in ensuring the Regiment's political survival when attacked by critics whose notions of the SAS had more to do with caricature than reality. This success contains the risk that hard-pressed governments come to believe that the SAS is a magic lubricant for any military crisis. In the author's opinion, some episodes in the South Atlantic were a disturbing illustration of the trend. SAS success made it inevitable, but SAS soldiers don't actually walk on water even if, occasionally, they appear to do so.

1. Malaya, 1950–59: The Inauspicious Beginning

Like Don John of Austria, the visionary leader of the last crusade against the Saracens, the post-war Special Air Service was 'risen from a doubtful seat and half-attained stall'. The Regiment had been disbanded at the end of the Second World War, together with the Army Commando, Popski's Private Army and other esoteric 'mobs for jobs'. And, when a special jungle force was raised for the long counter-terrorist campaign in Malaya, it owed more to the experience of Wingate than to Stirling. It was through a series of accidents that it became the SAS.

During much of the Malayan campaign the new unit's structure, style, and discipline were very different from, and inferior to, the ultra-professional force into which it subsequently evolved. Hard drinking, indiscipline, the 'fragging' of officers, as well as some good soldiering, all characterized those early days and it would be a long time before the Regiment would live down the reputation it had acquired. (The uninitiated should know that the word 'fragging' is derived from 'fragmentation grenade', originally the US M26 sometimes used by American conscripts against their own officers in Vietnam.) But even in retrospect, it is surprising that the Regiment got off to quite such a bad start, combining as it did some of the best that British Special Forces had created during the Second World War. That this did happen was due to the speed and ferocity with which the Malayan Emergency built up, leaving insufficient time for selection and training, and the fact that the war was for the hearts and minds of people, rather than for territory.

Such a war, at that time, was not one for which the wartime SAS had equipped itself.

No one who knew Malaya was surprised that it contained Communists. A small Communist Party had existed in that prosperous land since the 1930s. What caused the damage was the arming of Communist guerrillas during the war against the Japanese, without thought for the possibility that these guns might be turned on the British after the war. That this had not been foreseen is neatly shown by the presentation to the Communist guerrilla supremo, Chin Peng, of an OBE in the Victory Honours, and his participation in celebrations in London after the war. The justification for arming Peng and his underground army was that until the atom bomb was used against Japan, the Far East campaign offered no short-cut to victory. To assist the guerrillas in Malaya and elsewhere, the Special Operations Executive (SOE) sent a number of adventurous spirits into the jungle, some of whom had aided the partisans of Greece and Albania. One of these was the Regimental Adjutant of the SAS, Major C. E. (Dare) Newell, OBE.

Newell and his comrades were part of a cryptically-named organization called Force 136. In January 1945, he parachuted into Johor Baharu to meet with two British members of the Underground who had remained after the fall of Singapore. When, a few months later, Japan surrendered, the Japanese commander in Malaya, General Itagaki, did not believe it. Newell and his friends were ordered to remain in hiding until a member of the Tokyo Royal Family was brought to Singapore to persuade Itagaki that the war really had ended. By now, there were at least 4000 British and captured Japanese weapons in the hands of the guerrillas. If there was a moment when the Communists could have seized power in Malaya, this was it. The iron grip of the Japanese had been broken and the British had not yet returned in force. But the chance passed and the war ended with two gains for Chin Peng, in addition to his OBE. One was recognition of the Malayan Communist Party – withdrawn after the Emergency and whose restoration was to be a sticking point in negotiations to end the campaign against the British – and the other, a large part of the abandoned Japanese arsenal in the area.

In 1948, at a time when the gains of Mao's Communism confirmed in the minds of Chinese elsewhere their innate superiority over other races, a Communist convention was held in Calcutta. The British had left India and Burma, and had started to rule Malaya at one remove through a new Federation. The Calcutta conference seems to have inspired the Malayan Communists – most of them members of the Chinese community – with the belief that if Mao could defeat the superior Western-backed Nationalist Chinese Army in a protracted guerrilla war, they could follow his example in the jungles of Malaya itself. There were also internal stresses in the Communist movement in Malaysia following the defection of its secretary-general, which made it necessary to reunify the movement through an anti-colonial offensive.

Soon afterwards, 1200 wartime guerrillas returned to the jungle in ten 'regiments', only one of which was not exclusively Chinese. Long-hidden caches of weapons were dug up, degreased and prepared for the new offensive, and a clandestine support group among non-combatant Chinese, known as the Min Yuen, came into being to supply food, money and information. Between April and June 1948, the offensive began. Following the advice of a long-dead Chinese soldier, Sun-Zu, 'Kill one, frighten a thousand', foremen and other key figures in rubber plantations on the west coast were publicly executed by groups of armed Chinese, who lectured the horrified spectators about their war against imperialism before melting back into the jungle.

At breakfast time on 16 June, it was the turn of

Europeans to become ritual victims of the new order. Three young Chinese cycled into Elphil Estate in Perak and shot dead a fifty-year-old British planter, Arthur Walker. A few miles away, Ian Christian and his manager, Mr J. Alison, were bound to chairs and similarly murdered. Only the day before, Christian had called on an old Gurkha friend, Lieutenant-Colonel J. O. Lawes, to borrow a firearm because he sensed imminent danger. Lawes later recalled: 'I lent him an old Luger of my father's and said that I would try and bring some recruits out to the Estate pig-shooting the following weekend. . . . We were sitting on a volcano which was to erupt much sooner than expected.'

The Emergency – limited in its scope – was declared the same day, and thenceforth the war escalated rapidly from terrorism to jungle battles against regular soldiers of the six Gurkha battalions, many of whose troops were in poor shape. Three shiploads had arrived from India without boots or shirts; they included a large number of untrained recruits, many of whom were found to have tuberculosis.

The security forces now faced a tactical dilemma. Should they merely react to events and strive to protect the towns and plantations, or try to pursue the 'bandits' to their bases? Inland Malaya, as they knew from the campaign against the Japanese, was a guerrillas' paradise – mile after mile of slippery bamboo on the mountains, while in the valleys a canopy of trees rising above 200 feet obliterated the sun, reducing daylight to twilight. Below the trees, endless swamp. The first priority had to be defence of the towns, but as a gesture to offensive campaigning, an ad hoc group of veterans from Force 136 and a few volunteers from the regular army battalions was cobbled together in July 1948 into something known as the Ferret Force. Almost simultaneously, the first of forty-seven Dyak trackers from the Iban tribe – small, lithe tribesmen with high-pitched voices, who killed with blowpipes and removed their victims' heads as trophies – were imported from Borneo.

Ferret Force did not last long, because the services of the civilians and regular officers in it were needed elsewhere, but its exploration of the jungle revealed how great was the need for such a group. During its first offensive operation, in which it led in a battle group of Devons, Seaforths and Inniskillings from Singapore, as well as two Gurkha battalions, it had uncovered twelve permanent guerrilla camps. These were not primitive hides. They included lecture halls and accommodation for up to 200 men, and this only three months after the murder of Arthur Walker.

By March 1950, the Communists – now known as 'CTs' (Communist Terrorists) – had exacted an appalling toll on Malaya. A total of 863 civilians, 323 police officers and 154 soldiers had been killed. The CT had also suffered severely (1138 killed, 645 captured, 359 surrendered), but there was no sign of an end to the war, or even a pause in their campaign.

'Win the Aborigine'

In Hong Kong at this time, a British staff officer who was an acknowledged expert on guerrilla warfare was observing events in Malaya with growing impatience. A hard-drinking, hard-fighting idealist, his name was J. M. ('Mad Mike') Calvert and he was something of a legend. A physically tough character who had won a double blue at Cambridge, he had given up a commission early in the war in order to join a Scots Guards ski battalion destined for Finland. His wartime service included three years in Burma, much of that time behind Japanese lines. Calvert then commanded the SAS brigade in north-west Europe from December 1944 until it was disbanded in November 1945.

One day in 1950, General Sir John Harding, Commander-in-Chief of Far East Land Forces, called Calvert to confer about the explosion of terrorism in Malaya. The two men talked for some time, and Harding then instructed Calvert to produce a detailed analysis of the problem, with options for its solution. During the next six months, Calvert interviewed most of those conducting the campaign, covering 1500 miles, as he put it, 'unescorted along guerrilla-infested roads and only ambushed twice'. Much of his time was spent with the infantry patrols trawling through the jungle in a usually profitless hunt for an invisible enemy. This study, Calvert told the author, later formed the basis of a controversial new strategy named the 'Briggs Plan' after the Director of Operations, General Sir Harold Briggs, who put it into effect.

To isolate the guerrillas from the rest of the population, Briggs decided that 410 'villages' – many of them shanty towns inhabited by Chinese squatters – should be uprooted and their occupants moved to new, fortified villages. In June 1951, Briggs followed this with an equally ambitious plan to deny food supplies to the guerrillas. Both schemes demanded a uniquely stringent control of people and food, and over the next eight years they finally destroyed the guerrilla movement.

Another proposal contained in Calvert's study was the creation of a special military force to live in the jungle, denying the 'bandits' any sanctuary or rest. Calvert argued that British troops should be able to survive in such an environment for much longer than the seven days then regarded as the maximum for an orthodox infantry patrol. Linked with this was the suggestion that the key to winning the jungle war was the trust of its indigenous aboriginal population. Two months after submitting his report to Harding, Calvert was instructed to create the 'special force' he had in mind. He called it the Malayan Scouts (SAS), with the object of converting

Operations in Malaya, 1950-59

1. Kota Tinggi Jungle Warfare School
2. Belum Valley parachute drop, February 1952
3. Operation 'Hive', autumn 1952
4. Operation 'Termite', July to November 1954
5. Telok Anson swamp operation, February 1958

the Army to the idea of a series of special forces raised locally whenever they were needed, with a geographical identity linked to the SAS.

Calvert now began an intensive drive to organize and recruit the new regiment. His own retrospective view is that, in spite of acknowledged shortcomings, he was creating a foundation on which others could build, and that to be too fastidious in his choice of soldiers at such a time would almost certainly mean that the unit would never be formed. He had presided over the disbandment of the wartime SAS Brigade and he was determined not to lose this opportunity to resurrect the concept. Invitations were posted to units throughout the Far East for volunteers to join him and no particular criteria were laid down for selection. Some of those who responded were useful veterans of SOE, SAS, Force 136 and Ferret Force; others were men who were simply bored and whose units were happy to see them go elsewhere. One group consisted of ten deserters from the French Foreign Legion who had escaped by swimming ashore from a troopship conveying them to the war in Indo-China. Calvert, working from the premise that 'the best is the enemy of the good', accepted them. The consensus within the Regiment in later years was that this approach was unwise. Another profound difference between Calvert's thinking and the consensus was Calvert's theory that any special force (such as the 'Black and Tans') could be disbanded more readily than an established regiment of the line if this became expedient.

There were other pressures on Calvert at this time. Detailed administrative work was necessary at the Regiment's first base in Johor. A two-month training programme had to be started in the same area. Simultaneously, rapid results were expected from the Regiment's first operational area in Ipoh, hundreds of miles away. Such a task, combined with the search for more recruits, required the attention of four senior officers, but Calvert recalls that for many crucial months he was obliged to run things unaided. Despite the circumstances, however, a surprising amount was achieved in a short time. (Similar pressures were felt by the Gurkhas, many of whose new recruits were committed to the war half-trained.) The first priority, as Calvert saw it, was manpower. In search of this, he travelled 22,000 miles in twenty-one days, including a trip to Rhodesia which led to the creation of C Squadron from 1000 volunteers in that country. From Hong Kong he brought Chinese interpreters and counter-guerrillas, who had served with him in Burma, to join his Intelligence staff.

Another source of men was a squadron of SAS Reservists and Territorials (many of whom had served under Stirling) which had formed up in 1947 as 21 SAS Regiment. The genesis of 21 SAS was a compromise between those in the War Office who thought there would be a continuing need after Hitler's defeat for clandestine special forces such as SOE, and those who did not. From the argument there emerged a Territorial unit commanded by regular officers, of whom Lieutenant-Colonel B. M. F. Franks (a 'Terrier' before and after the Second World War) was the first. There is a conflict of recollection about the circumstances in which this contribution to the Malayan Scouts, the original B Squadron, was sent to join Calvert's force. According to the official regimental history by Philip Warner, the reservists were initially sent east in order to participate in the Korean War (which started in June 1950) and, when this scheme was abandoned, the men of 21 SAS were diverted to Malaya; but Calvert has since told the present author that he had simply asked for a squadron from the reserve and knew nothing of the Korean plan.

The force that now began to emerge as the modern SAS comprised three disparate elements: Calvert's original group of 100 volunteers (A Squadron); the Reservists from Britain (B Squadron); and the Rhodesian C Squadron. Training, as devised by Calvert, was directed at realism combined with domestic familiarity, with live rather than blank ammunition. To become familiar with grenades, for example, recruits ran between monsoon drains – narrow, concrete channels four or five feet deep – in the base area and, on a given order, they would leap for cover while one man threw the grenades. To learn jungle stalking, as Warner records, 'two men armed with airguns and wearing fencing masks would crawl towards the centre of a piece of scrub about 100 yards long. The aim was to shoot one's opponent before being shot by him.' Rifle practice, using live ammunition on ad hoc ranges such as the base football pitch, also took place.

Calvert's operational strategy in Ipoh, meanwhile, was to penetrate deep into the jungle with heavily laden patrols of up to fourteen people, including Chinese liaison officers and local police as well as the Malayan Scouts, to establish a firm base equipped with a radio. From this, smaller groups of three or four men would explore a large area of jungle so thoroughly that they could set up ambushes confident in the knowledge that they were covering guerrilla approach routes. Calvert recalls one such patrol, led by Lieutenant Michael Sinclair Hill, which remained in the jungle for 103 days, a remarkable feat at the time. When Sinclair received a message from the RAF asking the SAS not to invoke supportive bombing missions on Sunday, so as to give aircrew time to rest, Sinclair Hill responded: 'Tell us when it is Sunday.'

Other SAS innovations at this time, according to Calvert, were the creation of primitive clinics from which penicillin was distributed to cure aborigines of the skin disease, yaws; river patrols employing inflatable craft supplied by US special forces; and the first use of helicopters (initially flown by the Royal Navy) for resupply of troops in the jungle. Under Calvert, the Regiment also evolved some startling methods of clandestine warfare. One of these resulted from the discovery that local prostitutes were demanding payment for their services in bullets and grenades, rather than cash. This 'currency' was then passed to the enemy. Calvert's men were promptly used to pose as clients in order to supply self-destroying ordnance including hand grenades fitted with instantaneous fuses (to kill the users) and exploding bullets which, when fired, served the same purpose. Jungle food stores were booby-trapped and secret dead letter boxes supplied with notes and even government money addressed to Communist organizers, some of whom were then executed by their own side. It is not known how many enemy were killed during this inaugural phase of the post-war SAS. Fatal casualties among Calvert's own men during his command totalled four: a police officer; a Chinese auxiliary; an SAS soldier who was killed while staying with an aboriginal group, and another who died in a jungle fire-fight. Three others were presumed dead after a prolonged silence about their fate. But, Calvert revealed, 'they were found again living in a village on the east coast, where they had been having a bit of a beano. They had a good excuse. One of them had been wounded.'

By the time the first cadres of A Squadron were completing their initial operational tours in the Ipoh jungle, the other two squadrons were beginning their training in the Malayan Scouts base at Johor. The image of those first A Squadron veterans is still a subject of controversy within SAS circles. The disciplined, cohesive group from 21 SAS and the even more orthodox soldiers from Rhodesia were unfavourably impressed, to put it mildly, by what they found. Calvert himself, in an interview with the author, confirms that the London group was 'shocked to the core; maybe we went too far'.

There are opposing accounts of why this was. A faithful report, thirty years later, can only recount both versions. That of the newcomers was that orthodox discipline was manifestly absent; that there was too much drunkenness, and that the use of firearms in the base area was reckless. Calvert argues that such an impression is misleading and unfair, and reflects the incomprehension about jungle conditions of soldiers whose orientation was European. What the newcomers saw, he asserts, were recruits undergoing hasty battle training in realistic conditions; and the first operational veterans being deliberately encouraged to unwind therapeutically after weeks of hard living in the jungle. If anyone was shocked, Calvert believes that this was because, by the standards of jungle warfare to which he had become accustomed over the years, some of the newly-arrived reservist officers were, as he puts it, 'a bit soft'.

The truth was probably a combination of all these things. The pioneers of A Squadron were a hard, rough bunch, including some men who were totally unsuitable for special forces as well as some who were dedicated, professional soldiers by any standard. They included a senior NCO, formerly a boxing professional and Chindit, who occasionally dispensed justice with his fists in preference to the more orthodox, if bureaucratic, procedure of putting an offender 'on orders'.

Differences of leadership, selection and training style were resolved through the accident of Calvert's return to England about two years after his initial discussion with Harding. Calvert was invalided home suffering from malaria, dysentery, hookworm and the cumulative stress of twelve years' intensive soldiering. By then, as he later told the author, he was a 'very sick man'. But, whatever the criticisms, he had the satisfaction of knowing that he had resurrected the SAS.

The unit was taken over in late 1951 by Lieutenant-Colonel John Sloane, an orthodox infantryman who had been second-in-command of the Argyll and Sutherland Highlanders in Korea. He had no special forces background and no jungle experience, but he did know about good order and discipline. By now, as a result of Calvert's intensive recruitment campaign, the SAS had four squadrons in Malaya – A, B, C and D – plus a full headquarters. Sloane persuaded various officers who had thoughts of leaving the SAS – Dare Newell, later to become Regimental Adjutant, among them – to stay for a period of reorganization during which the Regiment was withdrawn from the jungle. As a result, old habits were relearned: weapons were kept clean, and basic administrative matters affecting soldiers' welfare were brought up to date. Some, though not all, of the Regiment's 'cowboys' were returned to their original units. Ultimately, according to the assessment of one expert, half of those recruited in Malaya would be disposed of in this manner. The remainder were excellent soldiers.

At this time, one of Calvert's best officers, Major John Woodhouse (later to command 22 SAS), prepared to return to England to set up a selection process better suited to the Regiment's needs. A former Dorset Regiment officer, he was not much interested in drill and uniform, but where battle discipline was concerned he hated sloppiness. When a soldier accidentally opened fire with a rifle, Woodhouse removed the weapon and handed the soldier a grenade from which the safety-pin had been removed. 'Carry that for a week,' he said, 'until you've learned how to handle a rifle.' If the modern SAS had a founding father, it was he.

Outside the jungle there was important work to be done. Much of this was connected with the controversial strategy of the new Director of Operations, Lieutenant-General Sir Harold Briggs, the planning of which owed much to Calvert. But in the short run, the use of the SAS to assist the Field Police Force at jungle forts and in 'jungle edge' patrols meant that Calvert's original concept of deep penetration had been put into cold storage.

Return to the Jungle – by Parachute

In February 1952, shortly before Woodhouse went to
England, where he was to remain for three years, the
Regiment returned to the jungle by parachute. The
purpose of the operation was food denial. In some areas
the guerrillas were already beginning to suffer from the
effects of Briggs's policies and had started to grow their
own crops. To do this in the jungle, however, they had to
fell trees in order to create clearings which would admit
sunlight. Such clearings could be spotted from the air and
were therefore vulnerable to attack. One of them was at a
spot near the Thai border known as Belum Valley. While
Gurkhas, Royal Marine Commandos, Malayan police and
two squadrons of SAS approached the site on foot, an
SAS squadron of fifty-four men parachuted into a
confined drop zone near the area. It was assumed that
some men might land in the trees, but it was hoped that
their canopies would snag the branches firmly enough to
belay the men safely; with this in mind, the planners gave
the soldiers 100 feet of rope each and some good advice
about tying knots. In fact, there were no parachuting
casualties on this occasion and thereafter, 'tree-jumping'
became an SAS speciality. Later experience would demonstrate that serious injury to someone on the drop
would occur almost invariably, and the technique was
abandoned at the end of the Malayan campaign.

While it lasted, such parachuting produced some good
newspaper copy. The *Straits Times* described an operation
that, for most of the men involved, was their first
experience of tree-jumping. 'They knew that if they
landed in bamboo it would splinter, and cut them deeply;
rocky or boulder-strewn areas, bomb blasted areas, spiky
and weakened trees could smash their necks and bones.
Aboard the aircraft, they joked and laughed for a few
minutes after take-off. Then there was silence. Some
slept, others read; a few glanced out of the windows,

fixing their eyes on the jungle. All faces were stern. Ten minutes to go. They checked each other's gear. One man munched an apple; another sucked an orange. A voice said, "Dropping Zone, two minutes to go." Then, "Stand up. Action stations." A crew member stood near the door, tapping paratroopers on the shoulders, yelling "Right, right, right", as each approached him in turn and prepared to jump.' Major John Salmon, second-in-command of 22 SAS, explained later: 'When you are in the doorway, you're scared. You have to conquer the butterflies. There's no turning back, so when you feel the tap on your shoulder you don't hesitate. Next thing you know, you are floating through the air and it's one of the most wonderful feelings in the world; then you see the trees coming. You are coming down beautifully, steering for the middle of the trees. The hot air makes you swing violently, as if a giant had caught hold of you. You let the air spill out of the 'chute and look for a good, healthy tree. Sometimes you make that spot; often you don't. It's hard to tell until you are a few feet away. When you hit a tree you don't know whether you will stay there or not. Often the branch snaps, you hurtle down, smashing into branches on the way, until you finally come to a halt. If it holds you, then you know you are safe.'

The first man out on that operation, acting as 'drifter' to discover which way the wind was blowing, was Sergeant Ken Kidd, a veteran of more than 300 descents, but still wary of tree-jumping, nervous of the odds-on chance that he would 'find himself dangling in a tree top with his spine or ankle broken'. Kidd 'spun into a tree and he was lucky. His feet and body smashed into the branches and the 'chute caught. He was 150 feet above the ground and all he could see through the branches and leaves was the thick undergrowth of the jungle. Above him, the Valletta aircraft kept circling. Now it began the first run in over the dropping zone. Inside the plane the green light flashed again above the door and the first stick of three steel-helmeted paratroopers was ready. Each seemed to half run, taking what looked like a hop, step and jump, and disappeared. The 'chutes opened 750 ft above the ground; 30 seconds later they were engulfed by trees, looking like jellyfish feeling their way into the depths of the sea.' On the ground, Kidd grinned with contentment. 'You need a lot of luck,' he said, 'but I would rather jump into trees than fly a plane. It's like anything else: you get used to it after a while.' Not everyone was so comfortable. Swinging from the top of one tree was Leon Harris, a thirty-three-year-old Australian who had just completed his first tree-jump. 'He shook so much 150 feet above the ground that it took him some time to get a cigarette into his mouth. At the foot of the tree, members of a ground party yelled, "Come on, Aussie" and Harris, securing his abseil mountaineering pack, called, "Advance, Australia fair. I made it. Here I come. Sydney or the bush".'

On another, similar operation, an SAS officer found himself dangling from a tree below which prowled an armed guerrilla. The officer was unable to reach the valise he had carried down, which held his rifle, and could only pray that the guerrilla would not look up. The episode led to a popular demand among some SAS soldiers for a supply of automatic pistols to cover that risk in future.

One of the first parachuting casualties was the man who succeeded John Sloane as Commanding Officer in 1953. Lieutenant-Colonel Oliver Brooke suffered a complicated leg fracture which required months of hospital treatment in England. Like Sloane, Brooke was a good regimental officer with no experience of special forces but, in contrast to the methodical Sloane, Brooke was a rumbustious, extrovert bachelor, quick to lose his temper, equally ready to bury the hatchet. His command of the SAS began eventfully.

In the officers' mess the night before Brooke formally assumed command, he and Newell were standing in a group, drinks in hand, in animated conversation. It was late. A number of NCOs and men from B Squadron who had celebrated too enthusiastically in the nearest town were returned to the camp by the Royal Military Police. At about the same time, some of the sergeants decided to 'frag' the reception going on in honour of the new Commanding Officer. They did so by setting off an explosive charge which blew down one wall of the mess. The table, around which Brooke, Sloane and Newell were standing, took off and landed some distance away. To Newell's surprise, Brooke did not appear to notice what had happened, but continued talking in an even, measured way. Next morning, having assumed command, Brooke took the unusual step of holding a disciplinary hearing on a Sunday, and ordered the return to their units of origin of a Senior NCO and sixteen other soldiers. They were out of the Regiment, and out of the camp, before lunch. (Surprisingly, the rejected men were among those who had formed the original, disciplined cadre from B Squadron, now diluted by newcomers.) This exemplary reaction had its effect, and discipline started to improve.

The effect of Briggs's policies of food denial and political isolation was to drive the CT deeper into the jungle. The security forces were therefore obliged to pursue the enemy there, which gave the SAS its second chance to prove its value. Armed with shotguns and the new Patchett carbine – an early version of the Stirling submachine-gun – they formed the spearhead of deep jungle operations in Pahang and Kelantan, entering by helicopter and parachute. Within the theatre as a whole, the SAS now constituted one of seven major units from the UK. There were also seven Gurkha battalions, one African and one Fijian, as well as eight indigenous Malay battalions.

While more orthodox units concentrated on harrying the Johor rebel committee, the SAS was making its first serious contact with the aboriginal tribes of the interior. Gregory Blaxland's masterly history of the post-war British Army explains that, 'The protection of the jungle-dwelling aborigines of the Seman and Sakai tribes' was the task. 'These scrawny little people had been completely at the mercy of the rebels and had been forced deeper into their service as the policy of food denial developed.

'Now the Special Air Service arrived by helicopter in groups of 15 and began to win over these nomad tribesmen, staying with them 13 weeks before relief.

'They built landing strips to enable them to market their supplies and brought them medical and engineering aid. Villages were turned into fortresses, in which police posts and even artillery were established. Much depended on the few lone persons who stayed to sell them the idea of self-defence. It was all part of the battle for hearts and minds.'

Resupply by helicopter, after its introduction in this role in 1954, presented peculiar problems. The noise generated by these machines was not conducive to security, so the SAS decided at one stage to try moving its bulk supplies into the jungle by elephant. On paper it looked like a good idea: the beasts were quieter than helicopters and not necessarily out of place in certain types of jungle. However, a thicket of bureaucracy had to be penetrated in order to arrange insurance for the animals. Only when this had been accomplished was it discovered that they would not enter the selected jungle anyway. It is one of the few recorded cases where even the SAS had to admit defeat.

Hearts, Minds and Head-hunters

For several months, the phrase 'hearts and minds' had reverberated around Malaya. Its author was the new, energetic Military High Commissioner, General Sir Gerald Templar. Asked in June 1952 whether he had sufficient troops, he had replied, 'The answer lies not in pouring more soldiers into the jungle, but rests in the hearts and minds of the Malayan people.' In fact, this was an admirable summary of the essence of SAS philosophy at the time, and has been so ever since. As one of the Regiment's planners of the successful Dhofar operation was to put it years later, 'It was not our numbers but our ideas which made a big difference.' It was also the concept which Calvert had dreamed of when forming the Malayan Scouts.

Such politico-military operations were not so popular with more orthodox troops. For two months during the autumn of 1952, for instance, two battalions of 2/7th Gurkha Rifles, D Company of the 1st Fijian Infantry Regiment and two SAS squadrons were enmeshed in Operation 'Hive' around Seremban in Negri Sembilan. The history of 2/7th summarizes what happened: 'Op "Hive" was designed to saturate a selected area with troops so that the terrorists' mode of life would be completely disrupted. A concentrated programme of police checks on roads and New Villages was planned in detail with the aim of driving the bandits back on to their jungle food dumps where they would be forced to eat up valuable reserves. Then the military units would move in to specific areas where it was hoped, by intensive ambushes and patrols, to force out the terrorists once more into the open or into the many "stop" (ambush) positions, established on recorded and likely tracks in the jungle surrounding Seremban. . . .

'A lot of men were required to close the chinks in the jungle, many more than were available . . . to search for about 100 bandits, hiding in an area exceeding 600 square miles. . . . Only 16 of the enemy were killed and in the opinion of one or two officers, not all this total was directly attributable to "Hive". . . . General Sir Gerald

Templar visited the Seremban Operations Room during "Hive" at a time when he was under considerable pressure from other districts to end the Operation so that troops could return to their normal duties. He was suitably impressed by the food denial aspect of the Operation and, with a typically terse "Stick to it", he allowed the Operation to follow its planned course.'

The impatience of the troops was understandable. But what they were learning was that there were no soft targets in the deep jungle. According to one estimate, 1800 man-hours were expended on patrol for every contact made with the enemy: the man-hour/kill ratio was even more daunting. In spite of this, there was competition among all units for a high body count, the greatest score being that of 1/10th Gurkhas with 300. The SAS, a late starter, 'scored' 108 during a nine-year period, which was the sort of return most infantry battalions achieved in one-third of the time. The SAS, however, was learning its fundamental role in life, a dual one of Intelligence gathering and perception shaping. Its real achievements, then and later, were much harder to quantify, and not dramatic enough to win medals: it was 1953 before the Regiment achieved its first Mention in Dispatches, and late in 1957 before the first Military Cross and Military Medal were awarded to it. What is of more significance, perhaps, is that between 1951 and 1953, when the SAS started to penetrate hearts and minds in the jungle, casualties among British forces dropped sharply.

From 1953 onwards, the SAS was living more and more in the jungle during a series of long operations. Simultaneously, it was deeply involved in training Iban trackers in the fundamentals of modern soldiering. The head-hunters were now formally recognized as a locally-raised unit of the British Army, the Sarawak Rangers. (So, at this stage, was 22 SAS: unlike the Territorial SAS, it was not yet part of the permanent Order of Battle.) The

Rangers were issued with rifles which they sometimes used with more enthusiasm than effect.

Typical of the operations from 1954 onward, when the enemy was becoming concentrated in certain identifiable areas of wilderness, was Operation 'Termite'. It lasted from July to November, and began with heavy bombing of the jungle by RAF Lincolns – an indiscriminate use of air power which was as likely to kill aborigines as Communist guerrillas, and one which the SAS regarded as counter-productive. (The mistake was not subsequently repeated in Borneo.) Two SAS squadrons, a total of 177 men, then parachuted into jungle clearings created by the bombs. That clearings had to be made in this way attests to the number of casualties suffered by the Regiment in its attempts to perfect 'tree-jumping'. Even then, the drop generated four casualties. Such casualties were occurring not just as a result of the unpredictable behaviour of parachutes as they were 'bounced' by the thermal effect of air above the trees: the technique of abseiling out of the trees was also proving defective. In theory, the soldier detached himself from his parachute, lashed a long webbing strap to a branch, and descended safely to the ground. The webbing bulged at intervals, where it had been stitched, and therefore snagged at high speed as it travelled through D rings on the soldier's harness. As a result, three men were killed and one seriously injured taking part in Operation 'Sword' in January 1954, one of the deaths occurring after a soldier in great pain had cut away from the harness and fallen 150 feet.

In addition to the SAS, four infantry battalions took part in Operation 'Termite'. It resulted in the death, capture or surrender of only fifteen rebels, but, as Blaxland records, 'the gain was in the conversion of the aborigines to allies'.

Between 1955 and 1956, there were critically important changes in SAS organization which at last set the

Regiment on a winning course. The formidable John Woodhouse returned to active campaigning as a squadron commander under a new commanding officer, Lieutenant-Colonel (later Lieutenant-General) George Lea. Lea wasted no time in weeding out officers who were not good enough for the SAS, and several were sent back to their original units. He was a large, tough character – 6 feet 4 inches tall and weighing sixteen stones – and had no time for the quaint customs of earlier days. (He was horrified, for instance, to learn that a sergeant who had hit the medical officer escaped with a reprimand and an order to shake hands with the officer he had struck.) Lea acquired good officers and promoted the best of those whom he inherited, such as John Cooper, who had started his career with Stirling in the desert. The new intake included Captain Peter de la Billière and Major Harry Thompson, red-haired and, like Lea, a big man, from the Royal Highland Fusiliers. Thompson would go on to become second-in-command of the Regiment in Borneo, where he died in a helicopter crash. This team was the core of the Regiment during its three most hectic years in Malaya.

Another decisive change was the replacement of the Rhodesian C Squadron with an equivalent group from New Zealand. The Rhodesians were tough, hard and willing; their leader, Peter Walls, would ultimately command all Rhodesia's armed forces after UDI; but some were also colour-conscious to a degree that was not helpful in the task of seducing aboriginal sympathies from the Communists. They were also peculiarly vulnerable to jungle diseases. The New Zealanders, by contrast, included a fair sprinkling of adaptable Maoris who made excellent trackers. Their presence in the SAS also encouraged the first Fijians serving in Malaya to transfer to the SAS. Most important of all, however, was the recognition that SAS soldiers could not be selected and trained in haste. The New Zealanders were hand-picked and given a thorough grounding in jungle warfare in Malaya's Jungle Warfare School before they went operational. (For a detailed account of the New Zealanders' exploits and additional insight into the Malayan campaign, see pages 310–18.)

In the same year, 1955/6, the SAS in Malaya was further reinforced by a squadron drawn from the Parachute Regiment in England, known as the Parachute Regiment Squadron, and commanded by Major Dudley Coventry. By 1956, five squadrons totalling 560 men were operating in the jungle, and the number of people killed by the guerrillas had fallen to about half a dozen per month. From now on, the military problem was the pursuit of the estimated 2000 CT thought to be still at large to their increasingly remote bases, which now more resembled sanctuaries than launch-pads for offensive operations. It was a time when the skills of the hunter – concealment, tracking, endurance, coolness and lethally-accurate snap shooting – were at a premium, and the time when 22 SAS came into its own.

The soldier who personified these skills at the time was Sergeant Bob Turnbull, a gunner from Middlesbrough, who combined a quick intelligence and good ear for foreign languages with the grinding determination of a human bulldozer. Turnbull befriended an Iban tracker called Anak Kayan, and achieved an eye for spoor as accurate as Kayan's own, reading the splayed toe-prints of the aborigine for what they were; the terrorist footprint, which invariably revealed cramped toes that had once known shoes; and spotting a fine human footprint imposed by the more canny walker on an elephant footmark in an attempt to blur the trace.

Turnbull once followed the tracks of four men for five days until he spotted the hut they were occupying. He then waited for an impending rainstorm to arrive, correctly guessing that the sentries would then take shelter, and drew to within five yards of the hut before killing the four guerrillas sheltering there. On another occasion, he pursued a notorious guerrilla leader called Ah Tuck, a man who always went armed with a Sten carbine, ready cocked. When the two men finally encountered one another in the bush at a range of twenty yards, Ah Tuck died still holding his unfired weapon.

According to one officer who served with him, Turnbull used a repeater shotgun with such speed and accuracy that it would 'fill a man with holes like a Gruyère cheese'. (The shotgun, its use perfected by the SAS for close-quarter battle, has ever since been the subject of intensive study by US as well as British forces.) One officer who went on his first jungle patrol with Turnbull was unwise enough to insist that the sergeant act as back-marker to an Iban tracker and the officer himself. When this trio encountered a guerrilla, Turnbull instantly fired over the officer's shoulder and had disabled the terrorist while the officer concerned was still reminding himself of the drill for such situations, 'First, safety catch off. . . .'

Into Telok Anson Swamp

One of the last major guerrilla hunts, near the Malacca Strait Coast, in Selangor, was also one of the hardest. In February 1958, thirty-seven men of D Squadron led by Harry Thompson parachuted into the Telok Anson swamp, which covers an area measuring about eighteen miles by ten, to kill or capture two groups of terrorists led by Ah Hoi, also known as 'The Baby Killer', after his murder of an informer's wife. She was pregnant. His accomplices held her down on a table while he slashed at her with a knife, before an audience of horrified villagers. Ah Hoi was now hiding in the swamp.

The drop was from a Beverley. By now, the accumulation of casualties from this type of parachuting was such that no training jumps were permitted. As one veteran of the Telok Anson operation put it, 'You just got out of the aircraft and hoped to God you would land safely in the top of a tree.' One man, Trooper Mulcahy, was unlucky. He hit a tall tree, but his canopy did not catch the branches. The canopy collapsed and he dropped like a stone into the tree roots, breaking his back. The Squadron's first task was to fell some trees so that a helicopter could evacuate Mulcahy. The clearance thus created was just enough to allow the aircraft's rotor blades to miss the foliage, but it was impossible to land because of the swampy terrain. Somehow, the pilot kept the machine hovering, with one wheel on a log, while the stretcher was taken aboard.

The initial search for Ah Hoi was led by de la Billière in a ten-day trek along river banks and through iron-brown water, the depth of which varied from shin to neck-height. The parts of the body that were submerged were the prey for leeches, the more enthusiastic of which could consume half a pint of the victim's blood before being detected; those areas not submerged were the target for the malarial mosquito and other insects. Each night, the patrol slung hammocks in the trees and enjoyed temporary respite from the swamp. A stay of more than one night made it worth the effort to construct a raft as a sleeping platform.

De la Billière's troop found several camps recently vacated by the terrorists, sites littered with the shells of turtles which the 'bandits' had eaten. Ah Hoi's men, it seemed, knew that they were being pursued. It is possible that the helicopter evacuation of Mulcahy had alerted them. De la Billière's route across the swamp followed the dominant feature of the place, the Tengi River. He reported his progress by radio to Thompson each evening, but made no contact with the enemy, who were now apparently heading up-river towards the centre of the swamp. Simultaneously, a second troop under Sergeant

Sandilands was moving on a compass bearing in that direction also, picking a cautious way through the swamp during the hours of darkness, noses alert for the smell of guerrilla cooking fires, ears straining through the cacophony of bullfrog croaks for the sound of a human voice. By day, Sandilands and his men put out sentries and slept.

Finally, at dusk on about the seventh or eighth day, soon after they had resumed the march, Sandilands' troop spotted two of the enemy about seventy yards away across a stretch of open water. Sandilands and a corporal eased themselves into the water to get closer, floating a log before them to conceal their approach. They opened fire from about fifty yards, killing one of the men. The other disappeared. Next morning, the troop cautiously followed a four-mile trail to a freshly-abandoned camp.

Thompson now tightened the cordon round the guerrillas by moving his men to a point on the River Tengi miles upstream from the point that de la Billière had reached, before the two groups started closing towards one another in a pincer movement. Simultaneously, a huge military and police cordon was thrown round the swamp perimeter and barbed wire was laid along the coast, with a notice warning anyone who crossed it that he could be shot on sight. With the need for secrecy eliminated by the Sandilands contact, helicopters now flew daily missions to replenish SAS stocks of food and clothing and to scan any open spaces of water for signs of Ah Hoi. It was now twenty days since D Squadron had dropped into the swamp, and all the men were suffering from prickly heat and other infections. Thompson's legs, ripped by thorns and mildly infected, were a mass of ulcers.

Two days after the cordon had been imposed, a diminutive, emaciated woman in an olive green uniform emerged from the jungle and approached a security forces checkpoint in a paddy-field. She was taken before a

Special Branch officer and identified herself as Ah Hoi's messenger, Ah Niet. Ah Hoi had a proposition for the security forces: a payment of £ 3500 by the government to each of his team and amnesty for those already in prison.

Ah Niet was told there would be no deal: Ah Hoi had a choice between surrendering within twenty-four hours, or death in the swamp where soldiers were already waiting for him. And if they failed, the RAF would bomb Ah Hoi out of hiding. Ah Niet, just 4 feet 6 inches tall, dissolved gnome-like, back into the jungle. Thompson, alerted by radio, flew with a troop of his men to a paddy-field and at dusk, shining torches, Ah Hoi and some of his men emerged. A contemporary account by Brian Connell reported, 'He was still arrogant, still ranting that the Reds would win in the end.' Given the choice of prison or exile in China, he initially chose China, then changed his mind, but was packed off to China all the same.

Ah Niet, meanwhile, led Thompson back into the swamp to make contact with another group of Ah Hoi's men who were ready to surrender. She led the way, swimming in total silence, 300 yards from a police post. It was her favourite entry-point and she had used it undetected for years. She was appalled at the amount of noise generated by the soldiers as they followed her. They did not find the remnant of the Ah Hoi band partly because Ah Niet's considerable strength now failed her. She was suffering from beri-beri, a vitamin deficiency disease. They emerged to surrender forty-eight hours later.

Whitehall Jungle Campaign

While the SAS was fighting on the ground to establish a reputation as a credible military force, a jungle war of a different kind was going on in Whitehall. In the long term, it was of even greater importance to the future of the SAS – if it had one – than Malaya. Argument about the role of special forces had been smouldering since 1945, and it had found early expression in the compromise function of 21 SAS, the volunteer Territorial regiment. Even this creation was regarded with hostility in some parts of the military establishment, which was suspicious of a 'private army' whose methods and objectives it did not understand.

Efforts to ensure the SAS a permanent place in the post-war regular army also hit opposition from officers who had a chip on their shoulders about the unit, either because they had been rejected for SAS service or because someone of, say, the rank of major had been treated to that terse form of advice – usually two words, of which the second was invariably 'off' – which SAS soldiers express when faced with obtuseness by higher authority. Such episodes should have no part in long-term military calculations, but armies are human organizations and some soldiers nurture grudges. It is also fair to say that some of the critics had a more substantial case, based on their contacts with the Malayan Scouts. The same men who had been company commanders in Malaya during those early days of 1950 to 1952 were staff officers in Britain by the time the political debate about the future of the SAS reached its climax between 1956 and 1957.

Another element in this domestic quarrel concerned relations between the SAS and the Parachute Regiment. The first SAS selection courses of post-war years in Britain were set up by Lieutenant-Colonel John Woodhouse in the autumn of 1952 at the Airborne Forces Depot, Aldershot. This was the home of the Parachute Regiment, an elite force for which, in those days, prior service with another unit followed by prolonged and stringent selection was required. Formal entry into the Regiment, marked by the award of parachute wings and red beret, took place only after parachute training. The SAS, by contrast, trained for parachuting after acceptance.

There were other, more profound differences. The SAS emphasized individuality while the Paras, despite their advice to 'use your Airborne Initiative' to solve otherwise insoluble problems, were still much closer to orthodox traditions of infantry discipline. These differences, added to the mixed reputation of the Malayan Scouts, generated an attitude by the Paras towards SAS men that was at best patronizing and at worst downright derisive. While they awaited posting to Malaya, SAS soldiers were used exclusively for menial, fatigue duties.

In the longer term, the SAS pioneers were disturbed by a possible takeover of their fledgling unit by the Paras. According to one account, the SAS Colonel Commandant of the day, General Miles Dempsey, accompanied the SAS course organizer, Woodhouse, in an abrasive discussion with the Parachute Regiment's depot commander, Colonel Pine Coffin, during which Dempsey apparently said, 'I hope it is clearly understood that there is no question of the SAS being taken over now or in the future by Airborne Forces.' In spite of that, attempts to absorb the SAS into Airborne Forces continued until about 1962.

In Whitehall, the long-term problem of the Regiment's survival particularly concerned Dare Newell and the very few others who were not under pressure to survive the next twenty-four hours in the jungle. That the SAS did survive to fight another day during that critical decade before 1957 was the result of a committee of inquiry into the role of special forces, headed by a Lieutenant-General. This group soberly evaluated the impact of all the private armies of the Second World War, including the Long Range Desert Group, Lovat Scouts, Popski's Private Army, SAS, Paras, Commandos . . . even, it is jokingly suggested, the Royal Corps of Tree Climbers.

The committee found that there was a requirement in a general European war for two types of special operation behind enemy lines – in so far as mobile, modern warfare would have 'lines'. One was for long-term, deep penetration; the other, for short-term, shallow penetration. The first role, the committee found, would be most appropriately performed by the Special Air Service, the second by Royal Marine Commandos. By 1955, the range of officially-proposed SAS targets deep behind enemy lines in a general war, embraced everything from the kidnap of 'important enemy personalities' to 'attacks on important industrial targets invulnerable from the air'.

In 1956, a new Prime Minister, Harold Macmillan, appointed Duncan Sandys as his Defence Minister to clean up some of the mess generated by the Suez operation and Britain's changing world strategy. Sandys was to 'formulate policies to secure substantial reductions in expenditure and manpower' in all the armed forces. For a start, National Service conscription would be abolished gradually. This meant long-term planning for a much smaller army of professional volunteers. In the subsequent debate about which regiments should survive, the advocates of the SAS relied heavily on the findings of the earlier special forces report as a document untainted by partisan calculations. Several former Directors of Operations who liked the flexibility inherent in the SAS approach to war, backed up this argument.

On 24 July 1957, the Army Minister, John Hare, announced the cuts, and many familiar cap badges were to disappear through regimental amalgamation. The SAS survived, though only just, to become part of the permanent Order of Battle, but the regular 22 SAS Regiment was to be reduced from four squadrons to two. Implicit in this decision was the belief that the SAS would not be engaged in continuous campaigning around the Third World.

In the short run, with the end of the Malayan campaign in 1959/60, it was not difficult for the Regiment to make the required cuts. Of the four squadrons serving in Malaya, one had come from New Zealand, to which it returned. Another was a Headquarters squadron. All the original British 'Sabre' (combat) squadrons – A, B and D – were well below their nominal, established strength. B Squadron was disbanded and its men absorbed by the other two. In Rhodesia, C Squadron was reduced in strength for several years. When it was raised again as the Rhodesian SAS Regiment, it continued to exist separately from the British 22 SAS both before and after the Rhodesian unilateral declaration of independence in 1964, at which point it became a 'lost legion'.

Although the SAS had won the first round in the battle for political survival, its existence continued to be questioned for several years. In Malaya it had justified itself, if perilously late in the day. What it now had to do was demonstrate that after nine years of jungle warfare it could function elsewhere. After all, the aboriginal Sarawak Rangers were also good in the jungle. . . . Briefly and brilliantly, in a politically sensitive environment, the SAS would make its point in Northern Oman within days of leaving Malaya.

2. Borneo, 1962–66: The Camouflaged Victory

The jungle war between Indonesia and Britain euphemistically described by both sides as 'Confrontation', lasted four years. It was fought by a mixed Allied force, never greater than 28,000 men, including Gurkhas, Australians and New Zealanders, in an environment no more tractable than that of Vietnam. The enemy was a professional army well versed in jungle warfare, which sought to de-stabilize the fledgling Federation of Malaysia, of which some Allied territory was part, through clandestine guerrilla warfare and terrorism. When that did not succeed, the Indonesian Government turned to all-out invasion, including airborne attacks on the Malay Peninsula.

The conflict ended in September 1966, with the clear-cut, unequivocal defeat of the invaders. Historically, however, the victory was mistimed. It occurred during a post-imperial epoch of British history – at home, the British were mesmerized by the hedonism of Beatles, Flower Power and the Swinging Sixties – as a result of which it remained entirely uncelebrated, its architect acknowledged only through the award of a bar to his existing brace of DSOs until three years later, when he received a belated knighthood. Walker's friends attribute this enigmatic behaviour by Whitehall to the General's fierce opposition to a scheme of drastic cuts in the Gurkha force, of which he was the Brigade Major-General.

In keeping with such a low profile success, the role of the SAS was also discreet to the point of invisibility. The

Regiment's task was a classic one of deep penetration and Intelligence gathering across enemy lines, in which combat usually implied that something had gone wrong. This did not happen often. To express journalistically the problem of reconstructing this campaign, there was no story because man did not bite dog: things went according to plan most of the time. Having obtained early warning from SAS patrols of Indonesian attacks, the Allies were able to hit back with mobile reserves from the roads, waterways and the air, as well as creating ambushes in the jungle.

To measure, objectively, the success of the SAS in Borneo is rendered even more difficult by the Regiment's characteristic neglect of archives and records until about 1970, and a traditional aversion to 'gong-hunting'. (This attitude, let it be said, is not due to excessive modesty, but more a sort of military existentialism: the important thing, in the SAS, is to be there when it happens, and then get on to the next operation.) There are, however, some historical hints about the Regiment's silent contribution to a muffled victory. The first overall commander there, General Sir Walter Walker, rated the value of a few SAS soldiers equal to a thousand infantry, not because they had equivalent firepower, but because their Intelligence gathering and ability to shape civilian perceptions could save that number in battles won without a fight. Even Whitehall was happy. It was able, perhaps uniquely, to fine-tune offensive operations to achieve a precise political outcome as a result of SAS reconnaissance.

During the three years preceding the Borneo operations, the regular SAS had been learning for the first time to live through a period when it was not involved in active operations. Since the end of the Malayan campaign in 1959 and the intensive, but brief, intervention in northern Oman in the same year, there had been much discussion in the SAS about whether its future lay in

Europe, or in Britain's shrinking share of the Third World.

'Third Worlders' v. 'Europeans'

The Regiment was effectively divided between the 'Europeans', who felt that the long-term future of the SAS, politically as well as militarily, lay in finding a deep penetration and reconnaissance function with NATO forces; and the 'Third Worlders' who suspected that this course would smother the SAS under the bureaucracy of the British Army of the Rhine. Better, they said, to forage for an immediate place in a real campaign than play games in a mock war on the North German plain. Some had joined the SAS to escape from precisely this fate.

Influential people outside the Regiment, however, were beginning to question its cost effectiveness. Some in Whitehall, thinking aloud, wondered whether it would be a good idea simply to absorb the two SAS squadrons into 16th Independent Parachute Brigade. A lack of knowledge among senior Army officers about what the SAS was supposed to be doing, and the skills it had acquired, did not discourage such thinking.

By the autumn of 1962, at about the time of the Cuban missile crisis, it seemed that the 'Europeans' had won the argument. The Regiment was now retraining with the United States special forces for its new role and the long-term, hypothetical operations that implied. Its commanding officer, Lieutenant-Colonel John Woodhouse, had been a pioneer of the Malayan days, and had made a special study of Communist philosophy. As a result of this he encouraged the process, evolved by the Chinese, of continuous self-criticism. Among the 'thinking bayonets' of 22 SAS there was criticism anyway, but Woodhouse institutionalized it. The decisive moment for setting the new policy in concrete apparently came

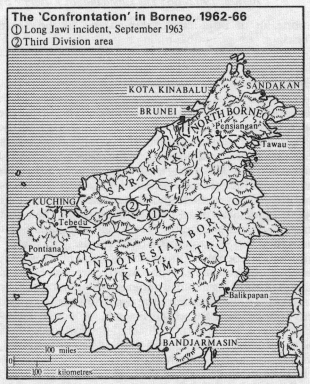

The 'Confrontation' in Borneo, 1962-66
① Long Jawi incident, September 1963
② Third Division area

KOTA KINABALU   SANDAKAN

BRUNEI   NORTH BORNEO

Pensiangan

Tawau

SARAWAK

KUCHING

Rajang

① ②

Tebedu

Pontiana

R. Kapuas

INDONESIAN BORNEO

KALIMANTAN

Kutai

Balikpapan

Barito

BANDJARMASIN

100 miles

0

100 kilometres

when the Director-General of Military Training,
Lieutenant-General Sir Charles Richardson, visited SAS
teams training in the USA. The men were learning
foreign languages and advanced field medical training of
a kind unthinkable in Britain. Stray dogs collected for
destruction were anaesthetized before being killed. Gun-
shot wounds were then inflicted on the animals, which
SAS 'bush doctors' learned to repair with basic surgery.
Richardson, a pragmatic Royal Engineer, was impressed
by the unique potential of 22 SAS and, within two
months, Ministry of Defence clearance was given for the
Regiment to be re-equipped and modernized. Even more

important was the change of political climate in Whitehall. In orthodox military circles the SAS was suddenly 'kosher'.

But Woodhouse, the Commanding Officer, was also at that time a convert to the 'domino' theory about Communist expansion in south-east Asia at a time when Vietnam was succeeding Malaya as the principal battleground of Asia. So he was hedging his bets and encouraging some of his men to learn Thai – on the basis that Thailand, a fellow member of the South East Asia Treaty Organization, might come under attack next. By doing so, Woodhouse also satisfied some of the aspirations of the 'Third Worlders'.

On 8 December 1962, however, simultaneous guerrilla attacks were launched against police stations, government offices, a power-station and other strategically important centres in the Sultanate of Brunei. Brunei was one of three British dependencies in Borneo; the others were the colonies of North Borneo (later Sabah) and Sarawak; all were relics of nineteenth-century paternalism. These territories, extensive though they were, represented only one-quarter of the island. The rest belonged to Indonesia, whose head of state, President Sukarno – irreverently nicknamed 'The Mad Doctor' by British troops – had been inspired by the Japanese example to dream of unifying south-east Asia under his leadership.

The Brunei revolt, although a home-grown product, had been carefully fertilized by Indonesia. In response, a hasty, shoestring military operation launched from Singapore by Gurkhas, 42 Royal Marine Commando and the Queen's Own Highlanders, freed European hostages taken by the rebels and restored order in the coastal towns within a few weeks. But it was clear that a new jungle campaign was about to begin. The only question concerned the form it would take. Another Malaya? A Kenya? A Vietnam?

Woodhouse, scenting action, called on the Director of Military Operations at the Defence Ministry in London. The commanding officer of 22 SAS wanted the Regiment to have a place in Borneo. His most persuasive argument was that in addition to the perfection of its jungle warfare skills during the painful, formative years in Malaya, the Regiment could provide for this new campaign the uniquely valuable service of reliable, long-distance Morse communication on the radios with which it had now been issued. As the Gurkhas were to discover to their cost on one disastrous occasion, Borneo's jungle atmospherics could be so bad that the normal procedure of standing-to – that is, preparing for action at the main rear base – every time an outpost failed to make its daily broadcast, had to be dropped. Woodhouse, as it happened, had been studying the problem of long-distance communications in the context of the European, nuclear role. He was very persuasive.

Three days later, accompanied by a signaller and some of the new radios, he arrived in Brunei. Walker had gladly accepted the offer of an SAS squadron for the campaign because he was then short of helicopters and, as a Gurkha who admired SAS parachute operations into the Malayan jungle, he believed that the SAS would be just the thing for use as a mobile, reserve company of infantry. Woodhouse, with vivid memories of the casualties that had resulted from Malayan 'tree-jumping', to say nothing of the loss of security caused by the need to evacuate the casualties, shuddered inwardly. He explained to Walker that the SAS was not trained for orthodox infantry tactics even in the jungle, and that a company of, say, the Parachute Regiment would be more suitable for the task. He went on to expound the SAS's peculiar value in Borneo. These were men who could operate in pairs, or alone if necessary, living among the tribes, speaking Malay – of which enough was known in Borneo to make it a lingua franca – and, most important, providing an Intelligence and communications network in the blank areas of Walker's knowledge. Like any sensible commander, Walker was worried about these blank areas. He 'bought' Woodhouse's proposition and, within three days, 22 SAS was flying to Borneo, the old hands slinging hammocks wherever they could find space in the aircraft, conserving their energy for the conflict to come.

One of the first people with whom they made contact was a British surveyor, Tom Harrisson, who had led an underground tribal resistance movement against the Japanese during the Second World War, and who had now raised his own aboriginal force to cut off the surviving rebels as they fled inland from Brunei towards the sanctuary of Indonesia.

The Regiment also renewed old friendships with veterans of the Sarawak Rangers, Iban tribal trackers and head-hunters brought to the Malay Peninsula in the 1950s as teachers and pupils of the SAS during that campaign. As pupils, the Iban had learned something about modern soldiering and firearms from the SAS; as teachers, they had given the Regiment a feeling for tracking an enemy in the jungle, silently and invisibly. Few of these Malayan veterans were still living their old life as hunters in the Borneo jungle – some had even taken to driving taxis – and in most cases their jungle sense had deteriorated. But the SAS proceeded anyway to regain its own former expertise and self-reliance in conditions that others, even the Gurkhas, sometimes found almost impossible.

The 700-mile Front

When the SAS arrived in Brunei in January 1963, the revolt had been extinguished, but Intelligence reports as well as Sukarno's public speeches made it clear that

Indonesia's campaign of subversion was not to be
confined to Brunei. Sabah in the north-east and Sarawak,
stretching east-west across the island, were equally at risk.
As Blaxland explains: 'The frontier lay open and unmarked across 970 miles of wild and mountainous
country, over which raids could, and undoubtedly would
be made without warning at any point, and the coastline
was very much longer and just as vulnerable. The total
area to be protected was slightly larger than England and
Scotland, and there were only five battalions (including
the Royal Marine Commando) available, controlled by a
brigade headquarters at Kuching and another at Brunei,
and with the need for a regular system of reliefs over an
interminable period, there was no immediate prospect of
any great increase.'

In an effort to fill the gap, SAS teams from A
Squadron, usually between two and four men, were
staked out across 700 miles. Each team was responsible
for a 10,000-yard front sited to block most of the obvious
approaches from Kalimantan, as Indonesian Borneo was
called; these generally consisted of natural faults in the
mountain ridge, which lay across the centre of Borneo
like a quiff, and down those jungle motorways, the rivers.

It would be clearly impossible for these minuscule teams
personally to watch over such an area. The trick was to
arrange matters so that the jungle tribes would act as
scouts for the SAS teams, who would be the reporting
centre for each locality. In an environment in which as
little as five miles a day might be an ambitious tactical
movement, a spoor even a day old was valuable information for a defence force equipped with helicopters.
Basically, therefore, it was the mixture as before, in
Malaya: the hearts-and-minds business to yield information; airborne assault plus familiarity with the jungle to
follow it up.

But this was a very special environment. As Blaxland
describes it, 'the interior was a roadless confusion of

jungle and rivers. . . . Innumerable village settlements or kampongs were to be found, either by the river or on a hillside, from which tribesmen of many varieties primitively tilled the land around them or went hunting for fish, deer, baboons, porcupines or the ever-pervasive snakes.

'They lived in longhouses which were made of attap wood, had foetid interiors and were apt to creak balefully on the stilts that had kept them out of the water for decades. The Iban of Sarawak . . . were small, cheerful and indolent people, who neither cut their hair nor dressed above the waist, regardless of sex, except when attired in ceremonial finery, which was worn for visiting soldiery who would be primed with rice-wine and invited to do a solo dance.'

There was no question here, as in Malaya, of forcibly transplanting populations into new, fortified villages. In any case, most of the tribespeople were well-disposed towards the British. For the rest, the troops had to rely on charm, quick wits and little else – the weapons of non-violence. Styles varied. One of the Gurkha regiments, with more men than the SAS, concluded that 'the old system of giving salt, tobacco, sugar and beads was wrong for Borneo. Tact, courtesy and, above all, infinite patience and human understanding were needed. . . . Bartering of a minor nature continued non-stop. . . . It was also important to uphold at all times the dignity and prestige of the local headman. One way of accomplishing this was by allowing him to take the salute at "Retreat".' At ceremonial dances, some British officers achieved a succès d'estime by performing the Twist.

Nearer the mountainous border, the SAS approach was to move into the village, cautiously and sensitively, and to live there for five months or more. Tom Pocock, in his biography of General Walker, recounts how 'at first some of the SAS men were sent up-country in civilian clothes; an unexpectedly difficult task because the shirts and jeans on sale in Borneo shops were cut for diminutive Chinese figures, not hulking British troopers'. But disguise was quickly discarded as unnecessary, and the patrols wore the usual jungle green denims and soft brimmed hats with a yellow band for identification.

The first step towards penetration was to build a secret hide in the jungle within walking distance of the selected village. Having kept the place under observation long enough to ensure that neither guerrillas nor Indonesian regulars were already established, the soldiers would walk in, smile, and make contact. Sometimes conversation was possible through the medium of Malay; sometimes a basic sign-language evolved. When this failed, as one veteran wearily recalls, 'they would sit and look at us, and we would sit and look at them'. This entertainment was somewhat one-sided, since the soldiers were probably the first Europeans most of the villagers had seen. On a good day, the SAS patrol would be invited into the animal closeness of the collective longhouse and offered rice-wine and food, before taking their leave to sleep in their hide (basha), endeavouring to conceal the trail as they went.

The next day they would be back. Their message was that evil men from across the mountain were coming, and that the soldiers were there to protect the village. This, when finally comprehended, did not always fill head-hunting tribesmen with awe. So, to close a growing credibility gap as well as to rehearse essential reinforcement tactics, A Squadron's commander, Major Peter de la Billière, devised the 'step-up' technique. For this, a full infantry company would be warned to be ready to move by helicopter to a remote forward location for a demonstration of quick deployment and firepower. On the day set for this exercise, the SAS soldiers would explain to the villagers that although the soldiers were only two in number, they had many friends, other warriors who could descend from the sky to their aid. It would be particularly helpful if the necessary space could be created for the flying soldiers to land safely. The tribesmen, who are adept at removing large trees with small, flexible axes, were fascinated by the prospect of such entertainment, and a helicopter landing zone was rapidly carved out of the jungle. The soldiers then radioed the message, 'Bring in the step-up party now!' About fifteen minutes later the helicopters would appear, loaded with business-like Gurkhas armed with sharpened kukris as well as modern firearms. The show usually brought the longhouse down.

Gifts of portable radios, simple medical aid and other favours rapidly ensured that the SAS team became an institution in the community, though with one exception, its aid rarely achieved the elaboration recorded by 2/7th Gurkhas whose native protégés 'made endless requests for trips to outlying kampongs (villages), movement of rice, planks, children, old people and pigs by helicopter. . . . The locals came to rely more on the soldiers and airmen than on the civil administration. . . .' One young and rich SAS troop commander expressed this hearts-and-minds offensive by flying out, at his own expense, hampers of Christmas food from Fortnum and Mason's exclusive London store to supply the nomads in his part of Borneo. Another unique contribution to village life was made by an SAS soldier of Romany origins, 'Gipsy Smith'. A natural improviser, he constructed a water-powered generator to provide the only electric light in thousands of square miles. For his next trick, he dismantled his Bergen rucksack and converted its metal frame to a still for making alcohol.

The message that accompanied these diversions was always the same: danger lay on the other side of the mountains and one day it would move closer. The villagers must help themselves by staying alert for anything unusual seen in the surrounding jungle, particularly the characteristic mark of a rubber-soled boot.

Could the villagers select one of their number to be a link-man with the soldiers? They could.

By now the SAS team would have its own quarters on the edge of the village, broadcasting daily reports to Squadron Headquarters. The team might be augmented by one or two members of the local police field force. Regularly the team would make a circular tour of the area, lasting up to five days, visiting a series of villages. Like village policemen, they moved on foot. Unlike village policemen they moved unobtrusively, in single file, the lead scout of the patrol followed by the commander and his radio operator, with a gun carrier at the rear playing 'tail-end Charlie'.

Only towards the end of this first five-month tour did something happen to remind even the SAS that the threat about which they had been preaching was real. In the early hours of Good Friday morning, 12 April 1963, a force of thirty guerrillas surrounded the police station at the border town of Tebedu in West Sarawak. After a brisk battle, in which a police corporal was killed and two others wounded, the raiders looted the bazaar.

When the news reached the local military HQ, a troop of Royal Marine Commandos was sent to the scene. The raiders had disappeared back into the undergrowth, leaving leaflets which purported to show that the action was a manifestation of the earlier revolt in Brunei. Later evidence was to sustain the intelligent guesses made at the time that the raid was probably led by Indonesian regulars.

At a remote border kampong known as Rundun, a four-man SAS team was preparing to hand over to a relief group from D Squadron. When the Tebedu attack took place, two of the soldiers from this group had already started the twenty-five-mile journey to the rendezvous, more than a day's march away, in order to guide their successors. Meanwhile, the remaining pair had received an urgent signal from the Squadron's operations room, telling them of the Tebedu affair, instructing them to stay at their location and to dig in. This phrase, conjuring up as it did, a vision of divisions massed on the Marne, caused some merriment. The team's reaction was: 'What, both of us?'

From now on, the war followed an inevitable course. More troops and helicopters were summoned to Borneo, and a search of towns in Sarawak brought to light plans by the Clandestine Communist Organization (CCO) for Malayan-style terrorism. The police began the confiscation of the 8500 licensed shotguns circulating among the Chinese community. There were more cross-border raids from Indonesian soil, and a night curfew was imposed on Sarawak during which the security forces could open fire without prior warning.

On the long, unmarked frontier there could never be enough men to achieve total security. But the success of the SAS in creating a defensive Intelligence network among the tribesmen encouraged General Walker to create, with the help of the SAS and others, the indigenous Border Scouts. This was a controversial decision, if only because experience in Malaya had shown that, while it may be expedient to arm tribesmen and train them as guerrillas in time of crisis, they are impossible to disarm when the crisis is over, with disastrous results for long-term internal security. A more short-term consideration was the role the Scouts would fill.

Inevitably, perhaps, the tribesmen, trained as Border Scouts by the Gurkha Independent Parachute Company in basic weapon-handling and battle tactics within three short weeks, more closely resembled orthodox infantry than the SAS pupils, who were encouraged to think of themselves as the eyes and ears, rather than the fists of their allies. As one Gurkha regimental history acknowledges: 'Although the use of the Scouts in this way involved border kampongs and longhouses in the defence of their own country and kin, their suitability for employment in defensive static positions was limited.'

The unsuitability of the Scouts for this sort of warfare, even under the overall command of such an experienced jungle hand as Lieutenant-Colonel John Cross, became tragically apparent in September 1963. At Long Jawi in Central Borneo, thirty miles from the border, the Gurkhas had established a Scout post consisting of twenty-one locals, two Police Field Force signallers and a six-man Gurkha team headed by a corporal. Just before dawn one day, a well-equipped company of Indonesian regulars fell upon Long Jawi. The signallers were killed as they tried unsuccessfully to summon aid. The raiders looted the village, destroyed it by fire, and withdrew.

The Gurkha HQ attributed radio silence from Long Jawi to bad atmospheric conditions until, four days later, one Border Scout and two surviving Gurkhas reached the headquarters, 'weak and exhausted, but with weapons spotlessly clean, and able to give a first-hand account of the battle'. Gurkha ambush parties were flown into the area, and during the next month most of the Indonesians were hunted down, sometimes in ones and twos, after their escape craft had been shot to pieces by Gurkhas waiting on the river banks. Vengeance had been exacted but the lesson, that such warfare was a matter for professionals, was not lost on Walker and his advisers. More SAS soldiers were needed, and urgently, in the border area. Meanwhile, on Walker's orders the role of the Border Scouts was changed – no more paramilitary work, and exclusive concentration on Intelligence-gathering activities.

Squadrons Restored

As a long-term measure, Whitehall approved the restoration of the two SAS squadrons that had been axed at the end of the Malayan Emergency four years earlier, in

1959. John Watts, one of the Regiment's most experienced soldiers, started work in England soon afterwards to raise a new B Squadron – for which recruitment teams toured BAOR – while the Parachute Brigade's Guards Independent (Pathfinder) Company was sent to Borneo to learn something like an SAS role on the job (as was the 2nd Battalion, the Parachute Regiment). Later, the Guards Company would provide the nucleus of the new G Squadron.

Also from Britain, the Headquarters of 22 SAS arrived to occupy a position overlooking the palace of the Sultan of Brunei. This building was known as the Haunted House: during the Japanese occupation it had been used for interrogation by Tokyo's Gestapo, and it was popularly believed that the spirit of a young European woman, a victim of torture, lingered there.

Almost coinciding with the attack at Long Jawi, a series of political events elsewhere generated SAS reinforcements from New Zealand and Australia. Less than two weeks before the attack, Sarawak and North Borneo (Sabah) were granted independence, and they promptly joined the Malaysian Federation. (The event was celebrated in the Indonesian capital, Jakarta, with a mob attack on the British Embassy, where the stone-throwers exposed themselves to a withering barrage of bagpipe music played by an SAS officer there, Major Roderic Walker, as he marched back and forth in front of the embattled building.) Since Malaysia was a member of the South East Asia Treaty Organization, the Australian and New Zealand SAS regiments each sent a squadron to Sarawak, the Australians responding to a visit by Woodhouse to their Perth headquarters early in 1964. As in Malaya in the 1950s, the New Zealanders – possibly because of the number of Maoris in their ranks – were to produce the best jungle trackers the SAS ever had.

This extra manpower enabled the next British squad-

ron on tour in the island – D Squadron, fresh from
training in West Germany and Norway – to concentrate
its efforts on the shorter frontier between Indonesia and
Brunei, which had chosen to remain a British protectorate rather than join the new Federation. The efforts of D
Squadron, as Philip Warner's official history of the
Regiment records, had tangible results: 'Several brisk
engagements, including one in which nine out of a party
of 21 rebels were captured, and the remainder fled,
leaving most of their weapons and ammunition behind.'
But fundamentally, in the autumn of 1963, it was the
mixture as before: long days in the villages, longer
marches between them, for five months. An anonymous
contributor to the regimental journal, *Mars & Minerva*,
described it thus: 'Four men, living as members of the
longhouse itself for months at a time, watch, listen, patrol
and report. . . . Day by day, the sick come for treatment,
the women bring presents of fruit and vegetables, the
men to gossip and bring news, the children to watch,
silent-eyed and the leaders of the community to discuss
their problems and to ask, and offer advice. The patrol
slips as easily into the primitive rhythm of the day and
season as the people themselves. Soon the cycle of
burning, planting, weeding and harvesting becomes part
of [the soldier's] life itself, and customs, rites and celebrations as familiar as the Cup Final or Bank Holidays at
home. . . .

'Here a strong patrol of five or six men will train ten or
twenty times that number of tribesmen in counter-
terrorist warfare. In each camp a simple longhouse
houses the Scouts; a similar, but smaller version, their
instructors. The daily programme is long and arduous,
though the syllabus is basic and directly related to the
skills required to be taught.

'The patrol embraces all responsibilities for its charges:
training, administration, discipline and morale. The language difficulty is ever present . . . pantomime is popular

and some are skilful exponents of the art. Helicopter training without helicopters is a useful test piece. Throwing live grenades presents other problems, but no pantomime is necessary. . . .'

In December 1963, this military idyll came to an abrupt halt when 128 guerrillas struck at the prosperous area of Tawau on the coast of Sabah, destroying a force of the Royal Malay Regiment in its own base twenty miles from the border. True, the raiders were all subsequently killed or taken prisoner by 1/10th Gurkhas, but the identification of twenty-one of the enemy as regular Indonesian Marines confirmed that this was no longer a routine counter-insurgency campaign.

Walker, the military supremo, himself characterized the year 1963 as one 'which began with the end of a revolution and ended with the beginning of an undeclared war'. Within a few weeks there were to be other, similar attacks. In January 1964, the British SAS Squadron moved back to the sensitive, unmapped mountain border of central Sarawak, known as the Third Division.

Cross-Border Operations: 'Those Bloody Ghosts'

It was not long after this that the Regiment started to mount its first cross-border reconnaissance missions, which would ultimately identify the camps from which the Indonesian regulars came and the exact routes they followed to their targets in Malaysia. Such operations were – and are – ultra-sensitive politically as well as militarily, normally requiring approval from the Prime Minister in London. In this case, such operations marked the decisive turning-point of the war in Britain's favour.

The first cross-border patrols were gentle, shallow probes over the ridge into Indonesian territory by four-man groups unaccompanied by local guides. The men carried exactly the same equipment and weapons that were being used in Sarawak. If wounded and taken prisoner, the men themselves, as well as their headquarters, would attribute their presence in Indonesian territory to a simple map-reading error. In the circumstances it would be a fairly plausible cover story. As Pocock puts it: 'The SAS was, as usual, a law unto itself and on reconnaissance missions would sometimes penetrate into what was certainly enemy-held territory.'

Another element in almost all SAS operations in Borneo, to which particular emphasis was now given across the border, was Woodhouse's policy of 'shoot-'n'-scoot' (to break contact with the enemy as soon as possible) whenever contact occurred. Woodhouse, as he admitted years later, was strenuously influenced by his own experience in a ten-man reconnaissance section during the Second World War, when only he and one other returned from a single operation. It had not been easy to find volunteers to replace the lost men.

In Borneo, conscious that he had only two operational front-line squadrons totalling about 120 men, Woodhouse was not going to allow heavy casualties to destroy the morale or the credibility of the Regiment in London at such a time. 'Shoot-'n'-scoot' was not popular with the SAS, and both officers and men said so; but there was much to recommend the policy for cross-border operations. As Woodhouse explained subsequently: 'There was a tendency in military circles to fear that the SAS would suddenly take matters into their own hands and that the first news of this to reach the top would be that 200 Indonesians had been shot up in bed. I used to emphasize that it was more important, for that sort of reason, that we should be seen to obey orders than anyone.'

The success of the first patrols into Kalimantan led to something more ambitious. The SAS was given the task of finding the exact river routes used by the Indonesians to move men and equipment up to the border. The recce patrols counted the boats and the men in them, mapped suitable areas from which the boats could be ambushed on the river bank, and quietly walked back over the mountain ridge to Sarawak. Next, the patrols were asked to find the kampongs and bases from which the boats had come. This was an ambitious undertaking which, if it went wrong, could not be dismissed as a mere map-reading error. By now, the first squadron commander to take part in the patrols had given much thought to the preparation of his men. By temperament a man who prefers to resolve problems before they arise, he typically organized random urine and blood tests to ensure that they were taking their prophylactic doses of Paludrin to avoid malaria. For these deep penetration patrols, he took men to the airport to weigh their Bergen rucksacks on the only available scales before they flew by helicopter to the jungle entry-point. If a rucksack weighed an ounce more than fifty pounds (later reduced to thirty) some-thing had to come out, for the emphasis now, unlike the situation in Malaya, was not upon how much a human being could carry, but how far he could travel and function as a soldier carrying the minimum of equip-ment. As one of his officers remarked: 'You can't go head down, arse up when you are in close proximity to the enemy.'

It was also decreed that nothing be left in enemy territory to betray the presence of British troops: no casualties who might be identified; no spent cartridge cases; no cigarette stubs; no identity discs, photographs or letters from home; not even the heel print of a standard British military boot. So the deep penetration patrols were equipped with the Armalite rifle, which had several advantages. It was the perfect jungle weapon – portable and powerful – and, although cir-culating in considerable quantities around the world, not standard issue to the British Army. Irregular footwear was preferred or, if this were impossible in the Borneo jungle, sacking or hessian was placed outside the boot to blur all marks indicating its origin.

Above all, the job was one for soldiers who were natural navigators and men who had a feel for the country, with one complete tour of Borneo duty under their belts. It was no time to get lost, since no rescue would be forthcoming. Furthermore, the only certain way to find the Indonesian bases was to follow the spoor left by the enemy's raiding parties. The reconnaissance groups had to be superlative trackers.

Having arrived at their destination, the SAS 'moles' were expected to establish not just the location of the base and its approximate strength but also to draw the most detailed sketch maps of the place they could. This meant penetrating the kampongs in which the Indonesian soldiers lived, without alerting sentries or dogs, and then slipping back to the blessed cover of the deep jungle.

When they finally emerged into friendly territory after three weeks or more, their uniforms sometimes hanging in rags, their appearance often appalled Allied troops. One, recollecting the emaciated condition of these military apparitions, said afterwards: 'They looked like bloody ghosts left over from the war against the Japanese. And they said nothing, nothing, except: "Hello. Hold your fire. We're British".'

Loss of body weight was inevitable when the men were obliged to live on dehydrated rations yielding 3500 calories per day instead of the recommended level of 5000. Upon their return, some men had to be debriefed (one day); allowed total rest (two days); and briefed for the next patrol (two days): a total of just five days in which to eat like hamsters and replace some of the lost weight before another trip across the border. After three of these patrols, most of the soldiers were so worn out that they needed recuperation in England. It was not surprising that Whitehall's attempts to extend SAS tours to six months or more – to reduce travel costs – were fiercely and successfully resisted by the Regiment's commanding officer.

The navigation for these operations was achieved through careful scrutiny of air photographs, cultivation of a photographic memory for such features as ridges and rivers and the compass bearings on which they ran, as well as a finely-tuned sense of distance walked to calculate a dead reckoning of mileage covered by reference to time-on-march. Tracking required the knack of seeing, as if they were motorway signposts, traces of human urine, crushed grass, muddied river crossings, bruised moss and broken bark on exposed tree roots. It required also the knowledge that fallen leaves, when brushed aside at the right spot, could reveal a perfectly shaped boot-print impressed in the soft earth beneath.

The recipe for concealment was that which General Walker had laid down for the Gurkhas when in ambush: 'No chance . . . if he smoked, chewed gum, washed his hands with soap, cleaned his teeth, Brylcreemed his hair, whispered or coughed. In ambush, a man is lying in wait for a dangerous, hunted animal whose sense of smell and eyesight can be phenomenal.' The nerve needed for these clandestine operations could not be taught. They involved a form of stress that scarred even the most stable SAS soldiers in some way. After they had experienced weeks of silence and near-silent communication, their comrades noticed, on their return to England, that some veterans of the Borneo patrols could not break the habit of whispering to each other, even when exchanging a joke in the men's room behind their favourite Hereford pub.

Such labours bore fruit a few months later in mid-1964 when, faced by increasingly bold attacks from the Indonesian side, General Walker sanctioned counter-strikes, first by artillery, then by 'killer' groups drawn from the best infantry battalions and led by SAS guides.

These were known collectively as 'Claret' operations and were hardly less sensitive than the reconnaissance that preceded them.

An Offensive with Golden Rules

'Claret' operations were governed by what were colloquially known as the 'Golden Rules' and they were graded Top Secret. The initial penetration depth permitted into Indonesia was 5000 yards and this was increased, for certain specific raids, to 20,000. The objective, according to Brigadier E. D. ('Birdie') Smith of the Gurkha Rifles, was: 'to pre-empt any likely build-up or attack, to harass by ambush and patrols the Indonesians, and to induce them to move their camps back and away from the border.... Initially, the guidelines were:

a. All raids had to be authorised by the Director of Operations (General Walker) himself.

b. Only tried and tested troops were to be used – in other words no soldiers were to be sent across ... during their first tour in Borneo.

c. Raids were to be made with the definite aim of deterring and thwarting aggression by the Indonesians. No attacks were to be mounted in retribution or with the sole aim of inflicting casualties on the foe.

d. Close air support could not be given except in an extreme emergency....'

For a time, Smith explains, only Gurkha battalions could be used for offensive cross-border operations in addition to SAS soldiers, and no unit was to mount more than one raid at a time. Finally, 'minimum force was to be the principle used rather than large-scale attacks which would have incited retaliation and risked escalation, turning the border war into something quite different, costly in lives and fraught with international problems'.

The guides for these raids were usually (though not

invariably) provided by the SAS, who found them almost relaxing after the nervous isolation of the earlier reconnaissance. As one SAS veteran said: 'Having done your recce, and crept around and done all the sneaky bits, when you came back as part of a Gurkha company you felt as safe as houses in the middle of their perimeter: all those little brown men with GPMGs going out in all directions to set up listening posts. . . .' Safer, yes, but on windless, silent days in the jungle, no less stealthy, as the history of 2/7th Gurkha Rifles reveals: 'No rifleman was allowed to eat, smoke or unscrew his water bottle without his platoon commander's permission. At night, sentries checked any man who snored or talked in his sleep. Whenever the company was on the move, a recce section led the way, their packs carried by the men behind. Because of the long approach march, each man carried six days' basic rations together with various lightweight additions and a small reserve in a belt pouch.'

The effect of the raids was often devastating. At one Indonesian Army camp, the enemy were breakfasting on roast pig when the Gurkhas arrived. In thick undergrowth, the patrol brought rocket-launchers, grenade-throwers and machine-guns into position. Then, as the regimental history records, 'the happy camping scene by the river was shattered as a 3.5-inch rocket flared across the water and exploded among the breakfast party. The hut disintegrated in a ball of flame, the men hurled in all directions. . . .

'As two assault platoons moved in to clear the camp they contacted a number of totally naked, panic-stricken enemy rushing from it. These were quickly dealt with and, covered by fierce fire from the support group, we assaulted the base. Resistance had ceased, but a number of dead lay scattered about the camp and blood was everywhere.'

Unaccompanied SAS units also began to attack enemy approach routes. According to Pocock's account, once formal government approval was received for such activities, the SAS, 'instead of watching and counting', would be given permission to begin interdiction: ambushing tracks and rivers and setting booby-traps where it was known that only raiders would pass. Sometimes their ambushes would be sophisticated affairs with electronically-detonated Claymore mines catching an enemy party's front and rear, while the SAS troopers' automatic fire raked the centre. Because the essence of SAS activity was speed of movement and reaction, they called themselves 'The Tiptoe Boys'. The ambush parties hit and vanished, leaving the counter-attack to find nothing but apparently empty jungle.

The impact of such operations was not always so one-sided. On both the reconnaissance and offensive patrols things could, and did, misfire. An Australian SAS trooper was gored by an elephant while in Indonesian territory. His companion bound his wounds and made him as comfortable as possible before starting a two-day trek for help from a Gurkha camp. The wounded man had died by the time he was found. Unusually, the body was recovered by helicopter. Deaths on such occasions usually meant the removal of all identification from the body and quick burial in an unmarked grave. In another episode, a 22 SAS sergeant who had contracted the jungle disease leptospirosis was lucky to survive his 20,000-yard march home while suffering from a 105-degree temperature and other symptoms.

Inevitably, SAS reconnaissance groups were occasionally ambushed by the opposition despite all precautions. As a veteran of the Borneo patrols explained: 'The man who is stationary in the jungle has the tactical advantage. We sometimes found it necessary to spend as much as twenty minutes in any half-hour period sitting and listening, and only ten minutes on the move.' Only once was an SAS soldier taken prisoner. A wounded trooper, seized after an ambush, was never seen again, but the Regiment subsequently learned from local tribesmen that he had been tortured so appallingly that he died before his captors could 'break' him. There were also some near-misses. Two SAS men had to be winched by helicopter out of the jungle so quickly that they were carried, still dangling from a rope, through the treetops for much of their journey. One of the men lost his rifle in the process, and a search had to be mounted to recover the weapon.

The Lillico Patrol

One of the best-documented cases of such an escape, recorded in the Regiment's journal *Mars & Minerva*, describes what happened to a patrol from D Squadron in February 1965.

'A small 22 SAS patrol was moving down from a ridge on a jungle track towards an old Indonesian border terrorist camp. The camp had been discovered the day before and appeared as though it had not been used for six months.

'As the leading scout, Trooper Thomson, ducked under some bamboo across the track – there was a lot of it in the area – a movement attracted his attention. He looked up and saw an Indonesian soldier six yards away to his right, just as the latter fired a burst at him. Several other enemy opened fire simultaneously.

'Thomson was hit in the left thigh, the bone being shattered, and was knocked off the track to the left. He landed in a clump of bamboo two yards away from another Indonesian soldier lying concealed there. As the latter fumbled for his rifle, Thomson picked up his own, which he had dropped as he fell, and shot him.

'The second man in the patrol, the commander, Sergeant E. Lillico, was also hit by the initial bursts and had collapsed on the track, unable to use his legs. He was still able to use his rifle, however, and this he did, returning the fire. Meanwhile the remainder of the patrol had taken cover.

'Thomson, unable to walk, hopped back to where Sergeant Lillico was sitting and joined in the fire fight. As he had seen Thomson on his feet, Lillico was under the misapprehension that he could walk and therefore sent him back up the track to bring the rest of the patrol forward, and continued to fire at the sounds of enemy movement.

'As Thomson was unable to get to his feet, he dragged himself along by his hands and, on arriving at the top of the ridge, fired several bursts in the direction of the camp. . . . The enemy withdrew. . . .

'During the remainder of the day, Thomson continued to drag himself towards where he expected to find the rest of the patrol. He had applied a tourniquet to his thigh, which he released from time to time, taken morphia, and bandaged his wound as best he could with a shell dressing.'

Lillico, meanwhile, 'pulled himself into the cover of a clump of bamboo, took morphia, bandaged his wound, and passed out. . . .

'The remainder of the patrol had decided that the best course of action was to move to the nearest infantry post close by and lead back a stronger party to search the area. This they did, starting back towards the scene of the contact late the same day.'

The following morning, Thomson continued to crawl back towards the border, and by evening he had covered 1000 yards, or about half the distance involved. He was found by the search party just before dusk, carried to a clearing next day and evacuated by helicopter.

On the second day, meanwhile, Lillico had dragged himself to the top of a ridge, 400 yards from the scene of the action. At about 3 pm, he fired signal shots to attract the attention of any friendly search party. Instead, the shots attracted more enemy troops, one of whom climbed a tree about forty yards from the spot where the sergeant lay quietly in the scrub. Twice during the day, Lillico had heard a helicopter overhead, but because of the proximity of the Indonesians he did not disclose his position. In the evening, the helicopter returned for the third time that day, identified Lillico's signal, and winched him to safety about thirty-six hours after the action. Lillico was awarded the Military Medal and Thomson was Mentioned in Dispatches.

The Superior Sergeant-Major

It was not only the small parties that hit trouble. From May to October 1965, Squadron Sergeant-Major L. Smith ran the SAS operations room for an area of the Sarawak border 382 miles across, the longest battalion front in Allied Borneo. Such a task, as the historians of 2/7th Gurkha Rifles point out, had not been the responsibility of any SAS rank below that of captain during post-war years. Smith, they reveal, was 'entirely responsible for mounting SAS patrols, maintaining liaison with battalion commanders and for the considerable work involved in mounting and running the patrol operations. He personally led several dangerous and exacting operations when detailed preliminary reconnaissance reports were needed.'

As a result of one of these patrols, a Gurkha company of forty men set off to ambush Indonesian water traffic. Instead, it ran into an Indonesian company of 100 men marching along the same track beside the river. A confused, close-quarter battle followed in which grenades, machine-guns and Claymore mines were used. Smith had not accompanied the patrol beyond an advance base position because of a cough which might have compromised the operation. But 'he had realized that something had gone wrong, so he had worked out a complete fire plan for the (artillery) gun support' and, as the first survivors straggled in, 'brought down a very close-in defensive fire which helped the Gurkhas to make a clean break'. As one Gurkha said later: 'Without his help we would have been faced with a running battle back to the border.'

Now it was discovered that some of the Gurkhas were missing. About thirty-six hours after the initial contact a New Zealand gunner captain who had been with the patrol walked into the forward base with the news that he had carried or dragged a wounded Gurkha sergeant-major through 6000 yards of dense jungle and swamp, an heroic achievement. SSM Smith now led the recovery party and, as the Gurkha history records it: 'In the jungle, SSM Smith was a tower of strength. He found a suitable winching zone, brought in the helicopter and supervised the lashing onto the stretcher of the wounded man. Had the evacuation been postponed further, the injured man would undoubtedly have lost a leg. . . . He was discharged from hospital without even a limp.'

Slowly but surely, towards the end of 1965 the Indonesians were forced to abandon their front-line bases, conceding control of the border to the Allies. Nothing had been said publicly by either the British or the Indonesians about the 'Claret' operations, but within Indonesia Sukarno was rapidly becoming discredited among his military commanders and the common people, who were finding the price of his dreams of glory exorbitant.

The British, meanwhile, were making plans to undermine the regime by spreading the guerrilla war to other parts of Indonesia including, if it were expedient, Sumatra and Java. Plans for these operations embraced such external Intelligence agencies as MI6 as well as the SAS, but they were overtaken by events. In March 1966, Sukarno was reduced to a figurehead by his military top brass.

The Last Invader

The last Indonesian invasion, by fifty soldiers into a Sarawak border area near Brunei, ended disastrously for them. An Indonesian coffee-tin label put a Gurkha battalion on their trail. At the first contact, the invaders fragmented into small parties which were assiduously pursued for many weeks. Their leader, a charismatic figure named Lieutenant Sumbi, who had boasted that he would seize Brunei Bay and the Shell oil installations, was captured on 3 September, three weeks after Indonesia had signed a peace agreement with Malaysia.

With the end of the war, General Lea, the SAS officer who had been Allied military supremo during the final, victorious phase, was promptly knighted. Walker, meanwhile, became the only general to be made an honorary member of the SAS. As the Army's historian, Blaxland, wrote: 'Thus ended what must surely rank as the British Army's neatest achievement during post-war years. What might so easily have been an interminable embroilment in the jungle, the kampongs, the villages and towns, with an ever-swelling flow of blood and hate, had been brought to a happy end in little more than three years.

'This had been achieved because the Army had won the confidence of the inhabitants and gained complete mastery over a brave and tough, if not very ably led, enemy. They had combined kindness to the defended with aggression against the attackers, two virtues not always regarded as compatible, and it had all been done with a lack of self-advertisement which must have had a deflating effect on the enemy. . . .'

The total number of British casualties was 19 killed and 44 wounded, while the Gurkhas had lost 40 killed with 83 wounded. The Indonesian dead numbered 2000.

3. South Arabia, 1964–67: The Lost Cause

What happened to the British Army in Aden, a territory which is now the Soviet satellite of South Yemen, is a well-documented example of how soldiers are obliged to continue fighting for a lost cause when their political masters attempt the impossible feat of leaving a colony, while at the same time remaining there. The abortive Suez operation of 1956; the emergence of Nasserism and its dissemination via the hot-gospel broadcasts of Cairo Radio; the 'shotgun marriage' of the South Arabian Federation between 1959 and 1963, linking the feudal, tribal sheikdoms lying between Yemen and the coast with the urban area of Aden Colony; the establishment of Britain's Middle East Command Headquarters in 1960: all these had generated intense local opposition to the British presence before the SAS arrived.

Most inauspicious of all, the hereditary ruler of Yemen, the Imam, was overthrown in a left-wing, Army-led coup in September 1962, which was instantly consolidated by the arrival of Egyptian troops. Recent evidence suggests that the Soviet KGB, aided by their British agent Kim Philby, had a hand in this. The new Republican government in Yemen promptly called on 'our brothers in the Occupied South' – Aden and the Federation – 'to be ready for a revolution and for joining the battle we shall wage against colonialism'.

What now occurred, in effect, was a war by proxy between two colonial powers: Britain on one side and Egypt, backed by Soviet Russia, on the other. The battleground was the whole of that desolate, mountainous territory lying between the Gulf of Aden and Saudi Arabia. In Yemen itself, the deposed Imam eluded his would-be assassins. During the next eight years or more, his Royalist guerrilla army was aided by the Saudis and stiffened by a mercenary force largely composed of SAS veterans using secret bases in the Aden Federation, an operation that enjoyed discreet official backing from Whitehall.

In the Federation, meanwhile, two distinctive campaigns were fought out simultaneously. A tribal uprising took place in the Radfan mountains adjoining Yemen, while in Aden State the British faced their first campaign of sustained urban terrorism. One of the paradoxes to emerge was that in Yemen an SAS 'old boys' team was part of a guerrilla force, while a few miles south in Aden's hinterland their successors in the regular regiment were striving to suppress a guerrilla campaign.

But the most significant battle, as usual, was the one for credibility. What were British intentions? Who would go and who would remain to run the country if the British left? There were many brave pronouncements from Westminster along the lines of 'No surrender', even when in July 1964 a Conservative Government set 1968 as the target date for the Federation's self-government. That promise of independence was accompanied by an arrangement that Britain would retain her bases in Aden and not desert the tribal rulers with whom she had maintained protection treaties since the nineteenth century. There were other reasons why Britain should keep her bases in the area. It was a time when shrinking British forces were still expected to maintain global commitments, particularly east of Suez. The Borneo campaign had started, unexpectedly, only a year before. Britain had important bases in Singapore and Hong Kong, so Aden was a strategically important staging-post as well as a port of regional importance (as the Russians would later demonstrate in their Ethiopian campaign of 1978). In

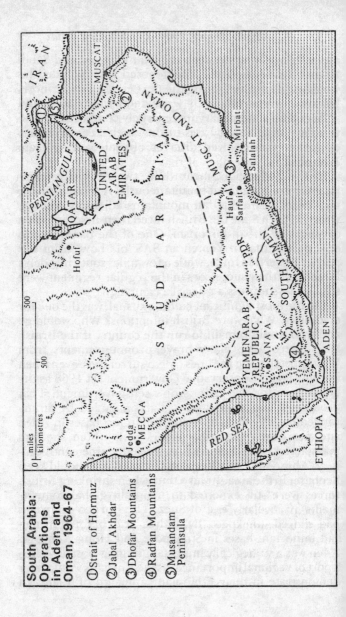

South Arabia: Operations in Aden and Oman, 1964-67

① Strait of Hormuz
② Jabal Akhdar
③ Dhofar Mountains
④ Radfan Mountains
⑤ Musandam Peninsula

IRAN

MUSCAT

PERSIAN GULF

UNITED ARAB EMIRATES

QATAR

Hofuf

SAUDI ARABIA

MUSCAT AND OMAN

Mirbat
Hauf • Salalah
Sarfait

PDR

SOUTH YEMEN

YEMEN ARAB REPUBLIC

SANA'A

ADEN

MECCA
Jedda •

RED SEA

ETHIOPIA

500
miles
500
kilometres
0

October 1964, Mr Harold Wilson's Labour administration swept to power on the promise of a society transformed by 'the white heat of technology' and other instant miracles. Within eighteen months, in February 1966, the new government announced a total evacuation deadline of the Aden base to coincide with Independence. In March 1967, the evacuation deadline was advanced to November of that year.

These decisions destroyed the credibility of British promises in Aden, and had the lethal result of nullifying the hearts-and-minds campaign that elsewhere had proved to be a more potent peace-making force than bullets. Nor, as events turned out, did a precipitate British evacuation bring more freedom to the people of Aden, despite the promises of Cairo Radio. 'Liberated' Aden became a drab military dictatorship in which those questioning the regime, such as the Chief Magistrate of the Supreme Court, simply disappeared. The Imperial British had at least doffed their caps at democracy through a limited franchise.

Britain's decision to withdraw from Aden also accelerated the guerrilla war against another of Britain's allies, the Sultan of Oman. During the final year of the Aden campaign, in 1966, Marxist rebels in a remote Adeni sultanate bordering Oman's warlike province of Dhofar, were supplying weapons to Dhofari tribesmen, effectively opening up a third front against the British. In Aden, the Irish Guards were used to attack the Dhofari bases with a spearhead provided by B Squadron of 22 SAS. This textbook infantry operation, a frontal attack, quite opposed to SAS methods, ended with the successful escape of the Dhofaris.

The ubiquitous Major John Cooper, the retired SAS officer who had served as a freelance soldier in Oman before joining the Royalist guerrillas in Yemen, took a more sophisticated interest in this extension of the war. From time to time he would appear at Aden's Intelligence centre, for which he carried a permanent pass, to scrutinize photographs of known terrorist leaders. A friend of those days recalls: 'At the time, John was based partly in Oman, partly in Yemen.'

The British left Aden on 29 November 1967. The political beneficiaries of the war were, quaintly enough, Israel, whose secret aid to the Royalist cause in Yemen tied down 60,000 of Egypt's best troops during the 1967 Six Day War; and Soviet Russia, which took over the base facilities in Aden. It can be argued that the secret war in Yemen – more fully examined in Chapter IV – also helped to prevent an Egyptian or Marxist takeover in Oman and other Gulf states. The significance of this prophylaxis would emerge only years later, after 1978, when the Iranian revolution and the Soviet invasion of Afghanistan plunged the world into turmoil.

Punishing the Radfan

The Emergency was declared formally in December 1963, after a grenade had been hurled at the High Commissioner, Sir Kennedy Trevaskis, and several Federal Ministers as they prepared to fly to London for a constitutional conference. The ill-defined frontier with South Yemen, across which Egyptian, Yemeni and Adeni nationalists were bringing weapons (including mines left in Egypt by the British), was then closed, at least on paper. But the border tribesmen, for whom guerrilla warfare was a way of life, were still supplied with money and rifles by Yemen, and a battle now began for control of the scorching, almost waterless Radfan mountains in which there were no roads.

Yet in April 1964, when A Squadron of the SAS arrived there, the strength of opposition and the general scale of the problem was simply not comprehended by the British. One eminent officer, who had served with Aden's

Federal Regular Army (FRA) as an Intelligence officer shortly before returning to the territory as officer commanding A Squadron, candidly admitted later: 'We did not appreciate the intensity of the violence of the tribal reaction to our presence. I expected a few dissidents to poop off a few rounds and then go home again. . . . So often, we underrate our enemy.'

Between the Emergency declaration in December and the arrival of the SAS in April, there had already been one attempt to subdue the Radfan area by a combined force of three Federal Regular Army battalions of Arabs with small numbers of British tanks, guns and engineers. Officially, this operation was described as 'a demonstration in force', but as Julian Paget's analysis of the Aden affair explains: 'There was no long-term plan as to what was to be done once the military task was completed; there were no plans to prevent further subversion, to finance development of the area or to initiate an intense "hearts and minds" campaign.' The real objective was punitive, and this in an area already in a rebellious mood and steeped in the tradition of 'an eye for an eye'. Paget records: 'There were many local officials, with a profound knowledge of the Arabs, who believed strongly that any attempt to subdue the tribes by force was doomed to be a waste of time and effort.'

The FRA battalions did occupy parts of the Radfan mountains for a few weeks, at a cost of five dead (one of them a British company commander) and twelve wounded. Then they withdrew to perform the even more important task of guarding the frontier. The tribesmen promptly reoccupied their former hill positions and began attacking traffic on the Dhala road linking Aden and Yemen. Meanwhile, Cairo and its puppet regime in the Yemeni capital of Sana'a announced the FRA's withdrawal from Radfan as a resounding defeat for the imperialists.

The Federal Government (a mixture of tribal rulers

and Adeni merchants) now sought more substantial British military help, despite the misgivings of that government's own Ministers responsible for internal security, who believed the deployment of British troops in so hostile an area would simply make matters worse. Not for the first time, however, the lessons of colonial history were forgotten. The British had first tried to bring the Wolves of Radfan – the Qotaibi tribe – to heel in 1881. From a desk in Aden, sixty miles away, they had declared the tribe nominally subject to the Emir of Dhala, a town on the ancient trade route linking Aden and Yemen. Until then the tribesmen had regarded it as their right to extort payment from travellers using the road, a protection racket deodorized by its antiquity. For years afterwards, the British sent punitive columns trudging into the inhospitable mountains, regiments lost to memory such as the Dublin Fusiliers, Sepoys, Bombay Grenadiers and Outrams Rifles, and they never entirely subdued the hill warriors. Throughout the 1930s, control (such as it was) was left to the RAF, which bombed the rebels from time to time.

In January 1965, in a study of the Radfan tribesman's character, Mr Harry Cockerill, a wartime SAS veteran who was already working in Aden when the Regiment arrived there, wrote: 'He will never surrender in battle and will endure shocking wounds, crawling away to die on his own rather than seek aid from his enemy. His territory is such that a few men can hold up a battalion. He is fanatically independent, a local saying being "Every tribesman thinks himself a Sultan". Unless a settlement is made that will allow him his independence . . . the Qotaibi . . . will take to the hills and it will all start again.'

In response to the Federal Government's request, a mixed force of brigade strength plus a squadron each of RAF Hunter ground-support aircraft, Shackleton bombers and Twin Pioneer transports, as well as about ten helicopters, was rapidly cobbled together. The vaguely-worded order to this force from the General Officer Commanding Middle East Land Forces, Major-General John Cubbon, was that it should 'end the operations of dissidents in the defined area'. This was subsequently refined as 'to bring sufficient pressure to bear on the Radfan tribes (a) to prevent the tribal revolt from spreading; (b) to reassert our authority; (c) to stop attacks on the Dhala Road'.

The troops were not deliberately to fire on areas containing women and children; villages were not to be shelled, bombed or attacked without a warning to the inhabitants by leaflet to move out. But once the troops came under fire, retaliation could include maximum force.

Exercise into Reality

At the time this plan was being constructed, the SAS Regiment consisted of only two squadrons, A and D. A Squadron was resting and retraining after five months in Borneo, and D Squadron was in Borneo. As it happened, A Squadron had already arranged to train in Aden during May and June as a refresher in desert warfare, and its commander, who was in Aden to prepare the ground for this exercise, suggested using his men for the Radfan operation a month earlier than the proposed exercise. His offer was promptly accepted.

A top priority 'flash' signal was sent to Britain to obtain the necessary permission from the Ministry of Defence. The Squadron's commander, having returned briefly to England, composed and typed the unit's manual of standard operational procedures for the forthcoming encounter – a tactical 'bible' – during the flight back to Aden with the rest of the Squadron. For security reasons, families were told that the Squadron was exercising on Salisbury Plain.

The men arrived at Khormaksar, the RAF base in Aden, just two weeks before they were to spearhead the Radfan offensive. Two weeks was also the period normally allowed for acclimatization to temperatures up to 150 degrees Fahrenheit; the SAS, as usual, ignored this requirement and drove immediately to a hastily-prepared base at Thumier, sixty miles from Aden and just thirty miles from the hostile Yemeni border. The same night, the Squadron moved into the nearby Radfan mountains for a twenty-four-hour proving patrol. In the darkness there was an exchange of fire with a group of armed men who were, in fact, British soldiers. One SAS trooper was slightly wounded. It was to avoid just such elementary failures of communication that this early patrol was mounted, but the episode was an augury of worse to come.

SAS officers discovered that Intelligence concerning the strength of the opposition was negligible. As one of them said later: 'In those early days of the Radfan campaign, no one knew anything about what would be needed. They didn't know whether there was water up in the hills, or anything about the people.' The improvised group that was to re-enter the Radfan now consisted of two battalions of locally-raised FRA infantry; 45 Royal Marine Commando with B Company, the Parachute Regiment, temporarily under its command; a troop of Royal Engineers; a battery of the Royal Horse Artillery armed with compact 105mm howitzers and a Royal Tank Regiment squadron equipped with Saladin armoured cars.

As an opening move, it was decided that two hill objectives code-named 'Cap Badge' and 'Rice Bowl', should be seized from the rebels during the night of 30 April. These were key points in the area because they dominated the camel routes from the Yemen as well as the only two fertile areas of the Radfan. The plan was that the Royal Marines should march seven miles from

Thumier on the Dhala Road into hostile territory, to climb and hold 'Rice Bowl', the most northerly objective. Meanwhile the Para company was to be dropped near the foot of 'Cap Badge'. Both groups knew that to be caught in the valley after daybreak, when the guerrilla picquets had taken up dawn positions on the heights, would be suicidal. Equally dangerous would be an attempt to land the Paras on an undefended and unmarked drop zone. The job of establishing such a DZ was traditionally that of the Paras' own independent pathfinder company, but this time the task was allocated to the SAS.

The Edwards Patrol

On 29 April, as dusk approached, nine men of 3 Troop led by Captain Robin Edwards set out in armoured cars, leaving the road and making their way up the steep-sided Wadi Rabwa. Edwards, a recent recruit from the Somerset and Cornwall Light Infantry, was a brave and conscientious young officer who had contracted poliomyelitis immediately after passing the SAS selection course. His determination made him fit enough for service with the Regiment twelve months later. Since arriving in Thumier, his troop had fired on a nocturnal camel train that had refused to halt: two Arabs had been killed and a third taken prisoner. Edwards's anxiety that he might have made a mistake was relieved only when local military Intelligence identified the prisoner as a much-wanted guerrilla leader. Edwards's men were mostly veterans of Borneo and Malaya, physically hard by any standard. The exception was the troop signaller, a slightly-built young ex-sapper named Warburton, who was already suffering from severe stomach pains, about which he did not complain, when the patrol left Thumier.

The patrol had to cover roughly eight miles to reach its objective and had about twenty-four hours within which

to accomplish this. Intelligence reports suggested that
opposition in the hills would not be serious if the patrol
moved discreetly. In the event, the opposition manifested
itself from the beginning. As the armoured cars nosed
their way up the Wadi Rabwa, away from the Dhala Road,
they came under continuous rifle and machine-gun fire.
In such terrain the cars could not move at more than a
snail's pace, and it became increasingly likely that the
vehicles would soon be forced to halt.

Making a virtue of necessity, the patrol dismounted
while the armoured cars' gunners replied to the fire from
the hills. By moonlight, each man hoisted his sixty-pound
pack on to his back and slipped quietly into the shadows.
Even after nightfall here, it was like a warm summer's day
in England, the heat stifling the airless, rocky bottom of
the wadi.

Each soldier carried four magazines for his self-
loading rifle, a total of eighty rounds, plus a bandolier of
the same ammunition and 200 rounds of .303-inch for
the patrol's Bren light machine-gun. The radio, and
enough water for each man – a one-gallon container and
four water bottles per head – were other essential items.
The Squadron's commander, an old Malaya hand, preferred mobility to firepower on such occasions, and the
weight carried was a compromise between two conflicting
priorities. For the same reason, the Officer Commanding
had stressed that ammunition was to be conserved
jealously if contact with the enemy did occur. As things
turned out, it was sound advice.

Despite these routine problems the Edwards patrol was
in good spirits. It had ducked away from the opening
battle unseen and was now tramping with quiet assurance
through dunes and rocks, up Wadi Rabwa. Off to the
right loomed the dark, sinister mass of the 3900-foot
Jabal Ashqab. It soon became clear, however, that young
Warburton, the signaller, was in poorer shape than his
comrades. Possibly he was suffering from a mild form of

food poisoning. Gradually, he fell back and the patrol waited for him. Edwards and his two sergeants, L. and Tk., decided to put Warburton in the centre of the file and redistribute the loads so that the radio, weighing forty-four pounds, would be carried by someone else. But after an hour or so Warburton was again struggling to keep up, and the patrol was now becoming dangerously divided.

At about 2 am, Edwards and his men paused to consider the situation. According to the original plan they should be in hiding on the objective before dawn at 5.30 am. They were then to lie concealed until dusk, when they would secure the drop zone perimeter and identify it with torches and an Aldis lamp for the Paras' night descent. In fact, it was now clear that they would not be able to reach the proposed DZ that night at their present rate of progress. Dead reckoning suggested that they were still about three miles away. To be caught in the open after sunrise would not only make them soft targets for the ubiquitous snipers on the hill-tops, but would also compromise the entire operation.

Despite all these niggling problems, there was also cause for optimism. From the point they had now reached, Edwards and his men had a downhill journey to their objective, and there would be ample time to cover the remaining ground at dusk on the morrow. They were now almost at the top of the highest ridge on Jabal Ashqab, though short of the precipice rising to the summit. Best of all, there were two ancient stone sangars (rock-walled firing-points built by local tribesmen) in which they could hide without attracting attention. As one veteran later joked, for the SAS to have built something without local 'planning permission' would instantly have attracted attention among hill people to whom every stone was familiar. The overwhelming logic of these factors was to halt in the sangars and give Warburton a chance to recover. At 2.30 am in his

headquarters tent at Thumier, the Squadron commander listened carefully as Edwards explained all this by
radio. Edwards was apologetic, but felt there was no
alternative.

At dawn, the patrol reviewed the situation. It was,
it discovered, only about 1000 yards above the hamlet of
Shi'b Taym, a meagre collection of mud-and-stone
houses. From the village, armed picquets tramped up the
hill some distance from the soldiers' position to begin the
long day's watch. Later, a group of children passed below,
chanting 'Allah yansir Nasir!' (God make Nasser victorious!) Still the patrol went undetected. All was quiet now,
and it seemed as though Edwards's gamble was succeeding.

At about 11 am however, the patrol saw a herd of goats
approaching, following a small wadi only a few feet
from their position. The animals were in the care of a
herdsman who shouted directions to a woman coming
towards the sangars from the village. Almost certainly
he was asking her to watch out for strays from the
herd. Edwards, without moving from concealment, softly
called to the soldier who was covering the herdsman's
approach: could the goat-herd be seized silently without a
fuss? Out of the question, the look-out replied; the
herdsman's companion would see it all. There was
nothing for it now but to hope that by some miracle the
herdsman would not spot them. If he did. . . . Suddenly
they all heard the Arab's voice raised in alarm only a few
yards away, shouting to his companion with new urgency.
The game was up. As he turned to flee, a single
high-velocity shot rang out from the SAS position. It was
a desperate means of buying time and the only one
available to the patrol.

The woman vanished, and armed tribesmen were soon
on the scene. They were taking no cover as yet, apparently thinking that the shot might have been an accidental discharge, but determined to establish where it had

come from. The soldiers, knowing that a battle was inevitable, decided to reduce the odds against them. As one survivor said later: 'We thought we might as well put a few away while we had the advantage.'

The tribesmen ducked into cover, crawling behind the boulders, still trying to locate the source of the shots echoing across the hillside. It was some time before they succeeded in this. Their solution was to observe the whole sweep of the hill from the ridge top about fifty yards away from the sangars, and twenty feet higher. Edwards had anticipated this and a crude but effective link was created between the patrol and two pairs of RAF Hunter ground-support aircraft. Under Edwards's control, Warburton passed directions by radio to the SAS second-in-command, Major Mike Wingate Gray, at Thumier, where the messages were amplified by use of a civilian transistor radio. The major relayed these instructions by field telephone to the RAF Brigade Air Support Officer, Squadron Leader Roy Bowie, in another tent at Thumier. Bowie, telephone in one hand, microphone linked to the Hunters in the other, repeated the fire orders.

As the first rifle shots struck the sangars from the top of the ridge, about two hours after the herdsman's death, the first pair of Hunters roared down to deliver withering bursts of cannon fire on the enemy position. The tribesmen scuttled back down the hill to the comparative safety of the rocks, and kept off the ridge for the rest of the encounter, which meant that they could not dominate the sangars. Equally, the SAS patrol had no means of escape. For the time being, it was stalemate.

The conflict which ensued was a tense, cold-blooded sniping duel in which the tribesmen fired from a range of only fifty yards at anything they could see – an elbow, a boot, the top of a skull. The Arab sharpshooters were good; even when their bullets scored no direct hits, they sent fragments of granite into the faces of their opponents whenever the British peered over the rock walls of the sangars. As a result, no member of the patrol escaped entirely unscathed. As each carefully aimed round hit their position, the men of 3 Troop called to one another: 'Anyone hurt?' 'Anyone see where that shot came from?' – 'No. They keep changing their positions.'

Overhead, the Hunters wheeled and dived with one eye on the identification panels originally intended for the DZ, and now spread on the ground between the two sangars. One veteran of this operation later recalled: 'We developed the air link to a point where we were getting messages up to correct the aircraft's course on its run-in to strafe the guerrillas.' The beleaguered troop also called down artillery support which one officer later described as 'fairly continuous and intense at times'.

Towards mid-afternoon, the SAS men noticed that the Hunter strikes were becoming less effective; the enemy was becoming more numerous and was creeping closer. The battle was being fought on the east side of Jabal Ashqab, which now began to cast a long shadow, first over the sangars, then over the hostile boulders below them. It was clear to both sides that by dusk the British patrol would lose its air cover completely. Until then, the guerrillas would bide their time. Their quarry was not going to escape, and there were blood-debts to collect. . . .

At about 4.30 pm, Lance-Corporal 'Paddy' Baker was wounded for the first time. He was inside the larger of the two sangars, but enemy sharpshooters spotted one exposed leg and fired. Two bullets hit him in the left thigh, causing severe flesh wounds from which blood began to flood. He called to the troop commander, Edwards: 'I've been hit, Boss.' From outside the sangar the voice of Trooper Bill H., with a bantering third person reference to himself, added: 'William's been hit as well!' Both men were lucky. Although the tribesmen were armed with accurate .303-inch rifles, their bullets were refills – old shell cases filled with a homemade charge whose velocity

was insufficient to penetrate bone. Bill H. later discovered that the round that struck him had creased his
back, leaving a wound like a whiplash across his shoulder
blades.

The patrol 'medic' threw Baker some extra field
dressings. As he strapped up the wounds, Baker thanked
his donor then asked caustically: 'But is this the best you
can do after all the expensive medical training you've
had?' Even as he made the joke, Baker was discovering
that his injured leg would no longer support him. In this
situation, the injury would be fatal unless he could make
the leg function again by dusk. . . . As he lay there he kept
testing the leg against the sangar wall. While he was doing
so, a sniper's bullet grazed the inside of his uninjured
right leg. His left leg recovered strength only a few
minutes before the guerrillas attempted to rush the
sangar. Two of the tribesmen reached the wall and
attempted to push it over. This was unwise. Baker, armed
with a rifle, and Sergeant Tk., with a Bren gun, rose
simultaneously. The tribesmen were still looking puzzled
as the sergeant killed them both with short bursts from
the Bren. One even attempted a gesture of 'Salaam', as if
surprised that his enemy was a white man instead of an
Arab soldier.

It was now almost dusk, and from the Thumier base
the Squadron commander spelled out what they already
knew, that air cover would have to be called off very soon.
Edwards told his men, spread around him in an area of
about fifteen square yards, that the original plan to mark
the Paras' DZ had now 'gone for a ball of chalk'. They
would have to break out just after dusk and make their
way back to Thumier; there would be no intermediate
rendezvous. By radio they requested an artillery barrage
on the sangars at 7.30 pm, by which time they would have
left the scene. All these plans were discussed with the
Squadron commander and contact with base ended with
his acknowledgement: 'OK. Good night – and good luck.'

For the major there was now nothing to do but sweat out the longest night of his life. He had tried to arrange a rescue of his beleaguered patrol by sending in another troop by helicopter, but the aircraft had been badly shot-up before it reached Edwards's position and had been forced to limp back to base.

At the sangars, Edwards's troop now smashed everything it could not carry, including the radio. From a separate morse set the soldiers extracted the vital crystals that controlled the set's operating frequencies. Each man carried only his weapon and belt equipment, consisting of water bottle, ammunition pouches and emergency rations. By this time, some of the patrol were still inside the larger sangar, while others had dispersed to the rocks outside. Those inside, the focus of enemy attack, were Captain Edwards; the signaller, Trooper Warburton; Lance-Corporal Baker; Sergeant Tk. and Trooper 'Darkie' B. Hiding among the rocks were Sergeant L.; the wounded Trooper Bill H.; Lance-Corporal 'Taffy' B. and Trooper T. This party would give covering fire to Edwards and the rest as they stormed out, through the rocks and down the hill. Edwards's group, in turn, would then take up positions from which to cover the retreat of Sergeant L.'s party.

There was a final, absurd formality before the break-out began. Edwards, conscientious to the last, and aware of the Squadron commander's insistence on routine preventive medicine, asked all within earshot: 'Has everyone taken his Paludrin?' It provoked some wry grins.

Now it was time to go, but as the party rose, ready to move, one man lay quite still in a corner of the sangar. Warburton, the signaller, was dead. He and his A41 radio set had been hit several times. 'All right, we're coming out now!' shouted Edwards. As the four men clattered clumsily down the slope, they were the target of a barrage of small-arms fire from the surrounding rocks, much of it from two large boulders immediately below them. Baker, in the lead, fired back with his rifle. From somewhere behind him, Sergeant Tk. was also blasting the hostile rocks with a Bren fired from the hip. Captain Edwards was between these two and 'Darkie' B. was back marker.

The leading man, Baker, lurched forward as fast as his injured leg permitted, then paused and turned to see whether the others were still with him. As he did so, a new fusillade of shots whistled past him and struck Edwards, who seemed to spin round under their impact before crumpling to the ground. The guerrillas concentrated their fire on Edwards now, and the combined force of their bullets pushed his body sideways across the slope. Baker and Sergeant Tk. continued their advance to a point fifteen yards beyond that of their covering party, and took cover themselves. Edwards lay silent and lifeless. There was nothing they could do for him.

The three survivors from the sangar – Baker, Sergeant Tk. and 'Darkie' B. – now called the original covering party to follow them. They did so stealthily, gambling correctly on the chance that the guerrillas would still be watching the sangar for any survivors. As the whole group tip-toed away at an angle to the valley, they heard a fire-fight continuing around the sangar where, in the gloom, two concentric rings of tribesmen were now shooting at each other. The patrol was least at risk so long as it kept to the high ground. This it did, following the contours of the hill as it swung round to overlook Wadi Rabwa and the road home. They had not gone far when the prearranged artillery barrage smashed on to the sangars. But by then – as later, grisly events were to demonstrate – the tribesmen had also retired, taking the bodies of Warburton and Edwards with them.

As shock and fatigue set in, the march back to Thumier took on a nightmarish quality in which the men's judgement and perceptions were becoming distorted. The two sergeants, with Lance-Corporal 'Taffy' B., 'Darkie' B., the medical orderly, and Trooper T., led the way, with the two wounded men, Baker and Bill H., following some distance behind. After some time, the patrol paused while 'Darkie' applied fresh dressings to Baker's still-bleeding wounds. He also cut away four old dressings which were now flopping round Baker's ankle. (Baker had been dimly aware that something was impeding him, but he was unable to comprehend what it was.)

The men resumed the march, struggling up and down the steep walls of minor gullies near the top of the hill, which fed the main wadi below them. The moon rose, and Sergeant L. called another halt. Barring their path, he fancied he saw a group of Arab tents. If the soldiers were challenged, should they fight? Bluff it out? Or what?

They decided to climb even higher to elude this latest threat. Below the 'tents' lay the main wadi and a track which was the direct route home. It was an enticing prospect, but fraught with the risk of an encounter with guerrilla picquets. Only when they had skirted the mountain for some distance near the summit, always marching south-west, and had examined the 'tents' from another angle, did they discover that the tents were rocks.

Farther still round the hill, the seven men struck a goat track which was going in the right direction, and they trudged slowly along it. Again, Baker and Bill H., the two wounded, fell back. Then Bill heard, or thought he heard, someone following them. Both men paused and glanced back. Some distance away a figure in white was padding quietly along the track in their wake. The two soldiers huddled behind the nearest bush, rifles slippery with sweat as they unlocked the safety catches. This time it was not a false alarm. The man in white was an Arab and there were three others following him in single file. Only the quiet tread of boots, as the rest of the SAS patrol continued on its unwitting way, broke the silence.

As the pursuing Arabs reached the bush, Baker and Bill H. rose, stepped on to the path and kept shooting until the four men went down. Baker, his rifle magazine empty, continued squeezing the trigger, bewildered – by shock, fatigue and loss of blood – that the gun no longer functioned. After some seconds of careful thought, he reloaded with a new magazine. By now, the rest of the patrol had halted, and the voice of Sergeant Tk. was inquiring: 'What's going on?' Baker replied: 'Hold your fire!' The two back markers, concerned that their comrades might inadvertently shoot them, hobbled even higher up the hill and approached the rest of the party in an arc. As they did so, Sergeant Tk., satisfied that they were safe, trained his Bren back up the path and fired three short bursts along it to discourage further pursuit. For some time they waited in ambush positions, but there was no sound except the groans of their dying enemies.

At last the patrol moved off again, even more cautiously, every man glancing back from time to time. An hour later, the back markers, Baker and Bill H., were certain that they were again being followed. Again they set up an ambush as their comrades marched on. This time the pursuers seemed to be guerrilla picquets from the ridge above them. These two were killed in a carbon-copy of the previous ambush.

It was now about 2 am. The men had been under extreme pressure for thirty hours or more, but the patrol followed the same drill as before, setting a careful ambush for any follow-up party, waiting, and then continuing the march. The soldiers were now far enough away from the scene of the original contact to make it reasonable to drop down towards the main Wadi Rabwa. From there to the camp was only a mile or so, but this, too, was fraught with danger. If they approached on foot, as someone suddenly recollected from the pre-operation briefing, they would certainly be fired on by the Arab FRA sentries at Thumier. So they walked, drunk with fatigue, down to the wadi itself, to hide and rest until daybreak. At the bottom of the hill they found a stream.

No one had any water left, most of the patrol having shared what they had with the two wounded men. So, ignoring an order not to drink from an unpurified source, the men slaked their thirst, hid in the scrub, and waited. Baker sank into unconsciousness.

At first light the patrol moved on again, their faces cut and bloodied by rock fragments from the sangar, the limbs of the wounded rebelling against further movement. After half an hour in the buzzing heat of the wadi, they heard the sound of salvation – the rumble of a Saladin armoured car as it foraged up the slope towards them. A radio message flashed back to the Thumier base, retailing the good news in terse, signaller's jargon. Now the wounded men, Baker and Bill H., were hauled into the vehicle for the last mile home. (Baker was to be awarded the Military Medal for his part in the operation.) The other five survivors marched back, grim-faced. No one spoke much. They had survived and, for the time being, that was enough. But the reverberations of the SAS skirmish at Shi'b Taym were to echo far beyond Aden.

The main operation in the hills, of which the Edwards patrol had been an essential preliminary, was restructured to seek more modest targets. Instead of a lightning strike at the 3700-foot Al Hajaf hills in the centre of the dissident area, which dominated two watered, cultivated valleys, the Paras and 45 Royal Marine Commando had to fight and climb their way in, peak by peak. Eventually, six major units required five weeks to subdue the area, after which the inhabitants were banished.

While this operation was still in its early stages, a few days after the loss of Edwards and Warburton, a strange and macabre Intelligence report about the fate of the two bodies reached the GOC in Aden, Major-General John Cubbon. Soon afterwards, on the evening of 3 May, Cubbon held a crowded press conference at which he was asked about a Radio Taiz Yemeni propaganda broadcast

claim that the heads of the two dead soldiers had been put
on public display 'in the Yemen'. The broadcast was
confirmed in Aden soon afterwards by two camel-
herders who had seen the display. According to *The
Times*, Cubbon replied: 'We have reliable information of
their decapitation and the exhibition of their heads on
stakes in Yemen. If this is true, I must express, on behalf
of all three Services in South Arabia, our deepest
sympathy with the relatives of the men and their regiments.' The timing of the question and the answer were
unfortunate. Not only were the next-of-kin unaware of
the deaths, but, like other families of A Squadron, they
had been led to believe that the men were on a routine
exercise on Salisbury Plain.

At government level, meanwhile, the row was only just
beginning. The Republican Government in Yemen, denying its own propaganda broadcast, now denounced the
decapitation story as 'a British lie'. In Taiz, the US
Embassy, which handled British interests in the absence
of UK diplomatic recognition of the Republicans, inves-
tigated and issued an ambiguously-worded statement to
the effect that there was 'absolutely no truth to the
rumours that the heads of two British soldiers had been
exhibited there'. In context, 'there' could mean the whole
of Yemen, or merely the city of Taiz. A row in the British
House of Commons followed, during which Labour's
front-bench spokesman, Mr Denis Healey, accused General Cubbon of relying on 'scanty evidence' for his claim.
But, as Julian Paget's study recorded ,on 13 May, ten days
after the press conference, 'a patrol of the Federal
Regular Army found two headless bodies buried in a
shallow grave in the area of the SAS battle. The FRA
patrol was itself fired on by some 25 rebels, but drove
them off by artillery fire. The bodies were recovered and
identified as those of Captain Edwards and Sapper
Warburton; there was no sign of the heads.'

A Squadron returned to Britain on schedule a few

weeks later, the object of intense press interest. Thereafter, like the Regiment's other squadrons (D and the
re-emerging B), it served in Aden for a few weeks during
retraining periods between each four-month stint in the
Borneo jungle. These episodes in Aden did not amount
to a consistent and continuous campaign. Yet, even if
accidentally, they served a number of useful technical
purposes which signposted the Regiment's future evolution through the Dhofar war of Oman to counter-
terrorism in Europe. In the Radfan, where the guerrilla
war smouldered on until the British withdrew in 1967,
SAS soldiers were regularly exposed to desert and
mountain operations for the first time since the Second
World War.

'Keeni-Meeni' in Aden

By way of contrast, in the foetid alleyways of Aden itself
the Regiment had its first taste of urban terrorist warfare.
Hitherto, nearly all its fighting experience since its
post-war resurrection in Malaya, had been in the jungle.
The urban campaign in Aden, so different from the
guerrilla tactics of Radfan and beyond, was also the
launching-pad for clandestine plain-clothes operations
later adopted by more orthodox regiments.

True, the originality of Major (later General) Frank
Kitson in Kenya's Mau Mau campaign – where 22 SAS
made a brief appearance – had produced the pseudo-
terrorist 'counter gangs', a mixture of former terrorists
and loyal tribesmen led by British officers disguised as
natives. It was true also that the same technique was used
subsequently in Cyprus to create undercover 'Q' units.
Here too, British officers performed a clandestine role.
But when the major commanding A Squadron of the SAS
in Aden set up a Close Quarter Battle Course for a
selected group of his soldiers, he knew that there was no

hope of 'turning round' Arab terrorists. Britain had announced her intention to leave the territory, and this extinguished any hope of active support even from her traditional friends in the area. So the new SAS units had to function more like the 'Q' squads of the Palestine Police. These had been started by Roy Farran, a veteran of the wartime SAS, and were manned largely by others from the same source. However, it was also remotely possible that, if some terrorists could be taken alive and interrogated, some break in the total, silent security surrounding Nationalist operations might be achieved.

The basic concept in Palestine and Aden, quite simply, was to blend into the local scenery and seize on targets of opportunity. The men chosen for this undercover work were those who most closely resembled Arabs. In the matter of pigmentation the SAS Fijians had, so to speak, a head start in spite of their height. But others who had the sharp, hooked nose and high cheekbones of the Semite looked equally plausible if they were well-tanned and dressed as natives. Such undercover operations were known in regimental jargon as 'Keeni-Meeni' jobs. 'Keeni-Meeni' was originally a Swahili phrase to describe the sinuous, unseen movement of a snake in the long grass. It also became a synonym in Africa – and later, via the slave trade, in the Arabian Gulf – for undercover work. British soldiers picked it up during the Mau Mau campaign in Kenya and subsequently in Aden.

The next criterion of selection for 'Keeni-Meeni' work was the ability to draw the heavy, thirteen-round Browning pistol from the folds of an Arab futah, and fire it with perfect accuracy. Farran had taught his men the then-unorthodox triangular firing posture known as the 'Grant-Taylor Method', and required them to be able to put six rounds through a playing-card at fifteen yards. The early SAS 'CQB' Course at Aden was not very different.

The 'Keeni-Meeni' squad of about twenty men operated from various centres in Aden, finally settling in 1966 on Ballycastle House, a block of flats formerly used as married quarters in the military complex at Khormaksar. From this centre they slipped out in twos and threes to make their way to the high-risk warrens around the Crater and Sheikh Othman districts.

Their main quarry was the group of skilled, Yemeni-trained assassins who were steadily suppressing the meagre Intelligence that was reaching the British authorities by the simple, bloody expedient of killing Special Branch officers and their contacts. Sometimes the SAS men would take with them a comrade dressed in Army uniform, or European civilian clothes, for use as bait in areas where the assassins lurked. Others used the idea, notably Major H. M. Tillotson of the Prince of Wales's Own Regiment of Yorkshire, who won a Queen's Recommendation for Brave Conduct because of his skill at this risky game.

Within the SAS it is felt that little of tangible value came out of the experiment except the acquisition of new experience and knowledge. But there were some contacts. A pair of Fijian troopers sitting in a civilian car in Sheikh Othman saw two Arabs approaching them with weapons drawn, ready to fire. The Fijians leapt from the vehicle, drew their pistols and killed the terrorists so quickly that the latter had time only to aim, but not fire, at the soldiers.

Occasionally, the 'Keeni-Meeni' patrol did arrest a terrorist. One was seized as he was about to hurl a grenade. Such attacks became increasingly frequent during 1966 and 1967, and parties of British schoolchildren were a favourite target for these 'Cairo Grenadiers'. This time, the grenade-thrower was picked up and taken back to SAS HQ at Ballycastle House for interrogation, but he was unwise enough to make a break for it as they arrived, and was shot dead. Later, the man was identified as a corporal in the Federal Regular Army, one of a growing number of terrorist converts among the local police and armed forces.

As in Northern Ireland five years later, the popularity of undercover patrols out-paced the elaborate training and co-ordination required for such delicate work. After an SAS plain-clothes patrol led by the redoubtable Fijian, Corporal Labalaba, had opened fire on a group of armed 'Arabs' in Sheikh Othman, seriously wounding at least two men, it was discovered, too late, that the Royal Anglian Regiment had put its newly-formed Special Branch Squad into the same area. Through the usual channels, the SAS had done its best to avoid exactly such a disaster, for unlike other regiments it was not committed to any given 'parish'. Against this tragedy, however, must be set the Anglian undercover squad's success. During a single, six-month tour, a ten-man team from the Regiment's 3rd Battalion captured 105 grenades, five automatic weapons, three pistols, two rocket-launchers, an impressive collection of bombs, ammunition and explosives, and fourteen terrorists including two members of the Cairo-backed FLOSY (Front for the Liberation of Occupied South Yemen) organization.

Back to Radfan

Meanwhile, those SAS soldiers who did not participate in the lethal 'Keeni-Meeni' games around Aden city spent a harsher time among the baking mountains near the Yemeni border, speculating cynically about the fleshpots the luckier 'urbanites' allegedly were enjoying. On a clear night, from the Bakri Ridge, one could see the lights of Aden, fifty miles away or more. . . . But in the hills there was the compensation of a more traditional hunt – a world of Hemingway rather than of Le Carré.

The presence of British soldiers in the Radfan mountains, following the initial operations of April 1964, had now ceased to be a novelty. Efforts to halt the flow of arms and guerrillas from their Yemeni bases in the north, as well as to control the war in the hills, made it inevitable and public. What still distinguished the SAS penetration was its covert nature.

The Regiment's task was somehow to create observation posts from which enemy movement could be observed silently and invisibly. It was a classic reconnaissance task aided by the terrain, but hindered by the climate. The heat in the mountains could wring, with alarming speed, the last drop of sweat from any living creature, however robust, leaving it dehydrated, exhausted and, if water were not supplied in time, dead of thirst. Medical experts fixed the minimum daily intake for British soldiers at two gallons per day, which meant laborious supply by helicopter and consequent disclosure of the OP position. The SAS overcame this problem in a variety of ways. Occasionally they would move into an overt position with an orthodox unit, remaining in concealment with extra rations for many days after the position had been ostensibly evacuated. They learned to conserve the water they carried inside their bodies by minimal movement during daylight hours, sneaking down to a local stream by night to replenish their stocks. But, even after dark, the exertion of foraging for water invoked the law of diminishing returns because much of what was collected had to be consumed on the way back. As a way of life, it was hard enough to make even the Borneo jungle seem alluring – one veteran describes the jungle as 'a gracious living' when set against life in the Radfan.

From their secret eyries, the soldiers directed artillery fire on to suitable targets. Time and again, guerrilla patrols, moving discreetly along the apparently safe route of some obscure wadi, had to scatter for cover as the hiss of incoming shells told them, yet again, that they were being stalked by an invisible foe. The tribesmen's reactions combined the fatalism of Islam with superstition: the guns, they assured one another, were new weapons devised by the diabolic British, guns with eyes 'which always seek you out, wherever you go'.

At the same time, the tribesmen took advantage of any target they spotted. One SAS attempt to transport men by helicopter on to Bakri Ridge, overlooking the forward base at Thumier, led to a heavy exchange of fire between guerrillas on the ground and the helicopter, which had been equipped as a gunship. That patrol had to be aborted.

Not all SAS personnel up-country were perpetually in the mountains. At least one officer of the Regiment became a temporary Political Officer, advising the local tribal rulers and calculating the political implications of individual military operations. His companion, a dogged bodyguard, also drawn from the Regiment, was never seen without his rifle; as a result local tribesmen nicknamed him 'Abu al-Bunduq' (Father of the Rifle). Both soldiers were fluent in Arabic.

A Friendly Early Warning

The nearer the projected withdrawal date came, the more essential were the SAS patrols, to give early warning of attacks on the main forward base at Thumier. The guerrillas, in their turn, now occasionally received early warning of SAS movements in the hills from Arab officers of the Federal Regular Army; they knew that, when the British left, their own lives would depend upon a record of co-operation with the rebels. On such occasions, the FRA advised the guerrillas to keep clear of any area where the SAS was operating, but they were seldom heeded.

In one of the last actions in this area, men of A Squadron were patrolling at Dhi Hirran, near the

Yemeni border north of Thumier. Below them, a patrol from 1 Troop saw dissidents moving along the bottom of the wadi. The tribesmen, who were equipped with a British Land-Rover, were dedicated Sha'iri supporters of the Egyptian-backed FLOSY movement. The SAS team called down an RAF Hunter strike in. one of the last offensive British air operations in Radfan. Politically, the effect of this action was to force FLOSY to merge locally with the more Marxist NLF, which had now almost taken power quite openly in the regional capital of Dhala, and would soon do so in Aden itself, after a bloody internecine battle at which the British would be spectators.

By now, the only major, cohesive British unit which dared to operate at strength outside the shrinking perimeter around Thumier was 45 Royal Marine Commando. Just before dusk on 17 June, only nine days before the final British withdrawal from the Radfan, an SAS observation post spotted three armed men moving along Wadi Bilah, about fifteen miles south-west of the base. The 45 Commando historian, David Young, records: 'Within ten minutes the fully kitted stand-by Troop, Nine Troop (Lt Phil Robinson), was embarked in Wessex helicopters prior to heading for the scene. . . . The Troop Sergeant, Sgt John French, takes up the story:

' "We leapt out of the choppers, having placed out two picquets – in case they tried to run away – and as we got out we saw the three men dashing up a low hill about 200 yds away. One stopped and fired at us. We were right out in the open and as there was such a din going on, I blew my whistle and told the lads to adopt a kneeling position for firing. This they did and two dissidents were killed outright, a great achievement as it is a most difficult position to fire from. The third ran over the crest of a hill slap into the picquet commanded by Cpl McLaughlin and was shot at 30 yds range. Throughout the entire engagement, only 80 rounds were expended, a fantastically small amount for three kills."

'At half past five, Nine Troop re-embarked in the Wessex and by 5.32 they were back in Habilayn (Thumier) with three dead dissidents. . . . This was the last occasion on which 45 Commando was to be able to show its outward aggressiveness in the Radfan. . . . For the last few days, the unit was literally fighting a rear-guard action.'

The handover of Radfan to the Federal Regular Army (soon renamed the South Arabian Army), on 26 June 1967, occurred immediately after Israel had crushed the Egyptian Air Force in a pre-emptive air strike of her own, and then destroyed the Egyptian Army in the field during the Six Day War. In Aden, the effect of the Egyptian defeat was to make Arab Nationalists almost mad with grief and hurt pride. Some smashed radio sets and televisions as they disseminated the bad news. For the British, what had been a long dying cause was now assuredly a lost one. It was not a situation likely to help military morale.

As Julian Paget, in his careful study of the Aden affair points out: 'It was difficult to find a political or national cause that was worth dying for. But there were other causes . . . for which the soldiers were happy to fight and die, and the chief of these was their Regiment.' Of no one was that more true than the politically, militarily and geographically isolated patrols of the SAS during those last days in the Radfan. Some months after Independence, in the spring of 1968, Harry Cockerill visited Thumier. There he discovered 'a few Brits' assisting the operation of the airstrip by the South Arabian Army. They included, inevitably, a recently 'demobilized' SAS officer.

4. The Mercenaries, 1962–78

In the world of the mercenary, the SAS Regiment suffers from the curse of the cuckold. It is burdened by responsibility without power. In an effort to distance itself from the problem, SAS Group Headquarters in May 1978 posted a confidential memorandum listing civil security firms, some run by former SAS officers, which were proscribed to soldiers serving with Territorial and Reserve SAS units. Some of the proscribed firms are merely inefficient; others are a disaster. For the Regiment, however, all of them, proscribed or not, could generate public embarrassment if they attract adverse publicity. Indeed, the greater the success of private enterprise in this field, the greater the potential embarrassment.

A similar difficulty afflicts the American Green Berets, the British Parachute Regiment and the French Foreign Legion. The charisma of these units is such that no mercenary soldier worth his fee will disclaim a connection with one of them – or in really ambitious cases, a permutation of several of these military elites – particularly if the fee is paid by a newspaper. For its part, the newspaper will wish to egg the pudding as succulently as possible, encouraging its sources to claim, or at least hint at, a special forces background. Thus the process feeds upon itself, despite the fact that most mercenaries – but by no means all – are, at best, mediocre soldiers whose morale is notoriously fragile if the unit they are serving with sustains serious losses.

By some mysterious law, it is also the case that such soldiers, some of them chronic fantasists seeking to compensate for broken careers and marriages, are often involved in military adventures that are doomed to failure. Their world is one of betrayal, loot and razzmatazz publicity. It is light years away from the disciplined, skilful, stealthy work of regular SAS operations, whose continued success demands as little publicity as possible.

The number of SAS soldiers who became mercenaries is a tiny fraction of the total. Some of them achieved little in the SAS before becoming freelance soldiers. In 1976, one of those who joined the mercenaries in Angola, for instance, had been obliged to leave the Regiment because of his uncontrolled violence. But soldiers of fortune are not invariably dogs of war, and there is an important distinction to be made between the 'cowboys' of the mercenary trade and the professional soldiers who work for a foreign power with the same degree of skill and dedication that characterized their regular service. Most evidence suggests that the very few exclusively ex-SAS 'firms' fall into the second category.

There is another reason why the word 'mercenary' is a dirty one. If one accepts the neutral, dictionary definition, that of a 'hired soldier in foreign service', then the mercenary's motive, by implication at least, excludes idealism as a respectable reason for soldiering. The consequent innuendo of political promiscuity inspires in the popular mind such pejorative labels as 'The Whores of War' and renders the freelance soldier the pariah of civilized society. This contemporary view of the mercenary was adopted by the International Red Cross, which in 1978 stripped from the mercenary the right to prisoner-of-war status and other benefits of lawful combat.

But, as the British Government discovered when it sought to legislate against mercenary recruitment after the Angolan shambles in 1976, the pariah image of the freelance soldier is an over-simplification. The International Brigade in the Spanish Civil War and the expatriate Americans who joined the RAF at the beginning of the Second World War are two examples of the non-mercenary 'mercenary'. As Anthony Mockler, in his historical study of mercenaries, points out: 'So strong is this instinctive feeling that to be a mercenary is itself immoral that it is generally forgotten how recent and how illogical this sentiment is. Throughout most of European history any such moralizing attitude would have seemed ridiculous.'

A Warrior Caste

The reason for this ridicule, prior to the nineteenth century, was that, with a few exceptions, soldiering was an acknowledged profession, a vocation even, and by definition the concern of a minority. The involvement of entire populations in modern warfare, starting with the massive and unnecessary waste of life in the First World War, changed the popular perception not only of the soldier, but also of such concepts as 'gallantry' and 'patriotism'. The SAS, uniquely, revived in the mid-twentieth century the characteristics of an exclusive warrior caste, fighting its wars in such a way that most of those involved were other combatants. It is not surprising that a number of its men, for whom this is a way of life, should have become mercenaries after leaving the British forces, particularly when actions fought by those forces have declined in proportion with Britain's withdrawal from the Third World. Paradoxically, it is precisely that withdrawal which has left in its wake a vacuum, which the freelance soldier has tended to fill. Personal bodyguards for heads of state; the organization of counter-coup forces; the training of indigenous government armies and professional strike forces; all have been provided, at one time or another during the past twenty years, usually with little publicity, by former SAS soldiers. On occasion, such services have resulted from links created during time spent with the regular Regiment.

One of the pioneers of the business in post-war years was the man who founded the Regiment during the Second World War, Colonel David Stirling. After the war, he worked in Rhodesia, devoting much of his time during the next twelve years to a movement known as the Capricorn Society, through which he spread a gospel blending racial equality with the ideas of meritocracy he had injected into his military thinking. In 1959 he returned to England, having won many friends in black Africa and having lost some among the more extremist whites in Rhodesia. His financial fortunes were at a low ebb, and he set about repairing them with a television programme syndication company, as well as winning the franchise to run Hong Kong's television service. He became involved in military affairs again as a result of events in Arabia and his own, powerful sense of patriotism.

The Yemen Adventure

In September 1962, the ruler of Yemen, the Imam Mohammed al Badr, was overthrown in an Egyptian-backed coup, and fled from his palace in Sana'a to the mountains in the north, near the Saudi border. As thousands of Egyptian troops poured into Yemen to stiffen the coup, the kings of Saudi Arabia and Jordan supported the Imam. An eight-year guerrilla war now began.

The British Government watched this stituation with growing anxiety, for Aden, immediately to the south of Yemen, was still a British Protectorate. British intervention in the Yemen fell into the hands of a club of Scottish lairds. When the Republican coup occurred, Lieutenant-Colonel N. D. I. ('Billy') McLean, DSO, was

visiting Saudi Arabia. McLean was a veteran of Special
Operations Executive during the Second World War,
having parachuted into occupied Albania to organize
partisan resistance there. Now Member of Parliament for
Inverness, McLean also visited Yemen before reporting
to his fellow Scot – the Prime Minister, Sir Alec
Douglas-Home – about the significance of the Imam's
survival and his campaign. With Stirling, and the tacit
blessing of the British Government, McLean discussed
the creation of an ex-SAS mercenary force to train the
Royalist Yemeni troops and ensure good communications in that remote mountainous area. Stirling was
excited by the idea: the British Government still needed
his services, it seemed, and that was satisfying. He was
also ready for another adventure for its own sake, now
that his commercial fences had been mended.

Stirling invited the ex-commanding officer of the
Territorial Volunteer Regiment, 21 SAS (based in London), to head the operation, and it was thus that
Lieutenant-Colonel Jim Johnson took leave of absence
from his job as a Lloyd's insurance broker to become a
mercenary organizer. Initially, a group of six ex-SAS
officers was recruited and flown to Yemen by way of
British-controlled Aden. The first of these was Major
John Cooper who, as a corporal, had been Stirling's
driver during the brave days of Commando operations
behind the German lines in the desert war of 1941/2.
After the war, Cooper became commander of A Squadron of 22 SAS and fought with the Regiment throughout
the Malayan campaign. He was also one of the leaders of
the assault against Saudi-backed rebels on Oman's Green
Mountain in 1959. After retirement from the British
forces he served as an officer on private contract under
the Sultan of Oman. Now, with other former SAS men
who had fought in the first Oman campaign, he was
sustained by his former enemy's paymaster, the Saudi
Government, as the Arabian Royalists united against a

common threat. With two comrades, Cooper marched into the Yemen from a safe house in Beihan, in up-country Aden, provided by the Sharif Hussein. Once over the border, the party moved by night, coming close enough to an Egyptian patrol on one occasion to see the glow and smell the smoke of their cigarettes.

Another prominent figure in the Yemen war was Colonel David Smiley, recruited under a separate contract by his old SOE friend McLean to make a series of tours of the battle zone and prepare reports for the Saudis. Later, for a while, he became the Yemeni mercenaries' commanding officer before being succeeded by two former SAS commanding officers. From 1958 to 1961, Smiley had commanded the Sultan's troops during Oman's Green Mountain compaign. On his return to England in April 1961, he was offered overall command of the three existing SAS regiments, but declined because promotion to brigadier did not go with the job. In his colourful account of the Yemeni campaign, Colonel Smiley muses over the irony that within two years of leaving Oman he would be 'in the service of my former enemies, the Saudis'. He comments: 'Although mercenary excesses in the Congo brought discredit on our calling, I maintain that it can still be an honourable one – with the important provisos that the mercenary's own conduct is honourable, and that what he is doing is in the interests of his own country, or in defence of his own ideals. . . . I was – and am – certain that what we were trying to do in the Yemen was in the interests of Britain.'

While mercenary recruitment of ex-SAS men was taking place in London, a parallel operation, with the tacit approval of the French Government, was going on in Paris. Jim Johnson's counterpart there was Roger Faulques, an enigmatic, scarred ex-Legion officer, one of the few French paras to survive a Vietminh prison-camp. During the year before the Yemeni operation started. Faulques, with discreet backing from the French

Government, was leading mercenary forces in their war against UN troops in the Congo.

According to Smiley, the force that eventually emerged from these sources 'at the height of the mercenary effort, when I was commanding them, never numbered more than 48, of whom 30 were French or Belgian and 18 British. They were broken down into small missions – usually one officer, one NCO wireless operator and one NCO medical orderly – and deployed according to the wishes and needs of the Royalist commanders.' Although small in number, the mercenaries, through their control of tactical communications, were in a position of extraordinary power and knowledge. At their most effective, the mercenary-led Royalists set up ambush positions to destroy Egyptian columns on the country's few roads. Bob Denard, one of the most flamboyant of the French mercenaries, during a break from his Congo activities showed Smiley the remains of such an action. Smiley wrote: 'The sight was indeed impressive. The Royalists had set their ambush in a valley between sand dunes and basalt rocks that looked like small volcanoes on the surface of the moon, and the grim relics of the battle littered the sand on either side of the track. There was a wrecked Russian T34 tank and the burnt-out shells of several armoured personnel carriers, and I counted – with my handkerchief to my nose – more than 50 decomposing bodies, half-buried by sand and half-eaten by jackals. I saw, also, six decapitated corpses – executed Republicans, they told me.'

Smiley's advice, to concentrate on the Egyptian supply lines guerrilla fashion, and forget about frontal assaults on Republican-held towns, was ignored by the Royalists, which did not enhance their chances of a military victory. But, given the air superiority enjoyed by the regular Egyptian forces, to say nothing of their use of poison-gas bombs, there was never much hope that the Royalists would produce anything more than a military and political stalemate. This, in fact, is what happened, in the creation of what is now known as North Yemen, but not before three British mercenaries had been murdered at what they believed was a Royalist road-block. They were asked to hand over their rifles and, surprisingly, did so. They were then shot and finished off by grenades thrown by tribesmen manning the road-block. Smiley records: 'All the dead men were married, with young children. One had been a good friend of mine who had served in the SAS under me in Oman. Like most of the British mercenaries he had come here to risk his life, not so much for the money, as for the adventure, and in the hope that he might be helping his own country as well; it was a tragic waste that he should lose it through trickery and murder.' By now, control of the operation had passed out of Johnson's hands: he withdrew in 1967, shortly before the British left Aden. But the episode left a shadow over relations between some former members of the Regiment for reasons other than simple grief. Disputes about compensation for the families of the murdered soldiers generated the belief that their paymasters had not kept faith with the men at the sharp end.

The mercenaries' activities had an even bigger – if less direct – impact on the Middle East outside the Yemen. From August 1963, Royalist supplies of arms and ammunition were parachuted into drop zones manned by John Cooper's team and others, who guided the planes by radio. These clandestine night flights involved a number of carriers, including Rhodesian Air Services and the Iranian Air Force (then under the control of the Shah), and were negotiated by David Stirling. But, as Johnson himself subsequently revealed, US pressure on her allies, including Britain, to back Nasser's pan-Arabism rather than antique monarchies, threatened these deliveries.

According to Smiley, it had become necessary by 1965 to charter aircraft with discreet pilots 'and – most delicate of all – to obtain the agreement of a Middle Eastern country to the use of its territory for mounting the operations'. Which Middle Eastern country? We have Johnson's word for it that the obvious candidates – Jordan, Saudi Arabia and even France, then controlling Djibouti – had regretfully declined to act as a base for the air drops. Royalist tribesmen who asked their British advisers on the drop zones where the weapons had come from were told, 'From your other enemy, Israel.' Johnson uses the anecdote only to dismiss it as a cover for the true source of the flights. The fact remains that so long as the Royalist arms were flowing, so an increasing number of Egyptian troops and aircraft became bogged down in the Yemeni desert. And, when the 1967 Six Day War occurred between Israel and Egypt, about 68,000 of Nasser's best troops and many of his MiGs were still there.

It is doubtful whether any military entrepreneur, however influential, could engineer such a risky political venture without government help. The precise involvement of Whitehall in the Yemeni war remains a matter of conjecture. But it is not without interest that in August 1967, soon after the Six Day War, the late Captain (later Major) Richard Pirie, the regular Adjutant of 21 SAS Volunteers, the London-based Territorial unit, alleged that his office had been used as a 'clearing ground' for mercenaries in the Yemen and elsewhere in the Third World. According to the newspaper, the *People*, he told two of its reporters that he had passed names and military records to someone at a secret address, and that the mercenaries usually heard something in a week or two. Even more astonishing, Pirie asserted that the men's wages of £250 per month were being paid through the Foreign Office and the Ministry of Defence. Both departments promptly denied Pirie's story in identical statements.

Pirie's approach, as he explained to the *People*, was: 'Why it should be so secret I don't know. The Egyptians must know that the Yemenis are being supported by the

British or British Dominion troops.' They did know. A
letter from Johnson's second-in-command, Flight
Lieutenant Anthony Boyle, ADC to the British Governor
of Aden until he became a mercenary under Johnson,
was taken from a Yemeni courier by Egyptian forces in
December 1963. It is also the case that Western Intelligence benefited considerably from the mercenaries'
operations. The former SAS men were able to obtain, for
example, indisputable proof of Egypt's use of poison gas.
They did so by collecting evidence for subsequent chemi-
cal analysis, including samples taken from some of the
victims. The analysis suggested that the gas had been
manufactured in China.

Peters in the Congo

At the beginning of the Yemeni operation, while it was
still being stage-managed by the 'Lairds' Club', a soldier
of a very different kind was making his name in the
Congo. John Peters, a dour – and in action, cold-
blooded – Yorkshireman, who was to succeed Major
Mike Hoare as the commander of the English-speaking
Five Commando, hated the traditional British officer
class and what he described as its 'lah-di-dah' ways. His
attitude represents even today, if in exaggerated form, a
distinctive element in SAS rank-and-file culture, that an
officer merits respect only if he is as good in action as his
men. Peters was an infantry sergeant in the British Army
before emigrating to Rhodesia, where he served on
attachment with C Squadron of the SAS. He then joined
Hoare as an NCO. Hoare describes him thus: 'A professional soldier with a background in the (Rhodesian)
Special Air Service. . . . A compact man of about 5ft 8in
with the build of a welterweight boxer, which he had been
in his earlier days. He had nerves of steel and a soldier's
conscience which recognises only the order and the

exigencies of the moment, backed up by a deadly efficiency in all weapons and every facet of soldiering.

'He was tough and untameable, as a Belgian volunteer had discovered when he made the foolish mistake of claiming Peters's camp bed for his own . . . an error which led to a knife wound for him and a severe reprimand for Peters. I hammered Peters frequently in our early days, but he always came up smiling.'

The view of one Rhodesian SAS veteran who was not in the Congo was that virtually all mercenary victories were empty ones resulting from 'automatic weapons versus knobkerries'. This is a popular impression among those who did not participate in the series of tribal wars that wracked the Congo after Independence. In some of the campaigns, the enemy was armed only with poisoned spears and ancient Mausers, plus a belief in invincibility induced by the liberal taking of drugs. They were also very numerous. Later, however, mercenaries were to fight battles against Ugandan regulars who were armed with modern missiles, mines, Browning machine-guns, 76mm cannon and armoured cars.

In 1964, four years after Independence, the United Nations force that had expelled a French mercenary group left the Congo itself, at a time when a revolt by cruel and superstitious warriors aged between ten and sixteen against central government was beginning to engulf one provincial town after another. For just over a year, the British and South African Five Commando – recruited by the Congolese Prime Minister, Moise Tshombe – performed the job that an affrighted Congolese National Army was incapable of doing, that of fighting pitched battles against the 'Simbas' ('lions'), who believed that they enjoyed magical powers, including protection from enemy bullets. Thousands of European missionaries of both sexes, farmers, technicians and their families were made hostage and suffered barbaric treatment ranging from the rape of their children to slow death and cannibalism. A fraction of these hostages were rescued by Five Commando's flying columns; many were murdered only minutes before their would-be rescuers arrived.

Unlike the SAS, which prefers to operate by night, the mercenaries did not care for night attacks, for they had been ambushed with devastating effect on the road after dark. However, if the rebels' supply line from neighbouring Sudan was to be cut and an enemy column overtaken before it dug into good defensive positions along the Nzoro River, a night march was essential. Hoare recalls: 'I sent for John Peters. I explained the tactical position as I saw it and affirmed that I would never give the order for our column to move at night ... but if he could find volunteers it would be a valuable night's work.

'Without so much as a second thought he decided to take the whole of Force John-John [Peters's elite fighting force of 100 men] at once. . . . Twenty minutes later the whole sky was lit up with a gigantic fireworks display. Force John-John had met the enemy column in the act of trundling on to the bridge. A lucky shot from Peters's jeep hit an ammunition truck and blew it sky high.

'The battle lasted ten minutes at the end of which Force John-John had annihilated the whole of the enemy column and captured eleven trucks and mountains of arms and ammunition. . . . Once more John Peters had risen to the occasion and by his magnificent personal example and bravery had turned the day. If the enemy had dug in on the Nzoro we would certainly have been held up for days. . . .'

Later, during a rebel counter-attack on the northern town of Niangara, 'John Peters had run from the other side of town to see a solid phalanx of Simbas approaching down a narrow road. Flinging a grenade into the middle of them and shouting the only words he knew in French – "Avancez les mercenaires" – his men joined battle. After some bitter fighting the rebels were pushed back over the bridge, leaving 80 dead behind them.' On another occasion, after leading a waterborne attack from Lake Tanganyika, Peters was seriously wounded but 'refused morphine and continued to direct the battle until weak with loss of blood'.

Hoare, an idealist who believed in prayer, and Peters, the essential warlord who fought to win, did not always find it easy to soldier together. To eliminate unnecessary civilian casualties, Hoare issued an order that anyone carrying a weapon was a rebel, but all others were to be regarded as civilians and left alone. 'At the next halt to clear a road-block, I noticed John Peters's jeep was stacked full of spears. One was issued to each dead rebel, posthumously, just in case. . . .'

With the end of the Simba revolt, Hoare went home to South Africa in November 1965, and Peters succeeded him as commanding officer of Five Commando, replacing the 'gentlemen' of Hoare's vintage with tough Afrikaners. Peters also wished to settle in South Africa, but his request was rejected. Mockler's history reproduces a long letter to the Pretoria government on Peters's behalf, claiming that Peters's efficiency ensured that South Africans serving with the unit – by now in the majority – or their relatives were properly compensated for death and injury.

A somewhat different picture of Five Commando under Peters is painted by Tshombe's biographer, Ian Colvin. During the year after the Simba war, Colvin asserts that 'these Commandos were not of the same mettle and morale as they had been when Mike Hoare commanded them. Some of the best volunteers had perished in battle. Others had been paid off. The newly recruited replacements saw no action in 1966 and were the victims of dangerous boredom. The rot set in. They took to carrying arms off duty and that led to violence, robbery and murder. . . .'

In 1967, Peters returned to London where he worked

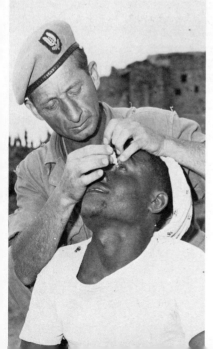

Above Malaya:
Sergeant Hanna, his
parachute draped in
the trees, joins the
Regiment's return to
the jungle.

'Squire' Perkins, an SAS
'bush doctor', treats the
inflamed eye of a
villager in the South
Arabian Federation
(now the People's
Democratic Republic
of South Yemen) in the
early 1960s.

What every well-dressed SAS soldier carries to meet a visiting
VIP in Aden.

Above Dhofar, c.1972. SAS soldier (right) in Arab headdress, with pupil.

Below Men of D Squadron in Newtownards, near Belfast, autumn 1969.

The new image of the SAS in its first dramatic, eleven-minute, siege-breaking operation in Britain. Wearing CS gas-masks and armed with HK MP5 submachine-guns, the CRW team members leap on to the Iranian Embassy balcony in London to begin the attack.

with the now-exiled Tshombe to prepare for a new, mercenary-led Congolese coup. The scheme never materialized because Tshombe was kidnapped at gun-point by a French agent aboard a privately-chartered British aircraft, taken to captivity and, ultimately, death in Algeria. Meanwhile Peters supplied freelance pilots to fly for the government of General Gowon during the Nigerian civil war. He was also confident that his services would be required in the Yemen. 'I'm certain I will be called in there within the next six months,' he told a journalist in November 1967. 'There is nothing I'd like better than to have a go at Nasser. There is a big future for mercenaries.' So there was, but not for Peters in the Yemen, where a firm with better connections had taken over the Royalist cause. Peters finally left London to live in the Far East.

Pre-Packaged Warfare

If the early 1960s was a period of ad hoc, freebooting mercenary activity (mainly in Africa) by individual soldiers who made their own way to the war of their choice, the late sixties and the seventies saw the development of something more sophisticated. This was the 'consumer' approach to freelance soldiering – the packaging of military services in such cities as London and Paris, far from the scene of conflict, the marketing style of which paralleled that of international corporations selling such consumer products as motor cars. There were many reasons for this. The end of the British, French, Spanish and Portuguese empires in the Third World created an indigenous demand for security. The growing cost of modern weapons meant that medium powers such as Britain and France were obliged to export war material in order to fund the modernization of their own forces. With those exports went government-sponsored military aid teams to train and advise client governments.

The British Government, fighting a festering counter-terrorist campaign in Northern Ireland from 1970 onward, refined a variety of techniques in 'low intensity' warfare. Other governments, concerned for their security in face of a proliferation of 'liberation' movements, were passionately interested in such techniques, creating yet another market for military expertise and hardware.

Stirling and his colleagues, alert to the trend, began meeting this demand in many parts of Africa and the Middle East. In 1967 they created the Guernsey-based Watchguard Organization, a cadre of ex-SAS soldiers that provided bodyguards and trained the corps d'élites of countries ranging from Abu Dhabi to Zambia, by way of Sierra Leone. Some of the contracts were less prosaic and included, for example, the creation of secret regimental 'command posts' to which a ruler could take his cabinet in the event of a coup d'état. It was an ironic commentary on the British withdrawal from colonialism. And, as the authors of a book dedicated to one Watchguard operation correctly point out, a process in which, most of the time, the firm's technique was to advise clients about security, but not to fight for them.

More debatably, they claim that Stirling's initiatives were 'leap-frogged' by the British Government. They assert: 'When President Jomo Kenyatta wanted more protection in the middle 1960s, Watchguard was nearly signed up, but lost the job to the SAS. In 1968, Stirling had quickly grasped that Sheik Zayid, the ruler of the wealthy little Persian Gulf state of Abu Dhabi, would be shopping around for protection. After the Sheik, with full retinue, had been to shoot grouse and stalk deer at the Stirling family estate in Scotland, David Stirling . . . visited Abu Dhabi to talk security.

'But the British Government considered the defence of the Sheikdom too important to leave to a private concern like Watchguard. Similarly, when Stirling offered to help the Arabian Sultan of Muscat fight off the threat from Marxist rebels in the province of Dhofar, Whitehall judged the stakes too high and again sent in the SAS. All these were situations where Stirling and his friends in Whitehall saw eye to eye about what needed to be done, but in which his little agency had been elbowed out of the picture by the official government arm.'

In fact, according to those closest to Stirling, he was never 'elbowed out of the picture' by the government. His approach was always to encourage the regular SAS to take on a job which would be, in his eyes, good for his country and his regiment. Kenya was a case in point and so was Iran. Stirling himself took on contracts of which the government approved, but which it did not wish to handle too directly. Stirling regarded the whole thing as patriotic fun even if, as sometimes happened, it were profitless.

In 1970, Watchguard proposed to King Faisal the creation of a 'Task Force' to infiltrate North Yemen. According to the *Sunday Times*, the force would have carried out 'destruction on a massive scale ... using relatively sophisticated sabotage techniques'. The main target was the Sana'a-Hodeida road, 'with the supplementary objective of destroying gas-bomb-bearing aircraft on the ground'. Stirling's proposal reminded Faisal that he had 'access to the Special Air Service of the British Army' and his Director of Operations, according to a document leaked to the *Sunday Times*, was an ex-commanding officer of 22 SAS and one of the Regiment's most successful and distinguished pioneers.

For the British Government, such initiatives created political problems as well as occasionally solving them. Military intervention in the Third World was now more than a matter of fighting battles. It had to be accompanied by diplomatic adjustment in British relations with the US or at the United Nations.

The 'Hilton Assignment'

Nothing came of the Faisal strike force, possibly because North Yemen was now ruled by a coalition government in which former Royalists were represented, but later the same year Stirling and his friends could be forgiven for thinking that a scheme to remove the new Libyan leader, Colonel Gaddafi, was politically copper-bottomed, in London at least. In September 1969, Gaddafi had seized power from the ageing King Idris in a bloodless coup. A dedicated disciple of Egypt's President Nasser – and an exponent of 'Nasserism' long after Nasser himself was disenchanted with revolutionary pan-Arabism – this young desert Savonarola had arbitrarily ended a multi-million-pound air defence deal with Britain and closed British and US bases in Libya. The scheme proposed to Stirling by a prominent Royalist Libyan exile was to 'spring' 150 political prisoners held in Tripoli's gaol as the catalyst for a general uprising to restore the monarchy.

Stirling's team, mostly former soldiers of the French SAS, would land on a beach a few miles out of town, at night, drive quietly along the desert road to the prison and blast a way in. Once the prisoners were set free, the two dozen mercenaries would withdraw to the sea, taking their dead and wounded with them. The outside world would never know that they had existed. It would be a crisp, uncomplicated operation which the Franco-Belgian team could mount with great confidence and a fair chance of success. Along the way, Stirling turned down a bribe of £ 2,000,000 to betray his own team and deliver those involved, including the backer, into enemy hands.

What became known as the 'Hilton Assignment' (a name taken from the ironic nickname given to the Tripoli prison) has been described in a book devoted to the operation by the *Observer*'s Middle East specialist, Patrick

Seale, and his co-author Maureen McConville. According to their reconstruction, the planners were warned off by the British Secret Intelligence Service almost at the eleventh hour. When a further attempt was made by a former SIS man, to whom Stirling delegated the job while recovering from a motor accident, Italian security men stormed aboard one of the assault craft as it was about to leave Trieste in March 1971. To Stirling's horror, the SIS man, who used the nom-de-guerre 'James Kent', later made details of the operation public. In addition to the vessel seized at Trieste, two other ships had sailed, but they were wrecked on the Algerian coast by a storm. Stirling was involved in prolonged negotiations before the men involved were set free.

According to the Seale/McConville version, both the Italians and the British were subject to pressure from the United States, which had decided that Gaddafi's Islamic fundamentalism made him sufficiently anti-Marxist to be worth protecting. That evaluation, of course, was in the innocent days before the emergence of the Ayatollah Khomeini's brand of Islam, and before Gaddafi's own demonstrated ability to reconcile Soviet aid with Islam. Whatever the truth about the 'Hilton' affair, it was soon after that episode that Stirling abandoned the business of freelance soldiering. Its growing emphasis on profit rather than patriotism, he confided to a friend, disgusted him. By the increasingly cynical standards of the seventies he was, like Hoare in the Congo, too much an idealist even to wish to succeed. He withdrew from all Watchguard activity in 1972.

Ironically, it was another British company with (albeit tenuous) SAS connections that would be training Gaddafi's personal bodyguard within a few years of the 'Hilton Assignment' despite Gaddafi's record of support for revolutionary groups including the IRA. The approach of this company, J. Donne Holdings, to military marketing was brash and typical of the new, apolitical, amoral style of mercenary entrepreneurs. Its glossy, six-page brochure offered courses in such techniques as 'silent killing', 'advanced sabotage' and 'advanced lock neutralization'. 'In-depth instruction is given in the use of explosives including the manufacture of "home-made" devices', it announced. Technical instruction was available using 'the most sophisticated equipment available', and so too were the tools of modern interrogation.

Donne Holdings' Training Director, Mr H. M. P. D. Harclerode, was formerly a lieutenant in the Irish Guards after which, on his return to civilian life, he became an officer in 21 SAS, the Territorial Volunteer unit based in London. In a letter to an American security expert in 1977 he claimed: 'We are fortunate in that we have recruited a number of former Special Air Service Anti-Terrorist Team members who left government service only in the last two weeks. They are, therefore, completely up to date on techniques and equipment.'

Negotiators and Assassins

The proliferation during the 1970s of such operations, many of which recruited former SAS soldiers, attracted much hostile publicity that inevitably damaged the image of the regular regiment. But some firms, such as Control Risks Ltd, a subsidiary of the London insurance brokers Hogg Robinson, appear to have performed a uniquely useful and merciful job, as well as a risky one, in employing former regular SAS officers to negotiate the release of kidnapped businessmen in many parts of the world. In September 1977, the *Daily Mail* revealed that two of these officers, Major Arish Turle (an SAS squadron commander who had been decorated for gallantry during the Dhofar campaign) and Captain Simon Adams-Dale, had spent eight months in Colombia, negotiating with the kidnappers of Mr George Curtis, vice-president of Beatrice Foods of America. Curtis was released from his prison, a tiny cellar, after a ransom of £ 240,000 had been handed over in four suitcases. Next day, Turle and his colleague were arrested and accused of being accomplices of the kidnappers, despite their claim that they had co-operated with the local police. They were released after six weeks and returned to England.

In its annual report for 1977, Hogg Robinson stated: 'Control Risks continues to expand.... Its kidnap and ransom service is now being used by Lloyd's underwriters as well as by many international companies both within the United Kingdom and around the world....' In 1979, Control Risks successfully negotiated, on behalf of Lloyds Bank International, the release of two of the bank's British officials after they had been imprisoned by guerrillas in El Salvador.

At the other extreme was a team of a dozen former SAS troopers and NCOs recruited in 1978 to trigger off a coup in the African state of Togo, of which assassinating the head of state was an integral part. The scheme misfired after discreet but effective intervention by MI6 and the Foreign Office. The retired Canadian officer at the centre of this plot appears to have had no special forces background himself, but, like others, he was attracted by the reputation of the SAS for efficiency in such matters. His team leader, a respected SAS veteran of Malaya and Borneo, twice Mentioned in Dispatches, and an ex-Watchguard employee, was recalled from Africa where, he insisted, he had been on business in Ghana.

Double Agent at Heathrow

One of the most extraordinary episodes of recent years

involved a former captain of 22 SAS, André ('Andy') Dennison. After serving as a troop commander with the Regiment's B Squadron in Borneo, he left the British Army. He commanded a force in the army of Botswana and then went to Northern Ireland, where he served as a regular training major with the Ulster Defence Regiment.

In May 1975, Dennison answered an advertisement placed in the *Daily Mirror* and *Daily Mail*: 'Ex-Commandos, paratroopers, SAS troopers wanted for interesting work abroad. Ring Camberley 33456.' The advertisement was placed by a former private soldier of the Parachute Regiment who had also served in Borneo with Dennison's original unit, the 2nd Battalion. His name was John Banks and he had been discharged prematurely from the Army, his discharge book being endorsed: 'Services no longer required'.

In the briefing that followed, Banks and his colleagues made it clear that the operation they were planning involved sabotage raids into Rhodesia from bases in Zambia. Banks opened his briefing with the warning: 'If you have any compunction against fighting for blacks against whites, leave the room now.'

At that time – and for long afterwards – the Rhodesian Special Air Service Regiment had good relations with its British side. As C Squadron of 22 SAS, it had been raised to fight in Malaya during the 1950s with Peter Walls (subsequently Rhodesia's military supremo) as its squadron commander. It took part in a 'training operation' in Aden in the 1960s, and it was still, unofficially, C Squadron long after UDI. What was more, Dennison had just been accepted for service in the Rhodesian Army.

After the Banks briefing, Dennison contacted his superiors in Salisbury and told them that he was staying in London for a short while on a 'private contract' that would be of interest to the Rhodesians. Dennison was selected as commander of the new mercenary force and it was as Major Dennison that he assisted in the final selection of the 200-strong Rhodesian squad at Banks's Camberley office, after the initial London briefing for volunteers. Simultaneously, Dennison was keeping the Rhodesians closely informed of the mercenaries' plans.

Late in July, a dozen of the mercenaries were assembled at the Skyline Hotel, near Heathrow Airport, prior to their departure for Africa. It was a weekend during which the mercenaries drank too much and fought among themselves, much to the delight of an attendant press corps. Dennison, according to one of those in the party at the time, remained notably sober, guarded and withdrawn. He had reason to be. He had just been warned by one of the organizers of the operation: 'We've heard from Salisbury that there is a spy in here somewhere. If he's found, we will have to "chop" him.'

Dennison's isolation ended after a weekend at the hotel during which his fellow mercenaries consumed an average of £200-worth of liquor per head, and the paymaster – never publicly identified – had decided that they frightened him more than the enemy. The operation was aborted. Dennison went to Rhodesia where he was later decorated for outstanding bravery while seriously wounded. He was killed in absurd circumstances while serving with the Rhodesian African Rifles. In July 1979 he was in the bar of the Zimbabwe Ruins Hotel near Fort Victoria when it came under guerrilla fire: he rushed out and was shot in error by a black Rhodesian police officer.

The Angolan Disaster

John Banks's paper army, put together in 1975, subsequently formed the nucleus of the most disastrous freelance military force since mercenary Genoese crossbowmen fled before English archers at Crécy only to be butchered by their French allies. In January 1976, hundreds of thousands of dollars were funnelled from the CIA to Holden Roberto, leader of the pro-Western FNLA faction in Angola after Independence. At least two other groups, the Marxist-oriented MPLA (and ultimate victor) and the centrist Unita group, were also in the field, following the withdrawal of Portugal. Roberto, in his search for mercenaries, recuited four ex-private soldiers of the 1st Battalion, the Parachute Regiment. Of the four, three had ended their British military service in prison and two had been described as psychopaths at separate courts-martial; one was said by his defending counsel to be a potential candidate for Broadmoor hospital.

In January 1976, after a week in Zaire, where Roberto had his base, one of the four, Nicholas Mervyn Hall, returned to London to find more recruits. He carried about £20,000 in new $100 bills whose numbers ran in sequence, a letter of accreditation typed in French on an English keyboard, and a photo-identification card describing him as 'Major' Hall. From the Piccadilly Hotel in London, he telephoned Peter McAleese, a former SAS sergeant who had been among Banks's recruits the previous summer. How Hall came into possession of McAleese's Hereford telephone number remains a mystery: the grapevine it represented had no connection with Stirling or his friends. Through an article in the *Sunday Times* written by the author, concerning the insurance of mercenaries for the aborted African operation of July 1975, Hall also made contact with Banks himself, and thus recruited most of the ill-fated advance guard of about twenty mercenaries who left for Angola, amid considerable publicity, about two weeks after Hall's arrival in London. The group included Peter McAleese.

The Angolan volunteers rapidly discovered that Roberto's mercenaries were engaged in a parody of skilled warfare which might have been funny if it were not also releasing some murderous fantasies. For instance, the mercenaries were issued with French army rations containing an innocuous, Pernod-flavoured powder contained in a sinister capsule labelled 'Boisson instantanée', an instant drink intended to make mere water more palatable. The mercenaries believed that the capsules contained cyanide – 'Poison instantané' – to be taken in extremis. It is possible that the prisoners who later appeared at the Luanda show trial were taken alive by their Cuban enemy because of this misunderstanding.

In the field, the mercenaries were led by Costas Georgiou, alias 'Colonel Callan', Hall's partner and former comrade in 1 Parachute Battalion. Georgiou ensured that his force alienated its own African support, such as it was, through arbitary execution of FNLA soldiers, sometimes for no better reason than to test a weapon, or because the executioners felt like it. The mercenaries also drove Land-Rovers at speed over roads they had mined themselves, with predictable results. It was not a way to win friends and influence people.

These events culminated in the execution, on Georgiou's orders, of fourteen newly-arrived mercenary recruits from Britain, an event known subsequently as the 'Maquela Massacre'. The most enthusiastic executioner was a former Parachute Regiment NCO, Sammy Copeland.

The SAS veteran, McAleese, meanwhile, was running his own reasonably well-ordered – if unsuccessful – campaign of defence training and food distribution among local civilians in the port of Santo Antonio do Zaire, a long way from Georgiou's grotesque reign of terror. After Georgiou had been taken prisoner by the Cubans, McAleese was appointed field commander of the mercenaries. With Hall, he participated in a court-martial of Copeland. In an effort to save Copeland, according to one painstakingly researched book on the Angolan adventure, McAleese proposed that another accused mercenary be executed in Copeland's place. This appeal by McAleese to the FNLA leader Roberto came to nothing when Hall insisted that Copeland should die as agreed by the court-martial.

Copeland's last-minute attempt to escape while the argument continued ended in a hail of bullets fired at him by other mercenaries. The coup de grâce was administered by one of the original four mercenary volunteers, another ex-member of 1 Parachute Battalion. According to the study cited above: 'He fired three times into the back of Copeland's head with his pistol. "That's him finished then," he said, returning his pistol to his holster and patting it.' In such a doomed enterprise, the distinction between friend and foe had all but evaporated. Soon afterwards, all FNLA positions were overrun by Cuban and left-wing Angolan soldiers of the MPLA.

McAleese subsequently joined the Rhodesian SAS, passing its selection course although he was now in his forties, during the last months before the country acquired a new identity (Zimbabwe-Rhodesia) and a black head of state. In Rhodesia, like other former members of the British SAS Regiment there, he received the same rate of pay as indigenous troops. Such expatriate soldiers were not motivated by a desire for instant loot but by the fact that active soldiering was a way of life and Rhodesia happened to be an available war zone. The only political peculiarity of the Rhodesian SAS was that it remained an exclusively white fighting force.

In the atmosphere that followed the Angolan shambles, it was hardly surprising that other British mercenary organizations attracted excited and hostile attention from journalists, who made no distinction between one 'funny firm' and another. Some of the criticism was dogmatically moralistic – 'The ruthless machismo of the mercenary creed does not easily lend itself to ideas of democracy, socialism or racial equality', declared Duncan Campbell in the journal *Time Out* – and much of it was directed at the SAS. Such a value-judgement ignores the

SAS tradition of meritocracy, irrespective of race, as well as Stirling's own declared commitment to racial equality.

Other enterprises which now received critical press attention included Thor Security, which has had former SAS officers on its board, and Donne Holdings.

Secrets for Sale

The most reasoned criticism of the activities of some of these freelance operators is that they appear to offer to their foreign clients data and techniques which are, or should be, official British secrets. Donne Holdings' material has been quoted already. Thor's sales brochure refers to new technology in safeguarding prison perimeters, and adds: 'Most of this information is classified, but can be available to Thor Security Systems for suitable government or civilian design contracts.' The nuance conveyed by the word 'suitable' is that official clearance would be required for the sale of such information, but such a claim is sufficiently novel to justify press interest.

There is little sign yet of official anxiety about the problem of mercenaries generally, despite the inquiry which followed the Angolan affair. No one has been prosecuted for the sale of any official secret; nor is it illegal to hire soldiers for freelance military operations outside the United Kingdom. Such inactivity derives from the fact that some freelance operators can be very useful to government from time to time, and that this consideration outweighs the occasional embarrassment.

The role of one such organization was the subject of parliamentary questions in July and August 1978. Mr John Tomlinson, Minister of State at the Foreign and Commonwealth Office, was asked about private security companies which the FCO had employed during the preceding five years. In Britain, the list contained such familiar names as that of Securicor. The Minister went on: 'Abroad, guards have been obtained through one private firm – KMS Ltd – to protect ambassadors at a very few particularly exposed posts. . . . The department looks for reputable firms able to provide a good and consistent standard of service.'

A few days earlier, Tomlinson had been asked about 'the hire of bodyguards from private firms such as KMS'. He replied that 'in a number of countries, the protection at our missions includes armed guards who have either been provided by the host government or recruited locally. At a very few particularly exposed posts, we have thought it advisable, with the agreement of the governments concerned, to strengthen this protection by sending out British guards from a private firm.' The initials 'KMS' in this context, do not literally represent anything. Less formally, they are an insider's joke, a sidelong reference to 'Keeni-Meeni Services'.

It is plausible to conclude that the parliamentary questions resulted, in part at least, from an article that had appeared in *Time Out* a few days earlier, identifying KMS as a mercenary organization, linking a number of prominent, retired SAS officers including Colonel Johnson and Major Andrew Nightingale. In spite of its critical tone – the headline, 'The Pedigree Dogs of War', said it all – the article did not specify what KMS did other than to recruit mercenaries and provide bodyguards.

An insight into Nightingale's role emerged through a parliamentary answer by Minister of Defence Frederick Mulley. Asked to state his policy on 'serving officers acting for hire through private companies', Mulley replied that when Nightingale accompanied Lord Carver on his 1977 mission to Rhodesia, he was on leave at the end of his military service. 'There are no regulations', the Minister added, 'to prevent people in this category from taking up civilian employment in advance of their release dates.'

For some time before the parliamentary questions, the

Regiment itself had been disturbed about the degree to which public perceptions of its character were being distorted by the links, sometimes tenuous as in the case of Donne Holdings, with the mercenary world. On 30 May, two months before the *Time Out* article and the parliamentary questions, soldiers in the SAS Territorial and Reserve squadrons were told that their service in the Regiment was incompatible with work undertaken for eight named freelance companies. 'This embargo', the Regiment announced, 'covers personnel who are not directly employed by these firms, but in receipt of a retainer's fee, awaiting employment. If a person employed by one of these firms resigns or leaves that firm, a clear six months must elapse between his time of leaving and his (re)enlistment into a unit of the SAS Volunteers). Any individual who gains entry to the SAS (V) by knowingly making a false statement about employment with one of these firms will never be further employed by the SAS (V) again.' To someone who has been accepted into the SAS family, such a sanction means everything.

There was a quaint postscript to this sonorous warning in 1980, when a team of ex-SAS soldiers, all of them good professionals, travelled to the strategically sensitive, politically non-aligned Maldive Islands in the Indian Ocean. Until 1976, the Royal Air Force had maintained a staging post on one of the islands, an atoll named Gan. Following the crisis in the Persian Gulf area resulting from the Shah's downfall, the seizure of US diplomats as hostages in Iran, and the Soviet invasion of Afghanistan, both super-powers were engaged in a search for bases in the Indian Ocean. The Maldives were perfectly located for such a base, but the neutralist government of President Gayoom politely declined to get involved in super-power war-games.

Then, with promises of £10,000 each, nine British mercenaries travelled to the Maldives to stage a coup d'état on behalf of an unknown backer. They tried, somewhat unconvincingly, to adopt a cover as 'businessmen on a diving trip' but, unaccompanied by wives, they stuck out like sore thumbs among bourgeois German and Swedish holidaymakers. According to their leader's plan, they were to rely upon surprise and a few .22in pistols to seize the National Security Service headquarters and armoury in the capital, Malé. But somewhere along the line, the Maldivian Government had got word of a foreign 'assassination team' in the country. This was sufficient to trigger-off a security alert.

The team quit the Maldives in the nick of time, after a heavy-footed reconnaissance 'holiday' which one government source described as 'more Laurel and Hardy than Dogs of War'. Back in England, the team disintegrated amid recriminations about unpaid fees and broken promises, in a pattern so familiar as to be a classic of its kind. But the hare-brained plan caused deep concern to 22 SAS – which abhors unauthorized freelance contracts – and the British Foreign Office. If the attempted coup had proceeded and failed – as it surely would have done – the appearance of ex-SAS soldiers at a political show-trial might have been the least serious result: at worst, the operation might have driven the non-aligned Gayoom into the arms of the Soviets.

5. Oman, 1958/9, 1970–76: The Wild Colonial War

The Sultanate of Muscat and Oman is a place of extremes where, according to a Persian proverb, the sinner has a foretaste of what awaits him in Hades. By day its volcanic rock acquires the heat and airlessness of an oven, generating a nocturnal summer temperature of 112 degrees Fahrenheit at sea level. On the northern mountains in winter, the temperature drops so far below freezing-point that it turns a metal water-bottle into a block of ice. Out of the valleys, the wind is incessant, and turbulence makes air travel a sickening experience. In the south, the summer monsoon brings incessant rain from which there is no shelter on the mountains of Dhofar. Everywhere, at all seasons, wounds fester with appalling speed.

The country is also a political anachronism, an absolute monarchy in a world of popular government, where political dialogue, when it exists, is traditionally violent. But, by an accident of geography, the Sultanate, through its inheritance of the Musandam Peninsula, commands the Hormuz Strait through which passes about 50 per cent of the non-Communist world's supply of crude oil. Successive British Governments have concluded that the protection of this strait is vital to the British economy, and successive Sultans have found it essential to rely on British soldiers for their security. It is a delicate arrangement, in which Britain has worked with some success to make the patriarchy of Oman less barbarous while safeguarding the monarchy itself (and one that uniquely defies post-war British policy of abandoning former colonies and protectorates to the wind of change).

By coincidence, a similar political interdependence has characterized the involvement of the SAS in Oman. The Regiment has fought two successful campaigns there, one lasting a few months in the winter of 1958/9; the second, a six-year war which ended with the government's victory of 1976. On the first occasion, the Regiment had just been included in the Army's long-term Order of Battle and was under pressure to prove that it could function, as it claimed, at short notice outside its now-traditional jungle environment of Malaya. The second Oman campaign began in 1970, at a time when the SAS – never a garrison regiment – had no fighting commitments and when its raison d'être was being questioned not only in Whitehall, but also within its own ranks.

Oman I, 1958/9: Mission Impossible

The first Oman campaign had its roots in a rebellion covertly backed by American oil interests and the Royalist Saudi Government in 1954. The revolt against the Sultan at that time was rooted in fertile soil. In 1958, an official from the British Embassy in Beirut reported that in twenty years' experience of the Middle East he had never seen, until he reached Oman, 'a people so poverty-stricken or so debilitated with disease capable of treatment and cure'.

The rebellion was led by three men. They were Suleiman bin Hamyar; Ghalib, Imam of Oman, the 'Lord of the Green Mountain'; and Talib, his ambitious younger brother, the most formidable of the trio. The 'Green Mountain' (Jabal Akhdar) is an elevated, fertile plateau, twenty miles by ten in area, on average 6500 feet above sea level, locked behind sheer cliffs of rock and shale rising to 10,000 feet above a sweltering plain. It has a climate and economy quite different from that of the surrounding countryside: it is almost an Arabian version of Conan Doyle's 'Lost World'. On the plateau, Talib had assembled an offensive guerrilla force of 180 sharpshooters supported by about 500 armed tribesmen. There were only twelve known easily-defended approaches to the plateau, and the rebels had ample stocks of modern weapons including .5-inch Browning machine-guns and quantities of mines with which, during raids on the surrounding plain, they blew up 150 vehicles including 18 British Ferret scout cars between March and November 1958. Although short of food and suffering from bombing attacks by the Sultan's air force, they were still a formidable enemy, apparently able to resist indefinitely.

By now, the conflict had already exploded one bit of British mythology about controlling tribes in the Middle East – that it could be achieved exclusively through the use of air power. As Phillip Darby's account puts it: 'The myth had persisted in air force circles that the RAF's air control method was an economical and successful way of dealing with local tribal quarrels. Thus when the Oman revolt broke out the RAF asserted that it could do the job unaided and the Government, acting on this advice, authorised rocket and cannon attacks on enemy held forts, and certain other operations. . . .

'In his statement to the House of Commons on July 23 1957, the Foreign Secretary, Mr. Selwyn Lloyd, was categorical that there was "no question . . . of large scale operations by British troops on the ground". Indeed, he went on to say that in view of the high temperatures in Oman at that time of year, it would be an example of military futility to seek to employ ground forces in the desert areas.'

So much for the received wisdom. The SAS was invoked in October of the following year, through a somewhat complex blend of realpolitik and coincidence.

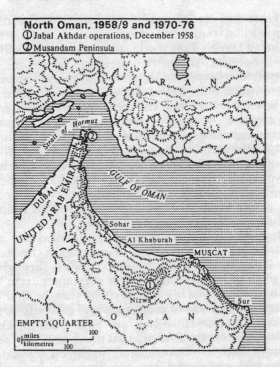

North Oman, 1958/9 and 1970-76
① Jabal Akhdar operations, December 1958
② Musandam Peninsula

In a sensitive War Office planning post at that time was
Major (later General) Frank Kitson, a pioneer of
counter-revolutionary warfare since the Mau Mau campaign in Kenya. Kitson's plan for seizing the plateau
involved the placing of carefully chosen British officers in
positions at the foot of the mountain, with a nucleus of
bodyguards and 'a substantial sum of money' with which
to bribe local informers. This, it was hoped, would bring
about the capture of guerrillas, some of whom would be
turned around to work for the government. 'I visualized',
wrote Kitson later, 'forming one or two teams of prisoners augmented by some of our own soldiers in disguise.'

These groups, he suggested, could then penetrate the plateau.

The Kitson plan was tentatively approved, with an elaboration added by the Director of Military Operations, General Hamilton: why not use the SAS? In the event, the Kitson plan was overtaken by the SAS's own, more direct method of attack. But the notion that the Regiment should take on a long-term Intelligence role, anticipating revolution before it actually happened, was one to which Kitson returned in later years, and which the SAS accepted only in so far as it did not change radically its existing role and character. A decade later, in Northern Ireland, some of Kitson's ideas – based, like those of the SAS, on an economic use of small numbers of carefully selected men – bore fruit in the creation of the plainclothes Military Reconnaissance Force.

In 1958, however, there were other reasons why the SAS was preferred to one of Kitson's 'counter gangs'. A quick military solution required climbing experts and an assault team that would operate in conditions of ultrasecrecy. Finally, there were indirect political considerations that more orthodox troops (such as Royal Marine Commandos and Parachute Regiment soldiers) would be hard put to meet – a requirement that no serious number of casualties would be suffered, to reduce the risk of adverse publicity at home, and a timetable that would ensure a conclusion before the next UN debate on the Middle East. What it all boiled down to was that the Green Mountain, unconquered since an abortive attempt by the Persians more than 900 years before, had to be taken without British casualties, in weeks rather than months.

Yet another political problem was the delicate question of relations with the Sultan and his British-officered, Arab/Baluchi army. The Sultan's new Chief of Staff, Colonel David Smiley, had been warned by his friend Julian Amery, Under Secretary for War: 'We give the

Sultan help; we sometimes give him advice; but we do not give him orders.'

The commanding officer of 22 SAS at this time was Lieutenant-Colonel Anthony Deane-Drummond (an Arnhem veteran who had eluded captivity after that operation by hiding for three days in a cupboard in a German-occupied house). After conferring with Kitson in Oman, he returned to Malaya to gather up D Squadron, under Major John Watts, for the new operation. The Squadron was spread around a remote area of the Malayan jungle near the Thai border, still mopping-up the campaign that had kept it busy since 1950. Now it had to retrain and be on the ground in Oman within fifteen days.

The force was brought back to Kuala Lumpur within forty-eight hours, through a series of forced marches and journeys aboard improvised river rafts. It then went through a hectic retraining period lasting sixteen hours a day, during which the favourite SAS jungle weapon, the sawn-off shotgun, was exchanged for automatic rifles and rocket-launchers. When the Squadron arrived in Oman early in November 1958, its men learned that of the fifty British troops attached to Smiley's staff, forty-five had been flown to hospital suffering from heat exhaustion, while two others had died of it. Furthermore, the risk of being shot on the slopes of the Green Mountain was such that virtually no Arab would act as guide. Two attempts by the British to seize the jebel in battalion strength had failed.

For the first few days, the Squadron pursued its own, energetic reconnaissance programme, and the dangers rapidly became apparent. One corporal – a soldier on temporary attachment from the Royal Army Medical Corps as a specialist – was riding in vehicles which were blown up on the two occasions he left the SAS base; he refused to risk his luck a third time and had to be evacuated by helicopter. Another corporal, 'Duke' Swindells, an experienced SAS soldier who had won a Military Medal in Malaya a few months earlier, was shot dead by a sniper as he walked up a ridge. Given the government's insistence on casualty-avoidance, this was regarded as a very bad augury indeed.

Nights on a Bare Mountain

Swindells was killed while moving by day. The SAS response was to propose nocturnal movement only, unless the need to do otherwise was imperative. The received wisdom among the Sultan's officers was that the nature of the ground made this impossible, but the SAS went ahead with the new policy anyway, arguing that night had the additional advantage of avoiding the heat and exhaustion of daylight operations. As a result, the Squadron was able to move on the mountain with much more freedom. An early episode featured the Squadron's commander, Watts, who came striding down a precipitous path, quite alone, as an astonished patrol of the Sultan's armed forces was feeling a tentative way upwards.

The new policy produced a limited success within a few days. Guided by a very nervous local sheik, an SAS troop climbed a steep track, once used by the Persians, on the north side of Jabal Akhdar. In the darkness they reached the lip of the plateau undetected. The track they had followed was punctuated by enemy sangars which, amazingly, were unmanned. At the top, near a twin peak called 'Sabrina', the guiding sheik fell on his knees and thanked Allah for salvation.

The two troops were led by Captain Roderic ('Rory') Walker, who subsequently came to public notice as the Piper of Jakarta during the Borneo campaign. His men occupied sangars 3000 yards short of a strong rebel picquet at Aqbat al Dhafar, and soon came under attack.

In one episode, 40 guerrillas armed with rifles and two Brens moved in on a forward slope position held by Sergeant J. Hawkins and nine men. The sergeant ordered his men to hold their fire. When the enemy was only 120 yards away, they let loose a barrage of Bren and rifle fire, killing five men and fatally injuring another four. The attack disintegrated.

In the same area, Walker led an exploratory raid against Sabrina on the night of 27 December. The two troops were detected just before they reached the top. One of them was climbing a rope up a fault in the cliff when the guerrillas above called, in English, 'Come on, Johnny', and opened fire. Walker hauled himself farther up the rope and lobbed a grenade over the top. One guerrilla was killed instantly and his comrades scattered. Walker was over the top now, his men following. In the darkness they killed another eight of the enemy.

Meanwhile, on the south side of the mountain, a small patrol had found a cave used by the guerrillas to guard the main approach to Jabal Akhdar. It was also a main store for weapons and ammunition. Two nights later, two SAS troops moved on it. One of these, under Captain de la Billière, made a ten-hour night march through enemy territory in order to approach the cave from an unexpected direction. It then crept to a point 200 yards from the cave mouth, lined up a 3.5in rocket-launcher, and waited. The only point from which the SAS could open fire was below the cave, and this meant that the rocket crew had to kneel or stand to use the weapon. The same firing-point was, faute de mieux, in a natural amphitheatre whose upper slopes were honeycombed by many small caves sheltering enemy snipers. At dawn, as the first of the guerrillas emerged, stretching his sleep-laden limbs and yawning, the soldiers poured a hail of missiles and machine-gun fire into the main cave. Describing the action subsequently, Deane-Drummond wrote: 'Even such withering fire did not cause the rebels to panic or surrender. They quickly dropped into fire positions and returned the best they could. Reloading and firing the 3.5in from the standing position became interesting.' What made it particularly interesting, as well as infuriating, was the failure of many of the SAS missiles to leave the launcher after being fired. They remained unfired but 'active' and had to be extracted immediately and replaced with another round, regardless of the recommended safety drills.

The battle instantly brought down rifle fire from the surrounding hills. Describing the encounter soon afterwards, the journalist Brian Connell wrote: 'Outlying rebel pickets retreated slowly and the SAS picked them off one by one. The rebels still had a mortar firing from a crevice behind the cave, but the SAS had laid on air support. As Venom aircraft came swooping in, one of their rockets made a direct hit. Mortar and men were destroyed immediately. "Right down the chimney!" the SAS shouted as it went up.'

In fact, it was not quite so simple as that. The Venoms were 'stacked' out of sight and sound, awaiting a simple radio signal for an air assault that was to last exactly fifteen minutes, during which the troop was to make an orderly, co-ordinated group withdrawal. This now became a fighting retreat, in which men moved back singly or in pairs, using every scrap of cover available. This lasted rather more than fifteen minutes, and was covered by a .3-inch Browning machine-gun manned by a regimental veteran, 'Tankie' Smith, from the nearest high ground held by the SAS.

As well as D Squadron, the Jabal Akhdar actions now also involved a Life Guards troop acting as infantry, two troops of local Trucial Oman Scouts, a few signallers and REMEs, a total of about 200 men. All shared the same harsh conditions. At night, the men's water-bottles froze. By day, the wind at 8000 feet blew incessantly. It was very different from the jungle, and an environment in which soldiers' lips, and their rubber-soled boots alike, cracked open within days.

Morale, Deane-Drummond asserts, was terrific, possibly because after Malaya, in which weeks of profitless jungle patrolling were relieved by a few seconds of action, the SAS had now found an enemy who stood his ground and fought. But, in addition to the hardships of the new environment, there were also some spectacular operational muddles. In the first attempt to deliver mortar bombs to the Squadron by parachute, twelve out of seventeen canopies failed to open properly and the bombs they carried exploded among the soldiers, injuring no one.

A Game of Bluff

By the end of December, it was clear that the Squadron's toehold on the north side of the plateau would remain just that unless more men could be brought in to assault it. True, a total of forty rebels had been killed by now, but this had merely stiffened enemy resistance. A full squadron would be required to seize and hold the plateau, while another was essential to maintain pressure on the flanks. And time was against success. Deane-Drummond decided to bring in a second squadron from Malaya and establish a tactical headquarters to co-ordinate the two forces.

Commanded by David Stirling's wartime driver and comrade-in-arms, John Cooper, A Squadron arrived in Oman on 9 January 1959. After less than a week's joint patrolling on the north side of the plateau with an augmented 'troop group' of the incumbent D Squadron, the newcomers were given the task of attacking the twin-peaked Sabrina, at whose centre was the main enemy gateway. This 'training-operation' as Deane-Drummond describes it, was in fact geared to bluffing the guerrillas into believing that this obvious route was indeed the main axis of the British assault; but, although a feint, it required a frontal assault up a narrow track that climbed 400 feet to a strongly-held position. A similar manoeuvre, launched from Tanuf, eight miles from Sabrina, would serve the same purpose. The third element of an elaborate hoax was a confidential briefing given to four local donkey-handlers, who were told that Tanuf would be the main assault route. The handlers, whose animals would carry ammunition, were threatened with death if they disclosed the secret. It was passed to the guerrillas within twenty-four hours.

While these bluffs were being enacted, the enlarged troop from D Squadron, which had taken part in the feint attacks, made a secret withdrawal in the darkness to join the rest of the Squadron for the main assault. It was a long march off the mountain to a pick-up point at Wadi Tanuf, from which lorries ferried the men fifteen miles to their rendezvous with the rest of the Squadron, and the beginning of another uphill climb. Planning a viable route to the plateau for the main assault on the south side of the plateau had finally become a matter of educated guesswork. The Sultan's Chief of Staff, Smiley, the commanding officer of 22 SAS, Deane-Drummond, and his squadron commanders Watts and Cooper, had all studied aerial photographs of the area. The consensus choice was a climber's route rather than a track, a fine line along a steep ridge extending like a fox's brush into low ground held by the Sultan's men near the village of Kamah. It required a nine-hour climb in darkness, up a 4000-foot slope, for which ropes were needed on one precipitous traverse. Each soldier carried at least sixty pounds weight, most of it ammunition. Behind the SAS Squadron came a troop of Life Guards on foot, and a company of the Sultan's Northern Frontier Regiment, hauling protesting donkeys laden with machine-guns.

This untried route was tested by de la Billière's leading

troop. Almost three-quarters of the way up, the troop found just one Browning .5-inch machine-gun whose two-man crew, as Deane-Drummond put it, 'could have mown down the attackers in the moonlight, but they had withdrawn to their cave secure in the knowledge of ten centuries that the jebel was impregnable'. The guardians of the Browning were asleep when the SAS reconnaissance troop found them. They were left to sleep on, with an SAS guard watching over them. Guerrilla picquets on the other side of the plateau, around Sabrina, had now been increased to 100, while the remainder of their force was concentrated at Tanuf.

From this point on, it seemed to the attackers that the way was clear, but it was now almost 3am. Watts, leading the Squadron, and the commanding officer, Deane-Drummond, therefore had a choice. They could continue to move a ponderous but well-armed force up the hill, with the risk that it would fall into the text-book trap of mountain warfare, that of being overlooked by the enemy at sunrise. Or the SAS Squadron could cache its heavy rucksacks and make a dash for the top with only a minimum of ammunition. This plan would also, had it misfired, have been fatal – costly in British lives if even a small group of guerrillas lurked unseen at the top, and politically embarrassing. Watts decided on a quick dash. The rucksacks were dumped on a false summit short of the plateau, in what was now a race against the sun, and the main force left to catch up later. With just their rifles and what ammunition they could carry on their bodies, the SAS men slithered down the steep incline leading from the false summit they had reached, to begin climbing once more.

'In the final stages', one of those who took part recalls, 'there was a race to be first on top since the Persians.' The front runners included Deane-Drummond, Watts and de la Billière. They arrived on the unguarded plateau 'absolutely shattered' by their climb, only to be scourged on by Deane-Drummond to advance and consolidate what was still only a tenuous hold on the guerrilla stronghold.

With the dawn came an air strike by Venoms and a parachute supply drop, which apparently convinced the few guerrillas remaining on the south side of the plateau that a full-scale airborne invasion of the area was in progress. Whatever the reason, the guerrilla leaders fled, leaving eight mortars, six heavy machine-guns, twelve Brens, quantities of mines and other ordnance, and a great deal of revealing documentation about the uprising. There was also an Aladdin's Cave, explored that morning by the SAS: a labyrinth full of boxes, which the soldiers opened by torchlight. They contained only clothes, but there were moments when the soldiers wondered if the next box might not just contain something approximating to the Crown Jewels. . . . The loot included a 6mm MAB pistol, belonging to one of the guerrilla leaders, which finally found its way to the regimental museum.

For many of those involved, there were more orthodox rewards. Deane-Drummond was awarded a DSO and Captain Walker one of four MCs. The others went to John Watts, de la Billière and Lieutenant Anthony Jeapes. Sergeant Hawkins received a DCM and Trooper A. Cunningham, an MM. Six men, including Cooper, were Mentioned in Dispatches. The comparative lavishness of the awards reflected, not only the military achievement, but also the gratitude of Whitehall for the fact that a highly embarrassing rebellion had been snuffed out, after more than four years of failure by the security forces in Oman. It was, declared *The Times*, 'a brilliant example of economy in the use of force'.

It was also a risky, lucky operation and one that was to have prolonged effects on British defence policy generally. The tide of independence movements in the Third World was already beginning to run counter to the traditional, imperial idea of big overseas garrisons of British forces. Additionally, the new emphasis on nuclear weapons was having an impact on conventional forces available for low-intensity campaigns outside Europe. As Darby cogently points out: 'Militarily, the Oman campaign was not much more than a skirmish, but it had important lessons for the policy-makers about the demands of British overseas commitments and the way in which they had to be supported.

'This minor operation in the arid wastes of the Persian Gulf, in support of the feudal ruler of a country which had not emerged into the twentieth century, powerfully supported the hand of those ministers who argued for a greater emphasis on conventional forces, and perhaps had more effect on the Cabinet's thinking about defence priorities than all the carefully balanced arguments of the preceding few months.'

Even more significant was the decision of the Chiefs of Staff in 1961 'that Britain must be increasingly prepared to intervene in Asia and Africa and that this would be her major military role over the next decade'. The policy from now on, until the 'Europeanization' embodied in the 1974 Defence Review, was strategic mobility, the 'fire brigade' approach to power projection, the first successful experiment in which was the SAS intervention in Oman in 1958/9.

Oman II: Defeat into Victory

By the spring of 1970, the Regiment had no suitable theatre within which to rehearse its 'training operations'. The classic counter-revolutionary campaigns that had started with Greece in 1944, and continued through to Aden/South Yemen in 1967, were now a matter of history so far as British interests were concerned. Early in 1969, an SAS officer, disturbed by the lack of action, analysed British military history and concluded that since 1830 there had been only one or two years in which the Army was not fighting a war somewhere. It seemed that 1968/9 was one of those years. True, from August 1969 onwards, violence in Ulster required the presence of about 14,000 British troops, but they were there initially as a peace-keeping force, UN style, rather than as counter-insurgency forces. Apart from one brief, unpublicized tour of Northern Ireland as orthodox infantry in 1969, the SAS was now living from hand to mouth: testing new weapons in Britain, testing the security arrangements at the country's newest prison (where they broke out over an 'unscalable' fence in less than two minutes), training special forces and paramilitary police forces of such allies as Iran, and even providing bodyguards for some friendly foreign heads of state. Some men serving with the Regiment at that time heard the rumours that afflict all special forces at such periods, that there was no future for them and that the unit was to be disbanded.

It was in this climate that a small group of senior SAS officers decided to turn their attention to one place where their services would be of value. Twelve years after their first campaign in northern Oman, the ageing Sultan Sa'id bin Taimur, the thirteenth hereditary monarch of Oman, now had a much more acute internal security problem in the southern mountains of Dhofar. The Regiment's interest in Oman was revived in 1969 when British Intelligence sources reported that an Iraqi-trained guer-rilla training team had started work among the primitive tribesmen of the sensitive Musandam Peninsula. As a result, a squadron of SAS soldiers was landed on the peninsula by Royal Marine Special Boat Section Gemini inflatables. One suspect was shot and wounded and one SAS soldier, Trooper 'Rip' Reddy, was killed during a nocturnal free-fall parachute drop into the area (proba-bly the first operational fatality of its kind in the British Army). The drop, by a reconnaissance free-fall troop, was peculiarly hazardous – a 'HALO' ('High-Altitude, Low-Opening') from 10,000 feet with equipment, into a near-vertical 120mph free-fall, to canopy deployment in a depression surrounded by 4000-foot mountain peaks. Reddy became unstable as the heavy Bergen pack he carried shifted its position: the result was a tangled canopy deployment and instant death.

Meanwhile, at the other extremity of Oman, 625 miles away on the border with Marxist South Yemen, the Sultan's disastrous conduct of his country's affairs had provoked a Communist-led guerrilla war and brought his own regime to the brink of extinction. Even within Oman, Dhofar is a faraway country of which the rest of the population knows little, a hostile mountain separated from the rest of the Sultanate by 400 miles of desert, a backwater described in the Book of Genesis as 'Ophir', the easternmost edge of the known world. It lies between the sand seas and gravel deserts of the Empty Quarter and the Arabian Sea, sandwiched politically between Royalist Saudi Arabia to the north and Communist South Yemen. It is about the same size as Wales, with 4000-foot peaks topping an escarpment that rises like a natural fortress from a narrow coastal plain. From June to September, a monsoon wind sweeps off the sea on to the hills, bringing low cloud and fine rain which runs off the hills, to be followed by months of sunshine. As a result, the narrow plain between mountain and sea luxuriates in vegetation, including frankincense. The lower slopes are cut by ravines, thousands of feet deep, through which secret paths wander beneath thick undergrowth. It is perfect guerrilla country, honeycombed by limestone caves where food and guns may be stored for months and in which men may live.

The hill people, perpetually short of water, have always had to fight for existence against their neighbours as well as nature itself, as they move with meagre herds of cattle, goats and camels from one scant grazing ground to another. According to one recent authority, 'the characteristic Omani settlement is a semi-fortified village

around a water source', a society in which arms are
carried as a badge of masculinity and status as well as for
protection. The hill man's ethnic links are with the people
of what is now South Yemen, while the ruling Sultan (a
client of the British since 1800) is traditionally a remote
and contemptible figure, a plainsman living behind
palace walls at Salalah, with an escape route to the sea
guarded by foreign mercenaries.

How Not to Win Friends

In April 1969, five years after oil had been discovered in
commercial quantities, a distinguished British economist,
John Townsend, arrived to help Sultan Sa'id begin 'a
cautious move forward into the modern world'.
Townsend recalls: 'My first meeting with the Sultan had a
dreamlike unreality: I met a strange, small old man with a
splendid set of Father Christmas whiskers, tended and
guarded by burly young men of undoubted African
origin who were known as "slaves". He gave me, in
excellent English, careful instructions as to whom I
should meet and what I might say. All the people with
whom I was to work were expatriate; I was not to meet
any Omanis. "Our people are not yet ready for development", was the explanation. . . .

'There was great poverty and disease . . . yet nothing
was done because the Sultan would not permit it. No man
could leave his village and seek work without the permission of the Sultan. No man could repair his house without
the permission of the Sultan. This remote old man, who
never left his palace in Salalah and ruled by radio-
telephone through expatriates, had instilled such a
fear in his people that very few of them dared defy him
and undertake any initiative to improve their lot.'

There were no schools, so Omanis who wished to study
were obliged to become political exiles. Some did so in

W.D.W. – F

Russia and East Germany, others elsewhere in the Middle East. There were no hospitals in Dhofar, and only one road out of the coastal plain. Almost all foreign goods were forbidden, and Omanis were prohibited from dancing, playing music, smoking, wearing sun-glasses, taking photographs or wearing Western clothes. As an official British press briefing document was later to admit: 'The penalties for disobedience were either flogging or imprisonment.' Such penalties were the minor ones. As one SAS veteran was to discover, Sa'id's collective punishments included the cementing over of water wells with catastrophic results for entire communities. Sa'id, the official brief concluded, was 'a medieval and somewhat despotic ruler'.

Across the border in Aden and South Yemen, left-wing Arab Nationalists had been engaged in a terrorist campaign against the British since 1963. It was inevitable that Sultan Sa'id's regime should also provoke rebellion. Dhofari tribesmen, trained in Iraq, started a sporadic campaign of armed ambush, mine-laying and assassination in 1965, and this led to savage repression by the increasingly isolated ruler. Within a year, the Sultan was the target of an assassination attempt by his own bodyguard, several of whom fired at him from a range of a few feet while he was inspecting them. They missed. It is part of the legend of Sultan Sa'id that he then drove himself to his principal Army garrison (leaving behind a wounded Pakistani palace guard commander) to tell its British commander: 'We seem to be having a little trouble down at the palace. I wonder if you would be so good as to come down?'

Not surprisingly, opposition to Sa'id prospered. Fred Halliday, a left-wing British journalist and academic who has studied the Oman campaign, records: 'In the first five years, up to 1970, the British were on the defensive and merely tried to hold out with their ramshackle army and colonial administration. The main tactics used were

traditional ones: villages were burnt to punish the populations, corpses of guerrilla fighters were hung up in the
main square in Salalah; the mountains were block-
aded and Salalah itself was ringed with a barbed-wire
fence so that no food could be taken out or weapons
brought in.'

In November 1967, a year after Sa'id's bodyguard had
tried to kill him, the British left neighbouring Aden.
Although the hinterland bordering Dhofar became a
battleground for two warring factions within what was
now South Yemen, it was clear that Sa'id's opponents in
the mountains would soon have more room for manoeuvre: the British were, almost literally, off their backs.
It is an axiom of guerrilla warfare that a sanctuary and a
secure source of war materials, perferably contiguous
with the war zone, must be established if the campaign is
to succeed. Clearly, the rebels would soon have just this.
The war would be lost if something were not done to
change Sa'id's disastrous conduct of affairs, and this
change occurred soon after the unexpected election in
June 1970 of Edward Heath's Conservative Government
in Britain. Townsend has recounted how the outgoing
Wilson Government of 1970 had announced that there
would be a British withdrawal from the Arabian Gulf at
the end of 1971, while 'the Conservative Government
which followed it was less inhibited about dabbling in the
affairs of other states. Both the Foreign Office and the
Ministry of Defence were worried that an unstable
situation in Oman could well prejudice the smooth
withdrawal from the Gulf in the following year.' There
was another, more pressing reason for anxiety in London: the flow of oil through Hormuz.

On the afternoon of 23 July, less than a month after
Heath's election in Britain, Sheik Braik bin Hamud bin
Hamid al-Ghafari, an Omani aristocrat and the Wali
(Governor) of Dhofar province, entered the Salalah
palace to demand the abdication of Sultan Sa'id. It was an

act of courage buttressed by Sheik Braik's knowledge that the Sultan's son and heir, Qaboos – Sheik Braik's close friend – as well as key British officers in the administration were part of the plot. The Sultan responded to the Sheik's unexpected appearance by snatching a pistol from his desk and opening fire. One round wounded the Sheik, another killed a palace servant and one or two more wounded the Sultan in the foot and stomach. (It is generally believed that the Ruler himself was the cause of all these injuries.) That night, the Sultan agreed to surrender himself to a British colonel seconded to his armed forces, and abdicate. Both Sheik Braik and the Sultan were then flown to a Gulf hospital aboard the same aircraft, separated by a curtain, and the RAF spirited Sa'id away to London where he spent the last two years of his life in seclusion.

Operation 'Storm'

A few months before these events, after comparing notes at the Hereford Headquarters of 22 SAS, three senior officers had spent the Easter holiday weekend of 1970 examining the Dhofar problem and devising a winning strategy. By now the Regiment had come a long way from its role as saboteurs during the Second World War. 'Low intensity' operations still involved hard, if unorthodox soldiering, but Confrontation in Borneo and the Vietnam war had shown that a winning strategy, in an age of revolutionary fish swimming in a proletarian sea, was a matter of shaping the perceptions and loyalty of the population at large. By Easter Monday, one of the three had produced a plan for what was to become Operation 'Storm' in Dhofar, the basic elements of which would change the course of the war there. The plan demanded, first, a vigorous but intelligent and coherent military campaign run by soldiers, in which indiscriminate reprisals would be avoided. The other basic elements of the strategy were:

1. A medical campaign to provide aid for the 50,000 or so people living in the Dhofar mountains, most of whom were then regarded by Salalah as enemies.

2. A veterinary campaign to improve farm stock, including the provision of that most scarce commodity, fresh water, as well as skilled advice about husbandry.

3. A coherent Intelligence-gathering operation that would embrace every scrap of knowledge about the opposition (as the rebels were regarded at Hereford) aimed at isolating them and breaking their morale as well as underpinning military operations.

4. A psychological operation to persuade the rebels to change sides, the basic ingredients of which were communication by air-dropped leaflets, offer of amnesty to tribesmen wishing to surrender and an aggressive civil-aid programme that would outbid anything the opposition could afford.

Possibly because Sultan Sa'id was still ruling Oman, such a change of style did not meet with universal approval in 'informed' circles. It was a risk strategy and one that required cunning co-ordination as well as greater discipline among the military leadership in Salalah. For example, the existing use of air power – then consisting of six BAC Strikemasters – was, in the view of one SAS officer, remarkably informal. 'At that time', he noted, 'the Sultan's Air Force operated in an ad hoc way. The pilots seemed to sit around the mess in Salalah, then someone would suggest, off the top of his head, "Let's go and hit such-and-such a place." Systematic air support for infantry operations did not really exist.'

The removal of Sultan Sa'id, however, gave the SAS the chance for which it had been waiting. Within hours of the palace coup, a small SAS team (officially an 'information team') was on its way to Salalah, led by the chief architect of the 'win strategy' document. It provided an instant bodyguard for the new Sultan, Qaboos, about which there is a story (possibly apocryphal) that it stood behind a two-way mirror while Qaboos received petitions in his palace. One petitioner was a venerable, bearded figure much given to florid gestures. He did not know that each time an arm swept towards his robe, the trained hands of SAS men behind the mirror moved towards their weapons.

One of the team's first operations was to organize a leaflet drop over rebel territory. Despite some mild mockery from the British Left, which criticized the leaflets' Arabic syntax, and scepticism within the Salalah old guard, and the real objection that only a tiny percentage of the intended audience was literate anyway, the operation produced an unexpected prize. The best military brains among the guerrillas at the time included Mohammed Suhail, a former soldier in the Sultan's British-officered Trucial Oman Scouts. Suhail had been sent to Mons Officer Training School at Aldershot, sponsored by the Foreign and Commonwealth Office. He was a good soldier: best rifle and machine-gun shot on his course, and top of the FCO sponsorship list. On his return to Oman, however, he was disillusioned with the Sa'id regime and joined the opposition in the mountains. The first leaflet, with its offer of amnesty from the new ruler, Sultan Qaboos (himself a British-trained officer), brought Suhail back again to work with the SAS and the Sultan's Intelligence staff, headed by an SAS officer.

The team in Salalah consisted initially of one troop of fifteen men, plus specialists including Intelligence Corps linguists, a doctor, a veterinary surgeon, and a 'psyops' expert to disseminate information among the guerrillas. As a first step to penetrating the community it started a model farm on the outskirts of Salalah, which included cattle and poultry as well as root crops. The SAS even sent a soil sample for analysis by British agronomists, via one of its officers on his way to London.

As it turned out, penetration worked both ways. First, two thoroughbred bulls flown by the RAF by way of Dubai (where they created a commotion aboard the plane, to the alarm of the air crew) were used to serve Dhofari cows before an appreciative civilian audience. But the SAS's prize cockerels met a less happy fate: local farmers, anxious to improve their stock, smuggled hens into the roost, and these passed on fowl pest to the imported cocks, which died in action as a result soon afterwards. The experience had a deadly familiarity. No regiment suffers so much from exotic diseases as the SAS – eighteen out of thirty-six men on a subsequent Oman operation contracted hepatitis in one hill locality – but the team's vet was undismayed. Asked how he liked working in Dhofar, he replied, enigmatically, that he preferred it to caring for homosexual goats at Harwell.

Only a fortnight after the coup, the SAS team leader was on his way back to London with a long shopping list of unmilitary equipment, including drilling gear with which to dig water wells. The Dhofari hill men and their livestock had been cruelly impeded in their nomadic pursuit of water as a result of both the war and Sa'id's repressive habit of sealing off such wells as there were. Water, above all, was the currency that was to prove decisive in winning friends and influencing people. The SAS took its request to the Army's Chief Engineer, Richard Clutterbuck, who is now a distinguished political scientist specializing in counter-revolutionary warfare. Asked to provide drilling gear to help dissident tribesmen in Oman he replied: 'That's what we're here for.'

At this stage, London would not sanction the use of SAS patrols into rebel territory. Political considerations as well as the need for the soldiers to familiarize themselves with the environment both played a part in the decision. And at this stage, too, a troop of fifteen men was just not sufficient. The politics of Oman as well as Britain made caution necessary. On 20 December 1970, the *Financial Times*'s Ralph Izzard reported from Bahrein that, although SAS soldiers wearing the familiar beret with its winged-dagger emblem had been spotted in Bahrein, Sharjah and Oman, their presence was officially denied at first.

'It is now explained', Izzard continued, 'that this denial was meant to save embarrassment to Sultan Qaboos who ousted his father in a palace coup in July.... He clearly would not want it to be thought his own British-officered armed forces were incapable of dealing with Dhofar's Chinese-trained guerrillas.

'Services spokesmen maintain that the SAS have been in Dhofar purely for training purposes. They had no contact with the insurgents and no shot was fired in anger.... Dhofar has special attractions as a training ground because it is partly covered with thick vegetation as a result of the summer monsoon.'

In Britain it was clear that the premature commitment of the SAS to action, with perhaps the risk of large numbers of casualties, would generate publicity that could have imperilled the whole strategy to retrieve Oman's security. In those early days of the campaign, then, the SAS worked at hearts-and-minds, dispensing medical aid in villages on the plain, setting up two- and three-man teams to assist the people in any way that seemed useful. In some cases the soldiers even organized an efficient postal service. Their olive green uniform was nondescript, though recognizably European garb, and cap-badges were not worn. It all helped to ensure that the incomers were accepted by the Sultan's men, expatriate British officers, as well as the locals. Because of the SAS's unique constitutional position in Dhofar, finally answerable not to the Sultan and his military command but to the Ministry of Defence in London, it was a delicate and vital exercise in credibility before military operations could begin.

Meanwhile the amnesty campaign – much criticized by some British soldiers as a double-edged weapon that supplied much war material to the rebels – was reaping a useful harvest of 'surrendered enemy personnel'. The price paid by security forces was that rebel camel-trains moved unmolested in and out of the Dhofar mountains. But the defections were accelerated in September 1970, by a split within the rebel camp between the Communists and Islamic traditionalists, which led to fighting between the two. A British Army brief records that 'the attempted counter-revolution was ruthlessly suppressed by the Communists and resulted in mass defections to the Government'. Between September 1970 and March 1971, encouraged by promises of cash as well as amnesty, a total of 201 rebels surrendered. Some handed over their Kalashnikov AK-47s and were paid an extra bounty of £50. The most useful men were then screened with the aid of Mohammed Suhail, and recruited into irregular counter-guerrilla units known as 'firqas'. The training, management and leadership of the firqas was one of the most important tasks taken on by the SAS in its role as a British Army Training Team. As the operation got under way, SAS soldiers were sent for intensive, ten-week courses in colloquial Arabic at Beaconsfield, before being attached in three- or four-man groups to firqa units in their own tribal areas. One such team was to be involved in one of the Regiment's most desperate actions of this, or any other campaign.

The Battle of Mirbat

On 18 July 1972, the British Army Training Team at Mirbat – a meagre group of ten SAS soldiers, despite its grandiloquent title – was looking forward to the following morning, a Wednesday. On that day, the men, drawn from the Regiment's B Squadron, would fly out of the desolate, barbed-wire enclave they had occupied for more than three months and return to England. They were glad to be going home. Even by Omani standards, Mirbat was not much of a place – a huddle of flat-topped houses and a couple of ancient, mud-walled forts flanked on two sides by the sea, forty miles from the provincial capital, Salalah. Children and insects were numerous, but not much else. More than most wars, this one was a long, grinding spell of boredom punctuated by brief spurts of action. In Mirbat even the 'action' was frustrating: the whistle of incoming mortar bombs or anti-tank missiles fired by an unseen enemy. On 28 May, six mortar bombs had hit the town. On 6 June, another six. Two days later, three 75mm shells. And that, throughout the tour, was that.

The training team – acronymously known as 'Batmen' – had kept busy and alert, training local forces, repairing vehicles and dispensing rudimentary medical care to human beings and camels in the quest for goodwill, while keeping their undisciplined allies in check through a prudent control of the ration stock. Their departure date was well into the monsoon season. It was a time of incessant rain, low cloud and damp clothes, and therefore a time when visibility towards the hostile mountain three miles inland was dangerously limited. The season favoured the Marxist guerrillas of the Dhofar Liberation Front, biding their time in limestone caves on the mountain, in another important way. It usually made flying all but impossible. In a tight situation, as both sides well understood, the British team might depend upon air supply for ammunition, reinforcement and casualty evacuation, as well as supportive aerial bombardment. On the eve of the team's departure it seemed that no such problems existed. As the soldiers turned into their sleeping-bags for their last night in the 'Batthouse', they could hear the wind screeching in from the Indian Ocean and buffeting past them to rage against the mountain.

But that night the guerrillas were also on the move, launching a silent attack on the town to begin the most ambitious frontal assault of their ten-year war against the Sultan and his British advisers. More than 250 of their best warriors had been assembled for this battle, armed with Kalashnikov AK-47 automatic rifles, light, heavy and medium machine-guns, mortars of various calibres up to 82mm, two 75mm recoilless anti-tank rifles and an 84mm Carl Gustav rocket-launcher. As well as ammunition for these weapons, each man carried a profusion of hand grenades. The guerrilla column marched south towards the town and the sea, and then broke into carefully-organized combat groups, each of about ten men, which spread out in a wide arc around the town. Another group made a circular trek east to the beach and then back again along the coast to penetrate the town from that side. Before dawn, the garrison was isolated with no way of escape.

Inside the wire, in addition to the SAS team, was a group of about thirty Askaris from northern Oman, 500 miles away, armed with accurate but slow-firing .303-inch rifles. They served the Sultan's representative, the Wali, as town gatekeepers, searching all who came and went for messages and supplies, including food, that might be going to the enemy on the hill. The Askaris occupied a fort near the water's edge, known as the Wali's Fort. Living in the town itself, armed with FN automatic rifles and light machine-guns, was the local 'firqa'. Nominally its strength was about sixty, but at least twenty of them were somewhere on the mountain on a reconnaissance patrol. The remaining forty were in bed with their wives. Finally, there was another force of about twenty-five men of the Dhofar Gendarmerie, armed with FN rifles and a single light machine-gun, in a second fort just inside the wire. In front of the fort was the dug-out position for a venerable 25-pounder artillery piece of Second World War vintage. The DG Fort dominated the town and Mirbat's only airstrip. It was a vital position. Apart from the artillery piece, the heaviest weapons available to the SAS, at their nearby Batthouse, were a single .50-inch Browning and an 81mm mortar.

About 800 yards outside the wire, on a hill to the north of the town, another eight Gendarmes were on picquet duty. Predictably, it was their position, known as Jabal Ali, that first came under attack. Completely surrounded, it was to have been suppressed in a silent attack, but, as the guerrillas crept up on the position just before 5.30am, the Gendarmes spotted them and a single high-velocity shot rang out. In the fight that followed, four of the Gendarmes were killed; the other four escaped. It was the start of a battle as remarkable as that fought at Rorke's Drift during the Zulu War.

Guerrilla mortarmen, realizing that surprise had been lost, immediately began raining bombs on the DG Fort, the Batthouse and the town itself. Inside the house, Captain M. J. A. ('Mike') Kealy, aged twenty-three, rolled out of his sleeping-bag, slipped on a pair of 'flip-flop' beach sandals, seized his automatic rifle and ran to the rooftop to see what was happening. What he saw was unlike any enemy attack of the war, and Kealy thought it possible that the firing was an appalling confusion caused by false identification of the friendly firqa patrol on its return. In the half-light of a grey dawn he could see groups of armed men running across open ground in front of the Batthouse, pausing to fire at the DG Fort away to his right. Men were also swarming over the picquet position on Jabal Ali: clearly it was already in enemy hands. Kealy ordered the team's only mortar, pre-laid to fire over the picquet to cover just such a situation, to open fire with high explosive and white phosphorous smoke to obscure the enemy's vision. Another of his soldiers, Trooper W., opened up with the Browning, raking the area between the two forts, while others, firing from the roof of the Batthouse, picked off targets with careful precision with FN automatic rifles and a light machine-gun.

Kealy was by now profoundly disturbed. A frontal assault of this sort on a government garrison must mean that the guerrillas had assembled an unusually large force and that they probably knew the real fighting strength of the defenders (effectively, about fifty men). He handed control briefly to one of his NCOs, Corporal B., while he drafted an urgent signal to the provincial headquarters at Salalah. The message safely away, Kealy prepared for a long, hard day by changing from flip-flops into desert boots.

By now, a well-co-ordinated assault was under way. Guerrilla combat groups moved as though presenting an infantry demonstration of fire and movement back home in Britain, one group advancing under covering fire until it could find dead ground from which to cover those who followed. From the overrun Jabal Ali, above the town, came accurate, considered bursts of heavy machine-gun fire, and mortar bombs were landing all round the DG Fort and the Batthouse. Even more sinister, stray enemy rounds were whistling in from the southern, seaward side of the town, 'overs' which told Kealy and his men that they were surrounded. The battle now raging round them was a three-cornered affair in which the Askaris were firing from the Wali's Fort near the water's edge on guerrillas advancing towards the DG Fort and gun position; the SAS mortar team under Corporal B. was identifying its targets from the flash of enemy mortars; and the DG Fort was hitting back with everything including the artillery piece. The 25-pounder was manned by an Omani gunner, Walid Khamis and two Fijian SAS men, Corporal Labalaba and Trooper Ti., who had run to the fort at the start of the fight. The noise was stunning.

None of this deterred the guerrillas despite the casualties they were suffering. As one group was cut down another replaced it, until they advanced to within a few yards of the perimeter wire. Once there they opened fire on the DG Fort with Soviet RPG-7 rockets and the Carl Gustav. At a range of only thirty metres the Carl Gustav's 84mm armour-piercing rounds had a devastating effect on the fort's ancient masonry: its tower crumbled in a plume of smoke and dust. Throughout the confusion, Corporal B. calmly indicated targets for the SAS mortar, the Browning and light machine-guns, using lines of tracer to emphasize his fire orders. He also picked off leading guerrillas with his own rifle. This firepower, such as it was, now turned on the leading group of guerrillas at the wire, manning the Carl Gustav, as it attempted to rush the fort less than a hundred yards away.

Kealy meanwhile was trying to maintain radio contact with the gun crew in its pit in front of the DG Fort and the Wali's men in their fort. Messages from the gun crew were laconic, giving little sign of a situation that was turning from bad to desperate. On the radio, Labalaba's voice, which had been indicating possible mortar targets to the Batthouse crew, announced, 'Enemy now very close. I've been chinned but I'm all right.' It was now about 7am. Within the Batthouse it was almost impossible to hear anything but a steady roar of battle as rounds from the Carl Gustav hissed across the roof to explode just behind the building. Kealy had already asked for strike aircraft at Salalah to stand by, but in these conditions, with cloud almost at ground level, it seemed a remote hope that the Air Force could do much. Now, in the light of Labalaba's last message, Kealy summoned a helicopter to attempt a casualty evacuation.

Both sides had been firing intensively at one another for about an hour. The guerrillas, although they had breached the wire, had not yet taken the DG Fort. Both sides needed to pause to see to their casualties and bring up more ammunition. In the lull that resulted, the firing became spasmodic – so much so that children gathered on the roof of a building behind the Batthouse to watch the action.

Kealy, concerned about the absence of any return fire from the Gendarmerie Fort and its nearby gun position, as well as continued radio silence, now took a brave decision. He would go to the fort himself. This meant crossing about 400 yards of almost open ground under enemy fire. It was also possible that by now the fort had been overrun. Others in the training team volunteered to share the risk, but he took just one man, his medical orderly, Trooper T. P. A. Tobin, to aid the casualties. Simultaneously, Lance-Corporal C. slipped away from the Batthouse, through the town to a helicopter landing-pad near the beach, to guide the machine in as a preliminary to clearing the casualties. Kealy and his medical orderly were en route to the DG Fort when the 'casevac' helicopter clattered in over the sea. On the landing site, the lance-corporal threw a green smoke grenade to indicate that all was clear. But, as the aircraft made its final approach, the guerrillas, reinforced and rearmed in dead ground around the DG Fort, started shooting with renewed ferocity. One of the first targets was the helicopter. Another was the man trying to guide it in. The lance-corporal stayed long enough to throw a red grenade to warn off the helicopter, and then dived for cover. The helicopter whined back into the cloud, its cabin pockmarked by machine-gun bullets.

When the battle erupted afresh, Kealy and his medical orderly were still 350 yards from the fort. From the Batthouse their comrades laid down a covering barrage from the Browning and light machine-guns, as the two men bobbed and weaved their way forward through the smoke, one pausing to fire while the other advanced. Luck was with them and they at last reached the gun position. As Kealy and Trooper Tobin slithered into the gun-pit and peered through the smoke, they found an appalling situation. Walid Khamis, the Oman Artillery

gunner, lay on his back seriously wounded. Above the
gun-pit on the parapet of the DG Fort, a dead soldier
sprawled across his machine-gun. Another dead Gen-
darme was in the pit itself. Both the SAS Fijians were still
fighting. One of them, Trooper Ti., was propped against
the wall of the bunker, bleeding from serious head and
shoulder wounds, still firing his rifle at the guerrillas. The
other, Corporal Labalaba, wore a shell dressing on his
face to staunch the flood from his chin wound. He was
loading and firing the 25-pounder unaided. The gun
itself, its shield riddled with bullet holes, had been
depressed through 45 degrees to be sighted down the
barrel and fired at pointblank range.

Labalaba reloaded the gun yet again as the medical
orderly set to work to dress Trooper Ti.'s wounds. From
the ammunition bunker, Kealy snapped a terse radio
message to the Batthouse calling for an air strike. Before
he had completed it, Labalaba was shot dead, and soon
afterwards Trooper Tobin had his jaw shot away. (Later
in the battle, the same man was to be wounded in the back
and hand by a grenade.) The bunker was now being
defended by two men, Kealy and the wounded Fijian
Trooper Ti. By now, the guerrillas were only thirty yards
away, moving on the gun-pit and ammunition bunker
from left and right. Both gun position and the fort
behind it were being hammered by small-arms fire and
shuddering blows from the 84mm Carl Gustav. Kealy,
from the right of the bunker wall, picked off first one
guerrilla who was about to shoot Trooper Ti., then
another who clambered out of a ditch towards their
position. Trooper Ti., still propped up, fired carefully-
aimed shots at enemy coming from the left. From
somewhere too close for comfort, a light machine-gun
fired at the two men, and Kealy felt a bullet pass through
his hair. Now came the enemy grenades, which burst
near, but not near enough to achieve their intention.
One, lobbed right into the gun-pit itself, landed among

the dead and dying, but failed to explode. From his position on the left of the bunker the obstinate, brave Trooper Ti. asked Kealy for more ammunition.

A hopeless position was retrieved at that moment by the arrival of two Strikemaster jets of the Sultan's air force, hurtling over the scene just above ground level and under a cloud base of only 150 feet. From the radio in the ammunition bunker, Kealy passed targets to the Batthouse: 500-pound bombs on a ditch where the guerrillas had gathered in force and 7.62mm machine-gun fire along the wire only sixty yards from both fort and gun-pit. As the guerrillas retreated, Kealy hastily draped an air identification panel over a body in the bunker to identify his own position to the jets. Even before the first air strike was over, Kealy was also issuing orders to his mortar position at the Batthouse, a few hundred yards away. The mortarman, Lance-Corporal H., found that the proposed targets were now so close that he could not elevate the barrel sufficiently by orthodox means. His solution was to pull the barrel up to his chest, lifting the supporting bipod off the ground, and to grip the weapon with his legs before dropping bombs down the barrel.

The battle around the bunker had now been going on for ninety minutes. From the Batthouse, Corporal B. directed the second wave of Strikemasters. One of these hit guerrilla machine-guns on Jabal Ali, overlooking the town, while the other made several attacks on the enemy hiding in dead ground near the fort and the wire perimeter. 'There are hundreds of them down there!' an astonished pilot reported . One of the aircraft, seriously damaged by heavy machine-gun fire at close range, cut out of the battle and limped back to Salalah.

While the pressure was off his position, Kealy gave water to the wounded and re-dressed their injuries, then went to fetch the DG Land-Rover inside the fort for use as an ambulance to the heli-pad. He found the vehicle unusable, its tyres and petrol tank holed by machine-gun fire.

If the air strikes had taken the heat off the fort for the time being, it was clear that nothing less than substantial reinforcements could save the situation completely. That they were on their way was due to a fortunate coincidence. Before B Squadron (to which Kealy belonged) could leave the territory, it had to hand over to its successor in Oman. This group, from G Squadron, had arrived in Salalah the previous day. When Kealy's first messages alerted the base, the men of G Squadron were dressed and armed to check their weapons on the firing range. Instead they flew by helicopter, almost at sea level, direct to Mirbat beach. Their arrival at 9.15am almost coincided with the second air strike around the fort. A party of eighteen from the first helicopter lift advanced inland in two groups, wiping out a ridge position held by five guerrillas. The new SAS group was spotted by guerrillas near the DG Fort, who fired at it before starting to withdraw. The tide had turned at last.

From the beach, a second wave of SAS reinforcements, operating in three-man teams, engaged in brief, vicious battles with three guerrilla positions on the southern, seaward side of the town. In another incident the SAS party covering the helicopter landing zone waited in concealment as three guerrillas came closer. They were only five yards away when an SAS officer stood up and ordered them to drop their weapons and surrender. They did so, instantly. It was almost 10.30 before the most seriously wounded – the medical orderly, Trooper Tobin, whose jaw had been blown away, the obstinate and thrice-wounded Fijian Trooper Ti., and the Omani gunner, Walid Khamis – could be removed by helicopter. The Fijian insisted on walking into the aircraft. By then, Lance-Corporal H., the man who had held the mortar between his legs, had moved from the Batthouse to the gun-pit to aid the wounded in the closing stages of the battle. By clearing Trooper Tobin's windpipe of blood, it seemed that he had saved the man's life; but Tobin was to die of his wounds later. The next group of wounded to be flown out included some of the enemy who had been taken to the Batthouse during the first lull in the battle. By lunchtime it was clear that the position was under control again.

Kealy, whose judgement throughout the battle had been impeccable, now decided to see what could be done to save the original firqa patrol still in the mountains. He took a group of men outside the wire and up to the Jabal Ali area, which had been the first position to come under attack that day. But by now there was no way of knowing whether the patrol had encountered the retreating guerrilla force and if so, where. The firqa limped back later in the day with four men dead and three wounded.

SAS casualties were two dead – Corporal Labalaba and Trooper Tobin – and two seriously wounded; the Gendarmes lost one man killed, one wounded; and the Oman Artillery, one dead. The retreating guerrillas left about thirty bodies and about ten wounded, taken prisoner, but their sources later admitted that the toll was much higher. Factional feuds provoked by the defeat at Mirbat caused further fatalities. Others died of their wounds and these, added to the list of surviving wounded and taken prisoner, left fewer than half of the guerrillas' original elite force unscathed.

When the war ended four years later, one authority concluded: 'The rebel forces never recovered from this defeat and were never able to deploy sufficient forces to mount a similar attack elsewhere.' But in Britain, the battle received no publicity. Gallantry awards made public four years later included a DSO for Kealy, a DCM for Trooper Tobin, an MM for Corporal B. and, posthumously, a Mention in Dispatches for Corporal Labalaba. In February 1979, Kealy, now a major, died of exposure while taking part in an SAS exercise in bitter conditions on the Brecon Beacons in Wales (see page 270).

Mirbat was the high point of the SAS campaign in Oman. The guerrillas had lost some of their best men. Worse, they had lost credibility in a warrior society through defeat in open combat when the odds were in their favour. But the decisive effect of the Regiment on the war was more diffuse, more subtle than its skill at arms. By the time the war ended in 1976, the combined anti-guerrilla forces numbered about 15,000 men. The SAS commitment most of the time was a single squadron averaging about eighty, and even this figure could vary by as many as thirty more or, more frequently, less. As one of those who had an important role in planning SAS operations in Oman argues, 'It was not our numbers, but our ideas which made a big difference.'

Running the Firqa

The action at Mirbat was not the only one of its kind. One potent reason for the success of the SAS was that despite frequent disciplinary problems with the volatile firqas, the irregulars learned from experience that their British tutors would sacrifice their own lives rather than desert an ally in trouble. On 12 April 1974, Captain Simon Garthwaite was killed while trying to rescue a firqa pinned down by enemy fire. Garthwaite's magnetism was considerable: that his SAS soldiers used his Christian name is a measure of their respect for him. A friend who wrote his obituary recorded that Garthwaite was uneasy at formal mess dinners, but at home on the jebel. 'Boots (no socks), shorts, a belt and his rifle were all that he carried. . . . He had an astonishing way with local soldiers. They were drawn to him and . . . whatever "the Captain" said, they would gladly do; wherever "the Captain" went, they would follow.'

This does not mean that the firqa technique was an unalloyed success. There were furious debates within the SAS about the problems that resulted from paying some of the irregulars better salaries than the Sultan's regular soldiers, as well as supplying the firqas too generously with automatic rifles, ammunition and blankets. One lobby argued for a 'lean-and-mean' style of management; the other believed that full bellies ensured loyalty. Certainly there was extravagance. At Mirbat during the first end-of-fast festival after Ramadan, the local firqa celebrated by firing 5000 rounds – almost the entire garrison stock – into the air and hundreds of FN rifles disappeared.

There were also chronic problems of command, which depended crucially upon the relationship between the SAS team leader and his tribal second-in-command. According to one British veteran, every firqa experienced a mutiny of some sort at some time, and a few units were disbanded. These problems were least manifest when the SAS leader lived close to his firqa, like Garthwaite, but only one SAS soldier immersed himself so totally in native culture as to dress as a native and speak the language fluently. In general, SAS teams were with the firqa but not of them. They lived and ate apart, preserving their identity, even if the space between the two groups was a matter of yards.

Finally, there was a growing tendency among the irregulars to demand more and more supportive firepower from the regular army and air force before they would go into action, a process that cancelled out their natural advantages of stealth and surprise, and the guerrilla techniques they understood. At its best, a firqa backed by regular military forces worked with a speed and efficiency unique to Dhofar in recovering lost territory. In an unclassified lecture, the operational commander during the final, victorious phase of the campaign, Brigadier (now General) John Akehurst, described how this happened: 'First, the firqa would select a base of their choice. Provided it offered good prospects for land access and drilled water we would mount a largely military operation, perhaps a whole battalion, to capture it. Military engineers would then bulldoze an access track and down the track would come a drill rig.

'Troops would then thin out to the minimum necessary to defend the base with firqa assistance. While the drill turned away, the Civil Aid Team set up a clinic, a shop (with Government rations which would be free at first but later sold, though at subsidised prices), a school and a mosque. Engineers would be building a distribution scheme for the water with water-points for humans and troughs for cattle and camels.

'All this probably took four weeks. Water is at a premium ... and people throughout the tribal area would bring in their cattle. ... The civilians, of course, were in regular touch with the enemy, many of whom were their relations. When they came in for water and other Government munificence the firqa talked to them, first to gain Intelligence, but second, to tell them to let the enemy know that they should not interfere with the provision of these good things. The enemy themselves were totally dependent on civilian goodwill and therefore were forced not to interfere.'

Firqa offensives did not always work so smoothly. In January 1975, the Liberation Front was being pressed back towards the border with South Yemen, with a growing intensity of conflict and increasing casualties on both sides. In a catacomb of limestone caves, almost invincibly protected by an ugly, dominating hill, the guerrillas had their main store of weapons and ammunition. It was a natural fortress, the conquest of which initially demanded speed, stealth and local knowledge. On SAS advice, a lightly-armed firqa unit was nominated for the task of spearheading a battalion assault. SAS climbers were on hand to assist in the final stages and, after the caves had been taken, the Regiment's demolition experts were to destroy them and their contents. But things did not work out that way. Before the firqa would cross the start line to begin the assault, they insisted upon a demonstration of supporting firepower from aircraft, artillery and armoured cars, and demanded that this be repeated every few hundred yards during the advance. This orchestrated barrage advertised the beginning of the operation: not only was surprise lost, but the subsequent ponderous advance gave the guerrillas ample time to prepare an excellent defence.

During the next two days, under increasingly accurate enemy machine-gun, rocket and mortar fire, the assault ground to a halt. Akehurst recalled in his lecture how the situation deteriorated: 'In an attempt to capture the caves the advance was ambushed by the enemy as it crossed open ground and the leading company lost 13 killed and 22 wounded in less than an hour.' The first to die, in a perfectly prepared ambush, was a British officer who was moving down an exposed forward slope with his company before attempting to cross a gully. This group was now hit by the full fury of well-sited machine-guns and mortars almost immediately above it. Attempts by back-up forces to save the now-isolated vanguard encountered more withering fire, and spectacular bravery was shown by individual officers and SAS troopers to recover the wounded. At dusk on the third day of the operation, the SAS Squadron moved forward to make withdrawal possible for the beleaguered company. Hitting back at rebel positions with accurate GPMG and rocket fire, they kept the enemy's heads down while the remnants of the advance guard fell back. (The SAS officer in charge of this rescue was awarded an MC and subsequently retired as a major, to freelance international security work.)

An operation originally intended to last twenty-four hours now ground on for three weeks, though without occupation of the caves by government forces. What did happen, however, was that the approaches to the caves were denied to the rebels by constant fire from 76mm guns mounted on armoured cars, and were never again used as stores caves. According to one officer involved in the campaign, it was from that point on that the guerrillas began to lose to the Sultan's regular armed forces in straight military battles. Like Mirbat, it was a body-blow to the guerrillas' credibility.

One officer recruited by the Sultan from the original SAS force as a freelance, contract firqa leader, did adopt the tactics of the true counter-guerrilla. Working under the direction of another SAS veteran who was now in charge of Dhofar's military Intelligence, he lived for months on the edge of the Empty Quarter, dressed like his Dhofari warriors and indistinguishable from them. He dropped and collected agents over the border with South Yemen, the guerrillas' main supply base, and in 1972 decided to blow up an army fort at Sinau, eighty miles inside Yemeni territory. The operation was totally clandestine, so much so that if he had been taken prisoner he would have been disowned by the Sultan's hierarchy, most of whom, including the British Commander-in-Chief, had no knowledge of the operation.

With two Bedford trucks each carrying 500 pounds of unstable gelignite, and eighty men, including a party of South Yemeni exiles trained in Saudi Arabia, he arrived unimpeded at the fort, where the small garrison surrendered without resistance. Little more than half an hour was needed to plant the gelignite, still in its fifty-pound boxes, in each corner of the two-storey stone fort, and to link these with detonator cord to a five-minute safety fuse in the courtyard. Having ensured that the engine of his escape vehicle was safely running, the British firqa leader lit the fuse and got out. Just after dusk, a spectacular explosion mushroomed red and orange in the desert sky destroying not only the fort but also a government shop

garages and a house. The object of such an operation was
to divert the resources of South Yemen's army from
aiding the guerrillas as these crossed into Dhofar farther
south, along the coastal plain. Although the Sultan of
Oman was impressed, his British military commanders
were horrified. Border crossings are a sensitive political
issue for Whitehall. The contract officer at the centre
of this adventure transferred to other duties in Dhofar
soon afterwards, in charge of another firqa. His direction of the Empty Quarter firqa was taken over by an
orthodox SAS team, and its cross-border operations
ceased.

The Unexpected Victory

The end of the war, when it came, was as improbable as
an Errol Flynn film. The final assault was to be launched
by helicopter at dawn on a day in October 1975. Its object
was to seize high ground above a 2000-foot-deep wadi
and elsewhere on mountains near the border with South
Yemen, while an armoured car-bulldozer column would
advance simultaneously from the plain to control the
foothills. But, at the last moment, what was to have been a
simple diversion became the main pivot of the attack. The
diversion was from an isolated, air-supplied mountain-
top position held by government troops at Sarfait. Such
an attack was, predictably, a kamikaze manoeuvre and
both sides knew it. The descent was by steps down a series
of cliffs, the first of which was an almost sheer 600 feet.
Government troops had tried to break out once in 1972
and they had failed.

   Nevertheless, on the night of 14 October the Muscat
Regiment probed its way downhill to take the first
plateau. There was no opposition. 'We learned later',
Akehurst has revealed, 'that the enemy considered anything from Sarfait would only be a diversion and we

believe they probably got confirmation of this from the firqa taking part. . . . In any event, they decided to do nothing.

'At about midday on the 15th, I sat with Ian Christie, the commanding officer of the Muscat Regiment, and contemplated our unexpected success. I asked him what he thought he would need to carry on down to the sea. After some discussion he decided two more companies. In the next two minutes I threw seven months of planning and 40 pages of operation orders out of the metaphorical window.'

The main attack went in from Sarfait the same night, and by morning the government forces held a three-mile corridor to the sea, cutting the guerrillas' last supply line. From now on, the guerrillas' chief priority was to reach the safety of South Yemen. For many of them it was a long, pitiless march along waterless tracks north of the mountains they had controlled for five years. The war ended formally a few months later with a ceasefire between South Yemen and Oman.

The full story of how the fortunes of this war were swung from the near collapse of government forces in 1970 to their outright victory by 1976 must await the memoirs of the operational commanders. Broadly, it is one of gradual penetration of Dhofari society, in which the firqas, trained and advised by the SAS, reoccupied the mountains using water wells as the ultimate currency of persuasion; and in which increasingly ambitious, orthodox military operations finally required thousands of Iranian and Jordanian, as well as Omani, soldiers to cut guerrilla supplies coming from South Yemen. This was accomplished by building a series of communication barriers, which employed barbed wire, booby-traps, mines and electronic ground sensors. Air and naval bombardment was used to soften up hostile areas before such operations took place, and everything that might aid the guerrillas, including cattle, was removed. The first of these barriers, the Hornbeam Line, covered thirty-five miles and took twelve months to build.

The closer government forces came to the border with South Yemen, the more they came under attack from 130mm artillery fired from within that territory by regular forces. Government helicopters and strike planes were constantly menaced by some of Russia's latest anti-aircraft missiles supplied to the guerrillas. Contrary to even informed left-wing opinion in Britain, the war was not a totally one-sided affair. If it had been, it would not have lasted for ten years.

Was it all worth it? Although the press reported that the SAS suffered 'scores of casualties', the Regiment in fact lost twelve dead during its six-year war. In the light of subsequent events in Iran and Afghanistan, and their impact on Western oil supplies, the strategic importance to British economic interests of winning the war can hardly be overstated. The victory also sustains in office – as Townsend, the Sultan's former economic adviser, points out – a regime in which trade unions are still outlawed and in which strikes, also illegal, 'tend to be settled by the police or the army rather than by negotiation.... When the apparently infinite cornucopia of material benefits begins to falter, the Omani people may demand more say in their government.'

Certainly the material well-being of the people of Dhofar is now incomparably better than it was in 1970, and the most petty restrictions on personal liberty have been removed. But what if the rebels had won? Townsend, a critic of many of the Sultan's policies from within the regime, does not conclude that life might have been better under a Communist government. The extremism and incompetence of the rebel movement, he believes, was such that it deserved to be defeated. 'Victory for the Popular Front movement would have resulted in a harsh and negative extremism far worse than that of the Sultan, if the example of South Yemen is taken as a guide', is his conclusion. Townsend does not defend Qaboos's absolute monarchy. He asserts that the Sultan can only survive if he realizes that he is almost the last absolute ruler, and that the facts of history are against his survival. By assisting that survival at a critical juncture, the SAS helped to buy time for more peaceful evolution within Oman as well as serving the interests of the British, and other Western economies.

6. The Irish Dimension, 1969–

When the Prime Minister, Harold Wilson, announced from Downing Street on 7 January 1976 that Special Air Service soldiers were being sent to Northern Ireland for 'patrolling and surveillance' tasks in South Armagh, his statement was greeted by many journalists and politicians in the province with scepticism. Mr Paddy Devlin of the Social Democratic and Labour Party, an amiable IRA veteran of the forties, expressed a widely held opinion when he said: 'It is only a cosmetic exercise. The SAS have always been here.'

In a sense, Devlin was right. With its chameleon-like talent for blending into the local scenery, the Regiment had been a presence that permeated much of the security forces' activity, on and off ever since the breakdown of law and order in Northern Ireland in that fateful week of August 1969. In reality, what the Downing Street announcement signalled was a change of role from one of Intelligence gathering, control and analysis by a few selected SAS officers and NCOs sent to supplement the work of other Intelligence gatherers, to one of combat by the Regiment's four regular squadrons on rota. This participation was not sought by the Regiment, unlike the campaigns of Borneo, Aden and Oman where the SAS had lobbied Whitehall to ensure a role for itself. The Irish commitment was imposed by the Prime Minister without warning and without reference to the Ministry of Defence. Furthermore, formal commitment of the SAS as such also represented an extraordinary about-turn by the government of the day which, until then, had taken the view that the Regiment's presence would be a political liability. When the murder of a number of Loyalists brought Protestant indignation to boiling point, it was as a political device that the SAS was sent to Ulster, for the same reason that it had been excluded hitherto. The 'bogeyman' image of the Regiment originally cultivated by the Republicans and their friends for propaganda purposes was now a positive advantage to Wilson in his efforts to reassure the Loyalists. Since the Republicans believed their own propaganda, this image would prove militarily useful.

Prior to 1976, the Regiment's Oman commitment (which ended, on paper at least, with the defeat of the Dhofar guerrillas in December 1975) had meant that there were assuredly not enough men to supply a squadron, more or less full-time, to Northern Ireland. If such a commitment were accepted, then the precedents of post-war years implied that the SAS would take on a fighting role that could be expected to continue for some years. Obviously, the conclusion of the Dhofar war may have helped convince Mr Wilson that the SAS was now available for another active campaign, though in fact the Regiment continued to have a commitment on the border between Oman and South Yemen for a considerable time after the formal end of hostilities in March 1976. By the time the Regiment was publicly dispatched to Ulster, it had missed the boat – or, as others would argue, the Regiment had not been allowed to catch the boat in the first place. Whatever the correct emphasis, the undercover war in Northern Ireland evolved new techniques which, for once, others – notably Brigadier (later General) Sir Frank Kitson – had developed during the years the SAS was elsewhere.

The Regiment's first foray into Northern Ireland occurred in 1969, soon after the breakdown of law and order. Men of D Squadron drained their glasses in bars near the Hereford base in response to the recall code, 'Free Beer', before returning to barracks to pick up uniforms and Bergen rucksacks. (This code had to be changed after one irate parent, already angry about her son's drinking habits, construed it as yet another invitation to a bottle party: there was some doubt whether she would pass the message on.)

By now, the situation in the province was extraordinarily fragile. For twelve months, a growing dialectic of violence between civil rights demonstrators and the Royal Ulster Constabulary backed by part-time officers of the 'B' Specials had convinced many Protestants that the civil war they had feared for fifty years was imminent. (They were wrong.) The Catholic communities, as well as some government ministers in Dublin, feared that a carefully-prepared pogrom was about to occur. (They were also wrong.) In Belfast, the police commissioner sought the aid of troops from the local garrison. A company of the Queen's Regiment was moved to a local police headquarters, then moved out again on orders from London. The most dangerous miscalculation of all was made by the politicians on both sides of the Irish Sea, in the Protestant Government of Stormont and the London Government of Harold Wilson. Neither side could agree about the terms on which troops would reinforce the police, and the compromise that emerged from this deadly tug-o'-war created the worst of all possible worlds: the soldiers were to be supplied initially only under their common law power to make citizens' arrests. A legal precondition of this was that Stormont the civil power, had to expend all its security forces, including the exclusively Protestant 'B' Specials, in a final attempt to restore order. Implicitly, this policy required a complete breakdown of law and order and the demoralization of the RUC before troops would become involved. In the event, this is what happened in August 1969.

Night of the Armoured Cars

This latest Irish tragedy culminated in an horrific episode in which a group of police officers, already exhausted by three days' fighting in Derry, were ordered to take to the sensitive, Catholic Lower Falls area of Belfast in Shorland armoured cars. The crews had not manned the vehicles before; they were unfamiliar with the Browning machine-gun mounted on the vehicles; and the guns had no night sights. The armoured cars came under petrol bomb attack and, in the darkness, one crew opened fire with the powerful Brownings at short range on a block of Catholic flats. The heavy-calibre bullets ripped through the building and killed eight-year-old Patrick Rooney as he sheltered in his bedroom. Later, the crew gave evidence to the Scarman Tribunal under codenames. In startling contrast to the treatment subsequently accorded to SAS soldiers in circumstances of equal apparent risk, the RUC men were not exposed to the threat of criminal proceedings. In the aftermath of this event, as well as a gun battle between the two communities in Belfast and the burning of Catholic homes, the Lower Falls became the city's first 'no-go' area, surrounded by barricades.

Only now, as Ulster creaked on the brink of a real civil war, were British soldiers sent in to control the situation. Initially, they were greeted as saviours by Belfast's Catholics. But the Intelligence available to the incoming troops was scarce and inaccurate. At the time, the total resources devoted to military Intelligence in the province comprised one Intelligence Corps captain and one sergeant. And, as a Hampshire Regiment major wryly put it: 'The Irish are long on "intelligence" but short on information.' Possibly as a result of this, a British general negotiated unwittingly with a leading Republican doubling as chairman of Belfast Citizens' Defence Committee in order to have the barricades removed.

One of the fears in the minds of those responsible for Ulster's security was that the traumatic events of August would at last precipitate a civil war. Troops were on stand-by in the Irish Republic to assist evacuation, and both communities were making efforts to smuggle arms into the province. The IRA, not yet divided between the predominantly left-wing, politically oriented 'Officials' and the warlike, traditionalist 'Provisionals', had contrived to produce only one Sten carbine and a few pistols to defend the Lower Falls. It also had some grenades which tended not to explode.

The men of D Squadron were more concerned with Protestant than Catholic guns at this time. During a tour lasting a few weeks, they paraded openly in SAS uniform and even laid a ceremonial wreath on the grave of the late Colonel Paddy Mayne near their Newtownards base. If the press did not notice their presence, it was because the main action was taking place in the cities of Belfast and Londonderry. The SAS, meanwhile, patrolled the countryside between the Glens of Antrim and the Mourne Mountains to establish whether the Protestant gunrunning operations of 1914 – when the Ulster Volunteers landed 3500 rifles at Larne – might be repeated. The Squadron searched incoming fishing vessels for the same reason, but no arms were discovered. That clandestine trade, by extremists of both communities, did not begin in earnest until months later; by then, as a unit, the SAS had found another and more familiar style of warfare in Dhofar. However, if no SAS squadron as such was permanently committed to Ulster before 1976, selected individuals were to serve with security forces there.

The disbanding of the 'B' Specials in 1969 greatly reduced the amount of street Intelligence flowing to the government, which in any case, as a matter of policy, had chosen to adopt a passive rather than an offensive Intelligence-gathering strategy. By the spring of 1971, following the emergence of the hard-line Provisional IRA and a bombing campaign averaging two explosions daily, the authorities had become desperate to penetrate the terrorist network. The Army did so by adopting the 'counter-gang' tactics developed during Kenya's Mau Mau campaign by Kitson. Ten proven IRA activists, including one who was a recently demobilized soldier of the Royal Irish Rangers, were arrested and given the choice between long terms of imprisonment or under-cover work for the British Army. They opted to join the British. Commanded by a Parachute Regiment captain they were known as the Special Detachment of the Military Reconnaissance Force (or more colloquially, as 'Freds'). Their guardians were ten volunteers for plain-clothes duty from the British Army. The 'Freds' lived in one half of a semi-detached married quarter in the heavily-guarded Holywood Barracks at Belfast, while their British guardians occupied the other half.

How would such men as the 'Freds' be 'turned around' in this fashion? In his autobiographical account of the Mau Mau campaign, Kitson suggests that 'three separate factors have to be brought into play in order to make a man shift his allegiance. In the first place, he must be given an incentive which is strong enough to make him want to do so. This is the carrot. Then he must be made to realize that failure will result in something very unpleas-ant happening to him. This is the stick. Thirdly he must be given a reasonable opportunity of proving both to himself and his friends that there is nothing fundamen-tally dishonourable about his action. Some people con-sider that the carrot and stick provide all that is necessary, but I am sure that many people will refuse the one and face the other, if by doing otherwise they lose their self-respect. On the other hand few people will choose the harder course if they think that both are equally consistent with their ideals.'

Initially, the task of the first MRFs was to drive round

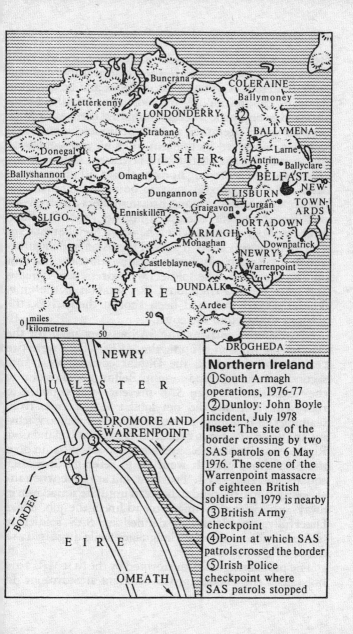

0 miles 50
kilometres
50

NEWRY

U L S T E R

DROMORE AND
WARRENPOINT

③

④

⑤

BORDER

E I R E

OMEATH

Northern Ireland
① South Armagh
operations, 1976-77
② Dunloy: John Boyle
incident, July 1978
Inset: The site of the
border crossing by two
SAS patrols on 6 May
1976. The scene of the
Warrenpoint massacre
of eighteen British
soldiers in 1979 is nearby
③ British Army
checkpoint
④ Point at which SAS
patrols crossed the border
⑤ Irish Police
checkpoint where
SAS patrols stopped

Belfast's Republican districts to identify erstwhile comrades in the IRA who were then placed under surveillance or arrest. It was a lethal, complex and bewildering game of cat-and-mouse and not many of the 'Freds' survived to enjoy the freedom promised them after MRF service. Some attempted to become double agents, and one was murdered by the IRA after his messages were intercepted by the British and rewritten. Others made the mistake of returning home to their Catholic ghettoes after a decent interval, only to be interrogated under torture by the IRA. Among British soldiers involved one was prosecuted for attempted murder, and acquitted, after the MRF team of which he was a member had hit four people with shots from a Thompson submachine-gun in the Republican Andersonstown district of Belfast on 22 June 1972. The soldiers were dressed as civilians and were using a traditional IRA weapon at the time. They believed they had been shot at themselves, the accused soldier told the court.

Surprisingly, perhaps, the SAS was not used for the clandestine work of running the MRFs. There were two reasons for this: first, the Dhofar commitment; and, secondly, political opposition in Belfast and London to the 'escalation' that an SAS presence was thought to represent. But this did not inhibit local people from blaming the Regiment for any undercover military activity. In June 1973, for instance, the Northern Ireland Civil Rights Association published advice about 'What to do if the SAS shoot you'. It went on to refer to 'SAS/MRF squads' and suggested: 'Provided you are alive when the shooting stops, pretend to be dead until the squad moves away, otherwise they might try to finish the job.' More cheerfully, one Irishman defined an SAS soldier as 'someone able to speak six languages while disguised as a bottle of Guinness'.

The pioneering work performed by the first MRFs did not satisfy the Protestant Government at Stormont. In

August 1971, against military advice, the provincial Prime Minister, Mr Brian Faulkner, persuaded London to introduce internment without trial. This was a political calamity, which alienated many hitherto uncommitted Catholics and exposed the poverty of the security forces' Intelligence system. Many of those rounded up had had nothing to do with the IRA for years, while volunteers who were currently active remained undetected by the security forces. Most of them, aware of what was in the wind, were not at home when the soldiers arrived. As the distinguished authority on terrorism, Richard Clutterbuck, has put it: 'The effect was disastrous. Of the 342 arrested on the first night a substantial proportion had no proven connection with the IRA and were quickly released. Of the remainder, 12 were interrogated "in depth" which involved long periods of questioning, with interruption of sleep and a bread and water diet; they were kept standing against walls in "search posture", sometimes with pillow cases over their heads and background noise to stop them seeing or hearing the others who were being questioned.

'Though the amount of information obtained was considerable, this kind of ill-treatment aroused anger and criticism both inside and outside Northern Ireland. Interrogation is a slow business and requires much patience especially if, as in this case, some of those arrested resist violently. For comparison, in major operations in Malaya, it was customary to limit the number of suspects arrested for interrogation in depth to 20 or 25 per month. Arresting 342 in one night vastly exceeded the capacity for interrogation in Northern Ireland.

'The result was a rapid escalation of violence. . . . While only 59 people in all had been killed in the two years from August 1969 to 9 August 1971, a further 231 were killed in the following six months. . . .

'British soldiers had carried out the arrests (though not

the interrogation) and borne the brunt of attempting to control the violence afterwards. The British Government told Mr Faulkner that they were no longer willing for British troops to be used under the direction of the Stormont Government, and that responsibility for security would have to be shifted direct to London. In March 1972 the Stormont parliament was prorogued and direct rule from Westminster was instituted. . . .'

A Cement for Disintegrating Intelligence

It was after this disaster that SAS soldiers, mostly officers and NCOs (who were, in some cases, Irishmen themselves), were posted as individuals to sensitive jobs in military Intelligence in Ulster. For convenience, some of them were attached to units already serving in the province. They were part of a much larger migration of Intelligence specialists of all kinds to Ulster over the next two years, which amounted to a counter-espionage 'gold rush'. As one Military Intelligence Officer put it later: 'Anyone who wanted to make his name in Intelligence was trying to get to Belfast.' Their world was like that of Gerald Seymour's novel about the underground war in Northern Ireland, *Harry's Game*, a world of petty but lethal jealousy and division among conflicting Intelligence agencies, a world of dirty tricks inaugurated by Military Intelligence Officers and their superiors, for which the SAS – by now not so much a military unit as a philosophical pantechnicon into which the Irish loaded all their suspicions – got the blame. To understand how this came about it is necessary to study the structure of military Intelligence in Ulster as it evolved between 1972 and 1974.

Attached to the Northern Ireland Office was an Intelligence supremo. His deputy, an assistant political secretary based elsewhere in the province, was for a long time seconded from the Foreign and Commonwealth Office. He was, in truth, a senior officer of the Secret Intelligence Service, or MI6 (also DI6), which is traditionally concerned with espionage outside the United Kingdom. The reason for this appointment (which caused resentment in the Home Office, the department traditionally responsible for Ulster as well as domestic counter-espionage, or MI5) was that, on paper at least, confidential exchanges of security information with the security services of the Irish Republic were an external affair controlled by the Foreign Office. The Secret Service was also keenly interested in monitoring a growing Soviet and Arab terrorist attention to the Irish conflict. Yet another, more pragmatic reason for the management of Intelligence in this way was that Harold Wilson, as Prime Minister until June 1970 and from 1974 to 1976, trusted MI6 more than he trusted MI5. The MI6 representative, through his boss in London, communicated with the Prime Minister with all the influence this implies, while in Northern Ireland he had at his disposal two 'executive' arms. These were the first plain-clothes MRFs and, separate from these, a Special Military Intelligence Unit, also working in civilian disguise with the police Special Branch from the RUC headquarters at Knock, on the edge of Belfast. There was also a traditional, if not explicit, link between MI6 and SAS people derived from the clandestine operations of the Second World War, Borneo, the Yemen campaign and elsewhere. Key posts in Military Intelligence, including the most senior jobs at Army Headquarters Northern Ireland and at Brigade level, were occupied by a succession of SAS officers, who returned to the SAS in Hereford or London after a tour in Ulster.

Meanwhile, the Intelligence supremo attached to the Northern Ireland Office, an MI5 man, also had his private line to Downing Street, as did the Army by way of the Defence Ministry. This spider's web suffered from grave structural disadvantages. For a start, all these agencies were jostling for control, offering conflicting analyses of what was happening on the ground and not revealing their thoughts to one another. The effect was sometimes to inhibit the Army while a fashionable intelligence scenario was being tested. An equally irritating effect of this divided counsel was that lines of command and responsibility within the rigid, hierarchical pyramids of the Army and RUC command structures were blurred when, for instance, an MIO captain or Field Intelligence NCO (a 'FINCO') working with the Special Military Intelligence Unit had a direct line to the MI6 Intelligence Chief at the army headquarters and through him to Downing Street, over the head of his local brigadier. Furthermore, because of the intimately personal relationships between the Army's undercover agents and their informers, who were constantly at risk, sources of information had to be kept within a very small circle, away from orthodox Army Intelligence staff at brigade level, or the RUC Special Branch, or both. Loyalties were further divided by the MI6 practice of marking certain documents in a way that effectively excluded the Royal Ulster Constabulary. The RUC, knowing what was happening, retaliated by withholding its best information and sources from the rest. To compound matters further, RUC Special Branch men and some of the Military Intelligence Officers working with them in the Special Military Intelligence Unit were running their own cross-border contacts with the Gardai Special Branch in the South, although these were ostensibly dealt with by the Foreign Office and MI6.

The confusion became total when the long-serving MI6 Intelligence Chief at Army HQ was moved to an overseas post and replaced by a less competent individual from MI5. It was after this change, according to two

MIOs active in Ulster at the time, that ten informers working for the Army Intelligence network run by an SAS officer were assassinated by the IRA. An MIO known as ·'Major Fred', who repeatedly crossed the border in civilian disguise, bearded, wearing dirty jeans and carrying a false driving licence issued in Dublin – in defiance of emphatic orders not to stray into the Republic – later described how the change affected his work. Hitherto, he had made his reports to MI6, but, following the departure of the MI6 representation, he explained: 'I had no-one to report to up at the top because I'd been told when I went up there by G1 Intelligence, this SAS major, "We're not working with MI5 because one of our lads has committed suicide. He had done four years here and handed over ten first class sources to MI5 who had just taken over, and within a week they'd all had a head job by the IRA, which means they've got a leak in their system. So under no circumstances give this information to the successors of the old Intelligence supremo. You must give this information to us, that is G1 Intelligence Army HQ, Northern Ireland." '

The suicide mentioned by this officer and confirmed by another former MIO was not that of an SAS soldier but of a FINCO of the Intelligence Corps, who shot himself at the Army's look-out post in Flax Street Mill, Belfast. The former Intelligence officer explained how this could happen: 'With an informer you get close, personally close. You know the man's family and you know the risks he takes to help us. To have a system which was incompetent because it was bureaucratic put people's lives at risk and made some of our own people crack up.'

Before this bureaucratization, the MRF groups had enjoyed much success. The 'Four Square Laundry', a creation of Army HQ at Lisburn, was a classic of modern Intelligence gathering. Until its cover was blown by an ex-IRA agent of the MRF, it was embarrassingly profit-able, since no official channel existed through which the revenue it yielded could be spent. As time went by, however, the MRFs also suffered some disasters. As in Aden, two of these plain-clothes Army patrols shot at one another. In one such encounter at Belfast's Springfield Road, each believed the other was an IRA active service unit. And the circumstances in which a Protestant ter-rorist quartermaster was shot and wounded with a silenced Sterling submachine-gun raised, even among RUC men, the suspicion more loudly voiced by the IRA that some of the security forces were engaged on their own assassination campaign.

In 1974, in an effort to impose order on the Intelli-gence mess in Northern Ireland, more SAS officers were drafted in to control agents in the field. This had the advantage that, without any overt structural changes in Intelligence gathering, there would be a cadre of people accustomed to working together who could act as a sort of cement to bond an organization that seemed, at times, to be falling apart. Many of their field agents were British soldiers not on the strength of the SAS but prepared to take extraordinary risks in impersonating the locals. Occasionally, as in the case of Captain Robert Nairac three years later, they were murdered when their bluff failed. (Nairac sustained his cover to the end. His killers thought he was a dangerous member of the left-wing Official IRA with which they had a long-standing feud that was then reaching a climax.) Other field agents were genuine locals who were now serving, or ex-soldiers; a few more, like the first MRF 'Freds', were IRA men who had been turned around.

Another effect of the Intelligence 'gold rush' was the emergence of hybrid units whose exact function was never really clear. Some had only tenuous links, if any, with the SAS. An Army free-fall parachute display team, which became very popular at charitable fund-raising events throughout Northern Ireland, consisted of two former SAS men, one MRF soldier and a Military Intelligence Officer. The team, appropriately named 'The Phantoms', never went armed. At Christmas 1974, one of its members parachuted into the grounds of a school at Crossmaglen, the IRA heartland of South Armagh, dressed as Santa Claus. He reasoned that not even the IRA would assassinate Santa.

The 'Doomsday' Plan

The year 1974 also saw the first excursion by an orthodox SAS squadron into Ulster, in spite of political resistance in London and Belfast to such a deployment at a time when negotiations with the IRA were going on in secret. During a raid on an IRA headquarters on 10 May in Belfast, the security forces had discovered documents including a 'doomsday' contingency plan for counter-attacks on Protestant areas if there were a repetition of August 1969 or worse. Army sources described the find as the most significant in five years of trouble. The plan, according to a British Intelligence source, was essentially defensive, but Harold Wilson, now back in office as Prime Minister, was influenced by an MI5 analysis of the IRA plan as an offensive one that imminently threatened a frightening escalation of the Ulster conflict. The reasons for this reflected the continuing rivalry between the two principal Intelligence agencies, MI5 and MI6, which, to do them justice, had never had to fight so closely on the same battlefield before and had, in Harold Wilson, a Prime Minister who was more than usually ambitious to 'fine-tune' events around him.

At the time, the Foreign Office, through MI6, was seeking a political solution, which inevitably involved secret exchanges with the IRA among others. The IRA, then down on its luck both militarily and in other ways, participated in these talks, but the MI5 analysis was that the terrorists were merely playing for time. If the Army could be taken off their backs for a time, it was argued, they would regroup. (They did.) The seizure of the IRA 'doomsday' document gave MI5 an ideal opportunity to discredit the hypothesis that the terrorists were serious about a political deal. Thus it was that the Prime Minister made a statement in the Commons to the effect that 'the documents reveal a specific and calculated plan by the IRA, by means of ruthless and indiscriminate violence, to foment inter-sectarian hatred and a degree of chaos ... to occupy and control certain pre-designated and densely populated areas in the city of Belfast and its suburbs ... its intention would have been to carry out a scorched earth policy of burning the houses of ordinary people as it was compelled to withdraw. ... An apparent IRA operation of potentially great danger has been brought to light.' As a result, an immediate growth in the Army's plain-clothes MRF surveillance operations was sanctioned and ultimately, by March 1978, the Minister for Northern Ireland, Mr Roy Mason, would announce that men from every unit in the province would be training for SAS-style undercover operations. But in 1974, as one of those involved put it: 'We couldn't get the soldiers trained quickly enough because the orientation process took time. We had suitable men who had volunteered for twelve months undercover work in Ulster, but how could we make them look, talk and think like Irishmen? Two of them went to a Paisley meeting with unshaven chins and in scruffy clothes. Not surprisingly, in view of the Orangeman's emphasis on smart turn-out, they were shown the door. There was also embarrassment when two of these volunteers didn't know the words of a favourite Protestant hymn. I sang with them as loudly as I could, but they weren't even moving their lips and they stuck out like two sore thumbs.

'Eventually it was agreed at Prime Minister level that

SAS soldiers should be sent to Northern Ireland, but not publicly. They were sent on the basis that, although they were members of the regiment, they were "returned to unit" and immediately posted to plain clothes duties. They were filling a temporary gap until we had trained sufficient soldiers from other units. Meanwhile intensive training of other volunteers took place in the UK and Northern Ireland.'

This peculiarly opaque period was attended by rumours of clandestine cross-border operations: if they ever occurred, they were contrary to the Regiment's insistence on staying within the law, if only because discovery of gross illegality would not be worth the political penalties involved. One example will suffice. On 8 November 1974, the Dublin-to-Belfast mail train was seized by armed men in the Republic and recklessly derailed near Portadown. The hijack was similar to IRA operations before and after this event. Yet, on the basis of hearsay, two former Army Intelligence officers were prepared to believe that the SAS had a hand in the derailment, the alleged purpose of which was to search Republican homes evacuated while the train was checked for explosives. As one ex-SAS soldier acidly observes, there were easier ways of accomplishing the same end. Yet the episode described is no more remarkable than a scheme entirely outside the ambit of the SAS, proposed to 'Major Fred' by his MI6 Intelligence Chief. The proposal was to substitute a doctored, exploding .303-inch bullet for ammunition an IRA assassin was about to use to kill a policeman. The scheme, confirmed by two former colleagues of 'Major Fred', was squashed by an Army brigadier. As Major Fred tells the story: 'I went to the brigadier and said, "Look Sir, I have a bullet here which is the top round of a clip of .303 ammunition that's going to assassinate a policeman on Saturday morning and I suspect that when it's struck it's going to blow the assassin's head off." The brigadier went absolutely mad with me and said, "I'll have no dirty tricks in my area. This is bloody disgraceful. You call yourself an officer?" So I immediately put this bullet in my cupboard and forgot all about dirty tricks.'

The SAS also had its critics among Army and police commanders, then and later, who felt that the introduction of the SAS somehow implied that they had failed. So when SAS soldiers failed to arrest a man in a Portadown pub after a fight, the news was greeted by the indigenous forces with a degree of schadenfreude. Soon afterwards, when two members of the Regiment were accused at Coleraine of bank robbery, the bad news spread more quickly. In a more general sense, it is not unfair to record that it was following the sharp expansion of undercover forces in 1974 that SAS veterans noticed a decline in the skill with which these forces operated. The decline is hard to quantify, and reflects subjective experience. Broadly speaking, it is said to result from a period of intensive recruitment into the SAS itself for counter-terrorism in Britain as well as elsewhere, during which (as ever) the veterans complain that standards dropped – increased bureaucracy surrounding clandestine reconnaissance coupled with official insistence that costs be reduced, and the general dilution of SAS reconnaissance techniques among men who had not passed the Regiment's stringent selection procedures.

The effect of cutting costs, for example, meant that the civilian cars used by MRF groups were resprayed less frequently. One officer, who was obliged to use an identical vehicle to trail an IRA suspect for five successive days in Belfast, was finally intercepted and shot in the head. An Intelligence officer responsible for the 'Q' cars solemnly registered each bogus vehicle with a senior official of the Belfast licensing authority, who retained the registration books and recorded the correct fee of £25 per vehicle. Each time a car was re-numbered and re-painted the same laborious process was followed.

Combat in South Armagh, 1976

Outside the cities meanwhile, long after the withdrawal of the SAS reinforcement group in 1974, one area of Northern Ireland that remained impervious to the successes of security forces elsewhere was the wild border country of South Armagh, centred on Crossmaglen. Never a natural part of the Protestant North, its inclusion in Northern Ireland was one of the more crass political errors of partition. The Irish Tricolour flies there as familiarly as the Union Flag in London. Throughout the troubles the IRA has sustained a classic, rural guerrilla war in the area, hopping back and forth across the multitude of border roads to friendly territory in the Irish Republic. This is not to say that the Dublin Government (as Mr Ian Paisley and other Protestant ultras allege) condones terrorism: the advantage to the IRA is that it does not recognize the border but the British and Irish security forces do, making hot pursuit in either direction, armed and in uniform, diplomatically impossible.

The IRA has had one other advantage in that area; skilled, professional military planning, which is attributed by British security forces to a renegade ex-colour sergeant of the Parachute Regiment. When Harold Wilson announced in January 1976 – apparently to the surprise of the Ministry of Defence – that the SAS was to be formally committed to the area, the 'score card' was: British Army dead forty-nine, IRA dead Nil. The peculiar advantage the IRA enjoys in the area is that it is an Intelligence desert, a sparsely-populated place in which even local people usually know nothing about what 'the Boys' are up to. The Army's border casualties included three young members of the Royal Regiment of Fusiliers who were surprised and shot dead in their observation post in November 1975. The only survivor, a lance-corporal, crawled to safety and 'played possum' while the

IRA called on the dying soldiers to surrender. They had been in the post for just thirty-six hours. One theory in military Intelligence circles was that their position had been leaked, without ill intent, by an undercover agent planted on the IRA, to increase his credibility with the guerrillas.

There was another reason for urgency in bringing South Armagh under control at that time. During the six months before the SAS was publicly committed to Ulster, twenty-one civilians were murdered in the border area as part of a tit-for-tat war of sectarian killing. During the week preceding the decision, ten Protestants were massacred in one episode and five Roman Catholics in another. The Wilson Government dispatched the Duke of Wellington's Regiment and 200 men of the Queen's Regiment as a response to this, but the Prime Minister concluded that this would be insufficient to satisfy an outraged Protestant community. Since the SAS was now assumed to be back 'on stream' with the end of the Dhofar campaign, he chose to make the maximum psychological impact with an announcement that they would now enter the Irish arena.

The initial advance party comprised only eleven men of D Squadron who had returned from Oman only days before. This fact rapidly came to the attention of the veteran defence correspondent Chapman Pincher, who described it as a mere 'token presence'. Wilson angrily denounced the story as 'a criminal misrepresentation of the facts', but Pincher was not led manacled to the Old Bailey or anywhere else. In spite of this propaganda mishap, the value of SAS mystique did count for something. The SAS, the IRA was led to believe, would wait in hiding for thirty-six days rather than thirty-six hours. In the ten months after the Wilson announcement only two men, both off-duty members of the Ulster Defence Regiment, were murdered in South Armagh. SAS strength in the area was gradually augmented to something approaching a squadron – in this case, probably about sixty men – as it had been in Dhofar. By 1977, according to one informed source, the number was 160, or two squadrons. Their target, according to an SAS officer who later in England talked unwittingly to a journalist with long experience in Ulster, was the top echelon of ten Provisional IRA ('Pira') leaders in the area. In December 1976, less than a year after being committed to their combat role, the officer revealed: 'We got four of them. The other six were chased away down South.'

One of the first to go was Peter Joseph Cleary, an IRA staff officer and a scrap-metal dealer, arrested while visiting his fiancée's home 100 yards inside the border and taken to a nearby field to await a helicopter. The chosen landing zone was a short sprint away from the sanctuary of the border. According to the officer quoted above: 'There were five of us. We radioed for a "chopper". . . . All of our men had to be used to hold up landing lights to let the machine down. Cleary was being held by just one chap. . . . He grabbed a soldier's rifle by the barrel and tried to pull it away. The soldier squeezed the trigger three times and got him in the chest.'

Another man, Sean McKenna, was brought before the courts where he claimed that he had been hauled out of bed in the Irish Republic by three men in civilian clothes. The SAS commander concerned said that McKenna had stumbled, drunk, into an SAS patrol near the border. Two others on the SAS list were arrested in the Irish Republic as a result of tip-offs to the police there.

In January 1977, just over a year after the Wilson announcement, the SAS scored a peculiarly satisfying victory. On 2 January, Lance-Corporal David Hinds of the Royal Highland Fusiliers was shot dead in an IRA ambush at Crossmaglen. A car in the vicinity was noticed by local civilians and, when it reappeared, the security forces were tipped off. On 19 January, in the gathering darkness of a Sunday afternoon, an SAS patrol waited as a young man approached its position. The man wore a black hood. He also carried a bandolier of ammunition – which later proved to be a strong buckshot used for deer hunting – and a shotgun the barrel of which was sawn short. As one of the patrol rose to challenge the man, he lifted the shotgun. The SAS trooper instantly fired several times. The impact of the shots hurled the gunman backwards. Simultaneously, the soldier came under fire from one or two other unseen gunmen using high-velocity Armalite rifles. The shots, about twenty in all, missed their target as the soldier ducked for cover. At the same time other members of the SAS patrol fired back twenty-eight times, aiming at the muzzle-flashes of the IRA weapons. Later, the soldiers found a trail of blood in a dyke beside the road. The first armed man they had shot turned out to be a twenty-year-old building worker named Seamus Harvey. He lived nearby at Drummakaval and was killed only 200 yards from the site of the observation post ambush in which the three British Fusiliers had been killed just before the SAS arrived. Two of his wounds were caused by the IRA Armalites.

The deterrent effect of such ambushes was dramatic. While soldiers and RUC officers continued to be killed regularly elsewhere in Northern Ireland after Harvey's death, the IRA attacks in South Armagh diminished almost to vanishing point for a year. When they were resumed, at Forkhill, the first casualty was a local pig.

Soon, however, the SAS was to learn that 'the Irish dimension' presented them with problems not even their previous campaigns, exotic though they were, had brought to light. Having declared a war of liberation against the British forces, the IRA was equally ready to claim the protection of the law, whether in the Republic (whose government it does not recognize) or in the North. Simultaneously, the SAS encountered covert hostility from elements in the police force on both sides of the border, although in theory all three were attempting to subdue a common enemy. The first and most famous episode led to the appearance of eight members of the Regiment (one a Fijian) in a Dublin court, charged with, among other things, the illegal possession of firearms with intent to endanger life. On conviction, the soldiers could have been imprisoned for twenty years on this charge alone.

The episode began on the night of 5 May near Omeath in County Louth, when a car containing a military plain-clothes patrol was halted at a police road-block 600 yards south of the Ulster border. In spite of appeals to let the patrol return the way it had come, a police officer manning the road-block insisted on taking advice from his Dundalk superiors and thereafter the affair escalated. Two other SAS vehicles, searching for the one that was missing, ended up at the same point at 2.15am and they also were detained. Weapons taken from them included Sterling submachine-guns, pump-action shotguns and automatic pistols. Army HQ Northern Ireland explained that the men had inadvertently crossed the border on an unmarked road as a result of a map-reading error. A *Sunday Times* journalist who went over the same ground concluded that the patrols had missed 'a faded, but still visible, large yellow cross in the narrow road painted by the Army to warn troops that they were coming to the border'; that they had made a 180-degree compass error and had also missed two road signs at a crossroads just before they arrived at the Gardai road-block.

The press, finding it incredible that two SAS patrols could make the same map-reading error, looked for a more plausible explanation and, they thought, found it. Nine terrorists had tunnelled out of the Maze Prison shortly before the SAS teams got lost. Further, a stolen car had taken six men from Forkhill in South Armagh and crossed the border earlier the same night. But this ingenious reconstruction, it was claimed by the Regiment after the trial, was wrong and ignored the simple, embarrassing truth that the whole episode was 'a foul-up', a comedy of errors which escalated out of control once an arresting officer in the Republic referred the matter to higher authority. Certainly this was the impression given during the Dublin trial by the police officer who arrested the SAS men. Asked what the soldiers had said at the moment of arrest, the officer coughed away his embarrassment, then quoted one of the accused, Corporal Nicholson: 'I was hoping to make it as a sergeant but after this fuck-up, there's no hope.'

The Law v. Political Rhetoric

Legal limitations on a regiment accustomed to the freedom (as well as the perils) of the battlefield have emerged in Northern Ireland as well as across the border, in spite of the televised pronouncement of Mr James Chichester-Clark, Stormont's penultimate Prime Minister, the morning after the first British soldier was shot dead in these latest troubles, in February 1971. 'Northern Ireland', he declared, 'is at war with the Irish Republican Army Provisionals.' Prime Minister Harold Wilson echoed this sentiment in his House of Commons statement about the 'doomsday' plan in May 1974: 'We are not talking of a peacetime situation,' he said. And, following the murder of Lord Mountbatten in August 1979, Prime Minister Margaret Thatcher voiced similar sentiments. The ordinary soldier might be forgiven for the belief that he was expected to react as though this were a war. In spite of the political rhetoric, the problem of adjusting a military campaign to the legal fiction that there is no war is one that has faced all soldiers in Northern Ireland. The SAS has encountered the problem in an acute form because of its rôle in capturing or fighting armed men in isolated ambushes laid by both sides, of which there are usually no witnesses except the combatants. The essence of the law governing the British soldier's conduct in Northern Ireland, as it has painfully evolved since the common-law arrangement of 1969, is that he may not shoot at an armed terrorist without risking criminal proceedings for murder unless he is in imminent danger, or can plausibly claim that he believed himself to be. This means that it might be illegal for a soldier to shoot at a gunman who has just killed one of his comrades, but who is now in the act of fleeing from the scene and threatening no imminent danger to the soldier in pursuit. The SAS has never been in the business of offering soft targets to an enemy, adopting Bismarck's advice: 'Only a fool learns from experience; I learn from the experience of others.' It was inevitable that once the SAS was committed to combat in Northern Ireland, its philosophy would come into conflict with the legal niceties with which, for political reasons, that war is 'deodorized'. When it did happen, the circumstances were peculiarly tragic.

By now, internment without trial had been abandoned in favour of Diplock (juryless) courts at which legal proof of motive as well as fact was required, while the initiative for much military planning had passed from the Army to the police. A sophisticated enemy, less susceptible to the traditional SAS methods of winning 'hearts and minds' evolved in Borneo and Dhofar, the IRA was not slow to cash in on the opportunities this unique legal environment offered. The only 'hearts-and-minds' initiative that would satisfy the IRA would provoke a Protestant uprising. Thus it was that the SAS became entrapped, with so much of British political history, in the Irish bog. The shooting of sixteen-year-old John Boyle should be seen as part of that history, rather than as a tale of military callousness.

On 10 July 1978, John Boyle, the son of a Roman Catholic farmer, took a break from his work in a hayfield

at Dunloy, in an isolated part of County Antrim, and went
to a deserted, overgrown graveyard nearby. John was an
inquisitive lad, and there had been some discussion in his
home about the possibility of an ancestral tombstone in
the graveyard. What John found, in fact, was a blue
plastic sack hidden under one of the gravestones. He told
his elder brother, Hugh, about this find. Later the same
day, their father, Cornelius, a careful and methodical
man, heard about John's find. He checked it and telephoned Ballymoney police station, concerned that the
cache might contain explosives that could endanger the
lives of children he had seen near the graveyard. A
detective constable said he would have the matter attended to. Later that day, this constable and three other
RUC men checked the bag. It contained a detonator cap,
cordtex fuse, what appeared to be gelignite bound with
black tape and, in a separate fertilizer bag, what appeared
to be a rifle. The cache also contained a revolver. They
called in the Army.

At an Army base, a few miles away, Sergeant Allan
Bohan, aged twenty-eight, an SAS soldier with twelve
years' service, six of them in the Regiment, and his friend
Corporal Ronald Temperley, aged twenty-six, were
watching a television programme *The Waltons*, when they
were summoned, with three of their comrades, to
Ballymoney police station. Bohan later said that they were
told that the weapons were probably to be used against a
local Protestant march on 12 July, and it was expected
that more than one armed man would return to collect
them. It was now the evening of 10 July: clearly there was
not much time to set up an ambush if this supposition
were correct; no time, apparently, to check whether the
illicit rifle was loaded. In spite of this, there were two
briefings during which the soldiers were shown aerial
photographs of the site and told who lived where in the
area. According to Army and police witnesses, one of the
detective constables present, the man who had received

Cornelius Boyle's original telephone message, agreed to repeat an earlier warning to the family to stay away from the graveyard. Later, this detective constable denied giving such an undertaking though, in fact, he did telephone the Boyle family to reiterate the warning the following day, seven hours after the SAS ambush was set up.

The police officers involved went off duty at around 3am, by which time Bohan and Temperley were concealed in the undergrowth twelve yards from the arms cache, while two of their colleagues were hidden in a farm building on the road opposite the path to the graveyard. The soldiers believed that the family had been warned to stay away. 'We believed we would be up against three armed terrorists and our mission was to capture any person who came to recover the cache,' Bohan said later in a statement. But it was clearly a matter of fine judgement, and perhaps split-second timing, if any terrorist collecting the arms were to be caught in the act, as the law required, yet simultaneously unable to threaten any soldier who had allowed him to arm himself. This may explain why, at the briefing, a 'killing' as alternative to capture was mentioned during the planning of the operation. In Northern Ireland, as in Aden, a live captive was far more useful for Intelligence gathering than a dead terrorist.

The police warning to the Boyle family was given at 9.40 am, about ten minutes after young John had taken the family tractor out to the hayfield. For reasons about which learned counsel could only speculate later on, the boy returned to the graveyard to have another look at the arms store. There were two sources of evidence for what happened next. One was Sergeant Bohan, who opened fire on Boyle, killing him; the other was Ulster's Assistant State Pathologist, Dr John Press. Bohan, from the outset, asserted that a man resembling a terrorist whose photograph he had seen walked straight up to the cache and extracted the rifle from it. 'He stood up . . . turned bringing the weapon to bear on us and I thought our lives were in immediate danger. I fired and he fell and as soon as he fell I stopped. I fired not more than twice and probably once.' As Bohan fired, so too did Temperley.

If this story were true, then clearly the first bullet to strike Boyle, who was facing Bohan, would have entered his body from the front. But it was contradicted by an autopsy report prepared by Dr Press, who insisted that Boyle was hit by three bullets, one through the head and two through the body, all entering from the back. Not long after Press's postmortem, the contents of his report were leaked to journalists with predictable results. The journal *Time Out*, for example, reported: 'Five high velocity bullets fired from less than four yards killed Boyle. All the rounds were fired from behind, the fatal bullet entering through the nape of the neck and blowing off the top of his head . . . the four men who murdered him were members of the Special Air Service.' In the fullness of time, Bohan and Temperley were charged with murder and brought to trial, almost a year after Boyle's death. By then, an independent autopsy by the distinguished British pathologist, Professor J. M. C. Cameron, had cast doubt on Press's findings. Cameron concluded that Boyle was shot in the head from the front, and that his body was turned by the impact of this bullet so that the two subsequent shots hit him in the back. Even more telling was Cameron's discovery that the basic measurements of Boyle's body and the site of the bullet wounds according to Dr Press were inaccurate. Having launched its case on the basis that Boyle was shot from the rear, the prosecution found it necessary, well after the case had begun, to float the theory that Bohan may have made a noise deliberately to induce Boyle to turn in Bohan's direction, 'and then you shot him'.

The Lord Chief Justice of Northern Ireland, Sir Robert Lowry, summing up the case described Dr Press as 'a most important' Crown witness, whose evidence was 'a clear indication that the deceased was shot in the back and that the defence of self defence . . . could not possibly stand up'. But defending counsel, Mr Michael Lavery, had cross-examined Dr Press 'with such a wealth of convincing anatomical and scientific detail as to cast the gravest possible doubt on the reliability of his [Dr Press's] principal conclusion'.

'Put shortly, counsel achieved a position in which the witness [Dr Press] admitted that the wound at the back of the head was for several reasons characteristic of an exit rather than an entrance wound. . . . The argument as to the wounds on the deceased's back was more complex, but identified a number of unsatisfactory features of evidence such as wrong measurements, faulty relationship of various "landmarks", failure to record objective signs on the existence of which the witness [Dr Press] later relied when pushed by counsel into a difficulty, and a number of facts which did not seem to support his essential hypothesis of the bullets having entered only at a slightly downwards inclination.'

The defence, by contrast, 'was suggesting a plunging effect which would indicate either firing from a considerable height (which was extremely unlikely) or (as defence counsel suggested) firing on the level into the body, the relevant part of which was almost parallel to the ground because (he suggested) the deceased, having been struck in the head, was falling as the two bullets of parallel height struck the trunk.'

'I consider', the Judge continued, 'that the most probable thing is that Soldier A [Bohan] shot the deceased in the head when the deceased's head was facing A, and slightly inclined to the left; that the deceased fell forward with his left shoulder coming under his body and towards the right; that while he was in that position two bullets from Soldier B's [Temperley's] rifle entered the deceased's back (which would cause them to make a downward track towards the fifth rib and lung) and that the deceased's body finished up roughly on its left hip and back. . . .

'To put it no higher, a responsible tribunal of fact is bound at least to assume in favour of the accused that something like this happened and that the deceased cannot have been shot from behind in the ordinary sense. . . .'

The result of the case satisfied no one and reflected the messy ambiguities of an undeclared war dressed up in the legal trappings of a civil police operation. Prosecution counsel had argued: 'The security forces do not have a free hand to . . . claim the same immunity as if they were on the battlefield. . . . The Crown accepts that both accused soldiers believed John Boyle to be a terrorist. . . . The accused looked at the short-term advantage of eliminating a person whom they believed to be a terrorist in the knowledge that there was a rifle under the headstone and they could make it appear that the terrorist had armed himself.' But the Lord Chief Justice (sitting, under the Diplock formula, as a jury) found the two soldiers not guilty of murder because 'a collection of suspicious circumstances is not proof beyond reasonable doubt'. Once the medical evidence (of Dr Press) had to be discounted, the only way a defence plea of homicide in self-defence could be attacked was by not believing that the boy Boyle had pointed the rifle at the soldiers, and, said the Judge, 'I am not infallible on a pure question of fact.' At the same time, Sir Robert scourged Bohan as 'an untrustworthy witness' who had gravely mishandled the operation because his team had shot an innocent boy, 'whether or not he was holding the gun'. If the soldiers believed Boyle was a terrorist, they had time to capture him. Furthermore, 'if one accepts the defence case this was a badly planned and bungled exercise'. For good measure, the Judge rammed home the prosecution's message: 'I do not intend to give any currency to the view that the army is above the general law in the use of weapons.'

Following the case, the dead boy's father blamed both the SAS and the police for what had happened. The Republican Clubs and others attacked the acquittals as 'absolutely outrageous'. No one complained about those responsible for the original arms cache, though evidence had been given that the Armalite rifle picked up by John Boyle had been used in several murders and attempted murders in the two years preceding April 1978, and nitro-glycerine explosive from the cache had come from the Irish Republic.

The leak of the inaccurate postmortem report; the detective's denial of a pledge to reiterate a warning to the family; and an allegation that there was an SAS conspiracy to tamper with evidence after the shooting; all this did nothing to sweeten relations between the Regiment and the RUC (to which a soldier in Northern Ireland is answerable after any violent death in which he is involved). Nor did another propaganda coup shortly before the trial began, alleging that a doctor's wife had been raped in Belfast by a lone, unidentified SAS man. Details of the rape undoubtedly emanated from police records, but the smear was sufficiently vague to make it impossible to get at the truth. It elicited an unprecedented statement from the Colonel Commandant of the SAS Regiment, Colonel B. M. F. Franks, 'to rebut the ever-growing, ill-informed comment in the press and elsewhere about my regiment'. No SAS soldiers were known to be in Belfast at the time, Franks said. A deafening silence followed the rebuttal. Whatever 'evidence' there was for the smear was never deployed.

Yet the trial of Bohan and Temperley did serve one purpose. The details of Bohan's evidence threw much light on the way the soldiers there perceive their task, and the extent to which SAS ambushes are now orchestrated by a doctrine embodied in the Standing Operational

Procedures (SOPs), which have evolved from hard experience in Ireland. Immediately after the Boyle shooting, Bohan – who had maintained radio silence
hitherto – had snapped a terse message to his comrades
posted just outside the cemetery: 'Contact! Send QRF!'
The word 'contact' indicated that the first shots had been
fired; the QRF, or Quick Reaction Force, on helicopter
stand-by, was now summoned as a back-up force. Asked
why this should be necessary, Bohan had referred to the
case of 'an OP (observation post) taken out by the IRA'.
This, of course, was the Drummakaval Hill episode in
South Armagh after which the only survivor, a lance-
corporal, had failed to use his radio until it was too late.
Pressed about the tactics to be employed in arresting a
terrorist suspect, and how to time his challenge, Bohan
had repeatedly made the point: 'We don't dictate the
tactics to the terrorists. They dictate them to us.' He was,
he explained, concerned not only about Boyle but any
other armed men who might be covering him. Yes, he
had stood up out of cover as Boyle took up the Armalite,
and perhaps, as counsel suggested, it was a crazy thing to
do; but presenting oneself as a target was sometimes 'the
risk of being a soldier'. In another reply, Bohan said
laconically: 'Tactics are like opinions: everyone has one.'
When counsel suggested that Bohan was in a 'cool, calm
and collected state of mind', as he fired at Boyle's head,
Bohan replied: 'I don't think anyone shooting from 12
yards at such a target would be cool and calm.'
    Immediately after the shooting he had again followed
SOP in moving to the body, searching it, and then moving
forward to clear his area. Stupidly, he agreed, he had
emptied the arms cache on the same basis and, once the
Quick Reaction Force had arrived, he again followed the
procedure in returning to his base before the police
appeared on the scene. Asked whether it was part of the
SOP not to give his name to the police when they came to
interview him, Bohan replied: 'I believe that is part of an

agreement between the Army and the police but I am not absolutely sure.' (In fact, a soldier is required to give his name to the police.) And how did he feel when he discovered that John Boyle was not a terrorist? 'His actions indicated to me he was a terrorist. . . . Nothing else. . . . I was told that the person who had been shot was not a terrorist but I didn't accept it. . . . I cannot regard any person who points a weapon at me as being a completely innocent person.'

Such answers did little to reassure an uncomprehending and often hostile civilian population, which was disturbed by a mounting toll of people shot dead by the Army during the preceding months. Some were IRA bombers engaged in planting bombs. For once, Irish logic and legal doctrine were at one when the *Republican News* complained on 24 June 1978: 'In the early hours of last Wednesday morning a three-man active service unit of the Irish Republican Army was surprised and trapped while on a bombing sabotage operation against Ballysillan Post Office Telecommunications Depot in Belfast. The unarmed volunteers having been surrounded by British soldiers and RUC men were summarily killed. Also shot were two passers-by, one fatally.' The ambush party, as it happened, consisted of an SAS team accompanied by RUC men, and the operation brought bombings in Belfast to an abrupt halt for several months. If the *Republican News* was not impressed by the soldiers on this occasion, neither were the soldiers by the IRA appeal to a legal system that it does not recognize. But this is not to argue that the legal restraints are without effect both in controlling the soldiers and winning the unacknowledged war in Northern Ireland. They are, in fact, a potent element in shaping perceptions, and SAS soldiers are carefully briefed about them – and, the difference from earlier campaigns – before they operate in the province. Thus there is a school of thought within the Army which, relying on a counsel of perfection, argues that an SAS soldier who gets caught breaking the law deserves no special treatment. Yet, after the Boyle affair, it is not surprising that at least one SAS soldier, cynical about these unique ground rules, should explain: 'Letting the opposition shoot first is what we call the "Irish Dimension".'

What the Regiment has not been allowed to disclose, for security reasons, is the extent of its success in non-lethal activity in Ulster. Like the rest of the Army, its record of arms hauls and terrorist arrests without bloodshed in the province is one of its most impressive achievements.

A few months after the Boyle case, in August 1979, Lord Mountbatten was assassinated in a part of Ireland that he loved and where he felt secure. The same day, eighteen British soldiers were killed by IRA land mines near the spot where the SAS patrols had been arrested by the Irish police in May 1977. The new British Prime Minister, Mrs Thatcher, visited Northern Ireland and returned, according to some press reports, appalled by the conflicting Intelligence assessments she received from the Army and the RUC. Soon afterwards Sir Maurice Oldfield, a retired head of MI6, was appointed as Intelligence supremo to co-ordinate the two services. Plus ça change. . . .

The campaign of terrorism and guerrilla warfare in Northern Ireland seems certain to continue until the men of violence are isolated from their host communities. But – unlike the Third World – Ireland is not a place where that isolation can be achieved by building protected villages for non-combatants while converting large parts of the country elsewhere into 'free-fire' zones. In this case, this author believes, isolation of terrorists has to be achieved politically in men's minds, as well as militarily. That will only happen when the Catholic minority in Northern Ireland feels secure enough to support the security forces. But, so long as influential Protestants such as Mr Ian Paisley oppose power-sharing, and so long as influential Catholics in the Social Democratic and

Labour Party cling to reunification, then a political consensus favourable to military activity against terrorism will not emerge. And without that consensus the security forces are often without sound Intelligence about the opposition, and are groping in the dark.

7. War on Your Doorstep

On 6 May 1980, when an SAS counter-terrorist team abseiled from the roof of the Iranian Embassy in London to halt the murders (then in progress) of twenty-one hostages, they had the sort of worldwide television audience that terrorist propagandists lust after and sometimes – as in the Munich massacre of Israel's Olympic athletes – obtain. In this case, the high profile of SAS success in ending a six-day siege was of incalculable help in propagating the unfashionable idea that democracy could defend itself from terrorism if it had to. As at Entebbe, Mogadishu and Assen, the propaganda of the deed reinforced the credibility of the rule of law rather than the law of the jungle. This political magnification factor was the only element missing from the carefully rehearsed SAS scenario for Operation 'Nimrod', as the rescue was officially named. But it was an inevitable consequence of such a public success and shattered the anonymity with which the SAS had masked itself for thirty years.

With the London hostages freed, the British promptly suffered a rush of patriotism to the head. Crates of champagne were delivered to the Hereford base of 22 SAS Regiment, which had supplied the rescue team, together with invitations to accept the freedom of this or that borough (though Teheran was not among them). This well-intentioned amiability was received by the SAS with a degree of cynical amusement. Not only had the soldiers been regarded for a long time as pariahs, but, as the Regiment wryly observed, no one had noticed that only four days before the Iranian Embassy was stormed, an SAS troop commander, Captain Richard Westmacott, had died in forcing the surrender of a group of terrorists besieged in a house in Belfast, Northern Ireland. Both events ended with a display of white flags. That the London squad was personally fêted by the Prime Minister, while Westmacott was cryptically described in a brief Army statement as 'serving in the Grenadier Guards, attached to HQ Northern Ireland', had much to do with political expediency as well as with the conflicting priorities of psychological warfare.

The failure of the first US attempt, in April 1980, to rescue its diplomats imprisoned illegally in Iran, the Soviet invasion of Afghanistan, even rising inflation and industrial disruption in Britain – all these things rendered the subsequent seizure of the Iranian Embassy in London a peculiarly grim event, seeming to rub home the belief that democracy was impotent, and that 'good guys' tended to be losers. However, if the wider problems listed above appeared to be beyond solution, the latest terrorist siege in London at least had the advantage that given luck, daring and the right skills, it could be turned into a media event that would make government more rather than less credible. These grand considerations did not apply to the drab, familiar little war in Ulster.

There was another potent influence at work in shaping events at the Iranian Embassy. This was the threat to the lives of Westerners in Iran if the siege continued as well as the survival of the Iranian hostages in London, where the terrorist objectives were to publicize the cause of Arab nationalism and autonomy in the region of Iran that contains the richest oilfields, and to force the release of political prisoners in Iran. In Teheran, meanwhile, the xenophobic Iranians were convinced that the London siege was an Anglo-American plot to pressure Iran into releasing the *American* prisoners, following the US failure to rescue them by military means. In an increasingly febrile atmosphere it was predictable that Islam's hackneyed 'eye-for-eye' philosophy would assert itself. British hostages would be taken, or, more dangerous still for world peace, the existing US hostages (six months after being imprisoned) would be put on trial. Events were certainly moving that way. According to that remarkably alert London hostage, BBC sound recordist Sim Harris, the terrorist leader, 'Own', constantly monitored Teheran Radio broadcasts. On the fourth day of the siege, Own told his captives that the latest Teheran broadcast had claimed that the Iranian hostages had smuggled a letter to Teheran. The alleged letter expressed the hostages' readiness to die for their brand of Islam. This was untrue, and of course all the hostages, including the Iranian hostages, knew it to be. So what purpose did this particular item of propaganda serve? Linked as it was to the suggestion that British police were preparing to storm the Embassy (at a time when the police were seeking to end the siege peacefully) it was, almost certainly, a crude psychological device to prepare the Iranian people for more 'martyrs'. In the tit-for-tat world of Islamic extremism, compensatory blood would then be expected to flow as surely as night succeeds day.

So the credibility of democratic government, the risk of armed conflict between the US and Iran, the well-being of Westerners in Iran as well as the Iranian hostages in London – all were issues in what might have passed, otherwise, as just another terrorist incident in a troubled world.

The perceptions of the terrorists themselves, as they rode this tiger, were dangerously unrealistic. They had spent a month in London before the siege, enjoying the sort of social freedom denied to them in their country of origin, Iraq, including the delights of alcohol and a shopping spree for everything from children's toys to video equipment. Only one of their number, Own, spoke English, but even he needed the help of a Pakistani journalist during the siege to translate his most important pronouncements into plausible English. It seems that the terrorists had been misled by their political 'godfathers' into believing that democratic London was a pushover for their commando operation. What they expected was a quick harvest of publicity, an element of diplomatic recognition (however transient) by Arab diplomats in London, and a free flight back to Baghdad to await the arrival of their air-freighted shopping. Armed with Soviet-made RGD-5 hand grenades (which they handled with frightening ineptitude, according to their captives), as well as automatic pistols and carbines, they were persuaded by their controllers that, since London was the ideal place for terrorist blackmail, the risk was minimal. They had not been briefed, as they might have been, on the basic lesson of previous hostage-taking episodes in the West – that the murder of a hostage usually removes any hope of bargaining with government. Once that occurs, then the terrorist has the choice, as Robert Mark once put it, of 'going to a prison or to a mortuary'.

Predicting Events

The SAS anti-terrorist squad – more correctly, the Counter Revolutionary Warfare Team – had prepared for such a siege with rather more thoroughness than their opponents. For at least seven years, successive teams had trained relentlessly for just this situation. Each month, an elaborate exercise had been set up in which the scenario varied only in its location. The basic 'storyline', or exercise plot, was always the same and eerily predicted circumstances as they developed in the Iranian Embassy:
1. Terrorists seize hostages and incarcerate themselves in a building, an aircraft, a railway train, a bus or aboard a ship.

2. The police negotiate in good faith, offering media coverage of terrorist demands as a bargaining chip, a substitute, or surrogate achievement for the terrorists' declared aims.

3. The terrorist demands are directed not at the British Government but a foreign one over which the British have little or no control.

4. The negotiations begin to crumble when terrorists threaten to kill a hostage, and shots are heard within the siege area. Later there are more shots and the contemptuous exposure to public view of the victim's body.

5. A timetable of executions is then announced by the terrorists, and the SAS assault follows.

6. As soon as the siege is over, police investigators and forensic scientists move into the terrorist stronghold to reconstruct exactly what has happened during the brief period of military control of the area. This change of command is made at the request of the police. (In the particular case of the Iranian Embassy siege, the request went to the Home Secretary, William Whitelaw, who submitted it for approval to the Prime Minister, Margaret Thatcher. Once approval was granted, the Ministry of Defence was constitutionally in charge of the area. At the scene of the siege, meanwhile, the police officer in charge notified the SAS tactical commander that he was handing over control, and the decision was recorded in the police log of the incident.)

Afterwards, with control back in civilian hands, the police investigation includes pathological examination of the dead and ballistic analysis of the rounds fired and the weapons used. Thus, the SAS teams are aware throughout these dangerous operations of the legal implications of what they are doing and the possibility of legal action against themselves if they use more violence than can be justified by the phrase 'minimum force'. On siege-breaking exercises, the most testing and boring period for the soldiers is this time spent afterwards, waiting for the patient, careful police to 'trawl' over the ground.

This degree of sophistication is the result of long and painstaking cultivation. The origins of SAS counter-terrorism in cities can be traced originally to the 'Keeni-Meeni' period in Aden (described on pages 100–3). This experience gave credence to the notion that, if the enemy were disguised as a civilian, indistinguishable from the rest of the population, then the most effective means of matching the threat was for soldiers to be similarly disguised. Then, as now, the overwhelming priority was that the undercover soldier must be as near perfect as any human can be in the skilled use of firearms, to minimize the risk of causing innocent casualties. For a long time after Aden, however, the evolution of counter-revolutionary warfare (CRW) techniques as practised by the SAS was the result of a series of historical accidents.

The Aden campaign ended in 1967, after which, until the Regiment went to war in Dhofar in 1970, it had no active campaign. The Commanding Officer of 22 SAS at that time therefore offered the services of his best marksmen to the British Government to train body-guards for overseas heads of state who were thought to be at risk and whose removal would be contrary to British interests. 'There were hundreds of them, as it turned out,' one veteran of that period recalls, 'and we went all over the world in their defence.' It was a potent invisible export, which yielded Whitehall a rich harvest of good-will as well as military Intelligence. In a few rare cases, for brief periods the SAS provided the bodyguard until local forces could be trained to take over. (One such case was Sultan Qaboos of Oman during the delicate days im-mediately after the palace coup that removed his father, Sultan Sa'id bin Taimur.) Simultaneously, in Hereford itself, a special house was constructed to train marksmen in the perilous skills involved in shooting would-be assassins or kidnappers in the close confines of a room, without hitting the VIP being guarded. The house is formally known as the Close Quarter Battle (CQB) House and, less formally, as 'the Killing House'. On their return to England, the six-man bodyguard training teams coached more bodyguards at Hereford, based on the practical lessons learned overseas, and formal courses in this work got under way. To maintain the momentum, a CRW Wing was created, commanded by a single officer whose task it was to keep international developments in his field under constant review. But in 1970/1, following the commitment of the Regiment to Dhofar, there was no longer a sufficient number of SAS soldiers available to act as the world's best bodyguards, and the Regiment's commitment to this work was drastically reduced. The CRW Wing, meanwhile, remained modestly in being.

What started to change this 'caretaker' approach to CRW was the Munich massacre in September 1972. Seven Palestinian terrorists seized the dormitory occupied by Israeli athletes during the Olympic Games, killing two athletes and taking nine as hostage. The Black September organization then demanded Israel's release of 200 imprisoned Palestinians. Israel refused to give way. The West German Government, however, agreed to a safe passage for the gunmen and their hostages out of the country; but then, at the airport, as the party was about to leave, German security forces fired on the terrorists. In the battle that followed, all the hostages, five terrorists and one police officer were killed. These grisly events were watched by a worldwide television audience estimated to be 500 millions, and the image of the West German Government was profoundly damaged. Western governments were alarmed by the implications of Munich. They noted that, through the magnifying glass of television, public opinion tended to blame governments rather than terrorists for the violent end to hostage-taking. Equally alarming, it was borne in upon most of them that no Western country had military people trained to the degree of sophistication necessary to defuse a massive psychological warfare threat of the sort mounted by a few well-trained 'civilians', some of whom were already acquiring more operational experience of sieges than any security force. West Germany responded by creating the GSG-9 anti-terrorist squad under Ulrich Wegener (later to achieve fame with his two SAS advisers at Mogadishu). Other governments, including the French, took similar action, while in London the government turned to the SAS.

The Regiment was now given the resources it needed to create a small, permanent anti-terrorist team available at short notice to deal with hijacks and sieges – in short, any situation in which hostages had been seized for political reasons – anywhere in the United Kingdom. There was, and is, an orchestra of exotic equipment available for such missions, ranging from parabolic directional microphones to thermal imagers capable of identifying which flats in a given apartment block are occupied. But, at the end of the road, when all the cunning of 'gee-whizz' technology has been exploited, the central problem of the siege is appallingly crude: to save hostage lives by killing, if necessary, the terrorists holding them. The SAS solution is to train its close-quarter marksmen to an extraordinary degree of skill, honing their reflexes in action as if they were tennis stars being groomed for the men's final at Wimbledon. The difference is that the tennis star may merely miss a singles title for the sake of a millimetre's inaccuracy, while the SAS soldier, obliged to fire a head shot at a terrorist holding his hostage against him as a shield, carries a graver responsibility.

Second in importance only to the skill of the men is the armament they carry. As Dobson and Payne have argued recently in *The Weapons of Terror*, such is the velocity of modern firearms that 'the up-to-date bullets of law and order, when used without care, not only travel further [than required] but they strike in the cause of the terrorists they are seeking to overcome'. In other words, excessive firepower will result in a propaganda victory for the terrorists, even if the security forces win the military engagement. And, since terrorism is primarily about shaping popular perceptions as part of its psychological warfare, the more important battleground is not the individual siege but the one fought in the pages of newspapers, on our television screens – and ultimately in our minds. For all these reasons, low velocity and accuracy are the desiderata of anti-terrorist weapons for use in cities. Reliability is equally important, since a weapon prone to stoppages is worse than useless. So what is required is a weapon that fires rapidly, precisely on target and at low velocity, hitting the intended target without penetrating one body and striking another. A dramatic illustration of this philosophy in action occurred when the joint SAS/GSG-9 team burst into the hijacked Lufthansa airliner at Mogadishu: every terrorist was wounded in the first quick burst of gunfire, but the ensuing battle continued for eight minutes. A woman terrorist was wounded nine times, and later survived after medical treatment in custody. Initially, the SAS/ CRW team armed itself with the American Ingram submachine-gun, but on automatic fire it tended to spray bullets too liberally over the target area, with ominous implications for innocent hostages. Eventually, the Regiment chose the Heckler & Koch MP5. Experiments in West Germany, where the weapon is made, had led to the accidental discovery that a certain non-German bullet could yield unparalleled accuracy among such weapons, and stoppages caused by the new bullet were cured by redesigning the magazine, making it curved. The weapon was used in action by the SAS for the first time at the Iranian Embassy siege. The other firearms carried by the team include the thirteen-round Browning automatic pistol, a reserve weapon that lingers in the SAS armoury partly as a result of the experience of an officer who found himself suspended from a tree in Malaya in parachute harness, weaponless, while an armed guerrilla prowled around immediately below him. The heaviest firearm used is the Remington shotgun, to blast the lock from a door to a room known to be occupied by terrorists. Also carried are plastic explosives and concussion grenades – 'flash-bangs' – which are magnesium-based and have the shock effect of paralysing the enemy during the vital first five seconds of an encounter. CS gas grenades can be used if surprise has failed to overcome an adversary. Both the 'flash-bang' (an SAS invention) and CS carry with them the risk of causing an explosion or a fire or both. In an assault such as that which took place at the Iranian Embassy, team members wear protective gas-masks throughout the attack, so that if they use CS they will not need to waste time donning masks after the assault has started. Finally, the CRW team is equipped with a variety of specialized motor vehicles and aircraft, enabling it to travel with its equipment at short notice anywhere in Britain.

At the same time as this re-equipping was taking place, the Regiment expanded its CRW Wing to a permanent cadre, or cell, consisting of one officer and four instructors to be responsible for all aspects of training in hostage rescue, bodyguard work, Intelligence gathering about terrorist techniques, and so on. The CRW team, now about twenty men, drawn on rota from the four operational Sabre squadrons, was deployed in earnest for the first time in January 1975, when a civil airliner was hijacked at Manchester by an Iranian armed with a pistol which later proved to be a harmless replica. The whole affair turned into black comedy after the hijacker was persuaded that he had reached his desired destination (Paris) when in fact he was at Stansted Airport, Essex, where the SAS awaited him. The only casualty was a soldier bitten by a police dog as he left the aircraft. The hijacker, an Iranian, was sent to prison.

The next time the SAS were summoned to a siege, the mere knowledge of their presence was sufficient to induce the terrorists to surrender. In December 1975, a four-man 'Active Service Unit' of the Provisional IRA was trapped by Metropolitan Police officers in a flat at Balcombe Street, Marylebone, where they held the occupants, a nervous middle-aged couple, hostage. Through the wonders of fibre optics, it was possible for a controller at Scotland Yard to monitor what was happening in the flat from minute to minute. The terrorists had a transistor radio and, when the BBC announced that the SAS were on the scene and standing by to take over the building, the terrorists surrendered. But the revelation that the soldiers were on the scene, successful though it was, also prompted speculation about who is in charge of such a situation: the police, or the military authorities? The legal situation that has evolved to meet such a case is an effective British compromise.

In an exclusively criminal enterprise, such as the seizure of the Spaghetti House Restaurant in London in September 1975, total operational control remains with the local police chief, who has armed officers under his control. However, if a siege is an exercise in terrorism – that is, an attempt to coerce government for political reasons – then direction of the affair is in the hands of a government committee known as 'COBRA' (for Cabinet Office Briefing Room). This is chaired by the Home Secretary, and includes junior Defence and Foreign Affairs Ministers, with advisers representing the police, MI5 and the SAS. Thus, the Regiment has a direct channel to the top of the decision-making pyramid as well as operational links on the scene with the police, who remain in tactical control during the negotiating phase. This is as it should be, since the SAS is stringently subject to the rule of law, for which the police are responsible.

The Army's CRW teams are reminded of this by a litany of ground rules, more elaborate even than the 'Yellow Card' governing the rules of engagement for soldiers in Northern Ireland. It travels with the team for display in their tactical operations room near the scene of the siege.

True, there might be some practical advantage in a more organic arrangement through which, say, the SAS handled negotiations as well. But, as things stand, the CRW team members know that they are on scene in exactly the same way as military bomb-disposal squads might be elsewhere, as military aid to the civil power. Politically, they are not merely neutral, but 'neutered' also. There is another reason why the SAS – even in the view of the Regiment itself – should not be in the 'driving seat' at an earlier stage of the siege. This is that the use of force, albeit minimum force, is only one of several options open to government in defusing the situation. The others range from total surrender to terrorist demands, in the style of the Austrian and past West German Governments (as well as the British in the case of Leila Khaled), to a measured response that permits, say, a limited draught of publicity but nothing else. Interestingly, there are cases, still hypothetical in Britain though not elsewhere, where government might advocate a violent solution to break a siege, but where expert SAS advice might be that this would be unwise – counter-productive, even. It cannot be overstressed that the contemporary SAS is an acute instrument of psychological warfare, and is keenly aware of the political content and ramifications of the violence it can inflict. Most media men, for whom violence is an exotic and vicariously exciting beverage (along with group sex and drug addiction), usually fail to comprehend that the SAS does not share their perception of risk and violence. Like experienced drinkers, the SAS has learned the wisdom of avoiding intoxication, particularly if the party is attended by moralistic outsiders who are likely to accuse the Regiment of excessive violence, while using the excitement generated by that violence to improve newspaper circulation or television-viewing figures.

The Road to Mogadishu

Different considerations apply when the CRW team goes into action outside the United Kingdom, where political control is in the hands of the host government. In October 1977, four Palestinian terrorists – two men, two women – joined seventy-nine normal passengers on a Lufthansa flight from Majorca. The cursory baggage checks there enabled the terrorists to smuggle an assortment of weapons aboard the aircraft, which they then hijacked. The principal object of the operation was to force the West German Government to release the leaders of the notorious Baader-Meinhof gang, a team of chic middle-class revolutionaries then in prison in Germany. For good measure, the hijackers threw in a demand for a £9-million ransom. The hijack occurred six weeks after the kidnap of Hans-Martin Schleyer, a powerful West German industrial baron; his release, like that of the Lufthansa hostages, was conditional upon freedom for the Baader-Meinhof team, and he was still imprisoned when the Lufthansa plane was seized.

Such was the crisis of credibility faced by the Bonn Government that much normal administration was being paralysed by the need to manage the crisis. As so often before, government was in a 'no-win' position: a surrender to terrorism would damage belief in government's ability to govern; a hard line, if it resulted in hostage deaths, would provoke a storm of protest from society's professional humanitarians. The terrorists knew they were on to a good thing, since, until that time, most captured terrorists had obtained freedom within one or two years as a result of such blackmail by their comrades outside. (The unfashionable Moluccans tended to be an exception to this rule.)

A wild aerial journey followed the Lufthansa hijack, around various places in the Middle East and the Horn of Africa. Soon after it began, a German minister travelled to London, accompanied by a member of the GSG-9 team, to seek British help and, in particular, liaison with the authorities of Dubai, where the hijacked aircraft was about to land. (A member of the United Arab Emirates, Dubai has close links with Britain.) Initially, the purpose of the Germans' visit was to ask Whitehall to use its good offices with the UAE ambassador in London to ensure diplomatic clearance for GSG-9 to go into action in Dubai. As a subsidiary objective, the GSG-9 representative thought that his SAS opposite number might have equipment that could be useful in breaking into the aircraft. The Germans had not appreciated that the SAS knows the Persian Gulf intimately and that, for example, Dubai's elite presidential guard is trained and led by former SAS soldiers. During the London conversations, therefore, it became clear to everyone that an SAS liaison team on this operation would be a decided asset, and such a plan was instantly endorsed by the respective premiers, Callaghan and Schmidt. The two men selected for the job were Major Alastair Morrison, OBE, MC, a veteran SAS squadron commander, and Sergeant Barry Davies, BEM; with a specially crated collection of flash-bangs they left immediately for Dubai.

They arrived to discover that GSG-9's leader, Wegener, and two of his men were being kept 'under escort' in the international airport's VIP lounge – in the politest possible way – while the hijacked airliner, with its hostages, stood on the scorching tarmac. Morrison and Davies sorted out this bureaucratic nonsense, and then set about training the Dubai Royal Guard in the basics of siege-breaking with a view to providing a back-up force for GSG-9, whose main force was then in a pursuit aircraft in Turkey. But, before this elaborate scheme could be put into operation, the Lufthansa airliner with its hostages flew on to Aden. Obstacles might have been placed on the Dubai runway to delay the hijacked aircraft's departure, but at that point the terrorists could threaten the hostages effectively while the security forces could not convincingly match that threat. In such a case, the golden rule is that government must be able to 'put its money where its mouth is' if it is going to arrest, or even contain, terrorists, or pay for its failed bluff with hostage lives. So the Lufthansa plane, refuelled and replenished, took off, followed by another aircraft carrying Morrison, Davies, Wegener and his two aides. For a time, the hijacked airliner enjoyed sanctuary at Aden, while, for some hours, the Morrison-Wegener group flew in the vicinity seeking permission to land on the same airfield. But this was refused. Aden, now capital of the Marxist People's Democractic Republic of South Yemen, contained numerous East German and Soviet advisers, whose governments declined to put pressure on their Arabian client to assist GSG-9.

By now, Morrison and Davies had become de facto members of Wegener's team, and they stayed with him when the hunt moved from Aden to Mogadishu, in Somalia, where the German commander was joined by the main body of his force after a flight from Turkey. The whole rescue party got together just twelve hours before the rescue attempt. The role of the SAS men would be to throw the flash-bang grenades at the start of the operation if peaceful persuasion did not work. The Germans were in earnest about a peaceful solution: their pursuit aircraft carried the ransom – £ 9 million in cash – in a large metal box. But at Aden, the hijacked airliner captain, Jurgen Schumann, was murdered by the terrorist leader, 'Captain Mahmoud', after he suspected Schumann of secretly communicating with the security forces. The Lufthansa airliner flew on to Mogadishu, where Schumann's body was thrown from the plane. For many hours prior to that, it had lain on the floor of the aircraft, in full view of the terrified hostages.

From the moment the pilot's body was hurled onto the Mogadishu runway, there was no hope of a peaceful end to the siege and, five days after the SAS team joined Wegener, they threw their flash-bangs from each side of the aircraft to signal the assault. The attack plan, composed by the SAS team, was one in which fortune favoured the bold. The assault team entered the aircraft through the emergency doors set above the wings on each side of the fuselage, kicking in the doors as the flash-bangs exploded. Once inside, they had to tackle terrorist gunmen at the front and rear of the airliner. Aviation fuel as well as duty-free alcohol scattered by the terrorists inside the aircraft might have exploded, but it did not. During the eight-minute battle inside the aircraft, the terrorists rolled two hand grenades towards the assault team, but these exploded harmlessly beneath padded passenger seats. The hostages, strapped in their seats, were below the line of fire being exchanged between the terrorists and the raiders, and three of the four terrorists were killed. Later, their leader was identified as Zohair Akache, a professional assassin serving the Palestinian extremist V.adi Hadad. That he was operating on this occasion on behalf of the West German Baader-Meinhof group was a vivid illustration of the organic nature of international terrorism in the seventies. Within hours of the Mogadishu battle, the terrorist leaders who had hoped to be set free as a result of the hijack – Andreas Baader, Gudrun Esslin and Jan-Carl Raspe – committed suicide in their cells. And, six days after the rescue, Schleyer, the kidnapped West German industrialist, was found shot dead in the boot of a car.

Confirmation of the SAS involvement in the Mogadishu operation came immediately after the rescue from Prime Minister Callaghan, then in Bonn with Chancellor Schmidt. In front of television cameras, Callaghan told Schmidt: 'It should have been Dubai.' But even if the venue was changed, the event added new lustre to the SAS reputation, and it was good for Britain's relations with Europe. Within Germany, an agonizing political crisis had been resolved. And a secret agreement among West European governments to co-operate in the war against terrorism – made eighteen months before, at the time of the Moluccan siege at Assen, in Holland – was given operational reality for the first time.

Inside a Terrorist's Mind

The event was also to have momentous implications for the role of the SAS in future years. The quick-reaction CRW team was still little more than twenty strong and, in the light of the political crisis generated by expert terrorism within West Germany, the Callaghan Government took the significant step of authorizing a substantial increase in the British CRW force. From now on, each SAS squadron was committed in turn to the CRW role on rotation, between tours in Northern Ireland and training missions abroad. The implication of that decision was that Britain was now a potential SAS operational zone in a way not previously contemplated. The squadron dedicated to CRW would spend a prolonged period undergoing refresher training in the necessary techniques under the guidance of the permanent CRW Wing. During this British tour – 'the war on your doorstep', as one SAS man called it – the CRW squadron would then work up to the monthly siege-breaking exercise, usually in a new environment each time, followed by a prolonged debriefing, or 'washup'. At the end of the tour, the same squadron would remain on stand-by and assist its successor squadron's retraining in the role. The wisdom of this decision only became apparent two years later, when the scale of the problem at the Iranian Embassy was within the compass of a squadron (about eighty men) but far beyond the capabilities of the original team of twenty. Yet again, the SAS had made one of its unique evolutions into a new role to meet a need that others could not satisfy.

The period between Mogadishu and the Embassy siege, 1977 to 1980, was one in which London became a battleground for various Middle East terrorist groups in conflict with the Israelis and with one another, and during which – in July 1978 – Britain had to expel eleven Iraqi diplomats because of their involvement in terrorism. In Hereford, meanwhile, the increased emphasis on CRW was accompanied by more funds and improved training facilities, which, as one veteran put it, 'moved out of the world of Heath Robinson in the late sixties, to superb equipment in the late seventies'. Details of those new facilities are secret, and rightly so. In general terms, however, it may be said that they train the SAS teams to enter a terrorist stronghold by a variety of means and, once inside, to distinguish instantly between terrorist and hostage (unless, as happened in the Iranian Embassy, some of the terrorists neither fight nor surrender, but pretend to be hostages). In the 'Killing House', now furnished with a television and pictures on its walls, dummies representing terrorists and hostages are moved from place to place. The CRW team is divided into two specialist groups, the assault group, who enter the building, and the perimeter containment group, snipers who provide a cordon sanitaire around the scene. The assault group members have to be able to burst into a room in pairs and (as described on page 288) instantly fire two pistol rounds or short, controlled bursts of automatic fire – the 'double tap' – into each terrorist, aiming for the head, without causing injury to their fellow team members or the hostages. Each two-man team has its own room to deal with and each man has his own arc of fire so that, once one room is cleared and the next squad has followed through, the possibility of an 'own goal', or battle accident, is drastically reduced. The use of balaclava masks, first introduced in the Aden days for certain operations, assists the process of instant identification in action while in Britain; and it also ensures that any SAS soldier accused of murder (for, unlike the terrorist, he subjects himself to the rule of law) will go on trial without the encumbrance of a jury that has identified him from newspaper photographs. In an age when the camera is ubiquitous, and terrorist resources enjoy the sophistication of government backing in Iraq, South Yemen, Libya and Lebanon, the mask also assures the future anonymity of SAS soldiers. Over the years, the dissemination of CRW training throughout the Regiment means that most CRW men have been prepared for the sniper's role on the perimeter as well as the assault role, greatly enhancing the mutual comprehension of SAS team members. Such is the stability of the Regiment that the same small group will work together for years. Two of those who stormed the Iranian Embassy in London fought together at Mirbat in 1972, and one was decorated for his courage there. The SAS team at Mogadishu were among those who flew to the relief of Mirbat.

What the SAS does not attempt to do is to assume control of the negotiations with the terrorists. (There are, as have been explained, good constitutional reasons for this.) Negotiating the release of hostages has become a technique for specialists, which the SAS studies carefully, but is not best qualified to practise. The aim of such negotiations is to ensure the release of the hostages, alive, but not at any price. Thus, the terrorists have to discover, once the siege starts, how far their demands are 'real' in the sense that there are some things no government could guarantee. Pressure on the Dutch Government by Moluccan extremists to arrange that part of another country – Indonesia – should be granted independence from Indonesia, over which Holland has no control, falls firmly into the category of total unreality. In practice, most terrorist sieges over the last decade have been aimed at securing the release of other terrorists from lawful imprisonment and, in general, it is a form of blackmail that has succeeded. At the other extreme from total surrender is the style adopted by the Israeli and French Governments, the full-frontal-assault technique, which affords the terrorists no scope for manoeuvre. This 'gung-ho' approach to the siege problem carries with it the lamentable by-product of dead hostages, which is politically dangerous.

Both the New York Police (whose motto is 'We bore them to death') and the Dutch security forces have pioneered the middle road of substitute, or surrogate achievement through the use of one subtle negotiator. His is the voice on the telephone, which, in a psychological sense, gets into bed with the terrorists, referring to the two sides – terrorists and negotiators – as 'us', or 'we', and the government and its security forces as 'them' or 'they', the outsiders. This Machiavelli gradually persuades the hostage-taker that if he kills any of his prisoners it will damage the terrorist cause. After all, the argument goes, the terrorist has commanded maximum media coverage of his grievance. Give it more time for the public to digest the lesson, Machiavelli continues, and meanwhile come out peacefully with clean hands to win respect by facing a bourgeois court. The argument is a seductive one for a terrorist who is trapped along with his hostages: it provides the terrorist with all the benefits of martyrdom without the unpalatable corollary of death, a bit like Mark Twain's description of attending his own funeral and being quite overcome with grief. But terrorists also read Mark Twain and much besides, and some of them have PhDs. Even the comparatively rustic Iranian Embassy terrorists had apparently equipped themselves with tranquillizers to help sustain the stress they were about to face.

The clever ones now add to the pressure on democratic government by launching their assaults at election time, when government is peculiarly vulnerable to the pressures of public opinion, which in turn is influenced by the media. The Dutch Government, faced with such a siege during an election in 1977, discovered that to 'play it long' in this way, became intolerable. The result, after days of negotiation, was a quick, brutal, military solution using Air Force jets as well as Marine Commandos.

Yet another psychological factor is the so-called 'Stockholm syndrome', by which is meant the emotional bond established between the hostage and his captor in joint opposition to the security forces. Such a bond is often created and, through various academic studies (usually American in origin), it has become a new orthodoxy that after a day or so the Stockholm syndrome will assure the survival of the hostages, provided the security forces do not precipitate a massacre by frightening the terrorists. But, as the murders of numerous European hostages in the Congo in the 1960s and the Iranian Embassy siege in London in 1980 demonstrated, the assumption underlying the Stockholm syndrome is a life-saver only if the terrorists share the same cultural values as the negotiators. Cultural assumptions about the sanctity of human life, and so on, are part of the fabric of Western democratic and essentially Christian society. The SAS CRW training scenario does not rely on the essential good nature of the terrorist, though the Regiment accepts that – to put it at its meanest – public opinion will demand a convincing effort to end a siege peacefully before unleashing the soldiers. Still, it is worth noting that the training scenario described above assumes that a hostage will be murdered *after* prolonged negotiations, during which, if the academics are right, the Stockholm syndrome should have started to show results. Indeed, to judge from the treatment of the Iranian Embassy hostages by the SAS immediately after they were rescued –

as Sim Harris put it, 'thrown from one man to the next, no compassion, no thought of minor injuries, and then tied up' – also assumes, correctly as it proved, that some hostages will try to help their former captors.

Basically, the British style of negotiation appears to be a pragmatic blend of the Dutch and the Israeli styles: to negotiate in good faith on issues that are negotiable, and to continue to negotiate merely to buy time once the murder of hostages begins. No doubt, in the light of events at the Iranian Embassy, the style will evolve still further. But, as that siege demonstrated, there is a limit to the extent to which even seven years' rehearsal can entirely remove the possibility of ill-luck and, therefore, disaster.

Seven Years and Eleven Minutes

The SAS assault on the besieged Iranian Embassy in London, which lasted a mere eleven minutes, began after the body of the Iranian press attaché, Abbas Lavasani, had been dumped on the steps of the Embassy at Princes Gate. Another hostage was to be murdered every thirty minutes, the terrorist leader Own announced, unless his demands for negotiations with three Arab ambassadors in London, as well as a guarantee of safe conduct out of Britain for the terrorists and their Iranian hostages were met. The police negotiators kept the discussions going, and successfully separated Own from the two British hostages (Police Constable Trevor Lock, taken prisoner in the first assault on the Embassy, and BBC man Sim Harris) as the SAS swung from the roof of the building on abseil ropes. Technically, this was an unusually hazardous operation if success, which the SAS defines as saving hostage lives, were to be achieved. The building had fifty rooms. There were now twenty hostages, fifteen of whom, all men, were in Room Ten, the telex room on the second floor overlooking the street. They had been moved there a few hours before, as tension increased and the terrorists prepared for an assault by the security forces. They were guarded by three terrorists, some of whom moved back and forth checking other rooms. Meanwhile, five women hostages, all members of the Embassy staff, were in the custody of one terrorist in Room Nine on the opposite side of the building, across a landing. Harris and Lock were near the telephone on the first-floor landing, where they had been with Own as he negotiated with the police until seconds before the assault began. To complicate matters further, the only feasible assault route at the front, across a first-floor balcony, was blocked by armour-plated glass which had to be blown in with an explosive charge. It was of critical importance, to preserve a shrinking advantage of surprise following the murder of Lavasani, that the SAS assaults on both front and back of the building should be simultaneous.

In the event, this did not happen. At least four pairs of SAS men appeared on the Embassy roof to begin their descent on two ropes down the back of the building, while another team, armed with framed charges of plastic explosive to blow in the front window, was stationed on an adjoining balcony. The first abseil team had started the descent when one of the pair swung against an upper storey window, smashing it with his boot. As this happened the terrorist leader, Own, put down the telephone and went to investigate. He was followed – perhaps stalked is a better word – by PC Lock, who had kept on his full uniform, top coat and all, throughout the siege to conceal the fact that he was still carrying a .38 in revolver. There was no question now of the abseil teams at the rear awaiting the sound of their comrades' explosions on the other side of the building before starting their own assault. It had to be done immediately.

The first pair dropped to the ground at the back a hair-raising speed, their descent recorded by an elec tronic camera smuggled into the area by Independent Television News. As they prepared to blast their way into the building, the second pair were already on the rear first-floor balcony, hacking at the window and hurling the first flash-bang grenade. But one of the third pair was trapped on the abseil rope, unable to move up or down. It is thought his problems resulted from the late discovery that insufficient rope was available and more had to be purchased in London. The new rope, although nylon, was of an inferior variety and overheated due to friction caused by the weights imposed upon it; it then ravelled into a knot, trapping one of the last men to use it. For the ground-floor team to set off their explosive charge now would certainly kill the man trapped immediately above it. They therefore followed the example of those above them, and hacked at the window instead, hurling flash-bangs as they entered.

Inside the building the terrorist leader, Own, was now taking aim at one of the SAS men coming through the back of the building when he was brought down in a rugby tackle by PC Lock. There was a violent struggle between Lock and Own, during which Lock drew the pistol he had been carrying for so long, but had sensibly not attempted to use. At this point, the SAS soldier intervened with the cry, 'Trevor, leave off!' Own now rolled clear and pointed his weapon at Lock, at which point he was killed with a cool, precisely aimed burst of fire from the SAS man's submachine-gun. On the front of the building, meanwhile, two more SAS soldiers were busy hitching the big frame, with its explosive plastic charge, to the window. While one man set the ten-second fuse, the other covered him. The fuse activated, the second soldier gave a hand signal to his comrades below, and both men darted for cover to an adjoining balcony. Two minutes after the abseil team had started their attack, an impressive explosion destroyed the armour-plated glass. The SAS men stormed into the room through the smoke and up the stairs while the building was still shuddering under the blast. Harris, groping his way out through a front window towards the balcony, encountered an SAS man who snarled at him, 'Get down!' He did so and, as the team swept past him in the wake of their own flash-bang grenades, Harris heard himself shouting: 'Go on lads, get the bastards!'

To the smoke and debris from the explosions was now added the insidious, sickening reek of CS gas, as members of the CRW team outside fired a cartridge into a front room near the top of the building where a sixth terrorist was hiding. Heavy drape curtains broke into flame, and soon a fire had taken hold of the place. At the back of the building, still trapped on his abseil rope, a soldier in the third team was scorched each time his weight swung him close to the window. His only remedy was to kick the wall and swing clear of the flames. His comrades, spotting his predicament, cut the rope and dropped him unceremoniously to the ground. He collected himself, and followed the rest of the team into the building. There, coming face to face with an armed terrorist, he shot the man dead.

Among the two main groups of hostages, meanwhile, some strangé things were happening. The terrorist in charge of the four women had thrown away his firearm and was hiding among his hostages when an SAS soldier found him. The women protested, 'Don't hurt him: he's a nice boy.' As the soldiers took him downstairs they searched his body for other weapons, and when he offered a flicker of resistance, he was hurled down the stairs before being dragged out of the building. The same pretence at surrender was adopted by the three terrorists in charge of Room Ten at the front. At the first sound of trouble, they started shooting their hostages, but abandoned this as the SAS men approached, and pretended to be hostages themselves. Although Room Ten was one of the first to be penetrated by the SAS – it was taken before all the terrorists elsewhere had been disabled – the terrorists shot dead assistant press attaché Samad-Zadeh and tried to kill the chargé d'affaires, Dr Gholam-Ali Afrouz. First, he was shot in the face by one of the gunmen and wounded; then, as he lay with a cloth over the wound on his face, he was shot again in the legs. A third hostage escaped injury only through the simple good fortune of a fifty-pence piece in his pocket, which stopped an assassin's bullet.

Seconds before the SAS team crashed into Room Ten, the gunmen threw away their weapons and began shouting in Farsi, 'Tasleem!' ('We surrender!') before hurling themselves onto the floor where the hostages already lay. According to the only British hostage in that room, Mr Ronald Morris, an embassy chauffeur, the terrorists did not give any signal that a soldier would recognize as one of surrender. No white flag was hoisted at this stage, and no one stood up to face a door or window with his hands in the air. No one sat with his hands on his head. 'The terrorists just sort of wormed their way in among us,' Mr Morris recalled later. The soldiers had but one objective – the rescue of the hostages, alive. They were also prepared, after a recent spell of duty in Northern Ireland, for booby-traps. Possibly, in view of the terrorists' earlier claims to have the Embassy wired to an explosive charge, the whole building was a booby-trap laid by people who meant what they said when they spoke of embracing martyrdom. The only certain way of saving the hostages' lives, therefore, was to kill the terrorists unless it was unequivocally clear that they were identifying themselves for what they were and were very plainly surrendering. This was far from clear at the time, and the building was now on fire. The soldiers demanded: 'Who are the terrorists?' When one of the hostages, apparently fearful that he might be mistaken for a gunman, pointed them out, the SAS team shot them as they half-sat, half-lay against a wall. As dead men, they would have no chance to blow up the building or attempt to 'surrender' while carrying concealed grenades. The speed and urgency of the decision is of a kind faced by, say, a family motorist who is travelling at high speed, his wife and children in the car, when a tyre blows out. He reacts instantly and takes no chances. Nor does the soldier on a military battleground, which is what the Embassy had now become.

Upstairs, the last terrorist was shot in the room in which he had locked himself. For some time, more shots echoed through the building as the SAS team blasted away locks to check other rooms. The fire had taken grip of the top of the building now, and the hostages, having been removed with expedition (if with some lack of diplomatic politeness), were bound and secured with straps on the lawn behind the Embassy. The women were still unwilling to identify their former captor – the only terrorist to survive – for what he was. This chore was performed by Sim Harris. Then, as he lay there, bound like the rest, Harris told another former hostage: 'Think yourself lucky you have just been rescued by what must be one of the crack squads in the world.' Later, in an interview with a BBC colleague, he ended his account: 'Thank you, SAS, for saving my life.'

This was a faint reflection of the emotional scenes that occurred immediately after the operation, in the SAS tactical headquarters near the Embassy. The wife of PC Lock, reunited with the husband she had so nearly lost, thanked the SAS soldiers who had saved him, again and again. Home Secretary William Whitelaw, who had advised the Prime Minister earlier in the day to sanction the use of the SAS, was also on the scene, his tears of joy and relief totally undisguised. The SAS were also relieved. This was the first time they had fought a battle on Britain's own doorstep. If it had gone wrong, the political and public backlash could have been calamitous. In all the circumstances, one scorched soldier, and another whose thumb was severely mangled by a bullet wound, were a small price to pay for crowning seven years' preparation with such a success. It almost made the publicity tolerable.

At the end of that memorable day, someone at the tactical headquarters suggested that the party, which included the Prime Minister, should watch the television recording of the rescue. Everyone, including the Prime Minister, agreed that was an excellent idea. In the darkened room, as the set came to life, there was a cheerful, impudent shout from one of the CRW team: 'Sit down at the front and let the rest of us see it.' Glowing with contentment, Mrs Thatcher sat down, cross-legged, on the floor. It had been a good day for the SAS, and an even better day for Britain.

8. A Funny Thing Happened on the Way to Everest

One evening in 1968, the British Rail signalman responsible for a stretch of track across the Firth of Forth, including the Forth Bridge, noticed something odd about the Edinburgh-to-Aberdeen express. The train was not particularly crowded, but three men appeared to be riding on top of it. The signalman took the sensible course of stopping the express, but not before one of the three had fallen from it, killing himself in the process. Subsequent inquiries revealed that all three men were volunteers in the Territorial SAS. They had become bored with the journey and started speculating about the possibility of climbing out of the train on one side, scaling the roof, and re-entering the carriage by way of a window on the other side. Their misplaced enthusiasm for this impromptu initiative test resulted in a bet worth £1.10s. and, after the inquest, some adverse publicity for the Regiment.

It was, of course, a reckless little adventure, which shed light on the lack of mature judgement of the lieutenant, sergeant and corporal involved. But it was also a reminder that the man whose judgement is entirely mature will tend not to gamble with either his money or his life: he will be a pillar of society, but entirely useless if society, to its surprise, requires the services of people who take risks. In a society in which risk-taking is only vicariously respectable (within the evidently fictional world of James Bond), the real climber, potholer, parachutist or hangglider is regarded with suspicion. More numerous casualties in the familiar and sedentary environment of motor accidents go almost unremarked, while the schoolteacher who seeks to take a party of children for a walk across calm hills is required to produce something called a Mountain Leadership Certificate.

Interestingly, it was a Labour Government that recognized how, within the armed services, the calculated risk has value as military training as well as its own, intrinsic worth. In 1964, as part of the withdrawal of military forces from the Third World for concentration in NATO Europe, the Prime Minister, Harold Wilson, suggested in a memorandum to his Minister of Defence, Denis Healey, that adventurous training be incorporated within the framework of official defence activity. This would enable service people on expeditions to enjoy the same pay and preferment as if they were on more routine duty elsewhere and, if hurt, to enjoy the same benefits that would follow a battle injury. Not surprisingly, SAS soldiers had not awaited the reassurance of Whitehall that Adventure was a Good Thing before finding out for themselves. The decision of one SAS officer, posted to Aden, to sail there in his own small boat was so routine as to raise only the most passing comment. After all, the same man had planned to ride home on a Lambretta motor scooter, until he was distracted by bitter fighting on Jabal Akhdar. (The journey home would have taken him from Malaya to Britain.)

The Regiment also pioneered high-altitude free-fall parachuting in Britain in the early 1960s. The military value of such techniques has yet to be proven beyond all reasonable doubt, but as an existential, life-enhancing experience it is the stuff that dreams are made of. No doubt there are smart intellectual explanations for such behaviour, that the artificial creation of a risk, and its resolution, are a source of security for insecure people, in the same manner that detective stories resolve anxieties among the less adventurous. But this misses the point that, in the detective story, there are no loose ends, no maverick, unpredictable factors. A real adventure is full of them.

There is an apocryphal story concerning a group of SAS free-fallers engaged in a night drop over Salisbury Plain ... at least, that's where they thought they were. Uncharacteristically, their navigator placed them in the wrong spot as they left the aircraft at something over 20,000 feet. The leader, a small light gleaming from his helmet, went out first with the others following on each flank, rather like a flight of geese. The jump was technically perfect and the men landed in a compact group, but, as they foraged in the darkness, it became apparent that they were not where they should be. They decided to ask, and approached a modest, suburban bungalow. They marched up the front path, between rows of pansies, the leader in the van, his light still gleaming, and knocked on the door. It was answered by a slight, elderly woman wearing hair-curlers and a dressing-gown. 'Good evening, Madam,' the leader said. 'Could you tell us where we are?' The woman's eyes darted along the line of strangely dressed figures. 'Earth!' she said, and shut the door.

Mid-Air Rescue

The basic and almost foolproof method of parachuting, used by armies since the 1930s and civilian novices still, is the use of webbing strap attached to a strong-point in the aircraft at one end and the parachute pack at the other. As the jumper leaves the aircraft, several yards of the strap – known as a 'static line' – pay out until the pack is removed from the parachute, which then opens. Well, usually.

On 17 September 1967, at a civilian sport parachute centre in the Midlands known as Halfpenny Green, thirty-six-year-old Sergeant Michael Reeves of 22 SAS was enjoying a weekend's 'fun jumping'. He was also acting as jump master for a group of novices, a familiar enough task for an experienced man, involving leaning out of the machine on its final approach to the drop zone and shouting corrections to the pilot to bring it over the correct spot. Once there, Reeves gave the instruction 'Cut'. The pilot cut the engine to diminish slipstream, and Reeves told the novice to get out of the plane, ready to go. The man did so and, on Reeves's shouted order 'Go!' he fell away. Only this time, instead of flying two seconds later beneath a normally-opened canopy 2500 feet above the ground, he was spinning on the end of a static line. For some reason, this had not functioned as expected.

The aircraft flew on over an increasingly urban area. Reeves leaned out of the plane again, and signalled to the alarmed pupil who, fortunately, remembered the emergency drill he had been taught and placed hands on helmet to indicate that he was conscious and aware. Reeves knew that, for the novice to survive, he would have to land under a normally-inflated parachute canopy; furthermore, that if the novice were to avoid descending on to a railway line, main road or factory roof, the landing must be back on the drop zone. He hurriedly consulted the pilot, and advised him to fly back over the drop zone and keep circling it until the problem was solved.

Reeves solved it by climbing down the static line, a knife in his own, free-fall parachute harness ready for the first stage of the rescue. Having reached his man, Reeves wrapped two legs and an arm around him, and signalled to the aircraft that all was well. They had climbed somewhat now, to give the two parachutists more height, and therefore more time, to accomplish a uniquely delicate operation. Having satisfied himself that they were back over the drop zone, Reeves sawed away at the static line, never releasing his fierce hold on the pupil's body. At last the line parted and they were falling, curling backwards as they did so. Reeves already had his hand on the man's chest-mounted reserve parachute. He grabbed the handle and pulled it away with ferocious urgency, then held on to the novice's body again. The white reserve canopy swirled past both of them and cracked open.

Both men might have landed safely under that one canopy, a similar model of which was to support an entire Cessna aircraft and its occupants in a near calamity a few years later. But the combined weight of the pair would certainly make for a hard landing. Furthermore, the way their bodies were linked would rule out an orthodox landing role, with consequent risk of a broken ankle, or a broken back, or worse. So, although they were now perilously near the ground, Reeves released his hold on the novice and hurtled away again into free-fall. He allowed a few seconds to pass, creating adequate space between himself and the other man, before opening his own main parachute. This, of course, was a free-fall 'rig', opened by the jumper by removal of the ripcord handle from the harness. Reeves's own canopy opened only a few seconds before he hit the ground. They were inside the official drop zone and Reeves did a neat, text-book landing roll. It was an exceptionally cool performance, requiring impeccable judgement, acknowledged through the award of a George Medal.

Between the recklessness of the Forth Bridge episode and the controlled courage of Halfpenny Green there is a spectrum of non-military adventurous stories involving SAS soldiers, which have become part of regimental folklore. The Regiment tends not to be good at organized ball games: it shines in tests of endurance, illustrated by Warner's account of the feat of Trooper T. McLean in rowing alone across the Atlantic in seventy-two days.

'He landed', Warner recounts, 'at Blacksod, County Mayo, on 27 July 1969.' His diet on the voyage was sardines, curry and tea. McLean, who was appropriately named 'Moby' and was twenty-five at the time of the 2500-mile row, had been an orphan since the age of two, and, perhaps because of that, had developed a high standard of self-reliance. 'He certainly needed it, for the weather was stormy all the way and once he woke up in the night in mid-Atlantic to find the boat swamped and sinking; he had another very narrow escape when he ran onto rocks off the coast of Ireland and took 1½ hours to get off. As soon as he landed he sprinted 200 yards along the beach because he felt a bit stiff and wanted to get himself properly fit again.' It is also likely that this was McLean's way of celebrating the fact that his feet were on dry soil once more.

What such episodes demonstrate is that a number of SAS soldiers would be exceptional people outside the military world as well as within it. Nothing could more completely lay the left-wing myth that they are really 'café-society gangsters', whose heroism is really a carefully-manicured propaganda exercise shrouded in military security for the wrong reasons, than the Everest climb of 1976.

A Climbing Machine

The expedition was set up by the Army Mountaineering Association (AMA), a club open to all soldiers, including those of the Women's Royal Army Corps. The selectors were not SAS people. They chose the team on the basis of climbing experience, age – no one younger than twenty-five – and temperamental suitability for team-work in adverse conditions. It was led by an ex-paratrooper, Lieutenant-Colonel Tony Streather, as a joint-venture with the Royal Nepalese Army backed up by a group of Sherpas. Interestingly, not only did two SAS NCOs emerge as the summit team, but the four-man support party for that team, which assisted in their subsequent rescue, included another SAS soldier, while one of the expedition's two doctors was a former SAS medical officer, a veteran of Oman. Of the twenty-seven British servicemen taking part in the climb, only the Parachute Regiment, with four representatives, was as numerous. Since the Parachute Regiment is still (in theory at least) three times numerically stronger than the SAS, the relative contribution of the SAS to the expedition was phenomenal.

The plan to climb Everest was conceived at an AMA annual general meeting in October 1971, but it was to be almost five years before the Government of Nepal was prepared to allow the soldiers to make an ascent. During that interval, the team made practice climbs in Britain, the Alps and the Himalayas. In 1975, the soldiers made an attempt on Nuptse, 25,850 feet and the lowest peak in the Everest triangle, generally considered to be a more difficult climb technically. The leading pair on that climb were near the summit when they fell to their deaths and subsequently two more men were killed on a particularly treacherous traverse. It was an unhappy beginning.

During both the rehearsals and the 200-mile walk-in from Kathmandu to the Everest base camp, two men emerged as clear starters for an attempt on the summit. They were Sergeant John ('Brummie') Stokes, BEM, and Corporal Michael ('Bronco') Lane, BEM. Stokes had joined the SAS from the Royal Green Jackets and Lane was an ex-gunner. They had climbed together for ten years. Although not the most accomplished technical rock-climbers in the party, their combined endurance added up to what one of their companions later described as 'a climbing machine'. Everest, in any case, is not a mountain for the elegant, balletic rock-climber. It is a monstrous, baleful challenge to human endurance.

In a book devoted to the expedition, *Soldiers on Everest*, the Scottish correspondent of *The Times*, Ronald Faux, describes Stokes and Lane during a rehearsal climb in

Wales, as follows: 'Somewhere on that Welsh weekend, out on the frozen Carnedds and hammering themselves implacably through the bitter winter day, were Brummie and Bronco, two figures around whom quite a mythology had grown in my own mind. . . . Even case-hardened paratroopers spoke of them with unqualified respect and although they were always regarded as a pair apart, one never somehow thought of one without the other; it was their self-sufficiency and unquestionable strength which made them the perfectly acceptable, a-political summit pair. . . . Regimental security overwhelmed them with Victorian reserve. At the sight of the camera they would slink away or regard the photographer with a cold stare. Was I going to cover the first conquest of Everest by anonymous men standing victoriously on the summit with their backs to the camera? There was no need to worry. . . . An oxygen mask on top of three months' growth [of beard] and snow goggles are perhaps the most daunting disguise.'

During the march-in, the Stokes-Lane team were invariably up and away before anyone else. Their occasional habit of sleeping in the open, as part of the hardening process, was not adopted by the rest of the team.

Climbing Everest requires sustained co-ordination by a team manager to keep a flow of food and oxygen moving up the mountain, with the obvious difficulty that the greater the number of men required to put essential supplies where they are needed, the faster the consumption. Above 20,000 feet, even the fittest and strongest climber finds his legs crumbling beneath him and his mind disintegrating into a soporific nightmare. A gnawing cold that hacks away at the body's core heat makes sleep seem the only sensible thing, but it is the sleep of death. Even the most perfect human calculations, however, can be crushed with Olympian brutality by the mountain itself. Capricious changes of wind and temperature, and radical movements of the earth itself, creating and closing fissures, generate risks that cannot be calculated. One member of the expedition, an experienced Royal Marine climber, simply walked from his tent at Advance Base Camp (about 21,800 feet) into a deep crevasse on one of the 'easiest' sections of the climb. Major Henry Day was dropped on the end of a rope into a hole as inhospitable as a deep freeze to recover, with considerable help from some Sherpas, the dying man. On another occasion a Sherpa was 'projected into the air like a paper pellet from a ruler when a crevasse closed as he was crossing it on a ladder which sprang free'.

The AMA route lay through the Khumbu Icefall, a place of avalanche and crevasse, and then by way of a series of camps hacked out of the snow to the South Col, a plateau 26,200 feet high, before ascending a massive ridge to the South Summit at 28,750 feet, and thence to the main summit itself, 29,028 feet above sea level. The first pitch, through the Icefall, was led by a party of eight, including the SAS team, on 27 March, and Camp I, 2000 feet higher up, was established one week later. Already, the hazards were emerging. Pat Gunson, a REME captain and one of the best climbers in the party, found himself swinging thirty feet above an ice wall when a crevasse opened beneath him. Above Camp II (Advance Base Camp) at 21,800 feet, the going was exhausting, and the daunting task of leading was spread among the team. As one group worked itself out, it was brought down the mountain for more routine tasks, including the movement of more stores.

An early casualty on the higher slopes was a Gurkha corporal, who developed a prolapsed intestine, complicated by piles, at Camp III, 22,800 feet. An operation had to be performed on the spot, and this was handled by Philip Horniblow, the ex-SAS doctor, assisted by Stokes, a qualified medical orderly. Recounting this episode, Faux writes: 'Philip's surgery, carried out in a tent at 23,000 feet, must surely rank as the highest operation ever performed, although as he admitted when he struggled into the open, hands dripping with unpleasantness, "I'm not sure I'd get my fellowship with that one".'

Camp IV was established on 29 April after a remarkable feat of endurance by several of the team, including the expedition's organizing secretary, Major (later Lieutenant-Colonel) Jon Fleming of the Parachute Regiment and his partner, Captain Sir Crispin Agnew, of the Royal Highland Fusiliers. At about 23,500 feet, they moved the summit gear required by Stokes and Lane, as well as their own equipment, without oxygen, each man carrying a fifty-pound load.

During the second week of May, two summit teams totalling four men, plus a small support group of six, reached the South Col and, on 14 May, with Lane and Stokes lightly laden and blazing the trail, the first summit pair, with their support group of four, started climbing towards the site of Camp VI at 27,600 feet, the last one before the summit. It was a weary and difficult climb up the South East Ridge, over loose rock covered by powdered snow, a climb that forced even Fleming to pause between each step to breathe oxygen. On the return to Camp V that day, Fleming writes that he could remember hardly anything of the final thirty minutes and 'the final shallow slope up to the Camp site very nearly defeated me entirely'. Waiting for him was the second assault team, Lieutenant John Scott (Parachute Regiment) and Pat Gunson; and a second pair in support, Captain Philip Neame (Parachute Regiment) and another SAS climber, Lance-Corporal Steve Johnson. Stokes and Lane were now on their own. All they required was twenty-four hours of calm weather to complete the climb.

Camp VI was about 1400 feet from the summit and it was about 3pm when the support team – consisting of a lieutenant-colonel, a brace of majors and a flying officer – withdrew, leaving the sergeant and the corporal to enjoy the privilege, as well as the hazards, of the last pitch. That night, however, a storm started blowing, which continued throughout the following day, and it was thirty-six hours after their arrival at this final launch-pad before Stokes and Lane were able to emerge from their tent. They were climbing, roped together, by 6.30 am and praying that the weather would not worsen again. If it did, the risk would be more than that of failure to reach the summit.

On the 55-degree approach to the South Summit they found, to their disgust, that the snow was not firm, but loose, powdery and resistant to swift movement. They had expected to reach this point after ninety minutes; the journey required six hours. At the South Summit, they paused and considered their position. It seemed sensible to turn back at 2pm. The alternative might be to succeed with a late assault on the summit and failure to reach the sanctuary of Camp VI before dark. Neither man was seeking posthumous recognition as an Everest climber. Before leaving the South Summit they cached two half-full oxygen bottles to await their return. They now had just one full oxygen bottle each for the last 300 feet of climb, working with increasing urgency to cut steps into the ridge before them.

Two o'clock arrived and they were not yet on the top of Everest. In fact, they had still to overcome the last technical obstacle before the summit, a thirty-foot wall of rock known as the Hillary Step. The account written by Faux and Fleming describes how, 'at the foot of a slight chimney, the two men stopped for a "Chinese parliament". "Do we go back?", inquired Bronco. "No way", replied Brummie.

'Bronco turned to the pitch and 45 minutes later both men were on the final slope to the summit. Suddenly there was nothing ahead, but a simple mound of snow like any other mound of snow. It marked the summit of the world. There was a quiet tumult of elation and satisfaction; they had made it and the expedition had put them there. It was a fine achievement; a few footprints to mark years of planning, hope and grief for the five people who had died in the attempt to put soldiers on the top of Everest, a few footprints which would soon be wiped away by the wind and which summed up the glorious inconsequentiality of mountaineering.'

The two soldiers paused just long enough to take photographs, and then began the return march. It was 3.10pm and they knew that their chances of reaching Camp VI before nightfall were diminishing. The light seemed to be fading long before they got back to the South Summit. On the way, in an effort to speed the progress home, Stokes removed his snow goggles. It was to prove an almost fatal error. Furthermore, his temporarily enhanced vision revealed approaching cloud, and therefore worsening weather. They were far beyond help here. Even if they had carried a radio to link them with the rest of the team, it would be practically useless because there was no helicopter in Nepal capable of reaching them at this altitude.

The point at which they had cached the oxygen bottles on the South Summit was 1000 feet above Camp VI. In rapidly gathering gloom, and near exhaustion after fourteen hours' climbing above 28,000 feet, they stumbled upon the half-full bottles by the sheerest chance. Both men now knew that they were not going to reach the tent that night. To make the attempt in the dark, in their condition, was the road to certain disaster. The alternative they now faced – a night in the open – offered the remotest hope of survival so long as the weather did not get too bad. . . . After all, it had been done successfully twice before, once by Doug Scott and Dougal Haston the year before, and in 1965 by an equally expert American team. But more, much more often, the gamble had failed. Stokes took the decision for them both. Removing his oxygen mask, he grunted through the ice hardening on his beard and face: 'We'll have to stop here and dig in somewhere.' Slowly and silently, like two drunken men, they staggered back and forth slowly clawing pawfuls of snow out of their survival hole. They were too tired for serious reflection that this was more likely their own grave they were digging in this benighted place. Like Scott during that final, doom-laden walk across Antarctica, they concentrated only on the job in hand ... 'Stick-it ... Stick-it ... Stick-it. ...'

It is a profound mystery, even to the two men concerned, that they did not drift away that night into the long, endless sleep of death. The instant they huddled into the hole together they were engulfed by a mind-drugging cold. It seems almost certain that it was watchfulness for the other's welfare that kept each man alive. First one nodded towards oblivion, then the other, and each time it was the urgent pummelling of his companion that staved off unconsciousness.

Alive, but Snow-Blind

There was a moment that night when it seemed that Stokes was dying. His eyes no longer focussed, and presently he lost his sight completely. According to Faux's account, Stokes's laconic description to his companion was to the effect that 'some bastard's been sandpapering my eyeballs'. To stay conscious in these conditions was bad enough if the eyes stayed open and aware, but eyes closed by snow-blindness – which was what was happening – monstrously reduced Stokes's ability to rouse himself from the temptation to let go, and lapse into deadly slumber. Lane fed his companion oxygen from his own bottle, and Stokes started to revive despite the fatigue and the onset of blindness. Miraculously, he produced from the depths of his layered clothing a piece of unpalatable-looking fudge. They shared it and felt better, despite the numbness that had now seized fingers and toes.

At about 3am the wind changed and started blowing directly into the snow-hole. They retaliated, blocking the entrance with rucksacks. Only two more hours to dawn, and they were in with a chance of survival after all. But they knew that they could no longer move without external help. The only place from which they could expect this was Camp V, on the South Col, about 2500 feet below them. In bad or even merely mediocre conditions, that could be a full day's climbing away. In their hole, Stokes and Lane staved off the implications of that, and tried to conserve their energy and the rapidly dwindling oxygen supply. At least the sun was now shining on Everest. It was a cracking day for climbing, Lane assured his companion. Stokes was in no position to disagree. He was now entirely blind.

The alternative summit team, led by 'Big John' Scott, found them at 9am. Now began a perilous recovery operation, initially involving Scott and his climbing partner Gunson, as far as Camp VI. By 10am, alerted through a radio message infinitely more optimistic than anyone had expected, the mountain was alive with activity. The imperative need now was to get Stokes and Lane back into an environment in which the insidious damage of frostbite and gangrene could be minimized.

From Camp V, on the South Col, the summit support party consisting of Johnson and Neame climbed urgently to assist the casualties down the steep, powder-snow gully that led from Camp VI. This accomplished, the next day the entire party set off downhill from the South Col, bound for Camp IV, at 1.15pm, but it was a bitterly painful climb down. On one exposed traverse, those accompanying Stokes had to place his feet in the holds and they were travelling at only 100 yards an hour. The operation to bring them down to base camp, where a helicopter waited to fly him to hospital in Kathmandu, required four days. For the later stages of the journey off the mountain, he was on a McInnes stretcher, though he had to negotiate one ice-fall, painfully, on foot.

Both Lane and Stokes were to lose several toes as a result of their determination, and Lane also lost the terminal phalanges of his right hand. Both men learned to climb again in Wales in spite of these disabilities, and in 1979, Lane was awarded a Military Medal for his military work in Northern Ireland.

One incident, quoted by Faux, encapsulates better than anything the spirit of these men. On the way down, 'Big John' Scott and 'Bronco' Lane were met by Jon Fleming, the Parachute Regiment major who had been involved in the organization of the expedition from the beginning, and from whom the overall leadership had been whisked away by the organizing committee at the last moment, after the Nuptse expedition. In the comfortable surroundings of the Army Staff College at Camberley, they had explained to Fleming that they saw him as 'a potential summit man; to lead the summit assault, perhaps'. At the foot of the Lhotse Face, just below Camp III, 'Bronco' hugged Fleming. 'Jon mate,' he said, 'we did this for you – to avenge last year.' Last year had been the year of Nuptse, a year of tragedy for the Army climbers, and Nuptse had been the reason advanced by the committee when they changed the Everest leadership for the need to strengthen the team, as they saw it. But, as Lane saw it, Nuptse was not just a tragedy, it was also an unspoken contract.

9. How to Select an Elite

In his study of military elites, Roger Beaumont argues that such forces tend to suffer from what he calls the 'selection-destruction cycle'. The most able volunteers are selected for the most hazardous missions and suffer higher casualties than other units as a result. Governments, he believes, like such forces because they reinforce belief in the myth of controllable, rationally waged war. Moreover, in an age when the citizens' army is being replaced by professional forces raised from volunteers, 'one might ask if Western leadership outside the neutral countries has not gotten into the habit of killing off the flower of its youth rather than risking the political feedback that might come from casualties suffered by the generally raised forces. In Vietnam, even relatively few losses toppled the Johnson Government. In a cynical vein, in view of that experience, it seems that the best balance of military forces in a society with anti-military values and an elected government, would be the use of elite forces and of conscripts and/or recruits from politically impotent elements of the population.'

The motivation and selection of SAS regulars is much misunderstood in a society whose feelings about the military community are at best ambivalent. The anarchist fringe, aware of the SAS's special role in counter-revolutionary warfare, has a vested interest in purveying a sinister image of the Regiment. Elsewhere, civilian incomprehension and suspicion are reinforced by the secrecy surrounding SAS activities and by the minority-mindedness of SAS men, which springs from their self-imposed isolation not only from the community at large, but also from the rest of the British Army. For psychological as well as security reasons, the Regiment has a feline appetite for walking alone, discouraging the interest of outsiders including even ex-members of the Regiment. Yet if Beaumont is right, the Regiment serves democratic society in a unique fashion by nominating itself as the elite military group willing to take risks that others, comfortable in their suburban semis, prefer to experience from the safety of a seat in the Odeon cinema (or, for that matter, the author's study). When hostages are seized in Balcombe Street or at Las Palmas to begin an enforced journey to Mogadishu, society needs such men as surely as it needs surgeons and public health officers.

The Reason Why

Why soldiers volunteer for SAS duty is as complex as the motivation of those who take part in such risk-sports as climbing and parachuting. The initial stimulus may be nothing more noble than adrenalin addiction. But for all dedicated risk sportsmen there is a learning curve: to overcome fear is to gain a self-respect, self-possession and freedom unique in a secure, but increasingly claustrophobic, society bound by no doubt necessary rules. To win acceptance among a group who have found the same road to self-respect is to join a community and achieve an identity not attainable in the fragmented isolation of urban life, the world of the 'electric light' people.

From time to time, SAS men are scrutinized by psychologists (one of whom was evacuated from Malaya some years ago in a state of collapse). The resulting conflict of cultures – the one expressing itself by action rather than talk, the other dedicated to intellectual abstractions – does not shed much light on why soldiers volunteer for such service except, perhaps, to destroy the myth that all SAS soldiers are incorrigibly immature personalities seeking to 'prove' themselves. Most of those who are finally accepted are in their late twenties with several years' hard soldiering behind them. Good judgement in spite of stress and fatigue is one of the most important characteristics sought by the selectors, and that quality is rarely compatible with immaturity. The chimera of trying to categorize the SAS soldier in the compartmental world of the psychologist emerges from Peter Watson's exhaustive study of such matters, *War on the Mind.* He reports : 'The psychologists [who test SAS recruits] look for those who, on the tests, are: above average in intelligence; assertive; happy-go-lucky; self-sufficient; not extremely intro- or extraverted. They do *not* want people who are emotionally stable; instead they want forthright individuals who are hard to fool and not dependent on orders. The psychologists do acknowledge that occasionally, with the SAS, there are problems of too many chiefs and not enough Indians.'

What finally links those who pass a rigorous selection process is a dedication to soldiering as such. 'We are a bunch of misfits who happen to fit together', is how one member of the Regiment puts it. In an anti-military culture it is an adequate working definition.

If there is a multiplicity of reasons why individuals volunteer for SAS selection, there is little doubt what the Regiment is seeking. In 1955, Major Dare Newell drafted a paper that still embodies the Regiment's basic philosophy. Newell explained: 'Selection is designed rather to find the individualist with a sense of self-discipline than the man who is primarily a good member of a team. For the self-disciplined individualist will always fit well into a team when teamwork is required, but a man selected for team work is by no means always suitable for work outside the team.' Volunteers, Newell recorded, were assessed for their reactions to loneliness, to unusual situations when tired, and their attitude to army life in general. The last criterion, apparently banal, seeks to weed out those who mistake the comradeship between officer and man in the Regiment – in which Christian names, or 'Boss', are sometimes substituted for Sir – for a relaxation of discipline; to exclude also the tough who 'is seldom at home on his own and without an audience ... soon loses interest'.

The essential qualities needed for soldiers who were to work for weeks and perhaps months in isolation were initiative; self-discipline; independence of mind; ability to work unsupervised; stamina; patience and a sense of humour. What they represent cumulatively is a spiritual toughness rather than a physical superiority over other troops, and in that sense the pun that an SAS trooper is one of Nietzsche's gentlemen is not far from the truth. Yet, as those who have served with the Regiment's fighting squadrons are aware, one of the paradoxes about SAS troopers is that they are not loners in the sense that, say, an espionage agent must be: they cling to the tribal security of a small, four-man patrol with total loyalty. Like all soldiers, they are essentially gregarious, but they function best in small, family-sized groups that do not swamp individuality. Because of the intimacy of SAS operations, the most important factor of initial selection is the subjective judgement of the Regiment's instructors as they observe the candidates. They are looking for people they could live with, basically compatible souls who are not rigid loners, manic teetotallers or fanatics of any kind. The comment, 'I don't like him' is probably sufficient to ensure a candidate's failure even if he passes other criteria of selection.

Phasing Selection

The selection course for the full-time, regular 22 SAS Regiment, based at Hereford, is a prolonged and elaborate business, best understood if its outlines are first sketched in. It begins with ten days' fitness training and map-reading on the Brecon Beacons – let us call it Phase I – in which the volunteer is one of a group of about twenty men. This is followed by another ten days in which he is engaged in long cross-country marches in the same area, alone. This period – Phase II – culminates in a forty-mile endurance march to be completed within twenty hours, in which the soldier carries a fifty-five-pound Bergen rucksack and a ten-pound rifle, and in which he may travel alone or with other volunteers, as he chooses. Phase II is known as Selection with a capital 'S' because, when it is over, those who are not suitable and have not left the course voluntarily are returned to their units.

The survivors are then sent for fourteen weeks' continuation training: Phase III, during which they are still being tested for their suitability as SAS soldiers. Phase IV is the standard Army parachute course (low-level jumping employing static-line parachutes that open automatically as the jumper leaves the aircraft, a technique that has not changed much since the Second World War). Finally, the candidate faces combat survival training (Phase V), including escape and interrogation methods. Some men are rejected on the final day of this exhaustive process. For the rest, a tiny proportion of the original volunteers, the hand-over of a new beret and cap-badge marks acceptance into the Regiment. In SAS jargon, the volunteer is now 'badged', though recognition of this fact by his new comrades may well depend upon his performance on a live operation. (The Rhodesian SAS – still unofficially described as C Squadron – used operational experience as an integral part of its official selection system during the long guerrilla war in Zimbabwe-Rhodesia.)

The volunteer's induction is followed by Phase VI, specialist training in one of the Regiment's basic skills –

Morse signalling, linguistics, field medical care, use of explosives, pistol shooting – combined with tactical assignment to one of four sixteen-man troops skilled in boat work, climbing, long-distance overland navigation in Land-Rovers, or free-fall parachuting. By the time this 'postgraduate' course is completed, the volunteer has been with the Regiment for almost two years and he is at last a trained SAS soldier.

His first tour with the Regiment is for a period of three years, after which, if he is still fit for service, he can remain for another three years, and so on. In a sense, therefore, only a tiny cadre of permanent staff are the true insiders. For everyone else, the ultimate disciplinary sanction is RTU – return to unit of origin.

Volunteers begin their phase of the prestige and agony of SAS service at a peak of fitness; for many of those who have been engaged with the operational 'Sabre' squadrons, it ends with health impaired by exotic disease or physical injury, or shattered nerves. No one remains unchanged by the experience of SAS service.

The 'Sickener' Factor

At the beginning of this selection process (until recent years) each cadre of volunteers was greeted by the Regiment's commanding officer at Hereford, or by his second-in-command, with a mordant welcome to the effect that 'It's nice of you all to come along; I don't suppose most of you will be with us for more than a few days'. In fact, Phase I is now intended to achieve two things: to provide simple fitness training to ensure that potentially suitable people will not fail the course because they have not had time to get into sufficiently good physical shape and to induce the 'passengers' – those seeking a break from the boredom of garrison duties in Germany and elsewhere – to drop out as quickly as possible. The first objective is accomplished by cross-country marches in which the distance covered, carrying pack and rifle, increases each day. The weight carried also increases from a basic twenty-five pounds. Until recently, this was clinically dispensed through an issue of numbered bricks from the SAS quartermaster's store; more recently, this policy has been changed so that the make-up weight comprises more useful items such as additional food or clothing. A veteran of the brick-carrying era recalls that his greatest moment of training was when he was ordered to return his bricks – which, in fact, simulate stocks of ammunition – to the store.

For some candidates, basic tuition in map and compass work must also be covered during this first phase. The SAS is dedicated to movement on foot across country, and good navigation is as important as sight itself. Since the only people permitted to join the SAS from civilian life must be members of the Regiment's voluntary, part-time Territorial squadrons, the majority of the candidates are already regular soldiers. Volunteers from the Guards and Parachute Regiment, who are numerous, require little tuition in basic navigation, but there is always a surprisingly high number of SAS men whose soldiering began in the various corps (Signals, Engineers, Transport, etc.) and who have to learn almost from scratch to read the contours of a hill rather than a road map. The end result is that the SAS contains quick learners with a bewildering assortment of individual skills. At this stage also, the candidate begins to learn something of the SAS approach to security. Map references should be memorized, never written. Even the map must be re-folded along its original seams so that it could not betray the soldier's ultimate destination to an enemy.

Disposing of 'passengers' was traditionally accomplished by at least two exercises conducted during Phase I, coarsely described as 'Sickener I' and 'Sickener II'. Sickener I, for example, has been known to include the Mud Crawl, in which the volunteer is invited to immerse himself in a gully containing not only mud, but also a liberal quantity of rotting sheep's entrails. There were other, less colourful, disincentives. At the end of a fifteen- or twenty-mile march, the tired volunteers would arrive at a rendezvous only to see the lorries awaiting them drive away empty. Candidates would be told that it was necessary after all to march another ten miles. At that point, several more people would decide to drop out of the course. Those who stuck with it would find that the transport was waiting, after all, only two miles away. Another ploy, introduced during combat survival, was to order the candidate to carry the contents of his Bergen pack from the penultimate rendezvous to the final destination without the aid of the rucksack itself. 'The sickener effect could be quite dramatic,' one veteran recalls. 'On my course we lost 40 volunteers out of 120 during the first weekend.'

During the 1970s, however, the emphasis of basic selection has turned away from this approach towards a positive incentive to succeed. Even the word 'sickener' has vanished from regimental vocabulary. To some extent this change came about because of a growing need for SAS soldiers, as a result of events in Oman and Ulster, and the growth of urban terrorism in Britain. But it also reflected a change in the nature of British society itself. The young men who volunteered for SAS service after the late 1960s were no less fit or courageous than their predecessors, but they had grown up in an environment in which hardship and rejection were less familiar, and therefore more likely to demoralize. The SAS discovered that the generation of the 1970s had to be educated in the ways of adversity before it could begin to learn to cope with them. One of the architects of selection puts it like this: 'We reached the conclusion that the soldiers coming forward did not have the same stamina as the wartime and immediate post-war soldiers. Those latter, the product of the lean pre-war and wartime years, were accustomed to a much harder form of life than those from a welfare state background. We decided, therefore, that our approach to the physical side of selection had to be adapted to the class of man available. This is not to suggest that "little Tommy is not the man his father was", but simply that Tommy has to be shown what his body can put up with if it has to. One of our greatest difficulties was to persuade the older NCOs and warrant officers that this was not a lowering of standards.'

One basic rule is that the SAS volunteer is never more than an arm's reach from his rifle while in the field. One man who walked twenty yards to a lake to wash, leaving his rifle behind, received an instant sickener. 'Do twenty press-ups,' an instructor shouted at him. The man was about to begin when the instructor added: 'No, not there ... in the lake.' After the victim had waded into the water and performed his task he was ordered to get up and rejoin the group. 'I can't,' he replied desperately, 'I can't get up. I'm stuck in the mud.'

Among officers who volunteer for SAS selection, the sickener factor, though no longer known by that name, is still apparent. For a week before the beginning of the basic course, they are taken on long and tiring marches round the hills, then brought back to the Hereford base to be given Staff tasks – for example, calculate the amount of fuel and ordnance required to move a troop to a particular objective and demolish it, and produce a plan for the operation. The officer must then present his plan to a conference of veteran SAS troopers and NCOs, who will treat it with derision. 'You must be joking!' 'Where were you trained, the Boy Scouts?' are not responses young lieutenants have been taught to expect from other ranks. For some it is a punishing emotional experience. The officer's reaction to such criticisms will be carefully noted. Of one who failed the course it was recorded: 'He is a good officer and a wonderful person, but he is not

SAS material.' The most insidious sickener is the inducement to give up the course without loss of face. Even before a man arrives at Hereford he is officially told that it is no disgrace not to be selected. The SAS itself is also genuinely concerned not to destroy the self-confidence of men it will reject, for they would be valuable soldiers in more orthodox units.

Phase II of selection begins in the early hours of the morning when the volunteer joins others in a routine muster parade and clambers into the three-ton lorry as usual. But this time, instead of starting the march with a group he is turned out alone at an isolated spot and given a map reference as his next rendezvous. If he is not very alert the lorry has departed before he has properly woken up. It is raining and he wonders whether he heard aright the six-figure number gabbled at him as the vehicle disappeared. Orthodox soldiering is essentially a gregarious, mutually-supportive activity, and this sudden isolation is a shock. He has yet to discover that to cover the route up to Pen-y-Fan and down again three times by different routes within the time set for the exercise, he will have to jog much of the way. In the rain, his Bergen gets heavier as it absorbs moisture.

This situation is one in which it is easy to brood upon the unfairness of the world. After getting lost once or twice, thereby adding to the distance to be covered, the volunteer arrives at the first rendezvous wet from the knees down after penetrating a bog, and soaked by his own sweat. The instructors sit drinking tea, apparently immersed in complacency. Until the seventies, it was normal for an instructor, with feigned solicitude, to say: 'You look all-in, mate. Hop in the back of the truck and get your feet up.' The wise volunteer knew that even to pause to consider the proposal was to invite rejection from the Regiment. To remove his pack at that moment was to ensure failure, even if his resolve weakened only for a matter of seconds. So, with a forced smile, he would reply: 'Piss off. I've got better things to do', and continue his journey. Today, the solicitude is probably genuine and the volunteer, far from being seduced into abandoning the march, will be reminded: 'Only another ten miles. You've come more than half way. Stick with it.' Furthermore, the trucks waiting at the end of the march will not mischievously disappear. Not all rendezvous are simple check-points. At some of them the candidate will be required to perform an unexpected task, such as stripping and reassembling a weapon he has not seen before – the physically maladroit are a liability in a section fighting its way out of an ambush – or, perhaps, prove powers of observation by answering questions concerning a dam or railway line he has passed en route.

The Endurance March

As the course continues, the volunteer finds that his judgement is becoming eroded by lack of sleep. Each day begins at about 4am and ends with a briefing at 10.30pm or later for the next day's exercise. The effect is cumulative over the whole twenty-one days, and it is at the end of that period that the selectors subject him to the endurance march. One of those who passed the course recalls that 'it is a test of strength, stamina and sheer will power: a real bastard. People worry about it and rightly so. Nothing that has gone before compares with this. Most people who are fairly fit can keep going for eight or twelve hours. This goes on for 20 or more. I took 21 hours which was regarded as rather wet.' By now, only the most determined candidates remain on the course, but it is likely that at least four to six more will be broken before the day is out. The minimum distance to be covered over mountainous terrain is forty miles in twenty hours. (Until recent years, the target was forty-five miles in twenty-four hours.) Allow for map-reading errors, bad luck, bad weather and bad judgement, and the distance may be considerably longer in fact.

The endurance march caused one fatality in 1979. Three others – two of them Territorial volunteers – died during preliminary marches over the next twelve months. Before this, only three volunteers had died during the twenty-three years that the initial selection course had existed, and one of those had suffered from a rare heart condition. Through a tragic irony, the first victim of 1979 was not a novice bidding for a place in the Regiment, but the hero of Mirbat, six years before, Mike Kéaly, now a major. In the early hours of 1 February 1979, he joined thirty recruits as they set off from Talybont Reservoir in conditions made treacherous by darkness, snow and ice underfoot and with visibility reduced to only a few yards by freezing rain, sleet and snow. Even on a fine summer's day, the forty-mile route would have been a formidable proposition for an experienced hill walker. That day, as events were to demonstrate, it was virtually impossible.

Though the men moved off in two parties, each of about fifteen, they were soon spread out across the hill in smaller syndicates of two or three men. To be completely alone made it harder, slower and therefore colder to walk on an accurate compass bearing in what one SAS officer later described as 'minimal visibility'. Two men, after all, could take it in turns to act as markers for one another if no other landmark were visible. A solo walker might be limited to the uncertain procedure of getting his 'fix' on a patch of bare snow a few yards in front. A further hazard faced the solo walker. To move too slowly in such conditions carried with it the risk of increasing cold in a biting wind, and with it the insidious onset of exposure, which hacks away at good judgement long before it reduces bodily warmth to a dangerously low level.

Kealy chose the loner's way. To some extent this was inevitable: he was not part of that selection course, though he had twice participated in the shorter, twenty-mile marches during the preceding three weeks. Also, he was a comparatively senior officer, somewhat older than almost any other participant, and regarded by them with awe blended with the suspicion that he might be one of the selectors. But why should he participate at all? After all, he had been in the Regiment for years and had a record of rare distinction in Oman. A sergeant in charge of the course explained later: 'He wanted to come on the endurance march to see if he could still do it in the time.' Now thirty-three, Kealy had been in administrative work after service in Northern Ireland, and was returning to operational duties to command his own squadron. To an outsider, what may seem uncommonly like menopausal recklessness was, to him, common prudence. He had to be fit enough for the next operation in any climate, and the only way to be sure of that was to demonstrate it to himself.

Yet in other respects his judgement was questionable. He had made up the back-pack weight of his Bergen to fifty-five pounds with bricks, and was not equipped with the waterproof storm suit issued to the novices. Once on the hill in driving rain, his smock and trousers were quickly soaked, causing a rapid loss of body temperature. At the weigh-in preceding the march, his pack was overweight and a brick was removed. Others on the course made up the correct weight with additional clothing and food. They did not carry bricks. And, though Kealy had gloves in his rucksack, he chose not to wear them. One of the survivors of the exercise found it necessary to wear two pairs, and he was still driven off the prescribed route because of cold.

Initially, Kealy moved fast, passing the first man to leave, Trooper E. But, after an hour or so on top of the ridge, this trooper and four or five other candidates overtook him. By now, conditions were so bad that, despite their foul-weather suits, they decided to get off the ridge and into the shelter of the valley below. As they turned off the original route, Kealy shouted, 'You're going the wrong way!' 'In a sense, we were,' Trooper E. later admitted. 'The major just went on his own and that was the last we saw of him.' By the time this group reached the shelter of a barn in the valley miles below and some hours later, one of their number was suffering from exposure.

Back-markers in the party later found Kealy staggering in the snow, and stayed with him when he finally slumped into a sitting position. But he threw away the gloves given to him by one man, and allowed a jacket placed over his shoulders to blow away, insisting that he was 'all right'. Further offers of help made him so angry that the two novices with him concluded that it was better to walk in front of Kealy and lead him off. He stumbled after them. Then they lost him completely in the darkness. Wind filled in the tracks Kealy made in the snow and after a fruitless search for him lasting well over an hour, the cold drove the two novices down the hill to shelter. At 9.30am, less than seven hours after the march had started, a captain and a corporal taking part in the march spotted what they thought was a rock protruding from the snow. As they got closer they saw that it was Kealy. He was unconscious now, but a feeble pulse could be detected in his neck. Hurriedly, the two men dug a snow-hole and slid the unconscious officer into a sleeping-bag. The corporal also entered the snow-hole and remained with Kealy in an attempt, almost literally, to breathe life back into him. The captain, meanwhile, set off to raise the alarm. For the corporal, it was to prove a long vigil.

By the time the alarm had been raised, several more hours had passed. The first message to reach Brecon Police Station, inviting general police assistance, was timed at 1.55 pm. The police contacted the Army only to be told that it would be sufficient to put the local civilian mountain rescue team on stand-by. Nevertheless, a police inspector made his way by road through thick fog to the SAS rescue HQ some miles away, only to be told, politely but firmly, that military authorities were organizing the search. The Army did not wish to duplicate matters by using police or civilians. In the event, it was 4.30am the following day, nineteen hours after Kealy had been found unconscious, before his body was lifted off the hill by helicopter. The corporal who had stayed with him, trying unsuccessfully to transfer the heat of his own body to that of the dying officer, survived the ordeal.

The SAS major in charge of the rescue, identified at a subsequent inquest under the codename 'Foxtrot', explained that when the alarm was raised about Kealy's problem other soldiers were still missing. The exercise was abandoned. Attempts by helicopter to reach the position where Kealy lay were defeated by bad visibility. Foxtrot was concerned about the loss of not just one man, however important, but possibly several. His first priority was to account for missing men and to direct those still on the hill, including instructors at prearranged rendez-vous, to come down. Furthermore, there were both Army and RAF mountain rescue teams at large. 'I had advice from an experienced mountaineer', Foxtrot told the Coroner, 'that it was unwise in those conditions to put too many men on the hill at the same time.' The only oblique criticism of this strategy came from the Coroner, who asked whether it would not have been opportune to invoke assistance from the local civilian mountain rescue team, who knew the area well. Foxtrot's answer, in effect, was that he had not discarded this idea, but that it was overtaken by events in a complex situation.

It is highly likely that another factor at work was SAS determination to keep the problem 'in the family' without external aid (but not for political reasons or because of misplaced 'macho'). What makes the Regiment unique is its unswerving belief in self-reliance, in the soldier's ability as an individual to complete his task unaided, if necessary, in the frightening isolation of hostile territory in wartime. In such a culture, more readily comprehensible to a generation that experienced the Second World War than to those who have succeeded it, a commissioned officer enjoys no special privileges. Indeed, as an article by Major Dare Newell, OBE, in the SAS regimental journal, *Mars & Minerva*, once explained: 'SAS operations require an officer, carrying the same kit as his men, to outshoot and outmarch them under most unpleasant conditions, without the company of other officers and those comforts that normally alleviate the officer's lot.' Regimental philosophy would also have shaped attitudes about the weather conditions that night. It is an article of faith in the SAS that its soldiers will operate in any part of the world, in any climate, without pause for a period of acclimatization. As Watson's study reveals: 'At the end of 1972, a contingent of the Special Air Service ... left its headquarters in Hereford bound for Malaya on a continuous 22-hour flight. Half a dozen psychologists had gone out before, armed with basic information about the men, collected in Hereford in the weeks prior to their journey.

'On arrival in Malaya ... the men were continuously monitored doing various combat and support tasks. As a result of these tests the psychologists were able to come to two important conclusions. The details are classified, but in general the psychologists found that the men who performed best on the first couple of days after the flight were by no means the men who performed best later on. ... Second, the psychologists found they were able to predict how well men would perform in a tropical climate on the basis of several psychological tests given in rural, and normally chilly, Hereford. The tests themselves are secret, but the results have now been put into effect in the selection of British SAS men who may have to serve abroad at short notice.'

Subsequently, Watson concludes that the best way to organize military 'fire brigades' would be to have specialist units that can travel and fight immediately for some days, to be withdrawn when the follow-up troops are ready to take over and 'this may be the way the British Special Air Service operates'. Certainly the notion of instant readiness to fight anywhere in the world is fundamental to SAS thinking. It is known, somewhat euphemistically, as 'environmental training', and there seems little doubt that it was with this in mind that Foxtrot allowed the endurance march to proceed on the Brecon Beacons the day Kealy died.

Kealy's death, caused by exposure, disorientation and hypothermia, probably could have been prevented if he had observed basic survival drills. So, too, could the second death, that of an exceptionally fit corporal who was a candidate for selection. This man ignored, or overlooked, instructions to stay away from a short cut on the day's route – the summit of Pen-y-Fan – on an August day when 60mph gales were destroying the Fastnet Yacht Race. Like Kealy, he became soaked by driving rain, suffered exposure and died of hypothermia, although the still-air temperature in the valley was a tolerable, if chilly, eight degrees Centigrade. The third death, in the autumn of 1979, was that of a Territorial volunteer taking part in a march on the Pennines during a week's selection course, who appears to have been swept away in the dark by a rain-swollen river. A common factor in all these cases is that the victims were regarded as being entirely capable of completing the course; all, however, could be said to have been over-confident of their ability to beat abnormal conditions. The fourth death, in March 1980, again occurred in extremely cold conditions. The soldier concerned, a Territorial, collapsed and died soon after passing through a check-point at which instructors felt the bodies of all candidates for signs of abnormal cold. This man appeared to be warm and was marching strongly.

Recruits who have completed the endurance march on time and who pass the initial three-week selection course for the regular SAS are gathered in a barrack room to discover that bad news rapidly succeeds the good. They are being allowed to proceed to continuation training, they are told, but only on sufferance, and it is by no means certain that they will be finally accepted into the Regiment. There is no cause for self-congratulation at having come this far. With that deflating message, they are allowed to take a long weekend's leave. It is not unusual for them to sleep all the way home.

Initial selection lasts three weeks. Continuation training – a refinement of selection – is an elaborate process spread over nearly four months. Much of this time is spent learning basic soldiering – fieldcraft, target reconnaissance, weapons-training from pistol to 81mm mortar, ground-control of air and mortar fire – because such a high proportion of those so far selected are not infantrymen. The course also includes an introduction to the use of explosives for demolition and sabotage, with tuition in the use of the standard SAS charge; four or five days devoted to field first-aid training; a language ability test; a 1000-yard swim in shirt and trousers; and a variety of initiative tests. There was a time when, on paper, these involved planning a bank robbery or raid on some other local target in Hereford, but after one such plan was left in a restaurant, with embarrassing results, the practice ended. Each short course ends with a test. 'The object of such tests', explains one former SAS soldier, 'is to weed out the total idiot who was fit enough and lucky enough to get through initial selection.'

Subsequently, as men specialize after acceptance into the Regiment, they develop a high degree of expertise in one or more of these techniques. The search for a quick learner, which is what this part of selection is about, is a change of emphasis from the Regiment's early post-war years, the years of Malaya, when the accepted philosophy was: 'Head down, arse up and march from one end of the jungle to another until you find the enemy.'

The first post-war SAS selection course in Britain was a simple one-week affair conducted in Snowdonia by Lieutenant-Colonel John Woodhouse, to check basic stamina and map-reading ability. During the course, he suffered an attack of malaria with the result, as he later recalled, that 'my endurance was more severely tested than that of the recruits'. In 1954, he submitted himself to selection, and passed.

Combat-Survival/Interrogation

One of the most testing and controversial elements of continuation training is a three-week, combat-survival course at Exmoor, in which candidates are stretched psychologically as well as physically. The point of such training is to prepare men to fight a guerrilla war behind enemy lines. Much of the course is run by a Joint Services Interrogation Unit staffed by SAS and other personnel. It is preceded by a special period of training at the Regiment's Hereford base. Both courses are a mixture of tuition in living off the land – identifying edible seaweed and fungus, learning trapping techniques to procure game or fish – followed by a realistic application of these lessons, in which the student spends several days and nights on the moor, being hunted by soldiers from other regiments. Cunning candidates have been known to pass some of this time comfortably as unofficial guests of people living on or near the moor.

The Exmoor course contains the usual 'sickener' element. Devices include a variant of the numbered brick, a five-gallon jerrycan of water to be carried over long distances. To eliminate the possibility of cheating, the water is dyed and the jerrycan checked by instructors.

At the Regiment's Hereford base and, subsequently, on the Exmoor course, SAS candidates are also subjected to interrogation of a kind that, to judge from the testimony of those who have passed the course, does not differ from the treatment about which terrorist suspects complained in Ulster in 1971, and which was studied by the Compton Commission. Already-exhausted soldiers have been subjected to physical hardship and sensory deprivation, including the use of a hood placed over the head for many hours, white noise and psychological torture. The object of these techniques is to force the combat-survival students to reveal the names of their regiments and details of the operations on which they are nominally engaged. Not all those participating are SAS candidates; Royal Marine Commandos and Parachute Regiment soldiers also take part. The difference is that for the SAS nominee to break is more than a chastening experience: it means he has failed to win a place in the Regiment. Those who fail at this stage are often the men who seemed best fitted to the physical rigours of the earlier selection process on the Brecon Beacons.

The experience of one successful candidate in recent years is that three periods of hooded interrogation occur during the two interrogation-resistance courses: a half-hour 'nasty'; an eight-hour period and finally, during the Joint Services' Exmoor Course, one of twenty-four hours interrupted only for periods of exposure to bright electric light while facing the interrogation itself. In one instance, hooded SAS candidates were hurled from the back of a stationary lorry by their over-enthusiastic captors, members of an infantry regiment, on to a concrete road as part of the pre-interrogation, softening-up process. One man suffered a broken arm as a result. A successful candidate on that course, who was still intact, recalls that he then spent eight hours sitting manacled in a puddle as a preliminary to questioning. During another period of interrogation, he was hooded and shackled to a strongpoint in a room in which white noise and coloured, flashing lights were used. After some time, guessing that he was alone, he contrived to remove the hood and regain a sense of reality. 'I looked around and there were all these flashing lights,' he said later. 'It suddenly seemed ridiculous to me. But until then it was a bit unnerving. Some people get frantic in there. I think there is a limit to how long you can stand it. After 24 hours you begin to wonder if they are on your side. At the time, while it was happening, I was told that the "treatment" would go on much longer and I was almost cracking.' At Hereford, as both victim and interrogator, he took part in more refined psychological brutality during a preliminary combat-survival course run exclusively for the SAS. Candidates were tied to a wooden board and immersed in a pond for up to twenty seconds before being recovered to face the same questions: 'What did you say your regiment was? What did you say you were doing?' One who survived this test later told his interrogators that he realized no one intended him to drown, but he did fear the possibility of a miscalculation, or that things would simply get out of hand.

An SAS interrogator with 'a Machiavellian turn of mind' so arranged matters that hooded captives thought they were about to be attacked by 'a perfectly lovable Labrador'. In an adjoining room, meanwhile, they could hear a beating taking place followed by the sound of vomiting and running water. The victim of the beating was an old mattress; the groans and vomiting were simulated by the interrogation team. An even more elaborate charade involved the use of a railway truck in an old siding, part of a disused ordnance depot. 'We had these guys handcuffed to the rails. By this time they were disoriented and tired. What they heard was a voice shouting from a distance, "Get those men off the line!"

The other guards then went through a pantomine. "Bloody hell, there's a train coming. Get the keys!" The prisoners could feel the vibration of the truck approaching. As it got closer one of the guards shouted, "It's too late. Jump!" In fact, the wagon went past them quite harmlessly on an adjoining line into the siding. Among the prisoners, reactions differed. Some positioned their hands so that the wagon wheels would cut the shackles and set them free. Some got themselves into a position where they would have lost an arm. Others went berserk and ended up lying across the rails. But every one of them thought that this was a real emergency and that we had made a monumental cock-up.'

The perception of another, older SAS veteran is that the account given above places undue emphasis on physical brutality. According to this source, the interrogation experts (who include at least one former captive of the Chinese) regard such brutality as counter-productive in breaking a prisoner's will. Furthermore, he adds, candidates are carefully briefed beforehand about what to expect from the interrogators. 'My experience was that the Exmoor course emphasized psychological vulnerability,' he said. In practice, in his case, this 'psychological' approach meant his being left naked in the snow for several hours before interrogation by a panel which included a woman. The size of his penis, much reduced because of the cold, was the object of sarcastic comment. This veteran, a particularly hard man, added: 'I wasn't always certain who was being trained: us or the interrogators. I think it was a bit of both, really.' What is undoubtedly true is that, in action, the most successful SAS interrogators in Oman and elsewhere are those who have used guile and elaborate bluff to penetrate captives' defences. Brutality, they believe, simply strengthens the will to resist.

Peter Watson's study concludes that neither sensory deprivation alone, used experimentally, nor simple physical brutality will break a victim during interrogation. He also points out that there is an inevitable difference in the climate of interrogation practised by friendly forces, and the real thing. 'So far as controlled laboratory experiments are concerned, there can be little doubt that, by itself, SD is not as horrendous an experience as has been painted. But of course there is a large difference between the laboratory situation and SD when used as part of "hostilities".' In the latter case, 'the captor-captive relationship is entirely different, the role of uncertainty and fear is magnified, and attempts to get people to talk will be far more assiduously pursued'. Watson also finds that 'the experience of captivity is far more disorienting than the experience of sensory deprivation, but together they are lethal. To counter them, soldiers have to have training in both. The world's armies are probably more aware of this distinction than non-military scientists.'

The two combat-survival periods – the preliminary SAS course at Hereford and the Joint Services course at Exmoor – end with a solemn, all-ranks dinner representing tastes acquired during this time, including seaweed, frog, hedgehog and rat. On one occasion, following total failure to obtain sufficient hedgehog in the wild, rats were collected for the feast from an Army veterinary establishment. 'What do you want these for, then?' the SAS messenger was asked when he arrived to pick them up. 'To eat, of course,' was the reply.

As well as resisting interrogation – or at least, coming to terms with the grim reality of it – combat-survival training also teaches escape and evasion. In winter exercises it is a long-standing military joke that the SAS man may be identified as the one who walks *backwards* across a patch of snow. The Joint Services Escape and Evasion course devotes a short time to lectures and demonstrations by police dog-handlers on eluding the dog by wading in water or through a farmyard where the scent will mingle with that of more pungent animals. SAS men are also taught how to kill a war dog, a skill some of the Regiment's soldiers used to remarkable effect during an exercise in friendly Denmark several years ago, to the outrage of the dog-handlers concerned.

The handful of men who complete the process of initial selection and continuation training – estimates of this number vary between five and seventeen out of every hundred – are welcomed into the Regiment by its commanding officer or second-in-command, and handed the beige SAS beret and cloth badge bearing the famous winged dagger.

Further Education: HALO, etc.

The new recruit is now ready for intensive specialist instruction. He can opt to serve in any one of four tactically different troops which make up each of the regular Regiment's four active-service Sabre squadrons. These are equipped for high-altitude free-fall parachuting; amphibious operations from small boats, canoes or even submarines, in ways similar to the Royal Marine Special Boat Section (though the ultimate purpose is different); mountaineering, including rock-climbing, ice and snow work; and overland missions by custom-built Land-Rover. The last group, known as the Mobility Troop, traditionally functions in the desert and is trained to use sun compass, theodolite and astro-navigation. Many SAS soldiers, who would serve in Norway or Denmark in a European war, must also learn how to use cross-country skis and other techniques of winter warfare. One squadron regularly sends men for training in Northern Norway.

As practised by the SAS, free-fall parachuting is more than usually hazardous and totally different from the basic static-line techniques used by the Army since the

Second World War. A six-week HALO ('High-Altitude, Low-Opening') course of about forty descents in Britain, and at Pau in France, drastically introduces recruits to the art of free-fall stability, with an initial descent from 12,000 feet, or about sixty seconds of unimpeded fall, after only three days' ground training. The basic task is theoretically simple: to remain stable in a face-to-earth, starfish posture, with the body's centre of gravity at about solar-plexus level. This is achieved by arching the back and placing the limbs symmetrically so that air pressure on them is uniform. After leaving the aircraft, the jumper will accelerate for the first twelve seconds of fall – about 1480 feet – to terminal velocity of 120mph.

The danger of this 'deep-end' method of training is that a novice can easily become unstable in the air by losing the symmetry of his position. If he starts an uncontrolled tumble at the moment when his parachute begins to open, there is a risk that it will snag on some part of his body, producing a 'horse-shoe' malfunction, instead of deploying unimpeded from the launch-pad of his back. The civilian sport jumper, by comparison, makes a first free-fall of no more than three to five seconds before opening his parachute in conditions of perfect stability, well short of the radical air pressures presented by terminal velocity. What is more, an expert civilian will expect to perform all the manoeuvres the sport involves – loops, turns, rolls, tracking – from about 7000 feet, and it is unlikely that he will often leave the aircraft above 12,000 feet, which is the height at which the SAS novice begins his parachuting.

The HALO course progresses to train the soldier to jump from 25,000 feet or more, by day or night, using oxygen, carrying a rifle against his body and an inverted Bergen pack slung across the back of his thighs below his main parachute harness. Because he carries so much equipment – the load may be 110 pounds – the SAS soldier's freedom to correct his posture in free-fall, so as to preserve basic stability, is severely limited. For example, the unencumbered civilian normally opens his own parachute with his right hand, while the left hand and arm compensate for this loss of symmetry by reaching out directly in front of the helmet to 'grab air'. The SAS soldier, burdened as he is, dare not attempt this manoeuvre except as an emergency drill. For this reason, his parachute is equipped with an automatic opening device. The risks of disaster escalate if, for any reason, the load being carried shifts during free-fall. It was because his Bergen shifted that an SAS trooper, 'Rip' Reddy, became the first British soldier to die during an operational free-fall descent in 1970. Because the load may vary on each descent, the aerodynamic problem of one jump will also differ from that of the last jump, or the next.

There are other peculiar hazards. As the exit height increases, so ice on goggles and chest-mounted altimeter becomes an acute problem. (So does the risk of frostbite.) The SAS soldier, if he is not to jump blind, must learn to rub the ice away with his gloved hands. Again, to preserve symmetry/stability he must use both hands simultaneously, at which point he will tilt head-down before recovering the basic starfish posture. And, because he jumps as one of a group, the risk of mid-air collision is significant. For some exercises, the canopy opening height is also reduced well below the usual 4000 feet (at which height the distinctive crack of canopy deployment is inaudible on the ground). In Norway and elsewhere, the soldier will travel into a valley in a 120mph free-fall with the walls of a mountain on each side of him. He must also learn to stay with the group. To close a gap he will have to manoeuvre across the sky in a tracking posture – arms and legs in a delta position, posterior raised – so as to make progress laterally as well as vertically.

Why use free-fall? Theoretically, it should enable a small party of men to leave an aircraft well away from their ultimate destination and to elude detection by radar. The radar cross-section of a human descending at that speed would resemble that of a bird, detectable only to an unusually experienced radar operator in ideal conditions. Jump suits made from radar-absorbing material further reduce the risk of detection. Behind a mountain screen, as in Norway, it could be the perfect, silent way to infiltrate a reconnaissance or sabotage party across enemy lines. So far, however, the handful of operational free-fall descents made by the SAS has not encouraged anyone to believe that free-falling has many advantages over the use of helicopters. Even the sound of helicopter engines, it is claimed, can be minimized to a point where it does not betray an operation. Meanwhile, free-fall parachuting, as well as being a tactical option, is also regarded by the Regiment as 'a good character builder'.

In its most dangerous form, free-falling into the sea is practised by the boat-troops, specialists in diving and other maritime skills, who do not always use boats. In 1970, the regimental journal, *Mars & Minerva*, described how 'the boat-troop, in their rubber suits, flippers, containers and parachutes waited nervously by the door of the Argosy aircraft for the green light and their "leap" into the sea. They all started as the voice of their favourite RAF parachute jumping instructor, Tommy Atkinson (who supervised the exits), rang in their ears: "One more point, lads. At Suez, we had some casualities in the aircraft door whilst waiting to jump. So now, I have orders to simulate this sort of thing by practising just such an eventuality as you make this jump." An amazed boat-troop looked goggle-eyed at Tommy as he made this statement, all frowning with concentration. "What I propose to do", continued Tommy, "is to punch every third man in the ear as he leaps from the aircraft." ... The boat-troop parachutists descend lower and lower, swaying through the dusk on their parachutes towards the inky blackness of the sea. Good grief, it really is black! The boat-troop dropped into a large oil-slick and emerged like Kentucky Minstrels. There were some who thought that this might have been one of Tommy Atkinson's tricks. He was that convincing. . . .'

On one occasion, 'the boat-troop Sergeant (a willing pupil of Atkinson) regarded the free-fall troop seriously as he briefed them for their annual swimming test in the cold, mid-winter Mediterranean Sea. "If you have any worries," he said, "raise your fists above your head and shout. My boys are in the Gemini pick-up craft and they will be with you almost instantly. Incidentally, I should warn you about the basking sharks that occasionally appear in the Med at this time of the year. Mind you, a man has not been taken here for about seven years, but just keep your eyes open." The free-fall troop had suddenly taken a new interest in their swimming. Some smiled in ridicule but nevertheless they all took a good look around as they jumped from the Gemini into the sea. Some five minutes had passed. All were swimming steadily towards the shore. Colin had drifted away from the others slightly, but was swimming well enough. Suddenly he felt a movement in the water close to him. With blurred vision, he peered under the water and sensed rather than saw the black shape flash past his legs; felt something sharp groping at his calf. His frantic cry of "Shark!" and consequent action were all that the books had ever portrayed. He was practically standing on the water. The rest of the free-fall troop promptly developed that gregarious spirit and formed an instant, protective, hysterical cluster in the water. The black shape, and yes, a fin were seen by all. Frenzied shouts. Why the hell were the pick-up party so slow in reacting? They seemed to be doubled-up over their boats. . . . Then, as a note of hysteria crept into Colin's voice, Bob, the boat-troop's ace diver, emerged alongside him. In the Geminis, the boat-troop laughed and laughed. . . .'

Signallers and Surgeons

Within each troop (one officer and fifteen men), whatever its tactical role, every soldier has to acquire one or more of the specialist skills needed when the troop or its standard sub-unit, the four-man patrol, is functioning on the ground. Communication is of such importance that a gifted signaller will be particularly cherished by the Regiment. The SAS is one of the few elements of the British – or any other – armed forces still using high-speed Morse. Not only does this make for better security, but there are technical reasons why Morse can be more readily transmitted 1000 miles across rough terrain than voice. The SAS basic signals course lasts three months. The need for a medical specialist well-versed in emergency first-aid and basic surgery, taught to SAS soldiers in this country and the United States, does not require a qualified doctor to satisfy it. If the situation is critical, a doctor will be flown or parachuted to the scene and the casualty will be evacuated. A good 'bush doctor' will know whether such assistance is imperative. He will also weigh against that need the risk that the turbulence and noise inherent in a casualty evacuation may 'blow' the security of a secret operation. The patrol 'medic' is also valuable in dispensing simple medical care to civilians and their farm stock in a primitive environment as part of SAS policy to gain the co-operation of the indigenous population. For the same reason, at least one man of the four needs an adequate command of the language of the war zone to which he is posted. Such courses are intensive and may be tailored specifically to SAS needs. They are held at the Royal Army Education Corps School of Languages at Beaconsfield. For historic reasons, Malay and Arabic have been most regularly taught to SAS soldiers, but more recently European and Scandinavian languages and Russian have become equally important.

Certain fighting skills are also developed to an awesome level of ability. Among these, the use of the automatic pistol in close-quarter battle (CQB) is among the most impressive. The object of this six-week course, for which a minimum of 1200 to 1500 bullets per man is provided, is to teach the soldier to burst into a room ostensibly occupied by several armed men and to kill or disable all of them with aimed shots from a thirteen-round 9mm Browning. It is assumed that each target must be hit in the chest by two bullets from up to twenty yards. The technique developed by the SAS in its specially-constructed 'CQB House' at Hereford, is to move continuously, rolling over and over on the ground if necessary, without pausing to fire accurately. Instant magazine changes and clearing jams in the pistol are also included in the repertoire. The ultimate effect of this training is deadly, as guerrillas and terrorists in Ireland, Aden and elsewhere have discovered. In a city or a crowded, hijacked aircraft, such training also minimizes the risk of innocent casualties that the enormous velocity of modern firearms makes all too probable.

The use of explosives is a basic tool of all SAS soldiers and forms part of the early continuation training. More advanced techniques taught to specialists in this field include the creation of booby-traps, knowledge of a wide variety of explosives and the use of sophisticated timing and trigger mechanisms.

The troop to which the SAS novice has now been assigned is part of a larger unit known as a squadron, of which 22 SAS, the regular regiment, has four. Each squadron consists of four troops plus a squadron commander (a major), a second-in-command, a sergeant-major, quartermaster and clerks – a total seventy-two men and six officers. Theoretically, the novice is not basically proficient until he has exercised with the whole squadron, though fighting actions involving an entire SAS squadron are rare.

At any one time, parts of the squadron may be

dispersed all over the world in small 'team jobs', either training friendly forces or on highly secret operations, often concerned with counter-terrorism in friendly states. But one complete squadron of 22 SAS is always on instant stand-by at Hereford, gear packed and a codeword, signalling an alert, memorized. Readiness is routinely tested, and men are extracted from their beds or their favourite pubs at unsocial hours. Some years ago the code was 'Free Beer!' As it echoed through the Hereford bars many of their regular customers left: back at Bradbury Lines barracks they collected their Bergens and assembled. 'This time it's for real, lads,' they were told. 'We're going to Ireland.'

Research and Intelligence

Also based at Hereford are other SAS groups, whose work is even more specialized. They include a separate signals squadron, an operations research group (evaluating new equipment and weapons), operational planning and Intelligence (colloquially known as 'The Kremlin') and a training wing that runs selection courses and prepares men for counter-revolutionary warfare. Within this complex structure, a variety of exotic skills flourishes, ranging from 'advanced lock neutralization' (safebreaking) to expertise in foreign firearms.

The soldier who emerges from this extraordinary training – perhaps the most varied and intensive military education anywhere in the world – does not stand out in a crowd. He tends to be a European, of medium height – only members of G (for Guards) Squadron are taller than average – of lean, athletic build (greyhound rather than bulldog), somewhat hirsute, and distinctly wary in the presence of strangers. A minority of SAS soldiers grow a luxuriant, cavalry moustache verging on a parody of stage whiskers. The custom is a relic of the days of jungle warfare of the early fifties, when most men wore beards and – ordered to shave on their return to England – retained as much facial hair as Queen's Regulations permitted. The SAS trooper's background is probably working-class, but he has learned to value such journals as the *Economist* as an aid to understanding the conflicts in which he might be involved at any time. (A junior Labour Minister, having been introduced, at his request, to a 'typical trooper', later accused his Hereford hosts of substituting an officer in disguise. The suspicion was unjustified.)

Within the SAS family, where the trooper's weaknesses as well as his strengths are public knowledge, he shares a ribald humour that mocks everything and almost everyone. It is a world in which the sonorous regimental motto 'Who Dares Wins' is transmuted into the plaintive question, 'Who cares who wins?'

A prolonged period of active service with the SAS involves great stress. The Regiment is well aware of this and, not wishing to waste valuable human resources, defies Beaumont's 'selection-destruction cycle' by regularly posting troops from tough operational jobs to less exacting posts in training at home or abroad, to operational research and elsewhere, where the latest experience of active duty can be fed back to those preparing for such work. Over a period of years, therefore, service with the Regiment is a sort of roundabout, from training to operations and back again. But in career terms, what is the cumulative effect?

Pay and Preferment

In an age when counter-revolutionary warfare has become the most common form of armed combat, expertise in internal security in all its manifestations is a marketable commodity in and out of the British armed forces. In the short run, however, the soldier who volunteers for SAS duty does not always help his orthodox military career. The effect on non-commissioned ranks can be particularly detrimental. A Guards sergeant earning, say £5000 per annum basic will be reduced, like all other ranks, to Trooper (the equivalent of private soldier) on acceptance into the SAS. During his first year of SAS service, he will continue to receive the same pay as he had before joining the Regiment; after that, like the rest of his comrades, he will be paid as a corporal, about £3650 basic per annum. However good a soldier he is, he may never achieve the same rank he had while serving with his parent unit, because 22 SAS, with a total strength of about 750, is not large enough to offer such preferment. Most volunteers treat the problem as another, permanent manifestation of the sickener factor, as well as a symbol of their commitment to soldiering for its own sake, and of their esprit de corps.

Young officers, by contrast, improve their position marginally by winning their SAS spurs. Most who come in as troop commanders are junior or senior lieutenants. As SAS troop commanders they are promoted to captain. Thereafter, it is not unusual for them to engage in a series of cross-postings between the SAS and their former regiments, with no loss of promotion. But the higher they reach up the ladder outside the SAS, the more difficult it becomes to return to the Regiment with the same rank. There are, for instance, about 200 brigadiers in the Army as a whole, but only one who commands the SAS Group (regulars and TA volunteers) based in London. At least one senior officer, Colonel David Smiley, is on record that he declined command of the three SAS regiments and left the Army in 1961 because, as General Bob Laycock, SAS Colonel Commandant at that time, explained to him: 'I know how you feel, David, but in fact the War Office simply isn't willing to pay a brigadier.'

There is also in the higher echelons of the British Army

a traditional scepticism about 'funnies'. Their elitism, independence, apparent informality, and special role out of mainstream operations in large-scale warfare, all make them a caste apart. This factor can act as an intangible blocking mechanism to officers' later promotion. Some, because they are supremely expert soldiers, do return to former regiments, such as the Green Jackets, to command a battalion with the rank of lieutenant-colonel after, say, a period at the Camberley Staff College. But many others find orthodox soldiering too tame and restrictive after a life of dangerous freedom with the SAS. Some of the best men, having become majors, quit the British forces altogether after SAS duty, to seek their fortunes as soldiers, or in some similarly risky occupation, elsewhere. The process was lucidly described by one officer who did this some years ago. 'One of the hardest things to assimilate, when you first join, is the dedication of the average Trooper. He is in the SAS for love, not money, nearly always sacrificing what he could attain materially elsewhere. . . . A troop is the most idealistic institution you can imagine. The troop comes before anything. . . .

'The Achilles heel of the SAS is administration. Soldiers come to the Regiment, often at great self-sacrifice, and serve it well. Operationally, they are well taken care of, but self-advancement and career planning leaves a lot to be desired. . . . Officer recruitment is an aspect of regimental life which needs drastic revision. . . . Perhaps the very excellence and freedom enjoyed with the SAS has caused many Regular officers to leave the Army at the end of their SAS tour, unable to face life in a battalion or regiment again.

'I could not have lived a more full life than the one I have been lucky enough to experience for the last four years. Britain, I feel, does not fully appreciate what a superb weapon she possesses in her armoury. If wise, she will look after it well.'

There are signs that this advice has been heeded at last. An SAS tour is now regarded as a bonus point in the promotion race. Following the election of the Thatcher Government in 1979, the new Minister of Defence, Mr Francis Pym, decreed that operational SAS officers would not be required invariably to pass the Camberley Staff College entrance examination (an essential step if a professional soldier is to rise above the rank of major). This unique dispensation recognizes that a professional fighter does not have the same opportunity for study as his less mobile colleagues, particularly those in garrison regiments. It also reflects changing attitudes to counter-revolutionary warfare as such. After a decade of urban terrorism in Europe, 'funnies' are no longer odd men out. They may be said to have come in from the cold.

10. The South Atlantic, 1982: A Military Gamble

Argentina invaded the Falkland Islands on 2 April 1982 and the separate British dependency of South Georgia, 800 miles away, the day after. When these events occurred a number of eminent people expressed surprise. It is a rare shock to the British political system that can precipitate the resignation of an entire team of Foreign Office ministers, particularly one headed by such an intelligent Secretary of State as Lord Carrington.

When diplomacy collapses it is the business of the soldier to pick up the pieces. This time, however, the pieces were 8000 miles from home and it was not at all clear how they could be glued together again. For once even the SAS – whose Intelligence staff tend to observe political violence with the professionalism of stockbrokers monitoring world markets – had not anticipated events. This was unusual, for while the Argentines were openly boasting about their intention to liberate the 'Malvinas', alert British journalists were making their way to Port Stanley to watch it happen, and to photograph the event. It was as if Britain's official mind, military as well as civil, were frozen into inactivity by a sense of incredulity. In fairness it should be stated that the Argentine people also seemed surprised – pleasantly so – but surprised all the same. So far as the Foreign and Commonwealth Office was concerned there had been many wolf cries from Argentina before which had come to nothing. Across the road, the Defence Ministry had no contingency plan to recapture the Falklands if they were lost.

As Lord Lewin (a recent Chief of Defence Staff) pointed out soon after the invasion, twenty years of defence reviews meant that 'opposed landings were excluded from future scenarios'. British forces were expected to operate on the basis of 'red carpet entry' in support of friendly countries which supplied the necessary air bases. By 1982, the concept of an opposed, amphibious landing had long since disappeared under a crushing weight of economic argument. It was a concept which had gone with big carriers, a large surface fleet and a policy of almost worldwide power projection.

The SAS, with its undiluted interest in Third World conflict, was an eccentric exception to the Europeanization of British defence thinking, tolerated because it added much to national prestige abroad without costing much money. If the Regiment suffered any disadvantage in the impending Falklands conflict it was that of being no longer accustomed to working within and alongside larger formations of NATO's amphibious and naval forces in the defence of Europe. Yet despite the fact that the Regiment was a prime tool for the job, it was offered merely two places in the initial British response to the crisis. The two men, both divers of G Squadron, joined 2 Royal Marine Special Boat Section at RAF Lyneham in response to a 3am telephone call.

Over the next two days, as the government determined that something had to be done, and swiftly, the SAS role grew. During that time the Regiment took a vacuum cleaner through the Ministry of Defence's map department and politely squeezed out of British Antarctic Survey officials every drop of relevant information about the area. But still events were moving too fast for an orderly appraisal of what was to be done.

The Commanding Officer of 22 SAS, Lieutenant-Colonel Michael Rose, first learned of the invasion through a BBC news flash. He immediately told D Squadron to be ready to move. He then telephoned Brigadier Julian Thompson, in

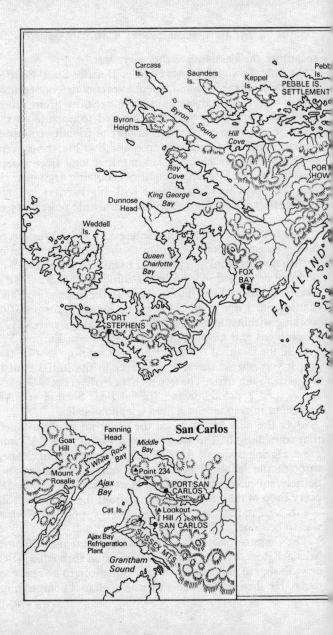

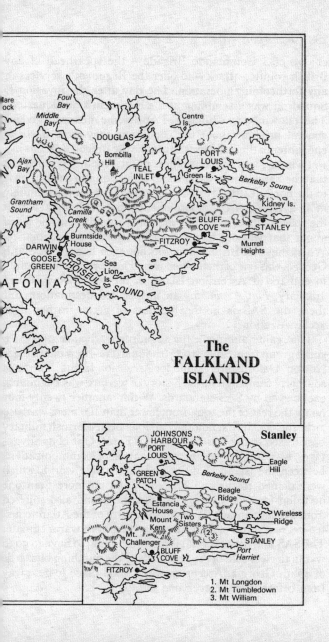

The
**FALKLAND
ISLANDS**

Mare
ock
Foul
Bay
Middle
Bay
Centre
Is.
DOUGLAS
Bombilla
Hill
PORT
LOUIS
ND
Ajax
Bay
TEAL
INLET
Green Is.
Berkeley Sound
Kidney Is.
Grantham
Sound
Camilla
Creek
BLUFF
COVE
STANLEY
Burntside
House
FITZROY
DARWIN
GOOSE
GREEN
CHOISEUL
Sea
Lion
Is.
Murrell
Heights
AFONIA
SOUND

Stanley

JOHNSONS
HARBOUR
PORT
LOUIS
Eagle
Hill
GREEN
PATCH
Berkeley Sound
Beagle
Ridge
Estancia
House
Mount
Kent
Two
Sisters
Wireless
Ridge
Mt.
Challenger
2 3
STANLEY
BLUFF
COVE
Port
Harriet
FITZROY

1. Mt Longdon
2. Mt Tumbledown
3. Mt William

charge of 3 Commando Brigade – the spearhead of any British counter-attack – to offer the Regiment's services in any forthcoming operation. The day after the invasion D Squadron was assembling at the Regiment's headquarters. The following day – Sunday, 4 April – the men were given a general briefing about the conditions they were likely to encounter in the Falklands. 'Just like the Brecon Beacons in a wet winter', was how one officer put it. Another pointed out that the Falklands lie as far south of the Equator as London is to the north. Little, if anything, was said about the infinitely more harsh Antarctic environment of South Georgia; within the space of three weeks the men of D Squadron would learn about that without having had the chance to acclimatize. When they left Britain they did not even know that South Georgia was one of their objectives. Their orders were simply to embark at Ascension Island in the Royal Navy's fleet auxiliary, *Fort Austin*, for an unspecified destination. But then, the SAS is in the business of action rather than acclimatization.

That same afternoon the squadron's advance party – a small group from Squadron Headquarters – flew out of Brize Norton, Oxfordshire, bound for Ascension Island. The most southerly campaign in the history of warfare was beginning, exotic even by SAS standards. Within another twenty-four hours the rest of the squadron, fewer than 100 men, was also airborne. Their first landfall had long been a British military base leased to the United States Air Force. One of its advantages was total governmental control of communications between the island facilities and the outside world, which were denied to the civilian population on more than one occasion for security reasons. But the island also suffered from a disadvantage. It sits in the centre of the Atlantic just ten degrees south of the Equator and enjoys a warm climate. The SAS and other special forces were going to have to go to war in the wet cold of the Falklands or the numbing blizzards of South Georgia. Ascension was a good place to get away from before it made everyone soft.

Operation 'Paraquet' Begins

It was several days before the Squadron, commanded by Major Cedric Delves, was able to move out with a battle fleet tailor-made for the rapid recapture of the former whaling base of South Georgia. The operation was originally codenamed 'Parakeet', and was then changed to 'Paraquet' and sometimes, jokingly, to 'Paraquat', a weed-killer. The details of the operation were revealed to those involved only after they had sailed from Ascension Island. While still waiting for this embarkation Delves was ordered to detach just one troop, a force of approximately 25 men, to sail on the mission. He persuaded the Royal Navy to include the whole Squadron because, as one of them explained, 'We didn't want to miss a scrap', even if no one knew yet exactly where the scrap was going to happen. One reason for the delay – a matter of three days, during which the Squadron lived in a disused school hall – was that Paraquet was already planned in London as a joint affair, with M Company of 42 Royal Marine Commando under the overall direction of Major Guy Sheridan. Sheridan's Royal Marine rank equated with that of an Army lieutenant-colonel.

M Company, about 150 men, is a colourful unit. Its nickname, 'The Mighty Munch', derives from some flamboyant nocturnal activities of an earlier generation during a night out in Singapore. On 9 April, the day the Munch arrived by air, the SAS Squadron embarked in *Port Austin* and the battle fleet put to sea. It included the destroyer *Antrim*, the frigate *Plymouth*, the fleet auxiliaries *Fort Austin* and *Tidespring*. Also waiting, thousands of miles to the south, was the Royal Navy's Antarctic survey ship *Endurance*, whose captain was one of the few people to hoist warning cones about the forthcoming crisis. Since the Argentine intrusion into South Georgia in March, *Endurance* had hung about in the South Atlantic, conducting a delicate Intelligence war.

Guy Sheridan's assets – his assault force – included about 25 men of 2 Special Boat Section, Royal Marines, as well as the Munch and D Squadron. The SBS has long historical links with the SAS of which, for some years during the Second World War, it was part. Like David Stirling's SAS it was a surviving fragment of General Bob Laycock's disbanded Middle East commando force, specializing in attacks from the sea by canoe and submarine. After 1945, as an élite element of the Royal Marines, the SBS evolved as a maritime and beach reconnaissance unit as well as a force specializing in underwater demolition. During post-war years it had found fewer opportunities than the SAS to practise its skills in operational conditions. True, it had been active in Borneo, Aden, the Gulf and Northern Ireland, in small numbers. The policy decision to avoid all opposed amphibious landings and to discard contingency plans requiring beach-storming had called into question, in some minds, the point of having an SBS at all. In fact it had, and has, a clear-cut place in British defence policy, through which it must concentrate almost exclusively on a potential war in Europe, the 'Priority One' task. This role has deprived the SBS of some of the valuable experience acquired by the SAS elsewhere. In recent years the SBS had played an offensive role as 'enemy' forces in NATO exercises in northern Norway and elsewhere. It had also been given the job of protecting Britain's North Sea oil installations from terrorism. In a sense it was living from hand to mouth, apart from a tiny handful of men working on ultra-secret operations not discussed here. Relations between the modern SAS and SBS during the South Atlantic conflict were to vary from the fraternal to the fratricidal.

The Glacier War

As a preliminary to the recapture of South Georgia – a prize much cherished by a politically embarrassed British Government – Sheridan and Delves decided that a covert reconnaissance of Argentine positions be carried out on 14 April.

Patrols by the submarine *Conqueror* and an RAF Victor found no trace of the enemy's navy. The approach looked good. Delves proposed that D Squadron's mountain troop land on the Fortuna Glacier west of Leith and proceed along the coast via Husvik and Stromness, to Leith itself. Meanwhile 2 SBS would go ashore at Hound Bay to reach Grytviken by way of the Moraine Fiord. Grytviken was the primary objective. On 12 April the SBS men together with D Squadron's mountain troop transferred by helicopter to the *Endurance*. Here, for the first time, SAS soldiers began to acquire firm information about the conditions in which they would have to fight. An earlier Falklands brief had said of those islands, 'Winter temperatures are similar to those in Great Britain, but the summer mean is more in keeping with that of Scotland.' This homely analogy did not hold good for South Georgia, the gateway to Antarctica, at the threshold of winter when downslope, katabatic winds propel blizzards at a malevolent 100mph. Mountain Troop had a new 'boss', a young officer recruited from the Green Howards only three months before. Captain (Gavin) John Hamilton was an accomplished climber who had already twice led his troop to the top of Mount Kenya. The approach to the target in South Georgia was essentially a mountaineering problem. The overall task, however, was a military one in an Antarctic environment. Hamilton and his men approached the job with professional military detachment.

Plans of obvious target areas – the settlements at Grytviken, Leith, Stromness and Husvik – as well as the British Antarctic Survey station at King Edward Point were rapidly produced. Maps of the entire operational area were photocopied after a grid had been agreed with the Royal Marines and superimposed upon it. Two SAS troopers worked round the clock drawing finely detailed street and building plans of the five settlements, from original plans provided by *Endurance*'s hydrographer. On the map of Leith, where the original (and illegal) group of Argentine 'scrap-metal' men were thought to be based still, the relevant map noted: 'Red 17 likely to be occupied by "scrappies".' Area 'Red 21' was the hospital. At Stromness even the piggery was marked as such. At Grytviken the British Antarctic Survey's Discovery House – now occupied by Argentine soldiers – was charted room by room. Such geographical details were backed up by carefully drawn moon tables. It was a cool, yet stunning display of the care taken by ordinary SAS soldiers preparing to risk their lives, and the very opposite of recklessness. All the detailed plans were photocopied aboard *Endurance* and a copy was provided for virtually every member of the squadron.

These painstaking preparations reflected an assumption that the main threat to the patrol's survival would come from the Argentine garrison rather than from the environment of South Georgia. Expert advice about the Fortuna Glacier itself was mixed. Few people had first-hand experience to draw upon. The explorer Shackleton had traversed it many years before. It had proved an extraordinarily hard and dangerous journey. Some in the British Antarctic Survey team aboard *Endurance* argued that the glacier was impassable at that time of year because of the weather and numerous crevasses. As one BAS meteorologist puts it, 'The glacier is a wind tunnel hemmed in by mountains and the winds are unpredictable.' Lieutenant Bob Veal, RN, who had led a recent climbing expedition in South Georgia, was against the SAS route. By contrast, a distinguished military climber, a veteran of Nuptse and Everest, who also knew South Georgia, thought the approach was feasible. At this stage, D Squadron was not required to watch Grytviken. That job had been allocated to an SBS team which was to be withdrawn after much effort, frustration and little success. The SAS was interested initially in the other settlements and there was only one approach to these from the enemy's 'blind' side, and that was from the glacier. The route made military sense. Delves and his team decided that the reconnaissance from that side was worth the try. With luck and a fair wind, it could come off. . . . In the event, the glacier was to prove a more implacable opponent than the Argentines.

Before leaving *Endurance*, Hamilton's team collected more suitable equipment than the Brecons/Falklands gear it had picked up on its hurried departure from England. Skis, snow-shoes, pulks (man-hauled sledges) and climbing equipment were issued. For good measure this was topped up with lightweight sleeping-bags and waterproof 'bivvy' bags to cover them, and more warm clothing. As things turned out, Mountain Troop was going to need every stitch.

Hamilton's men now moved base again by helicopter to the destroyer *Antrim*, affectionately known as 'the grey ghost' because, as one crewman put it, 'No one knows where the hell we are.' Already aboard *Antrim* was one other D Squadron troop and a compact Squadron Headquarters consisting of Major Delves, a staff sergeant, a senior signals specialist, and Delves's second-in-command, Sergeant-Major Lawrence Gallagher, BEM. Gallagher had risen the hard way, through fourteen years' continuous SAS service. The plans were discussed, the briefings gone over yet again. Hamilton's whole troop would land by helicopter well inland at a point 1800 feet up the glacier to the right flank of the most westerly coastal settlement, Leith. One patrol under Hamilton himself was to set up an observation post above the neighbouring whaling stations of Stromness and Husvik. A second, led by Staff Sergeant Philip Currass, QGM, was to watch Leith – the nearest target – while Sergeant Sid Davidson would command a third patrol which had the delicate job of finding potential beach or helicopter landing zones on the coast of Fortuna Bay. Currass had joined the SAS from the Royal Army Medical Corps ten years before. Davidson had nine years' SAS service. After they left the helicopters they would have to move down the Fortuna Glacier and cross the rubble of terminal moraine – silt, rock and sand – before starting work.

At noon on 21 April three Wessex helicopters attempted to place the troop on the glacier. Violent wind combined with dense snow to create 'white-out' conditions. Even for someone standing still on a mountain, as recreational skiers have discovered, a severe white-out can distort the sense of balance as well as direction. In a helicopter the problem is worse: the horizon (when the pilot gets a glimpse of it) jerks up and down like a badly projected film. Twice the helicopters tried to land the troop and twice they had to return to *Antrim*. At the third attempt the men bundled out, some thinking that almost anything would be better than this airborne version of blind man's buff. They were wrong. Things could get worse.

The soldiers landed in a 50mph wind which blew a scouring spindrift of snow into their faces and equipment. Very soon this fine spray blocked the feed trays of the troop's general-purpose machine-guns ('gimpies') and then turned to ice, rendering the weapons inoperable. There was nothing to be done except to get on with it and that is what Mountain Troop did. Sergeant John ('Lofty') Arthy, a Himalayan climber 'who could make frostbite sound exciting', led the arrowhead formation, followed by Corporal Paul Bunker, a free-faller as well as a climber, and another corporal. Each soldier carried about 80 pounds on his body in Bergen rucksacks and as belt kit, and had to take his turn in hauling the pulk. The troop had four of these vehicles and each weighed about 200 pounds.

A Choice Crevasse

The leaders moved cautiously, probing the ice for signs of a crevasse. One mistake in this situation would be one too many. Yet among determined souls, even a crevasse is not invariably hostile. Hamilton's troop, having covered less than half a mile in an exhausting, five-hour march during which it was halted time and again by white-outs, pushed back by wind and impeded by the inertia of the pulks, found an outcrop in the glacier and a small crevasse which offered some shelter from the relentless wind. There was no time to rest. They would not survive the Antarctic night, which was almost upon them, unless they obtained cover of some sort. To dig a hole was out of the question since there was insufficient snow covering the glacier's impenetrable ice. So Hamilton's men now attempted to erect two small green Arctic tents, each designed to accommodate two men. Even in the comparative shelter of the crevasse the tent poles snapped in the wind and one tent was torn from their hands to be swept away over the mountain. Five men, with sleeping-bags, contrived to insert themselves inside the second tent. They kept their shelter erect, after a fashion, by sitting against the side walls. Every hour, or less, one man had to leave the tent to remove driving snow which, ironically, now threatened to bury them. What of the rest of the troop, those who were outside? 'They kipped under the sledges or stayed in their bivvy bags with their boots on,' said one survivor later. 'We all had an uncomfortable night.' This was characteristic SAS understatement. Aboard *Antrim* the anemometer recorded a near storm force eleven wind, but the precise wind strength on the Fortuna Glacier that night was anyone's guess. By the following morning it was clear that Mountain Troop would not survive another twenty-four hours. Reluctantly, the men sent a signal asking to be lifted out.

After several attempts three Wessex helicopters – one bringing with it an anxious and determined squadron commander, Major Delves – did reach the troop but then only during a brief, fifteen-minute period of clear weather and aided by both green smoke and a search/rescue radio beacon (SARBE) carried by the soldiers. In continuing high winds which made flight near the ground very hazardous, the helicopters lifted off the men and most of their equipment. Of the three machines, an anti-submarine Mk 3 Wessex fitted with sophisticated navigational gear was leading the convoy with Delves on board. The flight plan was simple enough: follow the glacier down to a landfall, carry on out to sea and return to the ships. . . . You couldn't miss it. . . . But the capricious, volatile weather of South Georgia was not going to let the SAS off the hook that easily. Within moments of departure, as the Mk 3 swung down in a cautious right-hand descent of about 250 feet, the Mk 5 following it encountered a white-out. The pilot had just enough time to pull up the nose of his aircraft before it hit the ice. The tail rotor struck ground first and the machine whirled out of control before skidding to a halt on its left-hand side. Of the seven men on board – six SAS soldiers and the pilot – only one, Corporal Bunker, was hurt. Despite a back injury he climbed out of the main door along with the others. 'The good news,' said one survivor, 'was that the door was on the starboard side and therefore unobstructed.'

Within seconds, the remaining Mk 5, which had been following the crashed helicopter, and the leading Mk 3 had landed at the scene. Equipment on board the Mk 3 was discarded to accommodate three survivors, including a now spare pilot. All the soldiers aboard this helicopter now carried only their weapons and belt kit containing ammunition, water and very basic survival gear. Bergen rucksacks containing food, sleeping-bags and fuel had to be discarded. Aboard the remaining Mk 5, it was the same story as Currass, Armstrong and a corporal crowded in. The two helicopters lifted away again, their pilots nervously aware that the load they were now carrying made flying even more difficult. Again the Mk 3 Wessex led the way. Once again the view from the following aircraft was blotted out within seconds by a pancake of snow. The result was the same: a sickening, skidding crash onto the ice. This time, however, the machine lay on its starboard side. Delves, the Squadron commander, squatting over a machine-gun in the open doorway of the Mk 3, signalled to his fellow passengers that the Mk 5 was down. At that stage there was nothing the Royal Navy pilot, Lieutenant-Commander Ian Stanley, could do except note the crash site and return to *Antrim* as quickly as possible. Three helicopters had set out on the rescue mission that morning. It was a sombre return for the lone survivor. Back on board the destroyer, the rescued men were taken to an emergency medical post set up in the officers' wardroom. The Mk 3 refuelled and flew back to the glacier. News of the operation as it now stood – two helicopters lost and most of an entire SAS troop in dire trouble – dealt a body blow to the morale of Downing Street and the Ministry of Defence. For a time, the credibility of Britain's capacity to retake its lost territory was finely balanced. The public was not allowed to know what was happening.

A senior Ministry of Defence official described his reactions to author Robert Harris: 'You can imagine how we felt. This was the first real action of the war and it was a terrible reversal. It provoked hideous memories of the American helicopter disaster when they tried to rescue the hostages in Iran. The accident was so sensitive that it was agreed not even to raise it at the morning meeting of the Chiefs of Staff committee. With negotiations with Argentina still in progress, it was thought that news of the disaster might change the mood of the country and the House of Commons. It might even lead to the recall of the task force. . . .'

This last view was possibly exaggerated, but for Lord Lewin also, as he later admitted, it was one of the worst moments of the campaign.

By now, those stranded by the second crash had extricated themselves from the wreck, with some difficulty, and were 'making ourselves comfortable'. That is to say, they foraged a survival tent from the wreck, and much else of value from the scene of the first crash. The faithful Mk 3 Wessex, with Ian Stanley still at the controls, refuelled and immediately returned to the glacier. The men on the ice were able to report that they were in good shape and that there were no serious casualties. This information they had to relay by radio. At ground level, visibility was so poor that even Stanley was forced to postpone his latest rescue attempt. Later the same day he flew his seventh sortie over the glacier within forty-eight hours. He landed and watched, apparently impassively, as more and more bodies were crammed into the tiny helicopter. Including his navigator and himself, there were seventeen people on board. This anti-submarine Wessex is designed to carry five people.

With its single Bristol Gnome engine at full throttle and rotors creaking under the strain, the helicopter clawed its way into the sky. But with such an overload there could be no question of a normally cautious, hover-to-land approach to *Antrim*'s tiny flight deck. 'It was a one-shot, straight-in landing like the descent of a brick dung store,' said one participant later. All the survivors were now assembled and examined. The only evident injuries were a deep gash on Currass's cheekbone, which was stitched; Corporal Bunker's feet (which were suffering from frost nip) and his back, which was bruised. Next, the men of Mountain Troop invited themselves into *Antrim*'s wardroom (the officers' mess) to toast Ian Stanley and his crew and thank them for their bravery. Such behaviour by Royal Navy ratings would be unthinkable. For the SAS soldier, irrespective of rank, it was an instinctive and spontaneous expression of gratitude not to be blocked by naval protocol.

Next day, the Squadron tried again. This time it was the turn of the boat troop to set up viable observation posts. Delves and his team, re-examining the problem overnight, were now in no doubt that the environment was a greater hazard than the enemy, and that a brazen, frontal approach from the sea must be attempted. Five Gemini inflatable boats fitted with 40hp Johnson outboard engines were prepared for the attempt. As a precaution against any technical failure at the last moment, the engines were taken off the boats and started up on test rigs on *Antrim*'s deck. Once the engines were thoroughly warmed up they were re-fitted to the boats. The Geminis, each carrying three men, were then to set off to watch Leith and Husvik whaling stations from Grass Island in neighbouring Stromness Bay. That was the plan.

At the outset, this latest gamble looked good. *Antrim* was lying in Stromness Bay, in darkness, calm water and fine weather, a mere 800 yards from Grass Island. Astonishingly, in view of the care taken to nurse the engines, three of them would not start when the boats were launched. Boat Troop now faced an exceedingly tricky choice: to hold off until the engines were serviceable (missing a tide and losing at least twenty-four valuable operational hours) or to use the two functional craft to tow the other three. After a quick discussion between the Squadron commander, Major Delves, and the boat troop leader they decided to proceed immediately. They cast off and glided away from the big, grey destroyer into the darkness. Of the two functional Geminis, one was towing two of its disabled companions while the second towed the other.

The main characteristic of South Georgia's weather is its unpredictability, and its unusual knack of generating gale force winds in one spot only five miles or so from an area of total calm. This is partly an effect of the 'wind tunnel' of the Fortuna and other glaciers, decanting a powerful downhill airflow into a local sea area. Just such a wind now hit the Geminis with the force of a torpedo; part of a DSO citation for Delves refers to 100mph katabatic gusts blowing during this part of the operation. Under the impact of the sudden storm, the lines of two of the disabled craft parted and they were scattered into the night.

Three Geminis reached their objective. Of the two others one was found drifting, hours later, by the indefatigable Ian Stanley. Before they were winched into the helicopter one of the three men on board, a corporal, sank the Gemini to ensure that it would not be washed ashore to compromise the operation. The occupants of the second boat, meanwhile, were in an even more desperate situation. They were being carried past the last landfall for thousands of miles when they managed to wade ashore at Cape Saunders. After surviving on the ice for three days, they concluded that it was now safe to announce their position by SARBE. They were right. By now South Georgia had been recaptured and they were retrieved, still fit to fight, by helicopter. Meanwhile Delves, like other SAS squadron commanders before him, could only speculate about the fate of his missing men, and sweat.

While the SAS was attempting to set up its reconnaissance on Grass Island, the Royal Marine SBS team was about to make similar efforts elsewhere. Soon after midnight on 23 April, St George's Day, the marines landed at a spot known as Sorling Valley on Cumberland East Bay. The SBS team's hopes of crossing the bay in Geminis were destroyed when glacier ice, blown into the bay by strong north-west winds, punctured the inflated hulls of the Geminis. That evening the team was plucked off the bay by helicopter and brought back to the ships.

In the event, it was the re-insertion of this team which accidentally started a chain of events culminating in the Argentine surrender. The Argentines knew something was afoot. Radio signals intercepted by *Endurance* included at least one Argentine message suggesting that the British had put a team ashore. This signal the Argentines subsequently cancelled. They certainly knew also of the presence offshore of the mini-task force. Using civil Boeing 707 jets flying from the mainland, 1200 miles away, the Argentines were conducting regular reconnaissance of the area. One of these aircraft passed over South Georgia on 24 April, and on that day a deadly game of hide-and-seek began. The task force, aware that a submarine was in the area, temporarily withdrew to deeper, safer waters where it was joined by the frigate *Brilliant*. The obstinate *Endurance*, meanwhile, did not withdraw but lay quietly in Hound Bay, one peninsula away from Grytviken. Most of the British ships returned to South Georgia during the night of 24/25 April, leaving *Tidespring*, with M Company of 42 Royal Marine Commando, 200 miles to the north.

By a happy coincidence the Argentine submarine *Santa Fe* was tying up in Grytviken harbour that night, unseen by the British, to discharge marine reinforcements for the Argentine garrison. At first light on the 25th the *Santa Fe* put to sea to hunt down *Endurance* or any other Royal Navy vessel in the area . . . and Lieutenant-Commander Stanley, flying his Wessex, was returning to the *Antrim* after dropping the SBS men a few miles up the same inlet at Moraine Fiord. Glancing down at the cold, slate-grey waters of Cumberland Bay, he saw a submarine sitting vulnerably on the suface. Stanley promptly straddled the vessel with depth-charges which caused just enough damage to make it unsafe for the submarine to dive. Soon afterwards, alerted by Stanley, other helicopters – a Wasp from *Endurance* and a Lynx from the frigate *Brilliant* – followed up the first attack with a salvo of missiles and machine-gun fire which punched hundreds of holes through the *Santa Fe*'s conning tower. Leaking oil and listing, the submarine ran for the safety of the British Antarctic Survey station at Grytviken.

The Decisive Moment

The submarine's unexpected return was accompanied by confusion and panic ashore. As shore-based machine-guns fired long bursts towards the British helicopters, the submarine crew was seen fleeing for cover ashore. Delves, commanding D Squadron, and his Royal Marine colleague, Guy Sheridan, concluded that this was as good a time as any to move ashore in force and seize Grytviken. True, the assault force available was greatly outnumbered by the opposition, but as one observer of the operation explained, 'There comes a moment in any contact or battle when a decisive moment is reached. Delves and Sheridan felt that moment was at hand and whoever seized the initiative would prevail. The Argentines were already demoralized and had no way of taking any sort of initiative. So in spite of the odds against us, we were really in the commanding position.' The odds, none the less, were a formidable two-to-one against the attackers. The Marines' M Company was still 200 miles away aboard *Tidespring*, while marines in the frigate *Plymouth* could not be lifted ashore by the troop-carrying Wessex helicopter because *Plymouth*'s tiny flight deck was not large enough for the Wessex. So the only manpower instantly available for a landing 'in force' was aboard *Antrim*. Most of them were SAS soldiers.

Two troops, one led by Hamilton, plus a headquarters element including Delves and Sergeant-Major Gallagher, hastily put their gear together. This included NATO's new, lightweight anti-tank missile, Milan, as well as the general-purpose machine-gun. Other troops available for the assault included *Antrim*'s own Royal Marine detachment of ten men, a few of M Company, an SBS team and Royal Marine mortar and reconnaissance sections. The total fighting force totalled just 75 men, equal to about half the Argentine garrison. Thirty minutes before the assault a Wasp helicopter put ashore Captain Chris Brown, a Royal Artillery officer from 148 Battery, whose men are specialist Naval Gunfire Support Forward Observers, plus an escort. The unwieldy title, NGSFO, conceals adventurous commando-trained spirits who took their chances time and again during the South Atlantic conflict to direct the Navy's guns from covert positions in enemy held territory. Just before the Falklands campaign 148 Battery was threatened with disbandment as an economy measure.

John Hamilton's men were next to leave, the first patrol being led by Hamilton himself. They flew in the now familiar Wessex Mk 3 from *Antrim* to a flat, grassy area known as Hestesletten, two kilometres south-east of the BAS station. As soon as they had landed, the troops and Squadron Headquarters formed a tight defensive perimeter to await the arrival of Sheridan and his mortar team. From just over the hill, which rose away from their position, towards Grytviken, they could already hear the crump of falling shells as the 4.5in guns of *Antrim* and *Plymouth* put on an intimidating demonstration of firepower. The shells fell all round the Argentine positions, as intended, without hitting any building or causing a single casualty. But the message was obvious: surrender or die.

As the Marine Commandos arrived, Delves and his men moved off, up the scree and over the top. From this position,

avage Antarctic wind slices across *Antrim*'s decks as Sid Davidson
ont), Lofty Arthy and others prepare to attack Fortuna Glacier.
ces erased for security reasons are of men still serving. For all
ntline soldiers, this moment before they go over the top is one of
ital reality. (*SAS Regiment*)

ter a night on the glacier which they were lucky to survive, the
n were rescued by helicopter. But of three machines sent out,
ly one Wessex came back. The others, as this picture shows,
re wrecked in 'white-out' conditions. (*Ministry of Defence*)

For three weeks before the San Carlos landings and three weeks more until the Argentine surrender, SAS patrols relayed information about the enemy from behind the lines. The patrols' journey back meant long night-marches to a helicopter rendezvous. *Above* An SAS recce team returns safely to base. (*Paul R. G. Haley, 'Soldier'*)

After the Pebble Island raid, the wreckage of a Skyvan (foreground) and smaller Mentor trainers scar the runways. The Argentines were lucky. Only a failure of timing prevented the SAS from annihilating the garrison as well as destroying the aircraft and fuel stored there. (*Crown Copyright*)

The war intensifies as it nears its end. *Top* Heavily laden SAS soldier with Armalite passes Scots Guards team loading casualty into helicopter on Goat Ridge. (*Paul R. G. Haley*, '*Soldier*') *Centre* G Squadron mortar barrage on Wireless Ridge, supporting special forces' assault from sea twenty-four hours before Argentine surrender. *Below* Gazelle helicopter flying white truce flag carries Mike Rose, SAS Commander, to negotiate with Menendez. (*SAS Regiment*)

The attempt to count them all out from Argentine mainland air bases was the most secret reconnaissance of the conflict. In theory, 'burst transmission' – ultra rapid release of pre-coded messages whose split-second duration defies detection – was the way to do it. *Above* Soldier prepares to key scrambled message before transmission. Subsequent sketches (courtesy of *The Times*) show how radio back-pack transmits to command headquarters at sea where message is received, decoded.

Delves saw what looked like white flags around the Argentine positions. By radio he advised Sheridan, still in his helicopter, that D Squadron would go forward to investigate, a signal which Sheridan acknowledged. It has been suggested, erroneously, that there was a 'race' between Delves and Sheridan to be first into Grytviken. In fact, what followed was not a headlong dash by the SAS, but an ordered 'advance to contact' in which likely targets were engaged. Hamilton's patrol opened fire at least twice. To the soldiers' left, as they moved forward, loomed Brown Mountain, from which a spur ran across their line of advance, and down to the coast. On top of the mountain a suspected enemy position was hit with a Milan missile fired by Hamilton personally. The 'whoosh' of the Milan was followed by a resonant clang as the missile scored a direct hit . . . on an ancient piece of angle-iron. Soon afterwards, about 800 metres ahead near the coast, the patrol saw brown, balaclava-clad heads moving in the tussock grass. These were hit by SAS machine-gun fire and, at Hamilton's request, by shells from naval guns offshore. The troop, satisfied that a possible threat had been removed, continued to advance towards the ridge, still well ahead of the Royal Marines, only to discover that the 'enemy' in the tussock grass was a tribe of seven or eight elephant seals. 'They were now somewhat the worse for wear,' one SAS soldier said later. Another SAS team saw figures moving, then lie still in the tussocks. The recumbent 'enemy' this time proved to be penguins, sleeping contentedly.

From the top of Brown Mountain ridge the SAS men had a panoramic view of King Edward Cove, with Grytviken nestling ahead in the most sheltered corner. They had now been ashore for just over two hours. Outside Discovery House – an L-shaped building erected in 1925 to commemorate Captain Scott – the Argentine flag still flew. But every building nearby was decorated with white sheets. Hamilton's men could also see the submarine *Santa Fe,* berthed alongside the jetty and listing like a harpooned whale. But not a single human being was in sight.

After fifteen minutes, as the Royal Marines occupied positions on the ridge, the Argentine troops finally emerged from Discovery House and formed up alongside their flag. By now the SAS men led by Delves were scurrying towards them along the shoreline of King Edward Cove. On they came, past the wreck of an Argentine Puma helicopter shot down by the defending British marines three weeks earlier, through the deserted whaling station and into the area around Discovery House. There, as Hamilton's troop spread out round the enemy, pointedly covering them with Armalites and machine-guns, the garrison proffered the surrender of Grytviken to Delves. But first, Squadron Sergeant-Major Gallagher lowered the Argentine flag and produced from his battle smock a Union Jack which he ran up in its place, smiling broadly as he did so. Major Sheridan arrived by helicopter to complete, as senior officer, formalities of surrender, and his Royal Marines followed an hour later to take care of the prisoners. (Some weeks later another SAS officer would negotiate the surrender of the Falklands and, again, would leave it to others to complete the formalities.)

Meanwhile there was some urgent cleaning-up to be done around Grytviken. A few of the prisoners who spoke English could not understand how the SAS had avoided casualties. 'You have just walked through a minefield,' they explained. Corporal Paul Bunker and Sergeant 'Lofty' Arthy took their Argentine guides over the ground to defuse the mines, and mark their positions. The mines had been sited to oppose a beach landing opposite Discovery House and to protect three mortar pits and two machine-gun positions on a slope behind it, facing Cumberland East Bay. The SAS men were not unduly impressed. The mortar pits were half-full of water and weapons of various calibres had been thrown down haphazardly. From nearby Shackleton House Hamilton's men recovered a large haul of automatic pistols, revolvers and carbines including Israeli-made Uzis. Most of these, like those in the trenches outside, were still loaded and poorly maintained.

Next morning two troops from D Squadron together with an SBS team flew by helicopter into Leith, backed up by *Plymouth* and *Endurance*. After much Argentinian rhetoric about 'fighting to the last man', the Leith garrison – including Captain Alfredo Astiz, who was accused of torturing political prisoners in his own country – surrendered meekly. In London, the *Daily Mail*'s front page headline proclaimed in 1½-inch lettering, 'MARINES RETAKE SOUTH GEORGIA'. Leaving M Company on guard, D Squadron was back aboard *Antrim* within 24 hours, and a day later moved by helicopter to the frigate *Brilliant*. It was now 28 April and the Squadron was bound for the Falklands.

Already however, the repercussions of the recapture of South Georgia were world wide. As the DSO citation for *Antrim*'s captain, Brian Young, put it: 'The importance of this operation to the overall strategy of re-establishing British administration in the Falkland Islands . . . cannot be overstated. . . .' In the South Atlantic, the main task force now had a base nearer to the Falklands than Ascension from which to stage future operations. Public opinion in Britain was given the encouragement of a near-bloodless victory, and backing for further bold action swept through the country like a charge of adrenalin. The Argentine Government now faced, as never before, the prospect of a fight for the Falklands, and the American administration, having tried to maintain a neutral posture, at last came off the fence with promises of *matériel* (i.e., logistic and supply) support. In London, Prime Minister Margaret Thatcher, announcing the news in person in a chilly Downing Street, squashed all questions with the command, 'Rejoice! Rejoice!'

Strategic Stress

While D Squadron was setting the pace in the South Atlantic – a blistering pace which it was to keep up throughout the

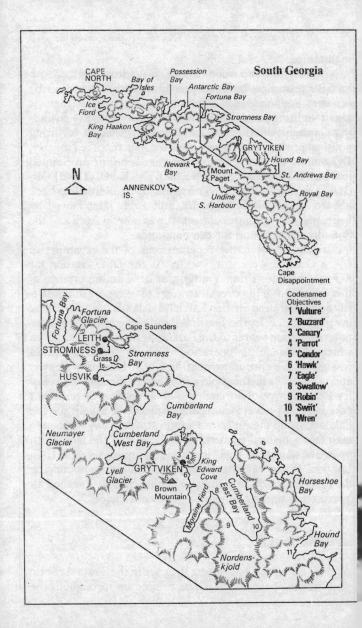

South Georgia

CAPE NORTH
Bay of Isles
Possession Bay
Antarctic Bay
Fortuna Bay
Ice Fiord
King Haakon Bay
Stromness Bay
GRYTVIKEN
Hound Bay
Newark Bay
Mount Paget
St. Andrews Bay
ANNENKOV IS.
Undine S. Harbour
Royal Bay
Cape Disappointment

N

Fortuna Bay
Fortuna Glacier
Cape Saunders
LEITH
STROMNESS
Grass Is.
Stromness Bay
HUSVIK
Cumberland Bay
Neumayer Glacier
Cumberland West Bay
Lyell Glacier
GRYTVIKEN
King Edward Cove
Brown Mountain
Moraine Fiord
Cumberland East Bay
Horseshoe Bay
Nordenskjold
Hound Bay

Codenamed Objectives
1 'Vulture'
2 'Buzzard'
3 'Canary'
4 'Parrot'
5 'Condor'
6 'Hawk'
7 'Eagle'
8 'Swallow'
9 'Robin'
10 'Swift'
11 'Wren'

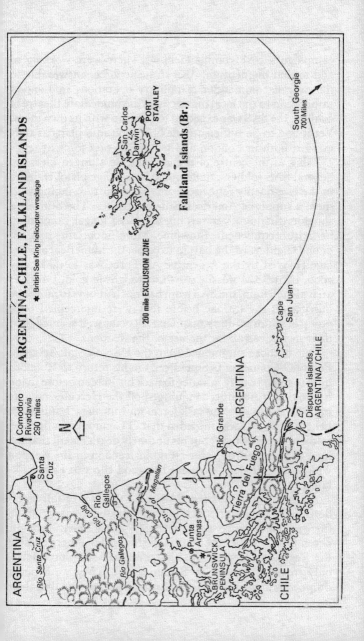

ARGENTINA, CHILE, FALKLAND ISLANDS

★ British Sea King helicopter wreckage

Falkland Islands (Br.)

200 mile EXCLUSION ZONE

San Carlos
Darwin
PORT
STANLEY

South Georgia
700 Miles

Comodoro
Rivadavia
290 miles

N

ARGENTINA

Santa
Cruz

Río Santa Cruz

Río Coíg

Río Gallegos

Río Gallegos

Str. of Magellan

Punta
Arenas

BRUNSWICK
PENINSULA

CHILE

Río Grande

ARGENTINA

Tierra del Fuego

Cape
San Juan

Disputed islands,
ARGENTINA/CHILE

campaign – SAS commanders elsewhere were working to add to that momentum. As a strategic force, answerable to the overall commander of military operations in London rather than to the local hierarchy in the immediate theatre of conflict, the SAS was expected to come up with its own ideas. Yet it had to be sufficiently flexible to fit into plans as they evolved both in London and within the task force at sea.

Being at the centre of things could be a mixed blessing. Several SAS soldiers, undergoing long-range pistol training in the US, hastily returned from that country bringing with them a supply of American Stinger missiles. The Stinger, a shoulder-fired anti-aircraft missile, has a longer range than its British equivalent, Blowpipe. More important, it is ten pounds lighter. In the battles to come, the numerical advantage enjoyed by the Argentine Air Force was to make any good, light SAM missile worth its weight in gold. On their arrival in Britain, the SAS team had not had time to move the missiles off the tarmac before they were intercepted by a group of senior military planners. All of these, it seemed, had their own ideas about the use of the weapon.

One of those summoned from the US was Staff Sergeant Paddy O'Conner of G Squadron. On his return to Hereford he was given twenty minutes to pack his Bergen before flying to the South Atlantic. He jumped off the Hercules tailgate into the sea to join the task force, murmuring, 'I still don't believe it. . . .' It was intended that O'Connor train the SAS soldiers to use Stinger, but his untimely death meant that the men of D Squadron received no instruction in the weapon which, nevertheless, they used to good effect in East Falkland.

An even more puzzled SAS team was a free-fall troop destined to be parachuted into East Falkland to carry out the first reconnaissance patrols there. These men, brought peremptorily under the control of strategic planners outside the Regiment, were flown 5000 miles to Ascension Island, only to be sent back to Britain again. They were never dropped into the war zone. The reason for this was that their transport, the RAF's Hercules, could not fly the 8000-mile return journey from Ascension Island to the Falklands without repeated in-flight refuelling. At that time, the Hercules were not equipped with the necessary probes. They were modified within a matter of days, but by the time this had been done the men of G Squadron with the amphibious task force at sea were almost within helicopter range of the islands. The planners now had to weigh the risk of incurring casualties by parachuting men into the windy Falklands against the perils facing helicopter crews obliged to fly 'blind' into enemy held territory. In the event, the men who drew the short straws were the Sea King helicopter crews of 846 Squadron, Royal Navy. This decision, ultimately, had to be a cold and professional one. At the very beginning of a covert reconnaissance mission, casualties, with their concomitant radio traffic and 'casevac' helicopter lifts, which could compromise the operation, were more likely to be incurred by paratroops.

The neatest and most successful long-range initiative taken by the Regiment concerned communications. Throughout the conflict – witness subsequent complaints from war correspondents attached to the task force – 'comms' remained a nagging problem for the strategists working in the Kafkaesque underground Fleet Headquarters, the 'Hole' at Northwood in Middlesex. Because of the great distances involved the only rapid and secure link was by satellite. Only one of these, Marisat (for 'maritime satellite') was available to a Royal Navy whose planning, for many years, had been geared to a crisis in the North Atlantic. Traffic on the only available satellite soon swamped the system, and prolonged delays ensued. This was acutely embarrassing since, for domestic and international political reasons, the need to show that the deployment of armed force was being orchestrated from London, was held to be at least as important as successful prosecution of the conflict on the ground. Yet there were times when the SAS, to the puzzlement and occasional pique of some in Whitehall, appeared to have tactical information from the front which was not several hours behind events. Former members of the Regiment are still coy as to how this apparent telepathy was achieved. It is believed that it might have been done through the use of miniaturized satellite communications.

Only once do the strategic discussions in London seem to have affected – and then only temporarily – the main thrust of SAS operations in the field. The departure of D Squadron from England to Ascension Island on 5 April was followed a day later by a regimental headquarters led by the Commanding Officer of 22 SAS, Lieutenant-Colonel Michael Rose, OBE, QGM, and by G Squadron. The HQ team worked aboard HMS *Fearless*, an assault craft designed also to act as a front-line HQ for battles ashore. Rose's team was part of a planning cadre known as R (for Reconnaissance) Group. Ostensibly, R Group would plan the first operations ashore including the initial Falklands landing, subject to the endorsement of its plans by London. The R Group was an integral part of 3 Commando Brigade Headquarters, the land forces HQ, headed by Brigadier Julian Thompson, Royal Marines.

As the Falklands crisis developed the British Government orchestrated its pressure on Argentina in an endeavour to avoid a land battle. For land battle, with the casualties it implied, would generate much bitterness and make the long-term diplomatic problem of resolving the future of the Falklands that much more difficult. Such orchestration first required a battle fleet to recover South Georgia, which is not part of the Falklands and is, unquestionably, British territory by any yardstick. This was followed by a larger Royal Navy battle group to enforce a maritime blockade round the Falklands, adding to the pressure without necessarily causing bloodshed. The final option, the use of an amphibious group to reoccupy the Falklands by force, meant keeping that group in reserve on Ascension Island until diplomacy – notably an American shuttle headed by Secretary of State Haig – was exhausted. To commit the amphibious assault force, including *Fearless* and the SAS commander, Rose, to the South Atlantic prematurely could have been unnecessarily provocative. It would, at the least, have exposed the soldiers to greater hardship and uncertainty, and reduced their fitness to fight. The amphibious assault group therefore remained at Ascension Island for about two weeks after the Falklands battle fleet had sailed.

It is clear from other published accounts of the campaign that R Group, aboard *Fearless*, did not enjoy the unquestioning support of either the strategic planners at Northwood or the overall task force commander with the fleet, Rear-Admiral John Woodward. Northwood, for example, promoted the swift recapture of South Georgia as a separate venture from similar schemes prepared by R Group. Woodward, properly anxious about a possible submarine threat to the task force carriers *Hermes* and *Invincible*, put to sea with his battle group on 18 April taking with him most of the men of G Squadron aboard the Royal Fleet Auxiliary *Resource*. As the initial Falklands reconnaissance team, it was not surprising that they should go with this first wave rather than remain at Ascension with the amphibious assault group. But so unexpected was their departure that some of the Squadron's vital equipment and manpower was left behind. On orders from Northwood one ship returned to the Ascension Island approaches so that the missing men and materials could be retrieved by helicopter. Meanwhile most of the Squadron continued on their voyage south, basking in the sunshine and lulled by a holiday atmosphere aboard *Resource*. ('The wine,' one officer recalled fondly, 'was excellent. . . . The atmosphere provided by the stewards very gay.')

During the last week of April, as the battle group bore down upon the Falklands, hopes of using the fleet as an instrument of diplomacy – a show of strength – broke down like a crumbling rock face under the boot of Argentine nationalism and obduracy. By the time the fleet arrived in the South Atlantic it is doubtful whether the Buenos Aires junta could have reached a peaceful settlement even had it wished. It was now trapped by the fury of the street mobs it had goaded with its own political rhetoric devoted to liberation of the Malvinas. So what had started in Britain as a knee-jerk response (even if for good reason, in a just cause) now became a deadly jigsaw puzzle from which several vital pieces were missing. One was the absence of sufficient air cover to repulse a determined, mass assault by the Argentine Air Force. It did not require psychic powers to realize that enemy air power combined with sea-skimming Exocet missiles posed a terrifying threat to Woodward's fleet. The necessary data was available to all in standard works of reference which made it clear that the Royal Navy had no weapon that could be relied upon to defeat the Exocet once it was within range.

Second only to this problem was the absence of hard information as to where in the Falklands the Argentines had concentrated their forces. Cloud cover over the islands rendered satellite reconnaissance data all but useless. In any case, Britain depended for this information on American sources, which meant a significant delay in relaying information to the task force by way of London. As the South Atlantic weather worsened with every day's approach to winter, the imperative need, if the Falklands were to be recovered by force, was for good, up-to-date reconnaissance. Without it any attempted landing could replicate the disaster of Gallipoli. The task of obtaining such information was a classic one for the SAS.

G Squadron Goes In

From G Squadron, four four-man patrols went ashore in Sea King helicopters of 846 Naval Air Squadron in the early hours of 1 May. The next night another three patrols went in and the third night, yet another. Simultaneously the first six SBS teams began their task of exploring the most important bays and inlets to identify the most feasible invasion points

Yet the honour of being the first returning British serviceman ashore in the Falklands went – fortuitously – to a Captain Chris Brown from 148 Battery, R.A. The first of May is historically memorable as the day on which 'the Empire struck back', when RAF Vulcan bombers, which had been consigned to the breaker's yard not long before, flew 3500 miles from Ascension Island and back – a 15-hour trip – to bomb Port Stanley at 4am. The attack was reinforced with strafing runs by Royal Navy Sea Harriers and a bombardment of airfield installations by the 4.5in guns of the fleet. Brown was spotting for the Navy's guns from a hovering Lynx helicopter which was obliged to make a forced-landing after being hit by enemy fire. He was on the ground for about ten minutes before the Lynx left, with him on board. The SAS and SBS patrols were obliged to remain ashore rather longer.

After a flight of 120 miles from HMS *Hermes,* the teams were placed under cover of darkness up to 20 miles from their final observations posts. First came the men, weapons in hand, boots squelching in the cold, soaking peat, then the Bergen rucksacks, backs buckling under the 100lb load. Welcome to the Falklands. . . . The helicopters lifted away, engine noise drowned by the crooning South Atlantic wind, and they were alone in enemy territory. The ration packs were sufficient for about a week, but they were going to have to last longer. It was the familiar SAS problem of weight versus mobility. One patrol, lying low above Port Stanley, was not to be relieved for 26 tense days.

Of these first patrols one overlooked Port Stanley proper and a second, the approaches to the capital. Elsewhere, other patrols watched Bluff Cove (where the tragedy of the bomb attack on *Sir Galahad* and *Sir Tristram* was to occur after D-Day) and Darwin/Goose Green. On West Falkland one team kept an eye on Fox Bay; another, on Port Howard. The siting of these OPs was based upon the meagre Intelligence available from Royal Marines repatriated after the British surrender; from civilians who chose not to live under occupation and from two RAF technicians who wandered about Port Stanley airfield freely for several days after the invasion a month before.

Each patrol's precise landing site was chosen by the team's leader after discussion with his Squadron commander, the Intelligence team and the Royal Navy's helicopter pilot. Such discussions, based on the meagre information to be gleaned from a 1:50,000 map, usually took place in the women's lavatory of the *Resource*. This was the only spare room on board and it became G Squadron's floating operations room. The team then flew on the basis of this intelligent guesswork to a spot where, hopefully, the enemy was not. The first part of the route into East Falkland, established as a 'safe' road and never varied much, was from the north across Bombilla Hill and thereafter along any convenient valley, but it was crucial that the outgoing patrol should know precisely where it had been set down. Its navigation on foot thereafter would depend upon a correct initial fix.

Such pinpoint accuracy and, indeed, the whole insertion operation was helped by new equipment which, for once, merited the overworked description, 'Magic kit'. American passive night goggles, issued experimentally to some of the Sea Kings' crews just before they left Britain, enabled them to fly in absolute darkness with complete accuracy and confidence.

With the Sea Kings' departure back to the security of HMS *Hermes*, the isolation of the patrols became acute. The nearest British ground forces in any strength were still hundreds of miles away at sea or 3500 miles distant on Ascension Island. There were no back-up squads, no quick-reaction forces to help any patrol which hit trouble. SAS Captain Aldwin Wight was decorated for his conduct during these operations. His official citation reads:

'Inserted . . . at a range of 120 miles, he positioned his patrol in close proximity to enemy positions, cut off from any form of rescue should he have been compromised.

This position he maintained for 26 days. During this time he produced clear and accurate pictures of enemy activity in the Stanley area, Intelligence available from no other means, which proved vital in the planning of the final assault. On one occasion he reported an enemy helicopter concentration against which an air strike was directed, resulting in the destruction of four troop-carrying helicopters essential to the enemy in maintaining flexibility and rapid deployment across the islands; a task complicated by the enemy's changing the location of his helicopter holding area each day. In spite of his exposed position . . . his Intelligence reports were detailed and regularly updated. The conditions in which he and his men existed were appalling, with little cover from view or the elements. The weather conditions varied from freezing rain to gale force winds, with few clear days.'

The troops approached their task with a canny mixture of caution and daring. The helicopter drop was sometimes made as far as twenty miles from the ultimate destination. As well as Morse transmitters, food, and as much cold- and wet-weather clothing as possible, the men also carried a large quantity of ammunition, which they hoped not to have to use, for this operation was the antithesis of D Squadron's attacking role. For G Squadron, there was no sudden spurt of action to burn off the adrenalin. Instead, just a steady, remorseless build-up of anxiety day by day, with no hope of release.

Costa Hypothermia

Once out of the helicopter the patrols' first priority was to get away from the landing zone at a rapid pace, on a compass bearing chosen during the planning stage aboard *Hermes*. After some hours there was a terse, whispered conference to decide how much farther the team should go towards its

objective before first light. Well before then, each man had to
be concealed in his 'scrape', a shallow trench covered by
hessian net, camouflaged with tussock grass or peat. The
soldiers quickly learned that to dig more than 18 inches down
into Falklands soil is to strike either granite or water. The
wise ones lined their scrapes with plastic, but these gravelike
holes were never dry and barely secure for observation.
Others were to find them even less tolerable. After the main
landing, according to Lieutenant-Colonel Malcolm Hunt, of
40 Royal Marine Commando, 'Positions almost on the crest
of the hills were filling with more than 2 feet of water. One
marine had tried to sleep in his trench despite such discom-
forts and had to be evacuated by helicopter suffering from
acute hypothermia. At one time during that morning his
heart had stopped.'

To brew up or cook anything on the tiny hexamine stove
was always a risk. By day the Argentines foraged around the
perimeters of their own positions on foot or – more effectual –
flew over suspect areas in helicopters. From these aircraft
any patch of carelessly disturbed soil would be vividly obvious. Cold rations such as biscuits, cheese and chocolate had
to suffice most of the day. Daylight hours, on the British
clock, were between approximately 10.30am and 6.30pm.
On almost every other day these 'daylight' hours were obs-
cured by sea fog. 'We could see the fog coming in off the sea
and over Port Stanley,' one man recalled. 'Once it rolled in it
usually stayed there all day.' After dusk the patrol, now
shivering with cold, would move on. Little things, like the
slow, painful return to life of numbed feet warming up in
perpetually wet boots mattered increasingly as the patrol
settled down to a lifestyle and a rhythm of its own.

No one spoke, except in a whisper, and then only when
absolutely necessary. It helped that the Argentines built
roaring camp fires by night. When these were spotted, a nod
of the head, a hand squeezing a comrade's elbow or a silently
pointed finger rated as conversation. The residual, unspoken
anxiety centred on the minefield risk. Too close to the enemy,

one foot placed on the wrong spot in the darkness, could bring crippling injury or death – and jeopardize the operation.

So just how far to go on each leg of the march was always a matter of nice calculation. Each part of the journey was treated as a self-contained operation requiring its own special reconnaissance before the entire patrol was committed to it. In the first days ashore the patrols played it 'safe' – comparatively – by lying up in an OP several miles from the nearest Argentine position.

The sense of isolation was emphasized by news from the outside world which they picked up by tuning their radios at minimum volume to BBC World Service broadcasts. Listening to the discussions about UN Resolution 502 and Haig's shuttle 'while grovelling in the peat watching Argentinians' could be disconcerting. During the first days of the covert reconnaissance operation, as the diplomatic quadrille danced this way and that, some of the more thoughtful SAS men speculated on the status of their mission. There had been no formal declaration of war, although this was assuredly a state of armed conflict. Was it another grey area, similar to Ireland? What if they 'bumped' some Argentines and killed them? What was their position if captured? Then came the news on 5 May of the fatal Exocet attack on the destroyer *Sheffield*. 'That night was the worst,' one patrol veteran recollected. 'The news was very alarming. From our point of view it seemed that the task force ships – our lifeline – were there for the picking.' The Exocet attack, 48 hours after the sinking of the *Belgrano*, impressed upon them, as had nothing else so far, that 'we were committed . . . for us, the sinking of *Sheffield* was as good as a declaration of war.'

There was one other potent element in the patrols' isolation; no one knew when they would be withdrawn. The original insertion could not be built around a specified cut-off date or even a precise method of extracting the patrols. Ideally, they would join up with advancing British forces . . . if they landed successfully . . . if they advanced far enough. . . . Such monumental question-marks were a nagging reminder that this was not an extended exercise, but the real thing.

After the long march in, the patrol's final OP was established in a less than comfortable hide on a windswept, eye-watering hillside, from which the men of G Squadron, using powerful telescopes, took turns to tabulate the enemy's movements. At the end of such a shift, despite their experience of similar work in Northern Ireland, eyes were red-rimmed with fatigue. In clear weather the target was more visible, but so was the OP. In the most sensitive hides even bodily functions had to wait, or be performed with minimum movement. As one man explained, 'Even then, you worried about being given away by rising steam. So you did it very slowly. If your feet got sprayed it didn't make much difference. They were already soaking anyway.'

Transmitting the information, so painfully acquired, in rapid Morse burdened the patrol with the most deadly detection risk of all: that of being 'DF'ed. 'DF' is military short-hand for 'direction finding', a simple electronic method of identifying the source of a radio transmission by taking two co-ordinates on the frequency. The Argentines, according to one specialist who has studied their equipment, were equipped with 'one piece of direction-finding equipment which could locate a transmitter after it had been on the air for a matter of seconds.' In addition to this problem, there was the risk of casual detection by local civilians. On the Falklands the virtual absence of a public telephone system means that everyone routinely listens to his short-wave CB radio. True, the casual listener could not break an SAS code, but he would certainly recognize the emergence of a powerful Morse signal as a sign that something odd was happening. Ultimately, the DF hazard was to cause the death of one SAS soldier and the capture of another. The risk of detection could be diminished by transmitting from a site remote from the OP itself, but this expedient was attended by its own hazard, movement across open country.

Hardest of all, for the boldest spirits, was the imperative that no target, however succulent, was to be attacked by an OP team. So, on occasion, Argentine Pucara aircraft as well as helicopters came and went and the sheep around them could safely graze. Wight's patrol, watching Port Stanley from Beaver Ridge, had to wait for several agonizing days before its target was hit by Harrier jets. At dusk, after the initial RAF bombing of Port Stanley on 1 May, the Argentines began moving their helicopters out to the wilderness of Mount Kent and Twin Sisters, west of the town. They could not afford to lose these aircraft, particularly the American Chinooks which could carry half a company of troops in one lift. The machines were the key to a defensive strategy depending upon mobile reserves held in Port Stanley. After sheltering in 'the camp' overnight, the helicopters would return to the capital at daybreak. The SAS patrol spotted them more than once, but were frustrated by communication problems in their efforts to report their findings. On one occasion they counted nine Argentine helicopters including two Chinooks. When, finally, they did get word through, they had the satisfaction of seeing the destruction of two of these big machines and two other helicopters.

Other patrols saw nothing of military significance. This was trying for the soldiers concerned who began to wonder if they were the task force's official bird-watching team, but to the Intelligence analysts 'negative' information, revealing gaps in the Argentine positions, was of priceless value. Finding such gaps, if the recapture of the Falklands was to succeed, was the name of the game.

Among those OPs which did have the satisfaction of being in a 'live' area the price paid in additional stress was enormous. At regular intervals a routine radio signal was expected from every team simply to report that it was on station and secure. One patrol could not risk even that short message for a period of seven days during which its position was surrounded by jumpy enemy soldiers equipped with excellent night sights and DF equipment. It is hardly surprising that after weeks of such pressure combined with lack of normal sleep and food, one SAS soldier was said to be 'in a dreamlike state, almost hallucinating' while others 'some of the fittest men we have, returned weak and looking like old men.' In addition to the effects of stress, most of the men suffered from trench foot, an unpleasant condition not generally encountered in the British Army since the First World War. 'But there's this to be said for it,' one Falklands veteran commented, 'If you're that isolated, no one on your side can interfere.'

Sergeant Joseph Mather was one of those who took the greatest risks. His patrol was watching the Bluff Cove and West Stanley areas for 28 days. 'In a totally hostile environment, with the only protection from ground and air search provided by the skill and stealth of his patrol, the reporting of Sergeant Mather was both accurate and timely,' a Military Medal citation records. 'In order to obtain the detail of the enemy disposition he was required to move his observation position to close and often obvious positions to gain the Intelligence required. This he did with great courage and skill knowing that if compromised his patrol could not have been extracted from any predicament caused by enemy action. In addition he communicated his information in an environment where the enemy were known to possess a Direction Finding capability.' Mather's leadership and example, the citation concluded, were in the highest traditions of the SAS and the Army.

The overall impression of the enemy generated by SAS Intelligence reports was that the Argentines were slovenly, inexperienced and badly-led soldiers. From this evaluation, some in the task force began to hope that once the enemy came under pressure, he would collapse without resistance.

Broadly speaking, this assessment proved correct. Given the numerical odds (12,000 defending the islands against 7000 attacking); the defenders' deep-dug positions commanding the high ground; the stockpile of food and ammunition; their air power, they should have been able to wreak havoc on a lightly-armed, under-strength attacking force. For brief periods the Argentines did fight vigorously. Then, as they started taking casualties, they surrendered or retreated with equal vigour.

SBS in Action

The SAS, as usual, were doing things the hard way, regardless of jibes from less intelligent members of other units that the Regiment was privileged. As a conscious policy, they decided not to make contact with Falkland Islanders who were potential allies. The SBS came from Britain armed with a list of such people, but decided against using it until the campaign was almost over. SBS men carried out valuable reconnaissance operations on the west coast of West Falkland – the nearest landfall to Argentina – as well as exploring many of the bays and inlets of the main population centre, East Falkland. In this work they had a uniquely useful yachtsman's guide to the islands, lovingly compiled by a Royal Marine officer, Major Ewen Southby-Tailyour. While serving with the Falklands garrison in 1978, Southby-Tailyour had sailed exhaustively. With the start of hostilities his book was classified as a secret document.

SBS reconnaissance patrols operated in similar fashion to those of the SAS, on which they depended for base communications at Ascension Island and elsewhere. Each man carried an extensive armoury: M-16 lightweight rifle (a superior Armalite), M-203 grenade launcher, fifteen high explosive grenades, one 66mm anti-tank missile, 200 rounds of rifle ammunition, smoke and phosphorous grenades, 9mm Browning pistol, and hunting-knife. For observation the team had binoculars, night sight, and tripod-mounted 60x telescope. The load was rounded off with sleeping-bags, quilted trousers in which to sleep, a change of clothes, Arctic dried rations and standard tinned 'compo' ration packs, which require cooking on an individual hexamine stove.

At 1.30am on 1 May one SBS team landed at Eagle Hill overlooking Berkeley Sound. A second was deposited at Johnsons Harbour, farther inland up the same stretch of water. Another two teams were placed on hills overlooking Salvador on the north coast. On the west coast, near the future British invasion site, a fifth squad established an observation post behind the refrigeration plant at Ajax Bay. A sixth concealed itself immediately across San Carlos Water on the Inner Verde Mountains. The following night more teams were set down, including a patrol committed to watching Port San Carlos for seven days. The name of the game was to identify suitable invasion beaches which were not garrisoned by the enemy. After clearing the landing zone as quickly as they could, the SBS men set up temporary bases on their way to their selected OP, checking their position with compass bearings before resting during the daylight hours. Of the four men in a team, three would dig while the fourth, acting as look-out, prowled the immediate vicinity. In one hand he held a fishing-line attached to a rucksack at the camp site. A tug on the line to rock the Bergen was his warning sign.

The SBS took exquisite trouble to make their two-man hides invisible, however temporary these might be. The ideal site was a fold in the ground covered by grass growing to 18 inches or so. From this they carved pieces of turf which were placed carefully to one side as if they were costly hairpieces. Then they dug deeper, putting the peat to one side. At a depth of 18 inches they lined the holes with waterproof groundsheets. Next they built a small earthwork round the hole, using the spare peat, so that the original fold in the ground was now level with the surrounding area. The hide – 8ft long by 5ft wide – was then roofed with chicken-wire stretched taut and pegged down. On top of that was placed a layer of hessian net. Finally grass was stuck in the hessian weave until the hole was invisible and the top 'hairpiece' matched the ground adjoining it. The Roman Army, which prided itself on its civil engineering, would have approved.

The SBS men said, 'We called ourselves "The Interflora Squad".'

Two hides, separated by no more than ten yards, each with a spyhole at both ends, were built for the four men. A third hide was constructed some distance away to conceal food and other stores. Each man knew how many paces and on which compass bearing this hide lay. Food for the day had to be drawn before first light. Immediately afterward the marines brushed upright the grass flattened by their feet, using foam camp mats for the purpose. By dawn they were under cover, invisible to the outside world.

For most of them time passed quickly. As one of them explained, 'There was a lot to do. By day each man was on watch for two hours and off for six. By night, when it is harder to stay awake, we had one hour on watch and three hours off. There's a lot to do during the "off-watch" periods. Cooking takes an hour or so. Everyone chooses his own menu and cooks for himself.'

By night the team moved stealthily across country to its ultimate objective after concealing all traces of the night's lodging. The group assigned to watch Fort San Carlos from Cameron's Ridge, facing the settlement across a narrow lead of water, spent two such nights before they reached their objective. There, luck was with them. A cave created by a rock fall was large enough for all four men, and little more than half a mile from the settlement. Expectantly the patrol waited for some sign of Argentine troops, probably in company strength. But the sergeant leading the patrol was flabbergasted to discover that none were present. 'We saw civilians moving about but the Argentines seemed happy to fly around checking the settlements before they disappeared back to base.'

After dark he examined the bay. 'We were looking for steeply shelving beaches into deep water, free from kelp but sheltered from the open sea, where landing-craft could come in without running around. But it was no use landing on a beach enclosed by cliffs. An exit point inland was equally important. We found Sandy Bay, a beach just a few hundred yards from Port San Carlos settlement, but out of sight of it behind a headland, and another, secondary beach below Fanning Head. Best of all was the absence of Argentine troops.'

Meanwhile the SBS patrol at nearby Ajax Bay was having a more eventful time. During the team's sixteen-day watch one Argentine helicopter landed only 100 yards from the hide while the pilot got out to relieve himself. Other helicopters also landed nearby, which convinced the men in hiding that they had been spotted. This, as we shall see, was to have some unexpected results. On another occasion a helicopter actually hovered over this hide, the downdraught of its rotors stripping camouflage away. The pilot, preoccupied with the map on his knees as well as flying his machine, did not notice what was immediately below him.

Tho most harrowing experience was that of an SBS corporal and a young Marine who had just joined the unit. They were peculiarly unlucky. The hilltop position chosen for their observation post by the R Group team on *Fearless* was also selected, at about the same time, by an Argentine patrol. The SBS men, moving stealthily in fog, had to choose between challenging the enemy – thereby compromising the operation – or allowing the Argentines to occupy the position, between the two men and the rest of their team. The two, going to ground at a safe distance, inevitably lost contact with their comrades and disappeared. They had no radio. They now followed a pre-arranged emergency drill, moving from one rendezvous to another, waiting at each for a specified time, hoping to be found. Day followed day and they were without food. The patrol's leader, meanwhile, was obliged to withdraw to meet a helicopter pick-up. Then with a fresh team he returned to hostile ground in an effort to find his missing men. By now, Special Force planners believed, it was an odds-on chance that the missing men were dead of exposure, or had been taken prisoner, or were hiding in a barn as clandestine guests of friendly locals. The search for them was concentrated upon the final rendezvous on the emergency list, though the agreed pick-up time there had long since passed. At this rendezvous, a bleak scrape in the peat, the corporal and his companion were found twelve days after the original incident. 'They were a bit thin,' said one of their comrades later, 'but glad to be found. We brought them back to the task force, fed them, debriefed them and sent them back to work.'

The SBS team watching Port San Carlos, meanwhile, reported that the area provided good landing sites with no Argentine garrison to guard them. The area, on 13 May, was 'clean'. D-Day was little more than a week away.

'Prelim' at Pebble Island

The SBS information, although vital to the main landings, was of no relevance to the first British land offensive on the Falklands. As events were to show, the SAS assault on Pebble Island, off the north coast of West Falkland, on 14 May depended almost as much upon good luck as the Fortuna Glacier reconnaissance in South Georgia. With hindsight, both the military and the journalists have tended to see the Pebble Island raid as part of some strategic grand design to soften up the enemy and persuade him that when the main invasion came at San Carlos it would be just the latest in a series of hit-and-run attacks. Like the 'disinformation' on this subject put out by the Ministry of Defence in London the raid did serve the purpose of throwing dust in the enemy's eyes, but it was originally intended by the SAS to have the same effect as a kick in the crutch: a blow not necessarily fatal, but which would certainly demoralize. The code name 'Operation Prelim' matches both interpretations.

When D Squadron first mulled over possible targets in the Falklands the only firm information about Pebble Island suggested that it held a small, isolated garrison of Argentine Army engineers and Air Force technicians working to prepare the airstrip as a dispersal field, a sanctuary for aircraft under attack at Port Stanley. Admiral Woodward, the task force commander, did not like the idea. It would require naval support and put valuable ships at risk. After the loss of *Sheffield* on 4 May, his caution is understandable. But then something happened to invest Pebble Island with a new significance.

A Harrier pilot returning from a raid on Darwin believed he had detected radar emissions from the new Argentine base. A radar system on Pebble Island would certainly identify an approaching invasion fleet, so it had to be removed. Woodward ordered a nocturnal 'elint' (electronic Intelligence) reconnaissance by aircraft equipped to read radar signatures. The operation did not confirm the Harrier's initial suspicion and D Squadron's proposed raid was again vetoed. The SAS persuaded Woodward to change his mind a second time, however, and the operation was finally approved.

Three days later, on 10 May, a reconnaissance team from one of D Squadron's boat troops – the same team which had gone ashore in faulty Geminis at South Georgia – was preparing to land near Pebble Island when severe weather obliged it to stand down for 24 hours. That night aboard *Hermes* the two four-man patrols went over the proposed route yet again: by Sea King helicopter to the remote Mare Rock peninsula on the most north-easterly point of West Falkland. From this delivery point the patrols were to use collapsible Klepper canoes to travel by sea round the Mare Rock headland and set up an OP facing Pebble Island across the fast-running, tidal Tamar Strait. Once they were satisfied that the coast was clear they would paddle across to Pebble Island. From this point they would still have to cover about ten miles to their objective, Pebble Island Settlement's airstrip. They would have to move on foot across a 'moonscape' which afforded no natural cover except for creases of dead ground. It was not a potential picnic. However, the very remoteness of the place led the planners to hope that the

Argentines would not patrol it. The briefing finished, some of the men settled down to play cards and Scrabble. Others checked their equipment, yet again.

In practice the first, routine snag was that surf crashing ashore at the West Falkland delivery point completely ruled out any hope of launching the canoes. The boat troop teams climbed back into the helicopter and flew closer to their destination. Now they had to march across a ridge at the end of the Mare Rock headland, carrying their canoes as well as other equipment. The only way this could be accomplished was by moving the rucksacks first, returning to pick up the canoes so that these, too, could be manhandled to the north shore. Once there they built an observation post and settled down throughout 11 May to watch Pebble Island. They saw nothing but sea-birds. At dusk the canoes were launched into the swirling, icy waters and the teams reached Pebble Island in the comforting safety of darkness.

At first it seemed that, for a change, a D Squadron reconnaissance was going to work as planned. One patrol stayed with the canoes as a firm base, with a radio link back to *Hermes*. The second patrol of four men then marched through the night until it reached the tight neck of land, girded by sea on both sides, which is the settlement. Day dawned, cold and grey above the airstrip. As the sky lightened, two things were dramatically obvious. The first was that there were eleven Argentine aircraft – a squadron's worth – dispersed about 2000 yards from the patrol's position. That was the good news. The bad news was that where the patrol lay and as far away as they could see, the ground was as flat as a football pitch with no protective cover whatever. The Argentine sentries were not alert but they were present. To try to walk away would have been suicidal. Even to crawl out with the bulky Bergens on their backs would have been to risk almost certain discovery. So the four abandoned the rucksacks and slithered away like slow, cautious serpents. When at last they reached dead ground they laid up throughout the day. The only equipment they had now were their Armalite rifles and belt kit containing ammunition and survival gear. That night they marched back to their firm base. Some time in the early hours of the following morning, 13 May, they signalled their findings to *Hermes* and preparations began immediately. The squadron's orders were to destroy all the aircraft and kill everyone in the garrison.

Time was of the essence now. The longer the raid was delayed the greater the risk that the reconnaissance team's abandoned equipment would be discovered. Equally oppressive was the pressure on helicopter time. Between 16 and 19 May the available Sea Kings were committed to a resupply of G Squadron's covert reconnaissance patrols. They had now been living hard for two weeks and resupply could not be put off. Aboard *Hermes*, D Squadron started drawing the weapons and ammunition it would need for Operation Prelim.

For reasons which are not clear, naval planners miscalculated the time it would take to bring the carrier within helicopter range of the target. This in turn meant a late dash into the target area, sailing at speed into a high wind, which ruled out movement on the flight deck. This meant that the helicopters could not be made ready. The result was that only one of the two original objectives – destruction of the aircraft – could be sustained. For the time being the lives of the Argentines manning the garrison were to be spared.

The revised plan of attack had the great virtue of simplicity. Only one troop – John Hamilton's Mountain Troop of about 20 men – would attack the airstrip itself. Another would remain in reserve to deal with any unexpected opposition. A third would seal the two approaches to the settlement. Finally, the remaining Boat Troop men not involved in the original Pebble Island reconnaissance (who were still staked out there) would protect the mortar team as well as the Royal Artillery officer, Captain Chris Brown, who was to direct fire from the destroyer *Glamorgan*. With everyone standing by and ready to board the Sea Kings, the helicopters were still not ready. After an agonising wait of 90 minutes – the worst point in any military adventure – the three 'choppers' whined off *Hermes*'s deck and away into a windswept morning. It was still dark.

Awaiting the raiders at the landing zone 45 minutes later was the Boat Troop captain and his reconnaissance team. Despite the great need of haste, weapons, ammunition and explosive charges were unloaded with fastidious care, and the helicopters departed. Then, in bright moonlight, the captain briefed Squadron and Troop officers about the target, a mere four miles away. This did not take long, and in absolute silence, the Squadron moved off behind him. As well as his own equipment each man carried two bombs for the 81mm mortar, an additional load of 13 pounds. These were deposited at the mortar position. The teams which were to seal off the settlement, and the one which was to attack the airstrip, were then guided to their destinations by scouts from the Boat Troop reconnaissance team. The Boat Troop captain personally conducted Hamilton and his assault squad to their target.

It was now 7am. According to the original plan this was the time at which the raid should have been concluded. D Squadron therefore had just thirty minutes in which to do its worst. For the Squadron to stay longer could have put *Hermes* at risk. She, after all, had to approach within helicopter range for the raiders to be recovered. Ideally, the recovery would be complete and *Hermes,* together with *Glamorgan,* would be turning for safer waters before first light.

At first, Mountain Troop did not tackle its task as an orthodox, text-book demolition job. With so little time to spare the men were at first content to blast away with small arms and 66mm rockets at the aircraft dispersed around them, a process known to soldiers as 'brassing up'. These aircraft were six Pucara ground attack planes, a Skyvan transport and four Beech Mentor trainers. By now, *Glamorgan*'s guns were firing on the Argentine trenches as a diversionary measure. The only response was a sporadic burst of small arms fire from the trenches, on the other side of the airfield.

As it became clear that the opposition was not going to interfere too seriously, Hamilton's raiders moved on to the airstrip proper, within sight of the trenches, and started to destroy the aircraft in a cool, systematic way, using standard SAS high explosive charges and more 66mm missiles. By now, Argentine ammunition and fuel stores were ablaze as a result of naval gunfire. Soon after 7am, one of the troop was hit by shrapnel in the left leg. Staff Sergeant Currass, a veteran 'medic', dressed the wound and the man continued fighting. By now Pebble Island airstrip looked like the scene of a spectacular military tattoo, but one aircraft remained apparently undamaged. Covered by Hamilton, Trooper Raymond ('Paddy') Armstrong, a demolition specialist, went forward and disposed of it. He and his troop captain that night shared the distinction of wrecking at least two Argentine aircraft each, and Armstrong was promptly nick-named 'Pucara Paddy'. Neither man was to live to see the end of the campaign.

Silhouetted against the burning aircraft the troop spread out and began to fall back off the airstrip, towards the agreed rendezvous. As they did so a landmine was exploded on command from the Argentine lines. It blew up in the centre of the troop, the blast hurling Corporal Paul Bunker 10 feet. Bunker, a mild-mannered Royal Army Ordnance Corps private turned SAS free-faller, was concussed. Miraculously he and his comrade, hit by shrapnel earlier in the operation, were the only casualties. That man, now faint from loss of blood, was given an escort of two men and told to go direct to the final rendezvous where the Sea Kings were to collect the whole Squadron. As this party reached the edge of the airstrip they heard four or five Argentine voices nearby, shouting towards the settlement. The wounded SAS soldier opened fire with a grenade launcher attached to his Armalite rifle, and kept firing until screams told him he had hit his target. So far as is known, this was the only Argentine casualty of the night. As things had turned out, the destruction of military hardware with minimal bloodshed appeared as a model of clinical, constrained use of force, though that had not been the original intention.

At 7.15, Hamilton's troop regrouped and with its wounded moved through the forward rendezvous manned by a captain and Squadron Sergeant-Major Lawrence Gallagher. At 7.30 contact with the enemy was broken off and the rest of the Squadron was on its way. At 9.30, right on time, the helicopters returned. First aboard were the injured men, swiftly followed by the exhausted reconnaissance team. No one spoke much during the eighty-minute flight back to *Hermes*. Everyone was trying to come to terms with an SAS raid modelled on the offensive style of David Stirling in the western desert. It was the sort of thing most of them had only read about until that night.

Only later did they learn that the Argentine garrison totalled 114 men, outnumbering the attackers by about three-to-one. The impact on Argentine morale elsewhere was devastating. First, South Georgia had fallen with no more than token resistance. Now a Falklands garrison was unable to prevent the destruction of eleven valuable aircraft. There had been no pursuit, hot or cold, by the defenders after the raid. One senior British officer (not an SAS officer) let it be known that the raid established the 'moral ascendancy' of the British Army even before its main forces were put ashore. Certainly this was the message promptly conveyed to the Argentine occupation army through Spanish language broadcasts by 'Radio Atlantico', an official British radio station hastily established at Ascension Island. The next time the phrase 'moral ascendancy' was used, was after 2 Para's battle for Goose Green.

The Pebble Island raid also had an odd postscript. On 25 May the destroyer *Coventry* was sunk by three Argentine bombs and 19 of her crew were killed. Task force planners suspected that an American-built mobile ANTPS-43 radar was still functioning at Pebble Island and had guided the Skyhawk bombers to sink *Coventry*. An SBS team, inserted by trawler, spent ten days scouring Pebble Island for the radar, without success. This team counted 120 Argentine servicemen at the base and a new attack was planned for 15 June. Two RAF Harriers were to bomb the airstrip, after which 34 SBS men were to wipe out any of the garrison who survived. In the event, the Argentine high command at Port Stanley capitulated 24 hours before this attack and, for the time being, the conflict was over. The SBS accepted the surrender of 112 Argentines at Pebble Island . . . and the SAS Boat Troop captain who had led the original reconnaissance of 10–14 May returned to look for his soldiers' missing rucksacks. They were still where the team had left them. Much later, Admiral Woodward summed up the operation: 'Easily the best example of a successful "All-Arms" special operation we are likely to see in a very long while. A short-notice operation carried out with speed and dash: no dead, one injured and eleven aircraft written off in one hour. Total time from start to finish, five days. Remarkable. But . . . because it succeeded on this occasion, it may be tempting to expect such operations to be feasible in this, or shorter, time scales at the drop of a hat. The time-scale will usually be longer and the assets needed . . . considerable.'

Sea King Disaster

The Pebble Island raid had provided the task force with an auspicious beginning to a week which was to conclude on 21 May with the stunningly successful landing of 3000 troops on the narrow beaches of San Carlos, without loss of life. For the SAS it was the week in which it suffered the greatest single blow in its post-war history: the loss of a Sea King helicopter with twenty men serving, in one capacity or another, with 22 SAS Regiment.

While the Pebble Island raid was taking place the finishing touches were being put to the invasion plan. On 13 May, the day when Royal Marine SBS patrols had reported that the proposed beachhead and the hills overlooking it were 'clean', individual assault units were assigned their beaches and places in the order of battle. A sense of expectancy and anticipation, mixed with anxiety, gripped the invasion fleet as it made its rendezvous with the carrier group led by *Hermes* on a flat calm sea on 18 May. Ashore the reconnaissance patrols of G Squadron were still fighting their private, silent war of information gathering.

D Squadron, meanwhile, had been briefed for a characteristically ambitious raid in the area of Darwin/Goose Green. The Argentine garrison had been identified by G Squadron; now it was up to D Squadron to tie it down long enough for the vulnerable landing force to get ashore unscathed a few miles to the north. On 19 May, two days before D-Day, D Squadron moved from *Hermes* to the multi-purpose assault ship *Intrepid* to prepare for this assault. Two hours after dusk, at about 9.30pm, the last elements of the Squadron clambered into the Sea King for the five-minute flight across the half-mile of water separating the two ships. One of those on board described it as, 'a routine flight; nothing exciting about it'. Most of those on the lift were men of John Hamilton's Mountain Troop, including the two men wounded during the Pebble Island raid. They had come from the carrier's sick-bay and were given the first two places aboard the helicopter. Not all the passengers were fully-fledged, 'badged' insiders of the SAS Regiment. Some were specialists attached to the Regiment who wore the same beige beret but kept their own, separate cap badges. Nevertheless, they went to war with the SAS and took the same chances. Among them were soldiers of the Royal Army Medical Corps and an RAF Flight Lieutenant, Garth Hawkins. An expert in directing air strikes to support special operations, Hawkins delighted in the vagrant, gypsy life he had discovered with the SAS. The Regiment regarded him as one of its own. Finally, there were the helicopter crew: pilot, co-pilot and navigator.

The two wounded men sat up front, on the port side,

behind the co-pilot. On the opposite side, almost facing
them, was the space from which, for operational convenience, the main door had been removed. As they settled down
the rest followed, glad to be on the move after a long wait. To
avoid further delays, no one asked for the cumbersome,
tight-fitting rubber survival suit which passengers are normally obliged to wear for a helicopter flight over water. One
of those on board later told the author that he was wearing
ordinary Army boots, socks, a blue boiler suit, heavy-duty
sweater, uninflated life-jacket, 'and that was it'.

As the helicopter lifted off into the darkness, *Intrepid* was
sailing abreast of *Hermes*, on the carrier's port side. Both
vessels were heaving on a rolling sea. The Sea King made a
circuit from the stern end of *Hermes*, away out to starboard
and then round *Intrepid*. The helicopter was not permitted to
land immediately, however, because another helicopter
which had touched down on *Intrepid* moments before had yet
to be cleared away from the flight deck. This meant that that
machine's engine had to be stopped and its rotor blades
folded before it could be stowed away. As a result, the Sea
King was obliged to make a second circuit.

When it was roughly midway between the two ships, some
of those on board heard a double report from the engine.
Others felt 'something like a sledgehammer blow' near the
front end of the Sea King. At that point the helicopter was
between 300ft and 500ft above the sea. 'Then we were in the
water, in complete darkness. Everything happened so fast.
One moment we were flying, then we were submerged. I told
myself not to panic. But there was no way of knowing which
way was up or down. At first I thought, "There must be a
way out". I was groping around and thought I was drowning,' said one man.

At this point, in fact, the Sea King was still afloat – just –
although capsized and becoming engulfed. 'Then someone
trampled all over the top of me and disappeared. I thought
there might be a chance for me, too. But the person who
trampled over me knocked the air out of my lungs. I reached

up, trying to find something. Because the helicopter had
rolled over, those of us who were sitting on the port side were
now nearest the door on the starboard side. When I found
something I grabbed hold of it and pulled myself up. In fact it
was the main door. But I was still trapped by something. I
think it was a life-jacket round my waist. I eventually freed
myself and bobbed to the surface beside the co-pilot.

He had a small automatic light on his shoulder and was
about 10 feet away. I made my way to him. I didn't have a
life-jacket any more and I'm not the best of swimmers. I
grabbed hold of his shoulder. He inflated a one-man dinghy
so I let go of him and grabbed hold of that. It was capsized,
but afloat. Then I found I couldn't move one arm. I was also
being sick. I held on as firmly as I could with the good arm
and hoped for the best. There were more and more people
coming towards us now. It was very dark.'

For another survivor the main recollection of the crash was
that he was hurled about in complete darkness, under water.
For him the journey to the surface seemed to take for ever.
On the surface, vomiting a mixture of seawater and aviation
fuel, he noted that the only remaining trace of the big
helicopter was one wheel which occasionally broke surface.
He, too, swam to the inverted dinghy. Soon ten survivors,
including the pilot and co-pilot, were clinging to it. When
their improvised life-raft rose on the crest of a wave they
could see lights aboard *Intrepid.* These seemed now to be a
long way off.

Those wearing life-jackets inflated them and held on more
grimly than ever, yet still talked to one another, encouraging
the injured not to let go. 'Hold on. Stay calm. They'll come
soon,' someone said. The aircrew were not going to leave
rescue to chance. Somehow they managed to make their
personal search-and-rescue beacons work and they fired
flares. By the time the first search helicopter found them,
hovering a few feet away, its searchlight probing the darkness, most of the survivors were near the fatal point of
unconsciousness. The machine circled, flew away and

returned seconds later. At first, the helicopter winchman tried to put his rescue loop round one casualty whose shoulder had been dislocated. The man merely shook his head. To release the tenuous hold he had on the raft with his one good arm already numbed by cold would mean the end. Around the raft the exhausted men discussed tersely who should go first. The corporal who was nominated still had the dinghy's painter, wrapped round his wrist. As the helicopter moved away so he dragged the dinghy with him . . . but only for a second. He released the rope in the nick of time.

The survivors had now been in the sea for thirty minutes, far beyond the time anyone could rationally expect to survive in those waters. They could not hope to last much longer. At this moment a small rescue craft from the frigate *Brilliant* found them. As they were hauled inboard several of the survivors collapsed, pole-axed by a combination of shock and exposure. Some were already verging on hypothermia. One SAS soldier, still wearing his bulky belt kit, could not help himself into the rescue craft even to the limited extent of reaching up an arm for help. One of *Brilliant's* crew, risking his own life, promptly jumped into the water to help the man to safety. He was characteristic of *Brilliant*, a vessel in the thick of every bit of trouble, usually in support of Special Forces operations.

All the survivors, except for the man winched out by helicopter, woke up aboard *Brilliant*. One of them came round after more than two hours to find himself curled up, totally naked, under a hot shower. It was a radical but effective way of dealing with hypothermia, a condition in which the body's core temperature, having fallen to a certain level, will continue to drop fatally unless drastic steps are taken to reheat it. His rescuers put the man into bed, where he lay awake throughout that night. Impressions of his ordeal came crowding back . . . the moment when he thought he was drowning and all he could think of, to stay alive, were 'the wife and kids'. . . the questions, most importantly, how many had been lost? All those who had clung to the dinghy clung also to the belief that somehow, the others would have been picked up. But in the isolated condition of all who have been 'casevacked' out of a military operation they were now out of the mainstream.

Firm information drifted to them only in snippets as they made their way back to Britain aboard *Canberra* (after the D-Day bombings) and the QE-II. What they did not know until much later was that they, the ten who had clung to the dinghy, were the only survivors. The full extent of the disaster reached Britain somewhat faster. Within twenty-four hours reporters in London had been given an outline of what had happened. Aside from speculative reports about SAS reconnaissance patrols, this was the only news about the Regiment to reach Britain prior to 6 June. It was to relieve the blow to morale caused to SAS families – which, through mail from home, might have had a knock-on effect upon the morale of SAS soldiers in the field – that the record was set straight. It was done through the medium of war correspondent Max Hastings. In a memorable, pooled dispatch he gave a graphic account of SAS successes.

The precise cause of the Sea King crash, like much else about the South Atlantic conflict, may never be known. It is significant that after the incident a mass of bloodstained feathers was sighted floating near the scene. This, combined with the double bang from the helicopter engine, convinced knowledgeable observers that this was yet another disaster caused by a bird. It is improbable that the bird was – as some inevitably speculate – an unlucky albatross. The Royal Society for the Protection of Birds suggests that the giant petrel, almost as large, with a wingspan of up to 6 feet, was the more likely cause. Flocks of these fly from the Falklands, following ships in search of food.

What is certain is that Hamilton's troop lost a significant percentage of its best men in the crash. The Regiment lost two squadron sergeant-majors. Mountain Troop losses from D Squadron included most of the veterans who had played an important part in recapturing South Georgia, and the

Pebble Island raid, including Staff Sergeant Philip Curass, Sergeant Sid Davidson, Sergeant 'Lofty' Arthy, Corporal Paul Bunker and Trooper ('Pucara Paddy') Armstrong. Also killed was the Squadron Sergeant-Major, Lawrence Gallagher, who had restored the Union Jack to South Georgia.

G Squadron's Sergeant-Major, Malcolm ('Akker') Atkinson, a former Grenadier from Barnsley, who had been with the squadron since its formation in Borneo, was another significant casualty. His career spanned twelve fully operational tours and he was a veteran of Mirbat. Other veterans were Staff Sergeant Paddy O'Connor (Irish Guards), the Stinger missile expert and an SAS soldier since 1966; Sergeant W.J. (Taff) Hughes (Welsh Guards); Sergeant P. (Taff) Jones, a former Welsh Guards regimental rugby player, latterly converted to angling, and an SAS soldier since 1975.

Yet another G Squadron casualty was Corporal Willy Hatton, QGM, the Regiment's first fully qualified diving supervisor. Hatton was originally a Royal Marine SBS diver who subsequently worked for a civilian company in the North Sea. He then joined the Army and was as successful with the SAS as he had been with the commandos. Indeed he was attached to 2 SBS during the Falkands campaign as one of a small team, including an SAS medic, which boarded and seized the 1400-ton Argentine spy trawler *Narwhal* on 10 May after it had been disabled by an RAF Harrier.

The SAS support arms lost Corporal William ('Paddy') Begley (Royal Corps of Transport), a small, lithe mountaineer; Corporal John Newton (REME) an armourer; Corporal Rab Burns (Royal Signals) signaller and bagpiper; Corporal Steve Sykes, signaller, marathon runner and cross-country skier; Lance-Corporal Paul Lightfoot and Corporal Michael McHugh (Royal Signals). Flight-Lieutenant Garth Hawkins, RAF and his signaller and partner, Corporal Douglas McCormack (Royal Signals) were an inseparable team and they died together. Hawkins, a forward air controller, was about to return to civilian life and had just bought a pub. Finally there was Corporal Edward ('Wally') Walpole, a Greenjacket, who had served as D Squadron storeman for five years and was, albeit unbadged, a regimental character.

In all, the SAS and support specialists lost twenty men. Others in Mountain Troop survived the helicopter crash but were sent back to Britain to recover. They included two of the men wounded at Pebble Island one of whom, still in his twenties, had also survived two successive helicopter crashes on Fortuna Glacier. He is now nicknamed 'Splash'. To replace the Sea King casualties, replacements including 'unbadged' signallers were flown from Britain by way of Ascension Island to join the task force. The last lap of their journey was a parachute drop from an RAF Hercules into the cold South Atlantic. Some of these men were in the water for 40 minutes before they were picked up by the Royal Navy, and were dangerously close to becoming exposure cases.

A Beachhead Compromised

The most critical reconnaissance of the entire Falklands conflict was in the hands of the SBS. This was proper. As amphibious experts they were the most appropriate people to examine the approaches to the invasion beaches and the tactically sensitive areas overlooking them. Without proper reconnaissance the slow-moving landing-craft, crowded with soldiers, would be sitting ducks. On 1 May, when the first 'advance force' recce patrols went ashore, four possible sites – one on West Falkland – were being considered as invasion beachheads. San Carlos, at that time, rated only third in order of preference. The SBS, with a mere 84 men available and denied helicopter transport at the most delicate phase of reconnaissance, had to land its parties, check each widespread area, withdraw, report exhaustively to the R Group on board *Fearless*, and then land again at the next site. There were not enough men or helicopters to keep all options under continuous scrutiny. The data required ranged from beach angles to the inland going for men and vehicles. It was too detailed to be sent by radio. The information gleaned from a 'simple' beach reconnaissance, one expert estimates, would require four hours' transmission time. Any signaller staying on the air for a fraction of that time would certainly be 'DF'ed. Despite such difficulties, General Sir Jeremy Moore was later to reveal that 'we worked throughout on allocating fourteen days to special forces' reconnaissance before the main landing.'

On 8 May, about three days before the final choice of beachhead was made, the SBS had to withdraw two teams from the San Carlos area. A third, at Ajax Bay overlooking San Carlos Water, remained hiding among the ferns in front of an abandoned refrigeration plant. On 13 May, when this patrol had been on watch for sixteen days, an Argentine helicopter landed only 100 yards from the SBS hide while the pilot dismounted to relieve himself. Even more daunting, six more Argentine helicopters – two Puma, two Huey, two unidentified – landed on Lookout Hill overlooking San Carlos Settlement. From these machines an Argentine Army search party started to sweep the area, which another SBS patrol had left a few days before. The Ajax Bay patrol, 'thinking their time had come', flashed a radio signal 'in clear' (uncoded) to report that their position was in imminent danger of discovery. For the special force commanders aboard *Fearless*, it was a particularly gloomy moment. Ashore, it seemed, the Argentines and SBS were missing one another as narrowly as characters in a bedroom farce by Feydeau. The British Government had vigorously declined to confirm that any of its forces were back on the islands. If the Argentines captured such men, the Junta in its turn would be under no pressure to confirm the captives' existence as prisoners of war. The implications of that grey area were not good. In the event, the SBS men who thought they had been discovered kept their heads down and held their fire. Their brief radio signal, so far as they could judge, went

undetected by the enemy and they were safely withdrawn
under cover of darkness on 15 May.

On that same day, the R Group planners received a tip
which they had to take seriously. This asserted that the
Argentines were in a position at Fanning Head known as
Point 234 which, the source said, was '4 kilometres north of
San Carlos'. This puzzled the R Group analysts. Fanning
Head is *14* kilometres north and several kilometres west of
San Carlos. The analysts now had to make the best guess
they could as to where the Argentines really were: in the
immediate vicinity of San Carlos, where the SBS men had
spotted them from Ajax Bay, or almost ten miles away on
Fanning Head, overlooking the approaches to San Carlos
Water. As one of them put it, 'we knew there were Argentines
in the area and said so. We did not know exactly where they
were. The analysts' best, and first guess was wrong.
Although one SBS officer noted on 13 May, a full week before
the landing, that a full enemy company might be either on
Fanning Head or Lookout Hill above San Carlos, the truth
was that both places were manned. The greatest Argentine
strength was in Port San Carlos settlement, immediately
overlooking the main invasion beaches.

The vital San Carlos reconnaissance operation was in
trouble in other respects. As we have noted, all the teams
except that at Ajax Bay were withdrawn on 8 May, when the
final choice of beachhead was still three days away. The Ajax
Bay team came out on 15 May when the narrow squeaks of
previous days made it appear that the team's time was
running out. Discovery seemed imminent. On 11 May, once
San Carlos was finally chosen as the main landing area, the
SBS tried to restore its coverage. But that scheme was stalled
by lack of Sea King helicopters to put the recce teams back
ashore. The aircraft concerned were by now committed to
the SAS raid on Pebble Island. Immediately after that raid,
Hermes, the Sea Kings' host carrier, sailed away north to meet
the amphibious force on its way south from Ascension
Island. The Sea Kings went with it.

   The SBS now made energetic efforts to reinsert reconnaissance patrols by ship. On 16 May the Ajax Bay OP was reoccupied after a gap of 24 hours. The same day, the frigate *Alacrity* landed another patrol, with a Gunner officer, south of Ajax Bay. During the next twenty-four hours this team marched to a spot overlooking San Carlos Water. It reported no activity in the Port San Carlos area which was, in fact, some miles from its position and the other side of a hill. On 17 May a third SBS recce team, specifically charged to watch Port San Carlos, was to be put ashore from the frigate *Brilliant,* at Middle Bay, well to the north of the target area. This position is on the opposite side of Fanning Head peninsula from Port San Carlos and screened from it by the mass of the peninsula itself. Approaching the shore in rubber boats, the SBS men needed no psychic powers to perceive that the area was occupied by Argentines. Their camp fires and voices conveyed the message that the approaches to the British landing site had been reinforced. For the team to follow its original orders and cross an enemy occupied hill, risking capture at such a late stage, could have compromised everything. So the Marines, after paddling quietly round the bay for two hours, returned to *Brilliant.* Their judgement was initially criticized by their SBS commanding officer, but applauded by the Brigade chief, Brigadier Julian Thompson.

   With little more than three days left before the biggest British amphibious operation since 1944, the R Group knew it had a problem. The enemy had reinforced the landing area, but no one knew exactly in what strength or how extensively. After another 24 hours, with the amphibious force closing on the approaches to East Falkland, the SBS again asked for helicopters to put their recce patrols ashore. Again the request was turned down. The most the SBS could hope for was a minimum number of aircraft to fly a force to Fanning Head six hours before the main landing. At best, the Argentines might be persuaded to surrender without a fight as at South Georgia. If they did it could repair the Intelligence gap at a stroke. For this reason the SBS team going ashore at Fanning Head was told that live prisoners were more important than dead enemy. The mixture was to be one of sweet persuasion and military muscle, if necessary. The mixture was to prove almost fatal for those who administered it.

The Fanning Head squad was allocated two Wessex helicopters which flew from the destroyer *Antrim*. Because of the need to store one aircraft with rotors folded while the other took off, the first Wessex was obliged to hover above *Antrim* for a long time while the second was made ready . . . So long, in fact, that when the second started flying, the first had to land again to refuel, while the second hovered in its turn and waited . . . All this in foul weather and darkness, just before a sensitive and difficult operation. When, finally, the whole party was assembled it included not only the SBS but also an SAS mortar team, a public-address device known as a 'bullhorn' and a remarkable Royal Marine captain named Roderick Bell, who speaks colloquial Argentine-Spanish. He was later to play a uniquely useful role in partnership with the SAS, in bringing the conflict to an end without prolonged bloodshed.

The operation started with a novel and startling success. Although the helicopters were older than most of the men they carried, one of them, a Mk V, was fitted with a piece of equipment with which police in the Home Counties had been experimenting to search for bodies abandoned in dense woodland. This device, a thermal imager, records the presence of a living or even a recently dead body by registering its heat. The imager can select from an entire apartment block which flats are occupied and which are not. The other Wessex, the anti-submarine Mk III piloted by Ian Stanley, carried the radar required to guide the Mk V through fog, rain and darkness for a 'hoovering' operation over the peninsula. Then, after several sweeps which drew a blank, tell-tale white spots indicating either sheep or men, appeared on the screen. In this, its first use as a war weapon, the imager identified 22 bodies hiding near Point 234. They were Argentines, and, as later became apparent, they were armed with two 106mm recoilless rifles and at least one mortar which could have caused hideous damage to the landing force.

The SBS men and their expert assistants, including a Gunner officer to direct *Antrim*'s two 4.5in guns, were set down about 1000 yards from the Argentines' position. The Mk V Wessex had to make five journeys from *Antrim* before the whole team was assembled. Each time the helicopter touched down on Fanning Head it needed the aid of lights, a highly dangerous undertaking on such an operation. Unlike the Sea Kings, it was not a 'PGN' machine which could see in total darkness. Once ashore the landing force divided into two groups, one to tackle the known position on Fanning Head; the other to sort out the suspect area overlooking Port San Carlos.

It was still dark when the Fanning Head party moved off. Finding the enemy was not a problem. The team had a man-portable thermal imager. Making non-violent contact with the Argentines was another matter. Bell went forward, unescorted, into the darkness and tried to make himself understood. It is unclear whether all 22 Argentines ever heard his words. A strong wind often obliterated his voice, as he stood calling into the darkness. The first response to his presence was a burst of machine-gun fire which ripped through an SBS man's rucksack at a range of 900 yards. The SBS did not return fire immediately for fear of hitting Bell with cross-fire and because their orders were to give first priority to taking prisoners. But with Bell safely back in the fold this restraint was removed. The first return burst by an SBS machine-gunner killed the Argentine who had started the shooting. Then *Antrim*'s guns were ranged on the enemy position. In the resulting slaughter another eleven Argentines were killed and three wounded. None escaped.

Meanwhile, the second SBS team, a four-man patrol, moved down the coast of Fanning Head peninsula to Port San Carlos beach. The original Intelligence reports, as well as military sense, suggested that any Argentine troops in the area would have taken up positions on the hills above the settlement. The Argentines had not fallen in with this logic. About half a company – some 60 men – were sheltering in the settlement itself when the shooting started on Fanning Head. Alarmed by the noise, they quietly started to pull out and make for the sanctuary of the hills. The SBS team stayed on the beach to await the first wave of assault troops from the Paras and 40 Commando, unaware of the enemy force just behind them, in the village. If the Argentines knew that a British reconnaissance force was only a few yards away, they gave no sign of it. Neither side pushed its luck. As a result, the first wave of troops from the main landing force, Parachute Regiment, were surprised by the evident presence of the Argentines inland about a mile away. When they came under mortar fire from the Paras they beat a hasty retreat but later that morning, they scored their first success, shooting down two Royal Marine helicopters as the aircraft escorted a Sea King ferrying ashore a Rapier missile battery. Three out of the four Gazelle crewmen were killed.

'Brassing-up' Goose Green

During that same long night, D Squadron of the SAS was in action again. Its march to attack a 1200-strong garrison at Goose Green was later described by one participant as 'the toughest hike I've ever done with the SAS'. The Squadron depleted as a result of the Sea King helicopter losses little more than 24 hours earlier, flew from *Intrepid* to land east of Darwin/Goose Green. It then began a fighting march of 20 hours' duration. Each man carried at least 80 pounds, mostly ordnance. The purpose of the operation – one of several diversionary raids that night – was to convince the Goose Green garrison that it was under attack from a battalion-size unit of 500–600 men rather than one of one-tenth that number. So the instruction was, 'Noise, firepower, but no close engagement.' To accomplish this the Squadron was armed with general-purpose machine-guns, mortars and the American M-203 grenade launcher used at Pebble Island. The anti-aircraft missile, Stinger, was also brought along. This firepower was augmented by the guns of the frigate *Ardent*.

Right on time, from the low hills north of Darwin/Goose Green, the Squadron laid down its barrage, pouring Milan missiles, machine-gun bullets and tracer into the Argentine positions. The SAS men were spread as widely as possible and shifted their positions frequently. The Argentines returned fire, but did not attempt to advance beyond the safety of their own perimeter. Meanwhile, 2 Para had landed at the head of San Carlos Water and was now advancing up Sussex Mountain, in the direction of Darwin/Goose Green. At daybreak the SAS broke contact and marched north to meet the advancing Paras. From the rendezvous the Paras watched as the small SAS column came over the horizon and marched down a forward slope. Then from a clear blue sky, the drone of an unfamiliar aircraft engine heralded a black shape which floated in a leisurely, menacing fashion from the same direction as the SAS men. It was a Pucara, the heavily armed, slow-flying counter-insurgency aircraft, specially designed to attack ground forces. The SAS column spread out, melting into the ground, but to the spectators it seemed certain that some of the men they had just seen would never move again. But warfare is full of surprises. From one SAS position a lone figure rose deliberately, something dark on his shoulder flashing towards the aircraft. The pilot seems to have become aware of his mortal peril when it was too late. As his aircraft exploded some of the men of 2 Para stood and cheered, waving their fists as if watching a goal scored at a football game. Robert Fox, a BBC war correspondent, recalls, 'We saw a cloud of blue smoke and a piece of material fluttering like an autumn leaf. Dangling underneath was a body; it was the parachute of a pilot whose Pucara had been shot down . . . by an SAS patrol covering the landing.' The Stinger had stung.

Later the same day, as Argentine air force attacks began in earnest, the same SAS soldier tried to add to his bag. From a carefully-selected firing point he released five more Stingers at incoming aircraft. To his disgust, they all missed. Then, with the rest of the Squadron, he returned by helicopter to the assault ship *Intrepid*. Neither the missile nor the man could be blamed for the five aircraft which got away. The only man with the task force trained to use Stinger was Staff Sergeant O'Connor, who had died in the Sea King helicopter crash. His training manuals were lost with him. D Squadron was having to learn to use the missile by trial and error. The first-round kill on Sussex Mountain was a lucky shot. The others, fired out of range, fell short.

The Squadron's maritime guardian angel did not get off so lightly. As the sun rose, the frigate *Ardent* – isolated from the rest of the fleet in Grantham Sound – came under savage attack from the air. At one stage, eleven enemy aircraft appeared to form a queue to hit the ship. *Ardent* destroyed one Pucara and carried on fighting despite the fact that she was now drifting out of control, her Seacat missile and 4.5in gun disabled together with her propulsion. Finally her skipper, Captain Alan West, ordered his men to abandon ship. He was later awarded the Distinguished Service Cross.

The intervention of both the SAS and SBS had removed three potential threats to the men of 3 Commando Brigade as they came ashore. Some units, discovering their assigned beaches covered by dangerously deep water, were obliged to check the depth themselves with poles before getting ashore where they could. A few blamed such problems on poor reconnaissance. They were unaware of an order from Brigadier Julian Thompson to the SBS to stay away from the precise landing places to avoid compromising them. Both naval and military top brass believed they had enough beach information without adding to the risk of detection at the last moment in an effort to reinvent the wheel. In general, the landings had gone better than anyone could have hoped. Even a hundred determined and well-armed men could have given the landing force a bloody nose. As might the Argentine Air Force have done, if it had struck earlier. But by the time the first air raid began in the 'Bomb Alley' of San Carlos Water on the morning of 21 May, most of the troops were ashore. When the enemy aircraft did appear, they concentrated their attack – as captured pilots told their SAS interrogators later – on warships and not the vital transports, including *Canberra*, whose supplies would sustain the expeditionary force ashore.

There was no good reason for the Argentines' sluggish response to the British landing. Argentine troops had been in Port San Carlos until the early hours of D-Day as well as on Fanning Head. The Argentines there do not seem to have made a convincing job of alerting their headquarters in Port Stanley before they fled. There was no Paul Revere to ride out with the warning, 'The British are coming!' That was our good luck. The landing of a 2400-strong expeditionary force 8000 miles from home on a beachhead already compromised, and with insufficient air cover, needed luck. During the first 24 hours after the landing, five out of eight warships lying in the approaches to San Carlos Water were hit by Argentine bombs. The frigate *Ardent*, supporting an SAS operation, was sunk and *Argonaut* was badly damaged. *Antrim*, *Brilliant* and *Broadsword* were more fortunate. Bombs which struck them did not explode. During the first 48 hours, eighty Argentine aircraft flew against the fleet, their pilots displaying the reckless courage of nineteenth-century cavalrymen. In that same period, the Argentine air force lost seven Mirage and four A-4 Skyhawk jets, three Pucara, one Chinook helicopter and one Puma. On 23 May, D+2, *Antelope* exploded spectacularly and sank, and *Glasgow* was hit by an unexploded bomb. Next day, the landing ships *Sir Galahad* and *Sir Lancelot* were also hit by UXBs. On 25 May *Atlantic Conveyor* was crippled by an Exocet missile and sank after only one of her valuable cargo of Chinook helicopters, and 14 Sea Harriers had been salvaged. That loss was to have sombre implications for the SAS. The same day, the destroyer *Coventry* went to the bottom. During this period, at least seventeen more Argentine planes, most of them fast jets, were brought down. In the eerie periods of calm between air attacks, the British were piling ashore tons of food, ammunition, Rapier missiles, tracked vehicles and other paraphernalia of an expeditionary force. On the beachhead it was a time to dig in, consolidate and wait.

Overlooking the scene from the chilly heights of Sussex Mountain, the men of 2 Para watched and waited impatiently. They could not advance yet. The SAS were still busy in the area ahead of them, around Argentine-occupied Darwin/Goose Green. The SBS, meanwhile, had established reconnaissance patrols 35 miles ahead of the beachhead, sprinkled along the north coast route to Port Stanley. From well out to sea, they penetrated miles inland along East Falkland waterways. One explored Port Salvador water, and withdrew just before the Argentines retreating from the Fanning Head/Port San Carlos actions arrived there. Another team, from 6 SBS, travelled 30 miles by small boat from *Fearless*, to land and hide at Green Island. From this position they ran close reconnaissance of Port St Louis and Green Patch for a week until the Commando brigade reached them. Soon afterwards, 2 SBS was inserted from *Intrepid* to carry out a careful survey of Teal Inlet. Before 3 Para arrived there the hard way, on foot, the SBS had discovered good news for them. There were no Argentines at Teal.

From the main beachhead the fastest and most direct route to Port Stanley, and victory, was the southerly one across which 2 Para now sat and waited. In time, the British would advance along both coasts. But first, in the south, was a threat which had to be removed.

The island of East Falkland is shaped like an egg-timer which leans eccentrically to the right at an angle of 45 degrees. The 'neck' of the egg-timer is a narrow isthmus on which lie, Darwin Settlement to the north, separated by a few miles from Goose Green Settlement to the south. The isthmus, at sea level on each flank, rises inland to a series of low

but easily defended escarpments. The approaches to it from
the north, the direction of the main British advance, are
screened by a series of low ridges rising to about 300 feet,
facing across a valley towards the forward downslope of
Sussex Mountain. It is not a place where the element of
surprise has much going for it. Yet for the southerly route to
be opened up, it had to be taken. The four-man SAS patrol
there, responsible for watching an area of about ten square
kilometres, had accurately reported the number of enemy
fighting troops. 600 men of 2 and 12 Regiments. Twelve
Regiment was a hand-picked Argentine mobile reaction
force. So long as it remained the Argentines could threaten
the British beachhead. It could not be by-passed.

Intelligence Controversy

The battle fought by 2 Para to win the isthmus has been
graphically described elsewhere and is only summarized
here. What should be noted is that the number of Argentine
prisoners taken by 2 Para totalled 1100. Another 200 of the
enemy were killed. The British battalion's all-up strength for
the assault was 450 and its fatal casualties, seventeen.
According to the *Sunday Times*, 'The Intelligence was wrong
. . . If the true odds had been known, the attack might never
have taken place.' The *Sunday Express* magazine team, however, after examining the evidence afresh, concluded that the
'faulty Intelligence' story was a myth generated by the unexpectedly large number of Argentine prisoners. 'Intelligence,'
it argued, 'did not predict the hundreds of "extras" – naval,
Marine and HQ elements – who were there but who played
little part in the battle.' Additionally, as two independent
researches show, some Argentine reserves were brought into
the settlement by helicopter from Mount Kent a few hours
before Goose Green surrendered. These reinforcements were
the result of 2 Para's move towards the isthmus being noted
(inevitably) by an Argentine observation post the day before

the battle. The Intelligence controversy may never be resolved satisfactorily. One of the author's sources is adamant that the true number of Argentines holding the isthmus was reported by the SAS to the Commanding Officer of 2 Para, Lieutenant-Colonel H. Jones.

Colonel Jones, in fact, personally debriefed the SAS reconnaissance teams on board the assault ship *Intrepid* just before 2 Para went into action. It is conceivable that H decided to disregard the Argentine 'extras' in weighing the true military odds, but he died, winning a posthumous VC, and we shall never know. Certainly there were other less celebrated cases in this campaign in which SAS reconnaissance provided information which, it later became apparent, did not reach the front-line soldiers who needed it. The accuracy of SAS Intelligence was degraded by last-minute Argentine reinforcements which might, or might not, have resulted from a Whitehall leak to the BBC suggesting that the Paras were within five miles of Darwin. This was broadcast on the World Service just before the battle began. In one of the earliest contacts an Argentine reconnaissance platoon, taken prisoner by the Paras, revealed that the garrison was stronger than the Paras had expected. According to Hastings and Jenkins, H was furious and demanded, 'What the hell have the SAS been doing down here?' Soon afterwards, as the Paras attacked the enemy-occupied Burntside House at Camilla Creek, the enemy fled leaving two dead. 'Inside, lying terrified on the floor, were four British civilians, two of them elderly women. Once again the soldiers cursed their Intelligence. They had been assured that Burntside House was solely occupied by the Argentines and had raked it ruthlessly with machine-gun fire . . .' These comments, according to a special forces operator who has no SAS connections, are unfair. 'Such reconnaissance patrols,' he believes, 'can only be expected to report that the enemy are present in an approximate strength.'

What is beyond dispute is that the SAS Goose Green reconnaissance team was no less effective than any other as the Military Medal citation for Corporal Trevor Brookes makes plain. He commanded the OP at Darwin/Goose Green for sixteen days immediately before the main landing. 'His position was most vulnerable at all times and the difficulty of achieving observation of the target necessitated his surviving under the main enemy helicopter route between Stanley and Darwin. Frequent enemy air searches and foot patrols were carried out in the area. He fully realised that no support was available to him, in the event of compromise by enemy action. His courage and leadership in this situation was of the highest order. The accuracy of his reporting was such that a successful air strike was carried out on his information against a petrol installation on the airfield at Goose Green.

'His information was of great value during the preparation for the successful attack on Darwin/Goose Green by 2nd Battalion, the Parachute Regiment. His performance as an individual and a leader was in the highest traditions of his regiment and the Army as a whole.'

Even if the numerical odds had been equal the Goose Green battle was certain to be a bloody affair, with no assurance of success by 2 Para. To attack a well-fortified position of this sort the British needed numerical superiority. 'We reckoned they were about a battalion, so it would be one for one,' the Second-in-Command of 2 Para, Major Chris Keeble, told the *Sunday Times*. If so, the tactical odds were still stacked against the Paras. A more professional enemy could have held the bridge, like Horatius, almost indefinitely. This operation, like others before it and since, was part of the great gamble of Operation Corporate.

The Argentines, packed into easily controlled, well-dug defensive positions, had a powerful arsenal: three 105mm guns; four twin 20mm and 30mm Oerlikon anti-aircraft cannon, which were used as battlefield weapons against the Paras; Pucara aircraft carrying napalm; a wealth of mortars, both 81mm and 120mm, machine guns and good supplies of ammunition. The Paras, by contrast, had as heavy support weapons, one 4.5in gun aboard *Arrow* (which jammed as the battalion crossed its operational start line); three 105mm artillery pieces; two mortars and a limited stock of bombs; Milan anti-tank and Blowpipe anti-aircraft missiles. Low cloud disrupted essential helicopter resupply to the battalion and, for most of the time, prevented Harrier jets from flying in support of the troops.

The battalion started its movement along the isthmus – just 400 yards wide at this point – in the dark at 2.30am on 28 May. The battle was to last all day. Almost as soon as the move began, Argentine shells began to explode around the attackers, causing surprisingly few casualties. With dawn at 6am, the Argentines fought tenaciously, trench by trench. Each was cleared at close quarters by the British, using grenades and anti-tank missiles.

On the east side of the isthmus Darwin Hill impeded the advance so badly that H, 2 Para's Commanding Officer, feared that the momentum of the attack was wavering. With his adjutant, Captain David Wood, he led the assault on what proved to be a series of well-concealed machine-gun positions. Both men were killed. On the other side of the isthmus two companies of the Paras led by H's deputy, Keeble, crawled for 1000 yards along the beach in order to outflank the other strong point, Boca Hill. They then hit it from two sides. As this position surrendered so did Darwin Hill, the scene of H's death. Only one strong point now remained between the advancing Paras and Goose Green Settlement. This was School House, to the settlement's immediate north. It was while accepting the surrender of Argentines here – signalled with a white flag – that three of the Paras were shot dead by Argentines in an adjoining trench. None of the defenders of School House was left alive in the fight which resulted. As dusk fell an Argentine prisoner was sent into the heavily defended, but now surrounded garrison of Goose Green, with a formal note from Keeble. This invited the enemy commander to surrender by 8.30am next day 'or take the inevitable consequences'. The Argentine commander, Air Commodore Wilson Pedroza, surrendered. Soon afterwards, 114 civilians who had been kept prisoner in a local community hall for a month were restored to freedom. The SAS was to make good use of the Air Commodore at a later stage of the campaign.

Leverage on Mount Kent

While the Goose Green surrender was taking place, British forces elsewhere were tightening their grip on East Falkland along the island's north coast. In a memorable 26-mile night march, 3 Para and 45 Royal Marine Commando reached Teal Inlet. But it was clear that the two-pronged coastal approach could be imperilled if a vacuum remained at the centre. The vacuum was large: about thirty miles separates Teal Inlet in the north from Goose Green in the south. The centre ground had to be taken and held as a pivot for the whole strategy to work. This task was given to D Squadron which, after its raid on Darwin/Goose Green, had transferred from *Intrepid* to the landing ship *Sir Lancelot*. The main initiative for moving into the vacuum came from the SAS Commanding Officer, Lieutenant-Colonel 'Mike' Rose. He selected an adventurous target for D Squadron. Mount Kent, many miles forward of both coastal prongs, is a 1400-foot hill which dominates the ridges rolling away to Port Stanley. For the Argentine garrison it was vital ground and certain to be defended. So, in spite of G Squadron's small, four-man OP already in the area since 1 May, a full-scale occupation of the area was an audacious move. Rose, studying G Squadron's reconnaissance report that nothing much was happening there, took a calculated decision to start something. He persuaded Brigadier Thompson to support his plan to seize the position.

Initially, Major Cedric Delves, the Squadron commander, was put in with a small patrol to verify that the move was possible. This patrol reconnoitred the area and passed back the invitation, 'Come on in. The water's fine!' In fact it was snowing on the mountain and the 'water' was deceptive. On 25 May, Argentina's national day, just 24 hours after Rose's scheme had received approval, another Argentine Exocet missile was sending to the bottom of the Atlantic three big troop-carrying Chinook helicopters and six smaller Wessex. All had been stowed aboard the container ship *Atlantic Conveyor*. For a short journey the Chinook could probably carry up to seventy armed men. The loss of the helicopters was a body-blow to the Army's mobility. One consequence of this was that D Squadron, committed to seizing Mount Kent, would have to dig in and hold it, with limited hope of resupply or reinforcement for an indeterminate period; certainly for longer than originally intended. But, 'Come on in . . . The water's fine' was an offer the rest of the Squadron could not refuse. So in they went, led by the new Second-in-Command, Gallagher's successor, to dig in, infantry style, on a strategically vital position 40 miles behind enemy lines. In the Second World War it was the sort of move which would have provoked a massive counter-attack. In East Falkland in 1982 it generated a series of small but deadly skirmishes between the SAS and Argentine special forces.

After one confrontation in the dark, an SAS soldier grumbled, 'Every time we get near an Argy patrol, they leg it . . . We ran into one the other night though. Took two, wounded two, killed three.' On another night an Argentine patrol and an SAS team met unexpectedly, face to face. The Argentine 'point man' hurled a grenade. Simultaneously the SAS lead scout opened fire with an Armalite. The SAS soldier was slightly wounded. The Argentine was killed. 'Our training paid off,' was the Regiment's terse comment on this engagement.

Prominent in these nocturnal firefights was Captain John Hamilton, leader of the Squadron's Mountain Troop. An official citation relates: 'His leadership and courage proved instrumental over seven days of continuous operations in seizing this vital ground from which the attack on Port

Stanley was ultimately launched. On 27 May he identified an enemy probe into the Squadron position and in the ensuing battle captured a prisoner of war. The next night he and his troop successfully held off another enemy attack and by doing so enabled 42 Commando Royal Marines to fly in as planned to reinforce the position on 31 May, an important step in the repossession of the Falklands. On the following day he ambushed another enemy patrol, wounding three and capturing all five members of the patrol.' On the Argentine side, Mount Kent was rapidly becoming a 'no-go' area. One patrol after another was sent to discover the British strength only to return, badly mauled or not to return at all.

Five days after D Squadron's arrival on Mount Kent, the SAS Commanding Officer descended to examine the ground in person. With characteristic panache he brought with him the war correspondent, Max Hastings. Hastings, prevented by censorship from announcing directly that this was another SAS initiative, slipped the comment 'Who dares, wins', into his dispatch as a way of making his point. His civilian presence emphasized the more serious idea which Rose was trying to convey, that Mount Kent was up for grabs. The reason why this should be, according to the Royal Marine journal, is that 'the Argentines had vacated their prepared positions on Mount Kent in order to reinforce Darwin and Goose Green. It was thus important that 3 Commando Brigade should seize this vital high ground which dominated the western approaches to Port Stanley, as soon as possible.'

With Rose and Hastings, therefore, came Lieutenant-Colonel Nick Vaux, commanding 42 Royal Marine Commando. Vaux brought his K Company, with two mortars and three 105mm light artillery pieces. But as they discovered on their arrival, not all the Argentines had left. An intensive gun battle was taking place less than a mile from the landing zone. Soon afterwards, D Squadron's commander, Delves, arrived to explain, 'No problem, boss. There was an Argie patrol up there, but we've malleted one lot and we'll sort out the others in the morning.'

Over the next few days the Commandos consolidated positions on neighbouring Mount Challenger, just seven miles short of Port Stanley, as well as on Mount Kent. D Squadron moved even farther forward to occupy Murrell Heights overlooking Port Stanley across Wireless Ridge. From this position on 1 June, military targets in Port Stanley were bombarded at a time when Argentina's radio claimed that the British were still on the beach-head of San Carlos.

An essential springboard for the final assault on the capital was now in British hands. This almost bloodless victory was marred by one tragic accident when a Royal Marine SBS patrol, not yet familiar with the terrain, overshot a grid reference (marked by a stream) and strayed into an SAS operational zone known as the Green Patch Area. In the exchange of fire which followed the SBS team leader, an endurance diver and skier, was shot dead. It was one of several battle accidents to demonstrate that in this respect the Falklands campaign was no different from other large-scale military actions. The SBS commander did not blame the SAS for what had happened. In fact, liaison between the two special force units became significantly tighter after this episode, and for a very good reason. As the British hardened their grip on the area around Port Stanley, the fighting battalions needed as much detailed knowledge of the area as they could get. The area includes a lot of water; Rose invited the SBS to attach at least one four-man patrol of scuba-divers to D Squadron. In fact, six SBS men joined first G, and later, D Squadron. The object was to improve the reconnaissance capability of the task force generally, and to explore ways of making underwater attacks on the Argentines through 'the back door' from the north. In the event, there were no scuba operations, but the SBS did link up with the SAS in the last hours of the campaign for one of the most spectacular battles of all.

Meanwhile, both D Squadron and the SBS turned their attention to John Bull's other Falkland Island. From a mili-

368 *Who Dares Wins*

tary point of view, West Falkland had seemed until then to be a sideshow. But since G Squadron's reconnaissance team had established that there were 800 enemy at Port Howard and another 900 at Fox Bay, plus an unknown number deployed elsewhere, this was not a case where ignorance was bliss. Several ugly possibilities existed and the SAS wanted to lay them to rest. One was that as Port Stanley was under constant threat by the British, an alternative route for supplies and reinforcements to the Argentine garrison might exist on West Falkland. There was also the risk of an unexpected Argentine amphibious or airborne assault against the San Carlos beachhead, mounted from West Falkland.

With the same possibilities in mind, the SBS had inserted its patrols into Pebble Island, Port Stevens, Weddell Island, Dunnose Head, Byron Heights, Carcass Island, Saunders Island, Keppel Island and Sea Lion Island. As one SBS officer put it, 'West Falkland was ringed. It became obvious that most settlements were completely free of Argentines. Our men went down and made contact with the islanders during the night, disappearing into the hills at dawn. During our visits to the settlements, the fatted calf was killed several times over. The islanders were a valuable source of Intelligence. They knew how many planes had flown in, what they carried, and where the Argentines were. It was a well informed grapevine. Perhaps we should have made contact with them earlier.'

As well as watching and listening, the SBS went on to the offensive on three occasions in West Falkland and in a way peculiarly suited to special forces. By using their observation posts for artillery spotting they were able to bring a barrage of naval gunfire to bear with fine accuracy on the Argentine garrisons of Port Howard and Fox Bay. It was a classic use of such troops as a 'force multiplier' without indiscriminate excessive force. It was also somewhat risky. One team paddled away from its island OP just before an Argentine patrol came looking for them.

Initially, D Squadron dedicated five four-man patrols to

its new operational theatre. Two of these replaced G Squadron teams on 5 June. The new teams quickly discovered that Argentine opposition was more aggressive than anything they had encountered so far. The Argentines' radio direction finding equipment was also in excellent shape.

Fresh from his adventures at Mount Kent, John Hamilton was assigned the hazardous job of watching the Port Howard garrison. For him, the nightmare which haunted all SAS soldiers running these covert OPs was now about to become a reality. An official citation explains that he 'managed to establish himself in a position only 2500 metres from the enemy, from which he sent detailed and accurate reports . . . Shortly after dawn on 10 June he realised that he and his radio operator had been surrounded in a forward position. Although heavily outnumbered and with no reinforcements available he gave the order to engage the enemy, telling his signaller that they should both attempt to fight their way out of the encirclement. Since the withdrawal route was completely exposed to enemy observation and fire' – he was overlooked as well as surrounded – 'he initiated the fire fight in order to allow his signaller to move first.

'After the resulting exchange of fire he was wounded in the back and it became clear to his signaller that Captain Hamilton was only able to move with difficulty. Nevertheless he told his signaller that he could continue to hold off the enemy while the signaller made good his escape, and then he proceeded to give further covering fire. Shortly after that he was killed.'

Hamilton, the survivor of so many tight corners since the beginning of the conflict, from Fortuna Glacier to Mount Kent, was awarded a posthumous Military Cross. As the citation put it, 'Captain Hamilton displayed outstanding determination and an extraordinary will to continue the fight in spite of being confronted by hopeless odds and being wounded. He furthermore showed supreme courage and sense of duty by his conscious decision to sacrifice himself on behalf of his signaller. His final, brave and unselfish act will be an inspiration to all who follow in the SAS.' Hamilton's service with the SAS had lasted just five months.

For his signaller, the odds were equally hopeless. He had run out of ammunition. After a brief pursuit he was seized, disarmed and taken prisoner. He was then confined in the cellar of a sheep-shearing shed until just before the final Argentine surrender five days later. He was not brutally treated. An Argentine officer who had witnessed Hamilton's death paid warm tribute to the courage of both men. But when the prisoner was discovered by a party of Royal Marine Commandos they were convinced he was an Argentine. The signaller, like a number of other SAS soldiers, is not a European. His dark skin made him suspect until an SBS man accompanying the Commandos recognized him and greeted him warmly.

Meanwhile the other SAS teams were still at work on West Falkland and remained so until the end of the conflict. One was particularly busy trying to identify the position of an Argentine observation post on Mount Rosalie, across the water from San Carlos. This position, rather than the mythical radar at Pebble Island, almost certainly acted as the 'eyes' for some of the aircraft raiding British shipping in Bomb Alley. A back-up party to attack this position was actually assembled but then, as the tide of war swept south towards Port Stanley, the scheme was abandoned. Equally disappointed in these last days of the campaign were men of an SAS Squadron new to the Falklands. B Squadron – which had broken the terrorist seige at the Iranian Embassy in London – now parachuted from Hercules aircraft into the Atlantic to take over from both G and D Squadrons, which needed rest. B Squadron's advance party, sent to a quiescent West Falkland, included Corporal Tommy Palmer, secretly decorated with a Queen's Gallantry Medal for storming into a room at the embassy where hostages were held. (Palmer was to die in a road accident a few months later in Northern Ireland.)

The problem facing those who were still where the action

was in East Falkland was that it was becoming a crowded little war with scant room for manoeuvre. G Squadron overcame their problem by liberating a civilian motor cruiser. The engine of this craft needed attention, but otherwise she was a vessel of which any Guards officer could be proud . . . given time. The team running her then sailed up Port Harriet water and went ashore within two miles of Argentine-held Mount Tumbledown. They then directed accurate artillery fire on the enemy garrison there for two days. Elsewhere, men of both Squadrons were based aboard the landing ship *Sir Lancelot* as a quick reaction force. Some were to take part in the last Commando raid of the conflict. This was an operation full of surprises, even for the SAS.

A Dose of Psyops

To those who do not know him well, Michael Rose, Commanding Officer of 22 SAS during the Falklands conflict, appears to be a slightly donnish figure whose affability only just conceals an evident shyness. This impression, although it matches his background – a PPE degree at Oxford (where he was a contemporary of Tariq Ali) a brief spell teaching in France and a well-stocked bookshelf – is deceptive. Like all successful SAS soldiers of whatever rank or background he thinks aggressively. He also thinks ahead. He had been fortunate in commanding the Regiment when it broke the Iranian Embassy siege in London. That experience had impressed upon him, as nothing else could, the value of talking to the enemy at the right time to soften the opposition's resolve. True, negotiations at the embassy had finally broken down and the affair had ended bloodily. But it might have worked.

Rose concluded that an elegant end to this campaign would be, not a blitzkrieg against Port Stanley – crowded as it was with civilians as well as teenage Argentine conscripts – but a civilized chat to satisfy the Latin sense of honour, followed by orderly surrender. In any case, as Admiral Woodward was to admit later, the British force was 'running out of steam' when the surrender finally took place. A prolonged siege outside Port Stanley in a Falklands winter was not on. Nor could an onslaught of the kind which happened soon afterwards in Beirut keep world opinion half-way favourable to the British case. Much earlier, long before D-Day at San Carlos, the SAS had considered hitting the Argentine high command in Port Stanley with a flying column of the sort that David Stirling loved to lead . . . and had dropped the notion as impracticable. So as the battle continued with tragic losses at Bluff Cove, savage fighting across the crags between Mount Kent and Port Stanley, Rose and his friends worked Jesuitically from the calm of the *Fearless* operations room to corrode Argentine resistance at source. They talked to the opposition leaders.

There are virtually no telephones on the Falkland Islands. Most people chat to their neighbours by radio and those who have nothing to do, eavesdrop on the conversation. It is a well-tried method of boredom relief during the long winter nights. A knowing Royal Marine Yeoman of Signals had already cashed in on this custom. On the long voyage from England aboard *Fearless,* he put together radio gear which would enable him to monitor civilian CB sets in the Falklands and, if he wished, transmit to them. Rose showed great interest in the equipment, and the idea. (This personal experiment in 'sig-int' saved at least one life. A civilian injured during a Harrier attack on Port Howard was evacuated to hospital by the SBS two painful weeks later. His condition was the subject of CB radio chat.) The yeoman-signaller became part of Rose's hearts-and-minds team, this time with a more orthodox SAS military transmitter on board *Fearless.*

As a special concession during the Argentine occupation, the military governor allowed Alison Bleaney, a British doctor in Port Stanley, to conduct a radio clinic for the benefit of people living outside the capital. These transmissions had an

Argentine 'minder' who monitored what was said. On 6 June, Dr Bleaney and her minder, a corporal, were astonished to receive a message in fluent Argentine-Spanish from someone claiming to speak on behalf of Major General Jeremy Moore, the British land forces boss. The voice was that of Captain Roderick Bell, Royal Marines. Initially, Dr Bleaney suspected that she was the victim of a practical joker, but the voice went on and on. It was the first of many such calls masterminded by Rose. General Moore, commanding land forces, was only half convinced by Rose's plan but agreed that he should give it a try. Rose, however, was entirely certain that he had the ingredients of a successful 'psyops' campaign, including the senior Argentine officers taken prisoner at Goose Green. The first attempt to make contact, by telephone from Estancia House to Port Stanley, failed because the line was cut. The psyops team then tried by radio.

The British approach was anything but bellicose. Please, Bell asked in Spanish, could the British military command talk to representatives of General Menendez about avoiding unnecessary casualties? The soldier who took this call made no promises, no concessions. But he agreed to pass on the British message. Next day at the same time another call was made. Dr Bleaney told the British officer that no Argentine was willing to speak directly to the British, but they had agreed that she could receive and pass on messages. These were finely tuned by Rose over the next eight days to reflect the growing pressure on Port Stanley and the growing threat to the survival of everyone in the town. To Bell's voice was added that of the war prisoner Wilson Pedroza, but his contribution simply enraged his former comrades.

When the psyops campaign began there was still plenty of fight in the Argentines. The two main components of British land forces – 3 Commando Brigade and 5 Infantry Brigade – had to battle their way through Mount Longden, Mount Harriet, Mount William and Tumbledown Mountain almost to the gates of Port Stanley itself, where British shells caused a handful of civilian deaths.

Five of these final actions were fought savagely at night against an enemy equipped with infra-red binoculars, more sophisticated than anything the British possessed. The battles required uphill attacks on bunkers with hand-grenade and bayonet, fighting of a kind the British Army had not experienced since the Korean War thirty years earlier.

'A Suicide Mission'

The SAS, whose covert OPs continued work in this increasingly crowded war until the very end, showed its mettle as a combat unit in the penultimate battle of the campaign. On the night of 13/14 June, the last night of hostilities, 2 Para were assaulting Wireless Ridge, a few miles west of the capital. The SAS volunteered to put in a raid from the sea, at the enemy's rear. This, it was hoped, would take some pressure off 2 Para by creating the maximum degree of confusion. Sentiment as well as tactics played some part in this decision. The SAS has a number of ex-Parachute Regiment soldiers in its ranks and the Parachute Regiment has officers – several decorated for their work in the Falklands – who have served one or more tours with the SAS. As one SAS officer explains, 'When your comrades are storming the hills and you are available, it would be unforgiveable to stand around muttering that it was time to hand over to the big battalions. We did what we could in the most effective way possible to assist their success.'

The raid was launched on the seaward end of Wireless Ridge, by way of a narrow strip of water immediately north of Port Stanley. One target was a huge ordnance depot. Initially, helicopters were to be used to carry the assault force. Because of bad weather, four Royal Marine fast power boats known as Rigid Raiders, driven by men of 1st Raiding Squadron, RM, from Plymouth, were employed instead. These craft were brought from San Carlos water aboard the trawler *Cordella*, put into the sea and taken by the attackers into hiding at Kidney Island. The raid was mounted jointly by two troops from D Squadron, one from G Squadron and six men from 3 SBS. This assault force, about sixty men, was supported by other SAS soldiers who descended from Murrell Heights on the north shore of the harbour approach and laid down a barrage of GPMG and Milan missile fire. The assault was also backed up by the guns of the frigate *Arrow*, but in spite of this, one participant conceded later, 'I think we bit off more than we could chew.' Another unblushingly described the attack as 'a suicide mission'.

To approach their target the attackers had to pass the Argentine fleet auxiliary *Bahia Paraiso*, then berthed as a hospital ship in Port Stanley harbour. Yet as the attackers went in, the crew of the *Bahia Paraiso* turned their searchlights on the Rigid Raiders. The SAS/SBS men now came under a hailstorm of gunfire from several directions. Both the Argentines on Wireless Ridge and in the Port Stanley area, convinced that the frontal sea assault they had always expected was beginning at last, opened up with every available weapon. The most intense flak came from triple-barrelled 20mm Rheinmetall anti-aircraft cannon which were depressed to their lowest trajectory. 'Being on the receiving end of that,' recalls one who got out unscathed, 'was rather like seeing that magical sword-beam weapon in "Star Wars". It was a long, continuous, glowing stream of hot metal.'

Since it was obvious to the attackers that withdrawal was the only alternative to being shot to pieces, they withdrew fast . . . all, that is, except a Rigid Raider which had lost part of its propeller. It could now travel at only two knots. The 'hospital' ship's participation was particularly resented since the British Harriers had taken exquisite care to avoid hitting her. So now, according to an SBS source, the Rigid Raiders on their way back drove straight towards the *Bahia Paraiso*, using her as a shield from the fire directed at them. Some Argentine 20mm rounds smashed into the ship's hull as a result. The Rigid Raiders reached sanctuary just in time. One sank slowly under the men climbing out of her. It was like a scene from a slapstick comedy. The other three vessels were so badly holed as to be beyond repair. D Squadron suffered just three minor casualties; the SBS, one.

At dawn next day, from Wireless Ridge the men of 2 Para stared down in disbelief as the Argentines, who had fought tenaciously until now, scurried away 'all running, running back to Stanley'. That same morning Dr Bleaney, adding her voice to the appeals of Bell and Rose, persuaded the Argentine Navy Commander, Captain Melbourne Hussey, to respond. By now white flags were appearing over Port Stanley. Recognizing the impossibility of his situation, General Mario Menendez agreed that the negotiators should come in.

Late in the afternoon a British Gazelle, white parachute trailing below it as a truce signal, descended into Port Stanley. Rose, Bell and an SAS signaller climbed out, only to discover that they were an embarrassing distance from their rendezvous at Government House. On their undignified way through hedges and gardens Rose saw a young woman watching him intently from the hospital balcony. Was she Alison Bleaney, he asked. She nodded, surprised. 'You did a great job,' Rose told her, and passed on through defended enemy positions.

At first Menendez would concede only a limited surrender. The Argentine could not speak, he said, for the West Falkland garrison. Rose insisted that a half-surrender was no surrender at all. If hostilities resumed, causing unnecessary bloodshed, history would judge harshly the man responsible. In London, thanks to the SAS's unique communications, the negotiations were being monitored almost paragraph by paragraph. The Regiment's communications 'net' was used in parallel with the orthodox link by way of *Fearless* to Northwood and then up the normal chain of command. As a result, Rose's outgoing messages went direct to Hereford while London's answers were relayed via Brigadier John

Waters, Moore's second-in-command, aboard *Fearless*. Menendez, by contrast, received no clear instructions from a demoralized Buenos Aires. He had to play the negotiations pragmatically to save as much face as possible. But this was like the closing stages of a decisive chess game and both men knew it. Rose also knew that his own High Command would, in fact, have settled at that stage for a surrender of East Falkland alone. The task force, as Admiral Woodward later admitted, was 'in a poor way' by 14 June and 'running out of speed.' The army was down to six rounds per gun. For this reason, no Press photographs of the occasion were permitted, in case Menendez changed his mind.

Rose, keeping his nerve, persisted. He wanted a complete surrender and he wanted it that day. Menendez, unaware that he had even one bargaining chip, gave way. The surrender would encompass all the islands. But at least his men – 11,313 in all – could be repatriated aboard Argentine as well as British ships? Rose promptly consulted London on this apparently innocuous detail. London, aware that outright victory was within its grasp, was not minded to reduce the Junta's public embarrassment. Menendez's personal defeat as well as his Army's was complete. He would return to Argentina aboard a British ship. But he shook hands, first with Bell, then with Rose. It was now 9pm. The substance of the Argentine capitulation was agreed. A little under three hours later, at one minute before midnight on 14 June, the formal instrument of surrender was signed by Menendez and Major-General Sir Jeremy Moore, the British land force commander. Argentine HQ staff extracted from their stock a bottle of Southern Comfort with which they toasted the end of hostilities. Afterwards, Rose went out and hoisted the SAS Union Jack on the Government House flagpost.

It was all over bar the inquests, conducted alike by two official inquiries as well as by a task force of journalists and MPs. This was right and proper. The gamble of Operation Corporate had paid off, though only just. For the SAS, whose leaders had effectively taken the surrender of both South

Georgia and the Falkland Islands, there were no intrinsically new lessons; just the reinforcement of old ones familiar to earlier generations of the Regiment. Of these, perhaps the most important was that no military operation ever works as originally planned. Success or failure depends on the skill, intelligence and nerve of the man on the ground. As a Soviet military aphorism pinned above the door of one of the Regiment's training offices puts it: 'Train hard; fight easy.'

Those Mainland Operations

For the historian, however, one tantalizing question about the South Atlantic war remains unanswered. Were there, or were there not, British special forces operations on the Argentine mainland? In this account of SAS history the author has tried to be faithful to the facts. But, in reading the entrails of the 'mainland' episode, we enter an area of – at best – intelligent guesswork.

The roll of those who subscribe publicly to the theory that there were such operations is too weighty to be brushed aside without discussion. It includes the writer Max Hastings, Robert Fox of the BBC, John Witherow of *The Times* (all correspondents with the task force) as well as other experts, such as R.J. Raggett, Editor of *Jane's Military Communications*. Enthusiastic investigative teams who argue that there was some sort of clandestine operation in Argentina also include the BBC's Panorama team and the *Daily Express*. In general, the view of this formidable lobby is that a special forces team drawn from, or linked with, the SAS was put ashore to count the Argentine aircraft out from Rio Grande and Rio Gallegos (if not back again) in order to give the task force early warning of impending attack. The absence of such early warning was a crucial factor. Had an Argentine air attack sunk one or both British carriers, the British military operation as a whole would have failed. The reason for such vulnerability was that the Royal Navy is custom-built for a war in the North Atlantic, where it can depend upon land-based aircraft flying from Scotland, Iceland, Greenland, Canada or the US for airborne early warning of enemy air attack. In the South Atlantic, no cover of this sort existed until the conflict was over.

The only tangible evidence that this gap was filled by special forces is the discovery on 20 May of a Sea King helicopter of 846 Royal Naval Air Squadron, burned out and abandoned about eleven miles south of Punta Arenas in southern Chile, a neutral country friendly to Britain and at odds with its neighbour, Argentina. Later a crew of three emerged from hiding after surviving unaided, they claimed, for several days in wild countryside. At a short press conference the Royal Marine pilot, Lieutenant Richard Hutchings, said: 'We were on sea patrol when we experienced engine failure due to adverse weather. It was not possible to return to our ship in these conditions. We therefore took refuge in the nearest neutral country.' Punta Arenas is about 500 miles from the Falklands and about 200 outside the British Total Exclusion Zone. It is only 140 miles from the Argentine air base of Rio Grande in Tierra del Fuego. It is 125 miles from Rio Gallegos, just across the Magellan Strait. Many air attacks were launched against the task force from both bases.

The helicopter crew received no further official publicity until the Falklands honours list was published after the Argentine surrender, though Panorama asserted that one of the three 'ferried SAS men on active service, has been on a course with the Special Boat Squadron, is a qualified frog-man, a weapons expert and a parachutist'. In the honours list, Hutchings was extolled for his skills as a Combat Survival Instructor as well as courage on eight operational missions. Like Hutchings, his colleague Lieutenant Alan Bennett, RN, received a Distinguished Service Cross for skill and courage 'despite the particularly hazardous nature of the missions in which he was involved'. The third survivor of the crash landing, Leading Aircrewman Peter Imrie, was awarded a Distinguished Service Medal for 'several missions in very hazardous circumstances'. The crew was exceptional in that all received high-grade gallantry awards, accompanied by citations that made no mention of the Falklands or South Georgia. Clearly, something happened: but what?

First it is necessary to test the military plausibility of such an adventure. In theory it would be perfectly feasible, given time, for an SAS reconnaissance team to watch an airfield, encode a signal describing preparations for an Argentine air attack and then transmit that information by modern 'burst transmission' in a second or less. The speed of such a message would defy Argentine efforts to pinpoint the source. (SAS teams such as Hamilton's would have had a much better chance of survival if they had carried such sophisticated gear. They did not.) Suitable vantage points exist outside the Argentine air bases, some in mountains suitable to SAS activity. The Argentines did from time to time search the hinterland around these bases, but could not commit sufficiently large forces to do the job thoroughly. Movement by Europeans in the area would not necessarily arouse suspicion, since most Argentines are themselves of European extraction.

There is also evidence that, as the Falkland campaign progressed, air alert warning of a general kind did improve. Robert Fox, with the task force, noted that 'early warning' of air attacks improved steadily throughout the campaign and sometimes over twenty minutes' prior warning was given before the Skyhawks and Mirages attacked land targets'. This implies that a Skyhawk, flying into the attack at 550 knots, would be spotted 180 miles away, a performance beyond the limit of any radar at sea level of the type available to the task force. If Fox is correct, therefore, then there must have been some other method of identifying the threat. Fragmented interceptions of brief radio exchanges between the incoming Argentine aircraft, which the task force did achieve, would not have been sufficient for the purpose.

Yet there is a vivid paradox here. A generalized alert was provided, but the Harrier pilots, who hoped to intercept the attackers, never received specific information about precisely where and when the enemy would appear. British Aerospace, sifting official records after the conflict, found that there was 'a lack of *any* advanced warning' of the Argentine attacks. A researcher who interviewed about twenty of the Sea Harrier pilots (roughly half of the total) told the author: 'All the pilots I spoke to deeply regretted that throughout the conflict they had no early warning, and none even hinted to me that there was such warning.'

As a result, the Harriers had to rely on flying standing Combat Air Patrols using one pair of aircraft in the hope of a chance contact, rather than being guided to a planned interception. Because the British carriers were 30 to 40 minutes' flying time east of the Falklands there was rarely more than one pair of Harriers over the islands at any time, apart from those aircraft engaged on missions in support of British ground forces.

This handicap resulted from the fact that the Argentines would quickly disappear from the sight of those watching on the mainland. Thereafter, flying low into the Total Exclusion Zone, they could sweep in at sea level and below radar detection. Max Hastings and Simon Jenkins suggest that intelligence teams on the mainland as well as British submarines reported the enemy's departure from Argentina. 'But at least 50 miles from the Falklands,' they add, 'the Skyhawks and Mirages dipped to sea level – low enough to come home with wings streaked with salt – and vanished from British radar surveillance. This was where the fleet's lack of airborne early warning became critical. The Argentine aircraft only appeared as they weaved between the hills or swung among the inlets on their final approach, often seconds before they bombed.' The aviation historian Alfred Price, who has analysed, with his American colleague Jeffrey Ethell, the Falklands air war from both sides for a forthcoming book, concludes that if a clandestine early warning system existed, 'I have found no evidence that it had any great effect. It did not make any difference to the way the Harrier patrols were flown.' The brutal reality that this blind spot existed throughout the campaign was reinforced as late as 8 June, only a week before the Argentine surrender, when the landing and supply ships *Sir Galahad* and *Sir Tristram* were hit by an air attack that left 53 dead and 46 injured.

There is another powerful objection to the plausibility of a mainland adventure. This is the risk it created for the credibility of British diplomacy in representing the United Kingdom as an injured party engaged in a minimum force operation of legitimate self-defence. If anything went wrong (and on such clandestine, cross-border operations something usually does) then the cost of compromise or capture of the SAS men involved would be at least as great as any potential gain for Britain if they succeeded. For a start, to quote a special forces' joke on the subject, 'What do we say at the press conference, boss?' Or, for that matter, the show trial? Support for Britain in the EEC, the source of the French-built Exocet missile, rested on a sanctions policy that was always ambivalent. Sympathy for Britain at the United Nations and – for what it was worth – at the Organization of American States would have evaporated, opening the door for instant replacement of Argentine losses. UN Resolution 502, calling for Argentina's withdrawal from the Falklands – the diplomatic card that justified the whole task force operation – would have been rendered valueless if Britain could be made to appear to be at least an equal aggressor in this quarrel.

And yet it is a fact that a British Sea King helicopter from the squadron flying British special forces at the time *did* land in Chile and its crew *did* go into hiding after destroying their aircraft. According to the BBC's Robert Fox, the plan was that this aircraft should never have been discovered. It was to have 'ditched' into the sea, to be lost without trace. So if a special forces team was put ashore, where did it come from?

The classic solution of hard-pressed governments in such a situation is to employ special forces that are 'deniable', people whose names – unlike those of regular servicemen in the SAS or SBS – do not appear in the Army, Navy or even the honours lists. Ideally, everything about them including their nationality should be blurred. They are soldiers of fortune who have worked through an intermediary, with no certain knowledge of who ultimately controls their operation. It seems implausible that between the Argentines' successful Exocet attack on the *Sheffield* on 4 May – which took the Royal Navy by surprise – and mid-May, there was sufficient time to recruit and brief a high-grade team of mercenaries (even ex-SAS soldiers), let alone put them on the ground in Argentina. So an intelligence-gathering operation on the mainland had to be performed by SAS or SBS regulars with all the risks this entailed, a risk which even the most dedicated SAS soldier might deem reckless.

This author concludes from the evidence as it stands, including the testimony of Hastings, Fox and Witherow, that the Sea King helicopter that was discovered in Chile had been stripped down to undertake a long range, one-way mission to put an SAS team into the mainland. Such a drastic decision would require clearance at the highest level of government and as such – like the sinking of the Argentine cruiser *General Belgrano* outside the Total Exclusion Zone – would be a political rather than a military decision. As we have noted, the risk involved, when set against the probable military value of the operation, would be hard to justify. An SAS identification of an all-out aerial onslaught at one time by every available Argentine aircraft would have justified the operation, but not even the Argentine air force was that reckless.

The author also believes that at least one team was deposited inside Argentina, too far from the target areas of Rio Gallegos and Rio Grande to make sufficient progress on foot remotely possible in the time available. Deposited in some confusion in a remote border area, the team reported that the plan had not proved a practicable proposition and then discreetly withdrew to neutral territory.

The evidence, such as it is, points to an operation that probably failed or one that, if it succeeded, did not affect the outcome of the war. The gamble of operating a vulnerable carrier force without airborne early warning was not a bet that could be hedged successfully through resort to special forces, however brave. For once, the SAS was asked to perform an impossible task, which might explain the conviction among some special forces personnel unconnected with the Falklands that, after the failure of the first team in Argentina, a second was assembled. Some of the men concerned, who had impeccable records, declined to embark upon an adventure they regarded as doomed. But such is the secrecy surrounding what the *Daily Express* described as 'Operation Eavesdrop', it is unlikely that we shall ever know for certain.

Appendix A
An Idea Spreads: The Overseas Regiments

The idea that David Stirling had in the 1940s has succeeded because it is inherently a good one. The SAS structure works because it embodies a flexibility unique among today's increasingly complex and bureaucratic armed forces, as well as a capacity for change in a world where soldiers and politicians alike are seeking quick, cost-effective solutions to military problems for which there are no precedents.

In post-war years, the Regiment has found itself in a sellers' market. Soldiers of 22 SAS served in at least twenty-six foreign countries during the year 1978/9, and many of these men were employed as training teams for other people's armies. Its three most durable offspring, so far, are the SAS regiments of Zimbabwe-Rhodesia, New Zealand and Australia. Each has acquired experience not shared by the others, but the lessons learned by each tend, within a short time, to be picked up by the others in that organic way peculiar to the SAS family.

Links with US Special Forces (the Green Berets) are of long standing. In 1962, Major-General William P. Yarborough, the Green Berets' supremo, was made an honorary member of the SAS Regiment, in recognition of the help received by the SAS in its US training in 1962. (Only one other man, General Sir Walter Walker, has been so honoured.) The two-way traffic continued in 1977, when a new US rescue force, the Delta Force, was formed under the command of Colonel Charles Beckwith. Beckwith, a Green Beret officer who had served on secondment with the SAS in Malaya, brought his new team to Hereford for basic training. By an historical irony – no fault of Beckwith or his team – he was obliged to call off an attempt to rescue American diplomatic hostages in Iran only weeks before the SAS rescued Iranian diplomat-hostages in London.

Rhodesians in Malaya

The first of the overseas SAS regiments was the Rhodesian, founded during the days of Brigadier Michael Calvert's desperate recruiting campaign for the Malayan Emergency. Calvert flew from Malaya to Salisbury and toured Rhodesia in 1950, addressing meetings in his efforts to find men. From the 1000 volunteers who came forward was created C Squadron of the Malayan Scouts (SAS). Their first commander was Peter Walls, then a major and subsequently the 'supremo' of all Rhodesia's armed forces. The military contribution of C Squadron to the Malayan campaign was not significant. Partly, this was because many of the volunteers were soldiers who had not experienced bush warfare in their own country, unlike their successors who fought the guerrilla war. The unit was peculiarly prone to jungle ailments, particularly scrub typhus, and at any one time a significant percentage of C Squadron was unfit to fight as a result. Two men were killed in action in Malaya. The main contribution of this formative period, in the view of one Squadron veteran, was 'the ultimate injection into the Rhodesian Army of officers and men who were thinking along SAS lines'.

After its return from Malaya, the Squadron was reorganized, and in 1961 it was based in Ndola, Northern Rhodesia (later Zambia) as part of the forces of the Federation of Rhodesia and Nyasaland, with a total strength of 250 officers and men. One of those attached to it at this time was John Peters, who achieved fame as commander of Five Commando in the Congo soon afterwards. C Squadron was itself deployed on the border with the Congo during the civil war in that country, notably when tension rose following the death in a Congolese air crash of the UN Secretary-General, Dag Hammarskjöld.

It was also during this period that the men of C Squadron became the first airborne troops in Rhodesia, and on 30 October 1961 a newly-formed Parachute Training School at New Sarum, Salisbury, started basic training. To begin with, the Squadron used standard X-type static-line parachutes and jumped from Rhodesian Air Force Dakotas. These parachutes had a tendency to oscillate in the prevailing air conditions, which in addition made for heavier landings than would occur in Europe. By 1970, the SAS had turned over to larger American-designed T 10 canopies, while a small cadre of soldiers would use more advanced, steerable parachutes for a high altitude 'stand-off' approach, totally silent under cover of darkness, to the most sensitive targets.

The pioneering days of the early 1960s saw the unit's first operational parachute deployment into Rhodesia's eastern districts, to pursue dissidents who carried on a campaign of arson against the area's pine and gumtree plantations. The Squadron also trained in Aden with 22 SAS from Britain.

The collapse of the Federation of Rhodesia and Nyasaland in 1963 led to considerable dilution of the Rhodesian SAS capability. With the reduction of the manpower and economic base provided by the Federation, the armed forces were also cut. In the ensuing struggle for survival, there was much jostling among senior military people naturally concerned about their own careers, the overall effect of which was not helpful to C Squadron. As morale in the unit declined, so many of the more experienced soldiers accepted 'golden handshakes' then being offered in exchange for redundancy, to start a new life in Rhodesia, South Africa or Britain. Others, including Peters, joined the Congolese mercenary force then commanded by Mike Hoare. Only a small cadre of officers and men remained to preserve the core of what would ultimately emerge as a reconstructed C Squadron. This was commanded by Major Dudley Coventry, who had led the Parachute Regiment Squadron of the Malayan Scouts (SAS) during the Malayan campaign, with Captain Peter Rich as his deputy. They had a few subalterns and about two dozen men. During the following year, as the constitutional conflict with Britain accelerated, the Rhodesian SAS cast its net wide in the search for suitable recruits. A former second-in-command of the Regiment, Major Mike Graham, recalls: 'We ended up as a fairly cosmopolitan crew: Rhodesian, South African, British, American, French, German, Greek and Portuguese. For a short time we even had a lad from Finland whose only English was the phrase, "Fetch my umbrella", which was not much use in the Zambesi Valley in the dry season.'

UDI and After

The reaction to Ian Smith's Unilateral Declaration of Independence in 1964 and the constitutional crisis that followed between Britain and Rhodesia seems to have provoked no conflict of loyalty in the minds of Rhodesian SAS soldiers. British public opinion over the issue was so divided (and so cunningly 'massaged' in Britain by the last Rhodesian High Commissioner and his team) that it seemed plausible to hope that there would be no military action against the Salisbury Government by Britain. Good relations established with the RAF crews of a Javelin squadron flown to Lusaka soon after UDI also reassured the Rhodesians. There was no British military action against the Rhodesians, so whatever doubts might have existed in both the British and Rhodesian armed forces about making war on kith-and-kin were never put to the test. Nevertheless, the Rhodesians (including the SAS) were prepared for a fight. Standing orders, issued about what they should do in the event of an airborne attack, included details of defensive positions to be occupied near Rhodesian Light Infantry barracks in the country, contingency plans for the removal of ammunition from a central ordnance depot and the mounting of a guard on the Kariba Dam. In anticipation of a waterborne attack by either British or African troops across Lake Kariba or the Victoria Falls Bridge, defensive positions including anti-tank weapons were dug-in and, in Salisbury, key positions were guarded against any attempted assault by British parachute troops.

By the late sixties, the Rhodesians were beginning to experience the first serious terrorist infiltration from other countries, including Mozambique, then still a Portuguese colony. Salisbury's reaction was to try to emulate the methods adopted in Malaya, and undertake a programme of military aid to the civil power, but the Africans proved impervious to a European-oriented hearts-and-minds scheme. When this failed, the SAS had to increase in size and recruit soldiers peculiarly suited to bush warfare. The men in question were young – some still in their teens – and exceptionally fit, as well as being sharp-eyed, superlative trackers. They were known as 'junglies' because of their love of the bush. After protracted operational periods in that environment, some of them would spend their leave hunting on game ranches. The risks of such a life were, as Mike Graham recounts, manifold. They included (in addition to the human enemy) elephant, rhinoceros, lion, leopard, hyena, crocodile, electric-barbel fish, mosquito, tsetse fly, snake, scorpion and other pests. In their turn, the SAS nomads were also predators, for game provided food. One anecdote illustrates this environment. According to

Graham: 'A young trooper, after admiring a large herd of elephant on a river bed, ran into a very large cow accompanied by her new calf. The elephant flipped away the soldier's FN rifle and in almost the same motion, beat him to the ground with her trunk. She then stood astride him and kicked him with all four feet in turn for some time. Not content with that, she then knelt down and pushed a tusk through the man's chest and lifted him into the air. The soldier, still conscious, grasped the elephant's second tusk in order to take the weight off his injured chest. At this, the elephant threw him to the ground, kicked him a couple of times and ran off after her calf.' The soldier was evacuated by helicopter and light aircraft to Salisbury, where he received immediate surgery. Ten days later, with seventy-six stitches in his chest, he was discharged to the Regiment's drinking club, 'The Winged Stagger'. He returned to duty after another six weeks, having spent his convalescence qualifying as an Outward Bound School instructor in rock-climbing. But other encounters by the SAS with the occupants of what was still, in theory at least, a wildlife reserve caused some distress to conservationists including National Parks officials. Like others in Rhodesia, they started to describe the unit as 'C Squadron, Rhodesian Special Air Safaris'.

Although they loved the bush, the 'junglies' regarded the early stages of SAS soldiering as less than satisfactory. The role primarily allocated to C Squadron at the beginning of the war was exclusively that of reconnaissance. One veteran explains: 'There was nothing more frustrating than watching the bandits from hiding, knowing that the information we would pass about them was going to units less combative and effective than we were.' This was, in effect, the Borneo strategy without the benefit of a Gurkha step-up party to do the killing. The tactical lessons acquired at that time were to be of great value when the Squadron began its own offensive operations.

Across the Border

It was inevitable that in such a vast area the Regiment's role would change from one of reconnaissance to that of a quick-reaction fire-force, responding to attacks that had already happened or begun. Air mobility, particularly through static-line, low-level parachuting from the vintage Dakotas into the bush to begin hot pursuit, was the chosen response. Simultaneously, the Squadron was also learning to work across the border. The guerrilla war had taken firm hold not only on Rhodesian soil but also that of Mozambique and Angola, both of them Portuguese colonies until 1975. Indeed, the Angolan war had started long before, in 1961. It was to improve Rhodesia's own security, as well as to enlarge their operational experience, that some men of C Squadron fought in Angola alongside Portuguese security authorities in 1967. From the early 1970s, there was also a long series of joint operations in Mozambique. The Rhodesian Air Force provided air reconnaissance of the Portuguese operational zone, after which small tracking units from C Squadron were placed by helicopter in an area where the guerrillas were training or operating. If the target merited the trouble, Rhodesian Hunter strike aircraft would also be employed. Guerrilla camps were destroyed and the Portuguese would promptly celebrate the creation of a guerrilla-free 'white' zone as the enemy slipped back to the sanctuary of Zambia. The SAS would then move to the next promising area. While they were thus engaged, the guerrillas would start infiltrating back to the zone that was officially cleared. One of the most dramatic operations in this series resulted in two helicopters each depositing four SAS soldiers inside a camp occupied by 300 anti-Portuguese Frelimo guerrillas. Instead of the customary SAS skirmish with a defensive Frelimo rearguard, the error generated 'a fairly exciting punch-up'.

After Portugal's withdrawal from her African colonies

in 1975, the bush war in Rhodesia intensified. As a result, the SAS was obliged to recruit younger, less experienced soldiers, including men 'who were in many cases no more than teenagers', as Graham puts it. 'We placed enormous responsibility on their shoulders and they did things that one would normally expect of seasoned veterans. But it would be wrong to expect the self-discipline we wanted to be evident in every single aspect of these young soldiers' lives. So back in camp, discipline was tight. We dressed correctly, marched properly and generally let Rhodesia know we were as professional on the base as on operations. Instead of joining a mad scramble for elitism, we quietly stuck to the rules. Along with the Rhodesian Light Infantry, which had the same attitude, we eventually got the lion's share of operations without indulging in histrionics or having a General deposited on us through every weekend.' When the rules were broken, 'our misdemeanours were skilfully disguised as somebody else's problem'.

In the peculiar, highly-pressurized circumstances of a country at war, Rhodesia evolved an intensive form of selection, which proved, according to a former member of the British 21 SAS who survived it, highly effective. The volunteers began in a camp near Salisbury with a period of harassment lasting between thirty-six and forty-eight hours. The men had to swim, play football, and run, always carrying bricks. No sleep was permitted. This 'sickener' period deterred a predictably large number of volunteers. It was immediately followed by the equivalent of Hereford's endurance march. Each man carried a forty-pound pack plus rifle, over a twenty-mile course in a hilly area south of Salisbury, in daytime temperatures exceeding 80 degrees Fahrenheit. A series of similar marches followed during the next two weeks, involving accurate map and compass reading and the completion of the route in a time that demanded much of it to be covered at jogging speed.

Even after nominal acceptance, the volunteer was not 'badged' until he had participated in one or more live operations, during which his performance was carefully evaluated. Operational experience, in turn, was only acquired after a period of continuation training, which included Scuba diving and canoeing, to equip members of C Squadron for the many water-borne Commando operations assigned to the SAS. There was also, inevitably, a static-line parachute course. By 1971, the Parachute Training School had recorded 12,000 descents, at which point the Squadron started operational free-fall training. This course, in which four out of ten operational Rhodesian SAS soldiers were trained, normally lasted six weeks and built up each man's experience, if the weather was good, to around fifty jumps from a maximum altitude of 12,000 feet. This included night descents with equipment and was, effectively, the C Squadron equivalent of the British 'HALO' course. One of those concerned with this programme told the author that operational free-fall had been invaluable in placing small teams into enemy territory for reconnaissance or limited offensive tasks, and as pathfinder groups for larger numbers of men who were dropped by more orthodox static-line parachutes. Most operational free-fall descents were nocturnal. The total number of descents of both types, by the time of the Lancaster House constitutional conference, was around 45,000.

As the war intensified, so the SAS specialized in launching surprise attacks against guerrilla bases both inside Rhodesia and across the border in Zambia and Mozambique. One man who took part in some of the raids concluded that they had two objectives: first, to inflict the maximum number of casualties on the guerrillas; secondly, to seize arms, documents and a few prisoners for interrogation. The arms, including Kalashnikov AK-47 rifles, RPG missiles and various anti-aircraft weapons, were taken for use by the Rhodesian forces rather than as propaganda souvenirs.

In a typical cross-border operation after Portugal had withdrawn from her colonies, the troopers parachuted from a mere 450 feet above ground from Dakotas in a dawn assault, only to notice on the ground below 'the enemy, hundreds of black dots like ants, running clear of the perimeter of soldiers dropping around their camp'. These airborne raids were often preceded by Canberra bombing and Hunter missile bombardment, which destroyed the camps but also removed any hope of surprising the occupants. The number of kills increased when free-fall parties led the way in the dark, and were already positioned as ambush 'stop groups' as the main assault began. As an alternative, the SAS were sometimes dropped miles away from their target and advanced to it on foot, in encircling groups in the dark. But this approach, while it preserved surprise, might require several night marches, and was not practicable as an approach to bases deep inside Mozambique or Zambia.

To War by Boat

Such raids did not always proceed according to plan. An attempt to destroy a base in Zambia after an approach by boat across Lake Kariba came to nothing when the assault team failed to find the target and simultaneously lost radio contact (which was by voice on high frequency rather than Morse) with its base. After two tense days and nights, the party re-established contact and was recovered by boat. This was just as well, according to one participant, who discovered that the initial radio exchanges had been intercepted by the Zambian Army, which then evacuated the target camp and waited in ambush for the SAS.

But other water-borne operations were more elaborate, and successful. Graham told the author that the Zambesi River and Lakes Cabora-Bassa, as well as Kariba, were all used as routes into enemy territory. 'Apart from the fairly standard equipment of Klepper canoes and Zodiac inflatables, we sometimes employed much larger "mother ships" equipped with radar and armed with Russian 12.7mm light anti-aircraft weapons which we acquired from people no longer capable of operating them.' Overland assaults by vehicle were also tried. 'We even built two specialized cross-country armoured vehicles based on German military Unimog chassis and fitted with 20mm Hispano cannons taken from inoperable Air Force Vampire jets. We claim no spectacular success with these because a guerrilla war in Rhodesia was very different from the North African desert in the Second World War.'

The operations that appear to have succeeded best were those more in the post-war tradition of the British SAS regiment, comprising parties of between two and eight men moving on foot and at night to mine roads and bridges routinely used by the guerrillas, to sabotage communications and ambush convoys before the patrol melted back into the bush. In this context, the Rhodesian SAS in the seventies was in a similar position to the British regiment in South Arabia in the sixties, acting as counter-guerrillas on one side of the border and guerrillas on the other. Much of the work on both sides was still close reconnaissance by four-man teams, which remained in concealment by day, keeping watch from a distance, and moving close enough to the target by night to obtain detailed information with the help of night-vision equipment. Some teams succeeded in remaining on station doing this stealthy work for weeks at a time, constantly feeding data back to Salisbury without detection. Yet the results of attacks on guerrilla bases that followed these arduous preparations were, as one of those involved observes, sometimes just a matter of luck.

'We sometimes hit the jackpot and returned elated. On other occasions we found that only a "caretaker" group was in camp when we hit it, the real prize having flown the nest between the time of our reconnaissance and the assault. . . . It's the sort of thing which happens to all soldiers, some of the time.'

Because of the very small numbers of men available to the SAS, planning and organization were peculiarly important to Rhodesia, and elaborate care was taken to reduce the risk of error. Until the formation of Combined Operations Headquarters ('Comops') in the mid-1970s, SAS soldiers were 'Army' troops exclusively administered by the headquarters of the brigade in whose area they were based, but for operational matters the Squadron had to report to the Army commander in Salisbury. Linked with this arrangement was a close liaison with the Rhodesian Central Intelligence Organization and the police Special Branch, both of which briefed the SAS on reconnaissance and sabotage missions.

Lessons from Entebbe

After the creation of 'Comops', all lines of command and planning led directly to the military supremo, Peter Walls. Mike Graham's experience was that this made it easier for the SAS to obtain air support, air-photographic reconnaissance and other forms of Intelligence. This development was soon followed, in July 1976, by the Israeli commando raid on Entebbe to rescue more than 100 hostages held by Palestinian and German terrorist hijackers. The Rhodesians studied film of the raid at a time when they were themselves planning an ambitious attack on Chimoio Camp in Mozambique. (That attack was ultimately launched in January 1978, and caused 1500 casualties among supporters of Robert Mugabe.)

An essential ingredient for such a raid, the Rhodesians concluded, was an airborne command post equipped with superlative communications, flying high enough to avoid all but the most sophisticated surface-to-air missiles. As Graham puts it: 'We had seen on the movies how the Israelis used a command Boeing 707, but since Air Rhodesia had only three Boeings we had to lower our sights a bit and ended up with an Air Force VIP Dakota equipped with an incredible range of radio sets and teleprinters and festooned with an incredible array of antennae. It worked excellently and General Peter Walls himself operated from the aircraft many times.'

The SAS's own Intelligence section also evolved to a sophisticated level. 'In addition to the map and air-photographic coverage of any target area, we had a team of seconded cartographers – specialists of great artistic talent – who made extremely lifelike models of the ground to be covered. Our routine in such cases was to start with a "think evil" session, initially with some of our own officers. We would then bring in the Air Force and go through the same routine. Eventually we were doing expert presentations to the War Cabinet.' ('Think-evil' was jargon for anticipating the worst, and for devising the greatest possible damage to the enemy.) 'The final stage was always a briefing to the men from the same model, without disclosing our plan. We outlined the task and set them various problems relating to the operation and placed the men in syndicates to find solutions. Then they came back and we listened to their opinions. Usually, the plan that emerged from the consensus of these sometimes heated discussions was the one we had already chosen, though with occasional modifications suggested by ordinary troopers. By the time we had rehearsed and given formal orders, again by reference to the models, every individual was thoroughly familiar with the task, so familiar that when the unexpected happened – as it usually did – the men were able to figure that out for themselves and react intelligently to changed circumstances. . . .'

Throughout 1977 and 1978, the strength of what was still officially known in Salisbury as 'C Squadron' gradually increased and edged back towards the 250 officers and men it had had in 1961. This development coincided with a general reorganization within the Rhodesian Army and, as a result, C Squadron was renamed the 'Rhodesian Special Air Service Regiment', 'Troops' became 'squadrons', and 'sections' became 'troops'. Interestingly, it was the veterans who were least pleased by this change of title: after enjoying for twenty-seven years the intimate comradeship embodied in the name 'C Squadron', some of them were less sure about the increased anonymity implicit in a full regiment. With the inauguration of black majority rule, many of the longest serving Rhodesian SAS soldiers returned to Britain or went to South Africa, some to join the armed forces there. Others soldiered on, uncertain what future, if any, the recently renamed regiment would have after Lancaster House and the confusion of the election campaign that followed it.

There was one other contribution to the Salisbury Government's war effort by the SAS that is worth recording. This is the birth of the Selous Scouts, a useful military unit, which finally ran out of control and was disbanded. Because of the SAS experience in infiltration techniques and the evolution of the Intelligence methods that those techniques required, it became almost routine for senior subalterns to act as Military Intelligence Officers during their period away from the SAS engaged in staff training. Other, more senior officers, were also seconded for special Intelligence duties with the Special Branch and the Rhodesian Central Intelligence Organization. One of these was Mike Graham, who, with Brigadier John Hickman and a Special Branch officer, recruited black soldiers, policemen and rehabilitated guerrillas for the risky game of penetrating enemy camps by bluff. They were sometimes joined by a few whites whose knowledge of African languages gave them an even chance in the more hazardous role of disguising themselves as Africans. The groups thus formed bore a close, but coincidental resemblance to the multi-racial 'counter gangs' organized by Kitson during the Mau Mau campaign in Kenya during the 1950s. Through these cadres, and as a 'shop window' for disguising more clandestine activities, there also developed a highly-specialized tracking element which could pursue enemy raiding parties to their bases accurately and without detection. What emerged was the Selous Scouts, one of whose members described to the author how the trackers, black and white, operated: 'We would follow a spoor only so long as the sun was on the slant, between the hours of 6 am and 10 am and from 3 pm until dusk. That way we could read the spoor as if it was a guidebook: the crushed grass, the traces of human urine, and so on. Sometimes we laid the ambush ourselves but more frequently we left that to others, having infiltrated the camp itself.'

When the Scouts was formally created, Graham was offered the post of second-in-command but preferred the atmosphere of the exclusively-white SAS, with its emphasis on professional soldiering and careful character selection. He was made a Member of the Legion of Merit (Rhodesia's equivalent of the MBE) for his pioneering work in the formation of the Scouts. Command of the Selous Scouts went to Colonel Ronald Reid-Daly, a former Malayan Scout and a contemporary of General Walls in that unit.

The Kiwi Squadron

The New Zealand Special Air Service Squadron was formed in 1954 to operate with 22 SAS, as New Zealand's contribution to the British Commonwealth Strategic

Reserve in South East Asia. Although New Zealand had had no airborne units as such during the Second World War, it was not entirely without experience and knowledge of such operations. A number of New Zealanders had served with the Long Range Desert Group after it had become parachute-trained. Others had joined the British Parachute Regiment and the original Special Air Service Regiment.

Applications were invited from civilians early in 1955, and a total of 800 were received. The Squadron required men of zeal and high morale who were physically tough and who possessed a high standard of discipline. It was made clear that volunteers must be prepared to undergo parachute training and, in addition to normal parachuting, to parachute into jungle or any other obstacles as was found necessary from time to time. Also, volunteers must be prepared to live for long periods in the jungle, to operate in small parties and participate in operations demanding self-reliance and leadership.

By imposing strict selection standards, the applicants were reduced to 138, and these, together with forty selected officers and non-commissioned officers who had volunteered from the regular Army, marched into Waiouru Camp to commence training on 7 June 1955. The Squadron establishment, which had been fixed at 133, allowed considerable margin for final selection, which was carried out during training. A total of forty-nine men were rejected during this period. Of the force that survived, about one-third were Maoris. Major F. Rennie, MBE, New Zealand Regiment, a regular officer commanding the new unit, was given complete freedom to select regular officers and non-commissioned officers.

The Squadron trained at Waiouru under the direction of its squadron commander. Emphasis was placed on developing physical and emotional endurance, skill-at-arms, minor tactical drills and the preparation for parachute training, which would take place in Malaya.

The new unit also adopted the maroon beret of British Airborne Forces, then still in use among 22 SAS in Malaya, as well as the regimental winged dagger badge and its motto, 'Who Dares Wins'.

Between 20 November and 10 December 1955, the Squadron flew to Malaya to come under the command of 22 SAS. It began immediate parachute training at Changi, Singapore. In addition to the eight descents required for basic military training, the Squadron's members also made on average a further six jumps, three from S-55 helicopters, as part of their continuation training. Two men who had been sent with the Squadron to Malaya without the screening of selection in New Zealand failed their parachute courses and one, who refused to jump, was sent back to New Zealand. Parallel with these jump courses, the Squadron was receiving instruction in jungle warfare during a three-week course in rugged, mountainous terrain in Perak, about 160 miles north of Kuala Lumpur. This initial jungle training was conducted by officers and NCOs of 22 SAS, assisted by an advance party of New Zealanders who had completed the course themselves only a short time before. The process of selecting and training the New Zealanders had taken more than six months, and the Squadron's subsequent performance in the jungle was to demonstrate the value of this cautious and coherent approach to the formation of such a unit.

By the time the Squadron became operational, the SAS had evolved a technique of identifying the enemy in a given area as specific targets. These were usually the terrorists' 'Special Liberation Army' organizations, controlling the aborigines. Having been allocated its target group of terrorists, an SAS squadron would then move deep into the jungle, make contact with the aborigines, and persuade them to move to new quarters such as a fortified jungle fort. It was an axiom of such operations that the confidence of the aborigines was not entirely won over until the terrorists who had controlled them were eliminated. On average, each operation now lasted thirteen weeks, with resupply by air during that time, and this was regarded as the minimum necessary to become familiar with the operational area as well as to influence the aborigines. The New Zealand Squadron's first operation lasted only five weeks, in fact, and it was carried out in Pahang. The target was the remnant of an independent Communist platoon, which had been responsible several years earlier for the murder of a senior diplomat. The operation was planned as a 'reconnaissance in force' to 'shake down' the Squadron as a cohesive fighting machine. The experience, although useful, led to no contact with the terrorist targets.

Ah Ming's Downfall

This operation was followed by two long operations, each of thirteen weeks' duration, in the Fort Brooke area on the Perak-Kelantan border. The main target was a terrorist ASAL organization of approximately eleven, which had controlled the aborigines for a number of years. The terrorist organization was led by Ah Ming, who had dominated the area and the aborigines since the Emergency commenced. During the two operations in this area, eight terrorists, including Ah Ming and his second-in-command, were killed and two terrorists were wounded. An aborigine terrorist was also captured. The Squadron had two casualties, one of them a leading scout who died of wounds after being hit in ambush. During these operations, the Squadron re-grouped a total of approximately 1200 aborigines into two main areas.

The last three long operations were carried out in the mountainous area of Negri Sembilan. The target was a group of twenty-four, consisting of the Communist State Secretary with a party of VIPs, and two armed workforces each under a District Committee member. The terrorist operations in the area were controlled by Li-Hak-Chi who had achieved considerable success against the security forces. The mountainous area was approximately 400 square miles and bounded by roads; it was particularly rugged and provided excellent hides for the terrorist groups. As a result of the Squadron's operations in the area, eight terrorists were killed including Li-Hak-Chi. Two were wounded and nine surrendered.

The original New Zealand SAS Squadron organization consisted of four troops and a squadron headquarters, but after six months' operation it was realized that the size of each troop could be reduced to create a new fifth troop. The Squadron also 'donated' approximately twenty officers and men to the British Special Air Service Regiment as its contribution to that headquarters, and a proportion were also left at the base in squadron administrative appointments. Never at any time did the Squadron deploy more than ninety personnel in the jungle operations. In all, troops spent seventeen months of the twenty-four and a half months in the jungle on operations during the tour in Malaya.

The following statistics give a fair idea of the Squadron's impact on the Malayan campaign in which twenty-six terrorists were killed for the loss of one SAS soldier:

Contacts (Squadron fired first)	10
Incidents (Terrorists fired first)	4
Kills	15
(+ 1 killed by artillery fire in support of the Squadron on Squadron information)	
Surrenders	9
Captures	1
Total eliminations as a result of operations	26

(+ 4 wounded)

Own casualties (died of wounds)   2
The following decorations were awarded to Squadron personnel:

Military Cross   2
British Empire Medal   1
Mention in Dispatches   4
Negri Sembilan Conspicuous Gallantry Medal   2
Negri Sembilan Distinguished Conduct Medal   3

Between operations, opportunity was taken to carry out continuation parachute training and to practise small-party raiding techniques, usually against Royal Air Force airfields in Malaya and Singapore. One large-scale raid with the entire Squadron taking part was carried out against the Kuala Lumpur Royal Air Force airfield.

In addition, members of the Squadron were detailed from time to time as members of a parachute rescue team that was on continuous stand-by to jump into aircraft crash sites in the jungle. One large-scale rescue operation was commanded by a Squadron officer. Also, some Squadron personnel carried out a limited parachute operation against a terrorist target by jumping into an unprepared jungle landing zone. Personnel practised this technique during parachute training, but, because of the hazards involved, it was only undertaken during active operations.

In November/December 1957, the Squadron returned by air to New Zealand and was disbanded, but, when the New Zealand Regular Brigade Group was created in August the following year, the Special Air Service Squadron was included in its permanent order of battle, and was resurrected six months later under the command of Captain J. A. Mace, a member of the original unit. The standard of the selection process imposed then, and maintained since, was such that on average only 25 per cent of those volunteering for SAS duty are accepted. The Squadron also included a nucleus of the Malayan veterans. Parachute training for the new squadron took place in Australia, with continuation training of all kinds being carried out in New Zealand. In 1961, a Territorial element was included to augment the regular squadron should the need ever arise. The reactivated squadron was tasked to function in South East Asia to perform classic SAS roles, including long-range, small-party offensive operations behind enemy lines against troops, materials and communications, as well as routine medium reconnaissance on foot or in wheeled and tracked vehicles.

In May 1962, a detachment of thirty men from the NZSAS Squadron, commanded by Major M. N. Velvin, was sent to Thailand, a fellow member of the South East Asia Treaty Organization, when a deteriorating situation on its northern border (where China, Laos and Burma meet) raised fears of a new guerrilla war. Based at Korat, the detachment assisted US Special Forces in training Thai soldiers and border police in counter-revolutionary warfare.

An official report records that 'the Kiwis' unorthodox methods posed problems for the Thai troops during training. New Zealand soldiers acting as "enemy" arrived in an area where Thai troops were defending a village. The New Zealanders set up a road block some distance away. When a truck appeared, carrying the Thais' prepared lunches, the "insurgents" captured it and drove unchallenged into the village. Recognizing the truck, the Thai soldiers knocked off for lunch and were "mown down" by a burst of concentrated – fortunately blank – fire from the vehicle as it sped through the village and out the other side. About five miles further on, the Kiwis stopped for lunch, having set an ambush party to frustrate any Thai recovery attempts. It was several hours before the baffled Thai troops could contact the American directing staff to transmit an appeal to the New Zealanders to return the food.'

When the crisis had passed, the Squadron was withdrawn from Thailand in September 1962, having received high praise from the Americans. General James L. Richardson, commander of Joint Task Force 116, said that the Kiwi SAS was a remarkable fighting unit. 'If the position in Thailand became worse again, I would be pleased to have you alongside us,' he said. One of Richardson's special forces sergeants commented: 'They're the best people I've met. I'm really sorry to see them go.'

A year later, the New Zealand Army commemorated the centenary of two of its most famous indigenous guerrilla forces – Major Gustavus von Tempsky's Forest Rangers and Major Harry Atkinson's Taranaki Bush Rangers – by renaming the Squadron the 1st Ranger Squadron, NZSAS. The Forest Rangers in particular had adopted guerrilla tactics and deep penetration patrols in pursuit of Maori war parties during the nineteenth-century Maori Wars. An official statement explained: 'The new name is more descriptive of the Squadron's role as an Intelligence unit trained to fight with its own or captured weapons, to live off the country for long periods and to operate by parachute, vehicle, small boat or on foot in order to move fast and stealthily through enemy territory.'

It was not long before the SAS Rangers were in action again in the region. Following a request from the Government of Malaysia, a detachment of forty men of 1st Ranger Squadron, New Zealand Special Air Service, left home in February 1965 to join the Commonwealth force in Malaysian Borneo. No. 1 Detachment, commanded by Major W. J. Meldrum, was located at Kuching, operating in the West Brigade area and sharing facilities with 22 SAS. After seven months, it was replaced by No. 2 Detachment, under Major R. S. Dearing, initially at Kuching and subsequently with 22 SAS Headquarters at Labuan. This detachment also participated in combined operations with the Special Boat Section of the Royal Marines. In February 1966, No. 3 Detachment succeeded No. 2 Detachment; commanded by Major D. Ogilvy it was based at Labuan, operating, like its predecessor, in the Central and East Brigade areas. The Rangers' final tour was by No. 4 Detachment, under Major D. W. S. Moloney, from June 1966 until November, when it was withdrawn to West Malaysia. Throughout the period of Confrontation, a small team of instructors from the Regiment was attached to the Jungle Warfare School at Kota Tinggi, on the Malay Peninsula, as specialists in the art of tracking.

In November 1968 it was decided to augment the New Zealand commitment to South Vietnam by sending an SAS troop to the country. The unit was known as 4 Troop, NZSAS. Based at Nui Dat, it operated in Phuoc Tuy Province, the tactical area covered by the 1st Australian Task Force. It was attached, not surprisingly, to the Australian Special Air Service Squadron and maintained its high reputation as a superlative tracking, jungle reconnaissance and Intelligence-gathering group. Operationally it received close support from helicopters of the Royal Australian Air Force. The troop returned to New Zealand in February 1971.

Aussies in Vietnam

The Australian Special Air Service was raised in July 1957 at Campbell Barracks, Swanbourne, in Western Australia, at a time when the Malayan campaign was all but over. It had a modest beginning as an independent 1st SAS Company, but ample scope – which it used – for expansion within armed forces that hitherto contained no special forces element. In the years since its foundation, the Australian SAS has acquired a monopoly of all commando operations, including those which in Britain would be performed by the Royal Marines and in the US by the Marine Corps. In 1960, the SAS Company became part of the Royal Australian Regiment. It was a brief, but useful, marriage which ended when the Commonwealth forces in Borneo urgently needed an increasing number of SAS soldiers. As a result, the Company was augmented to become the Australian Special Air Service Regiment, retaining the sand-coloured beret of its British counterpart as well as the regimental badge and wings. The date chosen for this expansion was 4 September 1964, anniversary of Australia's first combined land, sea and airborne operation in New Guinea in 1943.

During the four years preceding this expansion, the SAS Company had participated in exercises in Thailand, New Guinea (where Australia still has a military presence) and Okinawa, as well as in Australia itself. After expansion, the Regiment initially comprised a Headquarters, a Base squadron, 1 SAS Squadron, 2 SAS Squadron and a dedicated element of 151 Signals Squadron. A third Sabre squadron was formed in 1966.

The Regiment's first operational tour was by 1 SAS Squadron in Brunei in 1965; subsequently, 2 SAS Squadron saw service in the Kuching area of Borneo. Even fifteen years later, little is said about that period and, if official statements are to be believed, the Australian SAS took no part in the cross-border operations against Indonesia that were undertaken by the Gurkha regiments as well as British and New Zealand SAS soldiers.

Almost simultaneously with its participation in the Borneo campaign, the Australian SAS began operations in Vietnam, where the three squadrons served in rotation from 1966 until 1971. Most of this service was in Phuoc Tuy province, south-east of Saigon. There the Regiment often suffered the galling experience of identifying, through carefully-concealed reconnaissance patrols, large numbers of Vietcong guerrillas, only to lose the quarry in the slow, ponderous follow-up operation by regular American and Vietnamese forces. It was also sometimes difficult for the SAS to adjust its traditionally stealthy jungle tactics to the 'Prince Rupert', cowboy approach of helicopter-borne squadrons of US cavalry, as well as the high-profile, high-technology techniques generally adopted throughout much of the war by the more orthodox US forces.

The Australian SAS now consists of a Headquarters, two Sabre squadrons (1 and 3), a Base squadron, Support Squadron and 152 Signals Squadron. Selection is as stringent as in similar regiments elsewhere. According to Philip Warner, 'The Australian SAS Regiment has a "Recondo" (Reconnaissance/Commando) course in which those chosen to take part endure hunger, thirst, exhaustion and occasional physical danger for three weeks, for an average of only three or four hours of sleep a night. At one point in the course you may reach the coast in time to receive sea transport but if you do not make it you have the mortification of seeing the transport out at sea while you have to face further gruelling journeys because you have missed it.'

Continuation training follows the pattern familiar elsewhere, with a greater emphasis (in the absence of an Australian Marine Corps) on the maritime environment, including diving techniques employed by the Royal Marine Special Boat Section and the US Navy Seal team, with which the Australians run exchange postings. This illustrates one of the characteristics of the Australian regiment, which is its function as a clearing-house of information about special forces operations in much of the western world. While the Vietnam war was being fought, for example, Australian SAS instructors at the Jungle Warfare School in Malaya were relaying to British troops the lessons of that war, in particular the booby-traps – including lorry springs adapted as devices to impale a man against a tree – that the Vietcong had developed. Another example concerns the development of SAS weapons. In Malaya the British SAS pioneered the use of the shotgun as a modern fighting weapon, a lesson they learned from the terrorists. In 1952, a British study of the jungle war revealed that up to seventy-five yards' range the likelihood of hitting a fleeting target in the jungle was greater with a shotgun than any other weapon. The Vietnamese experience, years later, revealed that despite the tons of bombs dropped from high-flying B-52s, about seventy per cent of casualties inflicted on the Vietcong and North Vietnamese forces were caused by infantry weapons. It was an Australian who studied the work of his own SAS regiment in Vietnam and Borneo, Duncan J. Gordon, who followed the logic of contemporary jungle warfare by designing a convertible automatic shotgun able to fire belt-fed ammunition (like an orthodox machine-gun) or carbine-style ammunition carried in a box magazine.

The paradox of this ingenious and expert force is that its home base is remote from any obvious scene of conflict. How, therefore, does the Australian SAS justify its existence? It can do so by reference to two potential hazards to the country's security. One is the external problem of western security generally, in such sensitive areas as the Arabian Gulf. Australia depends on the infrastructure of economic activity in Europe and the US, so its defence interests are ultimately indivisible from those of its allies. At times of international crisis, such as the Soviet invasion of Afghanistan, the SAS is a valuable political instrument through which to express that reality as a military fact.

Somewhat more controversial, but equally important to Australia's military planners, is the potential need to defend a vast continent with a small, professional army. Although it is never officially admitted, and rarely acknowledged privately, Australia still has reason to fear that in an increasingly overcrowded world, its empty space and rich natural resources may make it a target for expansion by any one of several of its neighbours to the north. If Australia were faced, some day, with hostile landings at several widely separated points around its enormous coastline, then only the SAS possesses the mobility and the experience to generate training teams capable of leading local citizens' armies raised from the civilian population, leaving the regular forces to react in force in the area where the enemy attack is concentrated. This theory, expounded by some Australian SAS veterans, is one of the most novel in the canon of SAS military lore.

Appendix B
SAS Casualties, 1950–82

To stay alive, in SAS parlance, is to 'beat the Clock'. This derives from the tradition of carving on the Regiment's memorial clock at Hereford (a collapsible, portable structure) the names of those killed in training or in action. The clock was erected soon after the Regiment occupied its Hereford base in 1980. Each year, the list of those who did not beat the clock grows longer.

Malaya

Tpr T. A. Brown	1950
Pte G. A. Fisher	1950
Tpr J. A. O'Leary	1951
Sgt O. H. Ernst, Rhodesian SAS	1951
Cpl J. B. Davies, Rhodesian SAS	1951
Tpr F. G. Boylan	1951
WO2 W. F. Garrett	1951
Cpl V. E. Visague, Rhodesian SAS	1952
Tpr A. Fergus	1952
Major E. C. R. Barker, B.E.M.	1953
Tpr J. A. S. Morgan	1953
Tpr E. Duckworth	1953
Lt P. B. S. Cartwright	1953
Tpr B. Watson	1953
2/Lt F. M. Donnelly-Wood	1953
Lt (QM) F. S. Tulk	1953
Cpl K. Bancroft	1953
Tpr F. W. Wilkins	1953
Cpl P. G. R. Eakin	1953
Lt J. L. C. Fotheringham	1953
Lt G. J. Goulding	1954
L Cpl C. W. Bond	1954
Tpr B. Powell	1954
Tpr A. E. Howell	1954
Tpr A. R. Thomas, New Zealand SAS	1956
Tpr W. R. J. Marselle	1956
Lt A. G. H. Dean	1957
Cpl A. G. Buchanan, New Zealand SAS	1957
Tpr R. Hindmarsh	1968

Malaysia

Tpr N. P. Ollis	1969

West Malaysia
L Cpl R. Greenwood 1967

Oman (Jabal Akhdar)
Cpl D. Swindells,
  M.M. 1958
Tpr W. Carter 1959
Tpr A. G. Bembridge 1959

Borneo
Maj H. A. I. Thomp-
  son, M.C. 1963
Maj R. H. D. Nor-
  man, M.B.E., M.C. 1963
Cpl M. P. Murphy 1963
Tpr A. Condon 1964
Sgt B. Bexton 1964
Tpr W. E. White 1964
Pte G. H. Hartley 1964

Brunei
Sgt E. Pickard 1973

South Arabia
Capt R. C. Edwards 1964
Tpr J. N. Warburton 1964
Tpr J. Hollingsworth 1966
Tpr M. R. Lambert 1966
Tpr G. F. F. Iles 1967
L Cpl A. G. Brown 1967

Ethiopia
Cpl I. A. Macleod 1968

Oman (Musandam)
L Cpl P. Reddy 1970

Oman (Dhofar)
Capt I. E. Jones 1971
Sgt J. S. M. Moores 1971
Tpr C. Loid 1971
L Cpl D. R. Ramsden 1972
Tpr M. J. Martin 1972
Cpl T. Labalaba,
  B.E.M. 1972
Tpr T. P. A. Tobin 1972
L Cpl A. Kent 1974
Capt S. Garthwaite 1974
Tpr C. Hennessy 1975
L Cpl K. Small 1975
Sgt A. E. Gallagher 1975

France
Maj R. M. Pirie 1972
Sgt S. H. Johnson 1978
Cpl F. M. Benson 1978

Northern Ireland
S-Sgt D. J. Naden 1978
Capt H. R. West-
  macott 1980

UK
Cpl K. Norry 1962
Cpl R. Richardson 1965
Tpr P. C. O'Toole 1965
Tpr J. Hooker 1965
L Cpl J. R. Anderson 1967
L Cpl A. C. Lonney 1968
WO1 E. T. Nugent 1968
Cpl R. N. Adie 1968
Tpr C. P. Martin 1968
WO2 J. E. Daubney 1974

Maj M. J. A.
  Kealy, D.S.O.   1979

South Atlantic
Capt G. J. Hamilton   1982
WO2 L. Gallagher,
  B.E.M.   1982
Sgt P. P. Currass,
  Q.G.M.   1982
Sgt S. A. I. Davidson   1982
Sgt J. L. Arthy   1982
Cpl P. Bunker   1982
Cpl E. T. Walpole   1982
Tpr R. Armstrong   1982

SSM M. Atkinson   1982
S-Sgt P. O'Connor   1982
Sgt W. J. Hughes   1982
Sgt P. Jones   1982
Cpl W. J. Begley   1982
Cpl J. Newton   1982
Cpl R. Burns   1982
Cpl S. Sykes   1982
L Cpl P. Light-
  foot   1982
Cpl M. McHugh   1982
Flt Lt G. Hawkins,
  R.A.F.   1982
Cpl D. McCormack   1982

Appendix C
Operation 'Corporate': SAS Obituaries

(Courtesy of *Mars & Minerva*)

Captain G. J. Hamilton

John Hamilton joined 22 SAS in January 1981. He joined D Squadron and commanded 19 (Mountain) Troop until his death in action on West Falkland on 10 June 1982.

An accomplished mountaineer, he took 19 Troop to the summit of Mount Kenya twice earlier this year.

John was an officer such as to leave the stamp of his personality on all that he did, and a lasting impression remains with all of us who served with him.

His bravery and skill during the Falklands operations were an example for all.

It was his Troop who first landed on South Georgia. Having been forced to withdraw by blizzard conditions, they were involved in two helicopter crashes during their recovery. Despite this setback, it was only a few days later that he led his troop into Grytviken, the culminating moment in the defeat of Argentine forces in South Georgia. Again, during the Pebble Island raid he was in the fore. He personally destroyed four Pucara ground-attack aircraft. On Mount Kent his skill and direction contributed directly to the successful ambush of enemy patrols. Throughout these engagements he displayed a valour that he surpassed only in his last action.

His observation post above Port Howard was discovered by a strong Argentinian patrol. Despite being heavily outnumbered he engaged the enemy and conducted a spirited fight for some considerable time on ground offering little

415

protection. Early in the fight he received fatal injuries. John's courage and professionalism during this action won the praise and admiration of the Argentinian Commander.

WO2 Lawrence Gallagher, B.E.M.

Lawrence joined the Regiment from 9 Squadron Royal Engineers in January 1968, joining Boat Troop (17). His mild, gentle and relaxed manner earned him the nickname 'Lofty'.

About 1970 he was detached to IOSF in Bad-Tolz, where he made many American friends. For the rest of the last 14 years Lawrence has served with the Squadron wherever it has been. It was he who raised the Union Jack first when South Georgia was recaptured (the Argentinians, who were trying to surrender to him at the time, were told to wait).

Because of his strength and physique he was good at most sports, but never used his size to gain unfair advantage. He was impossible to upset, both on and off the sports field.

His honest, straightforward attitude earned him the deserved respect and affection of juniors and seniors alike.

Sergeant Philip Preston Currass, Q.G.M.
(Royal Army Medical Corps)

Phil joined 22 SAS in 1972. He was greatly interested in mountaineering and it was not surprising that on completion of his selection and continuation training he elected to join 19 Mountain Troop.

Here, amongst kindred spirits, he quickly established himself, not only in the mountaineering field, but also as an enthusiastic soldier.

He saw active service in Dhofar, completing a number of operational tours, later serving in Northern Ireland.

His efforts and enthusiasm earned him the award of the Queen's Gallantry Medal.

He and his troop, along with the rest of the squadron, found themselves operating in South Georgia in the very type of terrain they normally chose to climb in! He survived two helicopter crashes on South Georgia.

He was with the squadron on the raid on Pebble Island.

Phil's memory will always be with us, but more especially when in the hills.

24057552 Sergeant Sidney Albert Ivor Davidson

24057552 Sergeant Sidney Albert Ivor Davidson, known by his friends as 'Sid', joined 22 SAS in 1973. He served first in B Squadron, joining D in 1975, becoming a member of Amphibious Troop. He served both in Dhofar and Northern Ireland. During his time with the troop he became an expert on amphibious training, especially canoeing, eventually becoming an instructor in this field.

Sid was renowned for his professionalism, expertise and coolness in difficult situations, and was transferred to Mountain Troop where he again showed his versatility. He and Mountain Troop played an important role in the South Georgia operation where he survived two helicopter crashes. He took part in the successful attack on Pebble Island.

Sid's easy going, understanding attitude combined with his experience and professionalism will be missed by all his friends and colleagues.

Sergeant John Leslie Arthy (Welsh Guards)

'Lofty' came to the Regiment in 1975 and joined 18 Troop (Mobility). In 1977 he transferred to Mountain Troop (19) and was renowned for his climbing skill and boundless enthusiasm. He could make frost-bite sound exciting.

After completing the German Alpine Guides' course in 1979 he was chosen to go on the AMA 'API' Expedition to West Nepal. He was on the summit attempt, which reached 300 feet from the top, but was beaten by driving snow. Later the same year he was on another AMA Expedition, this time to China and Jiazi, where he and another member of the Regiment climbed Tshiburongi (5,928 metres).

He served with the Regiment in both Ireland and Oman and his Troop were responsible for the destruction of 11

Argentinian aircraft on Pebble Island a few days before the helicopter crash in which he died.

Like most big, modest men, Lofty was cheerful and good-natured, and had that rare gift of being able to pass his confidence on to those around him. His climbing skill will be sadly missed in the Troop, the loss of friendship and soldiering ability will be felt by the Squadron and the Regiment.

Corporal Paul Bunker (Royal Army Ordnance Corps)

Paul joined 22 SAS in August 1976 and was posted to 16 Troop, the Free-Fall Troop, where he proved to be a keen parachutist and a more than able and well-liked member.

He joined 19 Mountain Troop in May 1979 and proved to be an extremely capable climber.

With 19 Troop he served in Northern Ireland, West Virginia, Florida, Bavaria and the Falklands.

His troop was the first back onto South Georgia. They landed on the Fortuna Glacier, but their tents were destroyed by a blizzard. During the recovery the following day, two helicopters crashed with the Troop on board. A few days later it was Paul and his Troop who spearheaded the British attack on Grytviken. He was again in action on Pebble Island when the troop helped destroy 11 enemy aircraft.

Paul will always be remembered. His humour, strength and mild manner are a legacy that will long endure.

24110456 Corporal Edward Thomas Walpole (Royal Green Jackets)

Wally joined 22 SAS in 1977 and, until the night of 19 May 1982, when he died in the tragic helicopter crash, he served with D Squadron as Squadron Quartermaster-Sergeant's Assistant.

During this time his mild manner, endless patience and untiring devotion to his duties won him many friends throughout the Regiment and particularly in D Squadron who will recall that whenever they needed anything Wally never let them down. He was a friend who will be sadly missed.

Trooper Raymond Armstrong (Royal Green Jackets)
Paddy joined 22 SAS in 1979. His personal fitness, determination, strength of character and sense of humour stood him in good stead and during his time in D Squadron, Paddy met many people and quickly made a lot of friends. His success on specialist courses reflected his constant resolve to do a job well.

In the Campaign in the South Atlantic, both on South Georgia and the Falkland Islands, Paddy took part in all the D Squadron operations. On Pebble Island, in particular, his skill and professionalism in placing and initiating explosive charges that destroyed a number of enemy aircraft earned him the nickname 'Pucara Paddy'.

His death in the helicopter crash was a sad blow to all.

23969493 SSM Malcolm Atkinson
Malcolm Atkinson or 'Akker' as he was known to his friends, joined G Squadron 22 SAS in 1966. His career spanned 12 fully operational tours in Malaya, Borneo, Aden, Oman and Northern Ireland, a record quite exceptional, even for the Regiment.

Akker will be remembered for his exemplary professional standards, his good humour and his capacity to listen and then advise in the most patient and logical way. In spite of his formidable experience, as SSM of G Squadron he remained as always utterly approachable. His greatest and most unselfish concern was always the welfare of his men whether at a personal, social level or in ensuring that the training and preparation for operations by his Squadron were relevant, exacting and designed to give the greatest fulfilment to those involved.

It was while he was supervising the movement of equipment vital to the operation of his Squadron on the Falkland Islands that the helicopter in which he was travelling crashed. The loss of such a character, who had given so much and for whom a continuing and successful career was assured, is inestimable.

Staff-Sergeant P. O'Connor (Irish Guards)

Paddy came to 22 SAS in 1966. He was quick to impress on his arrival. A man of immense character and good humour, possessing an ever-present twinkle. He was a true professional, never afraid to speak his mind and always adopting an intelligent, honest, determined and responsible approach to his work.

He served with us in South Arabia, Belize, Northern Ireland, Dhofar, Norway and the United States. He was a specialist Signaller, skilful free-fall parachutist and a qualified Norwegian speaker. It is particularly tragic that Paddy, like others killed in the same crash, should lose his life in such a pointless and wasteful way.

He will be very sorely missed by his many friends in the Regiment.

24076141 Sergeant William John Hughes (Welsh Guards)

'Taff' joined 22 SAS in October 1972.

For three years Taff proved his utter reliability, complete application to his duties and a preparedness to work uncomplainingly for long hours. In 1975 he came to G Squadron as the Storeman, bringing with him all the attributes already described but also an irrepressible sense of humour. He soon became an invaluable and respected member of his Squadron, completing in the course of the next seven years, a total of 12 Squadron moves on operational or training tasks. Successive Squadron Quartermaster-Sergeants speak of their great good fortune in having Taff, with his great knowledge of accounting, equipment procurement and capacity for hard work, as the lynch pin of Squadron administration over this period.

No request was ever too much trouble. Totally uncomplaining, his loyalty to his Squadron and concern over his responsibility towards its welfare was absolute. On the night of 19 May 1982, while supervising the Cross Deck Movement of the Squadron Stores, the helicopter in which he was a passenger crashed. Taff was killed. He will be most sorely missed by his Squadron and many friends.

24154752 Corporal William Clark Hatton, Q.G.M.

Willy joined G Squadron 22 SAS as a member of the Amphibious Troop in July 1978 with whom he served until his tragic death in a helicopter accident in the South Atlantic on 19 May 1982.

His zest for life and inexhaustible enthusiasm were ideally suited to the varied tasks of an SAS Sabre Squadron. He became the first fully qualified diving supervisor in the Regiment. His foresight and inspiration in diving skills were largely responsible for the resurgence of interest and expertise in diving within his Regiment. He was present with his Squadron on four operational tours in Northern Ireland when his vast depth of experience in that theatre was of quite inestimable value. He spearheaded the involvement of the Regiment in the Falklands Crisis with a short attachment to the 2 Special Boat Section. He was instrumental, during this attachment in the success of the capture of the Argentine 'Spyship' *Narwhal*.

Willy, with all his attributes, his personality and personable companionship, achieved the undisputed respect of his Squadron and all those in the Regiment who were fortunate enough to have served with him. His loss has been a cruel blow.

Sergeant P. Jones (Welsh Guards)

'Taff' Jones died in the helicopter crash whilst serving in the South Atlantic. The loss of such an outstanding personality has been deeply felt by all the members of G Squadron.

From the start of his military career, at the age of 15 as a Junior Soldier, his strong open and cheerful character brought him immediate recognition. Whether playing Rugby for the Welsh Guards or as a young Lance-Sergeant with the Guards' Parachute Company, his intelligence, sound commonsense and ever present humour backed by endless energy and enthusiasm constantly shone through.

In 1975 Taff joined 22 SAS. During his time in G Squadron it was typical that he never missed an operational tour. When the Falklands Campaign started he was one of the first from the Regiment to go out. As one of the most experienced divers in the Regiment he had added to an already wide experience which promised him an exceptional future. There was also the ever buoyant, sociable friend and dedicated fisherman as well as professional soldier. Whenever and wherever possible the rods would appear and Taff would disappear fishing. We will greatly miss his direct and cheerful spirit.

24122095 Corporal William John Begley
(Royal Corps of Transport)

Bill Begley joined 22 SAS in 1978 and soon opted to try the Selection Course, which he successfully completed in August 1979.

'Paddy', as he inevitably became known to his friends, was small in stature but large in heart, humour and determination. His modest, unassuming demeanour concealed a durable, quick-witted character always striving to achieve the highest professional standards. His conduct on operations or training exercises was always immaculate. In his three years with the Squadron his contribution to operational tours, his example as an experienced mountaineer and not least as a devoted family man, has been an example to us all.

Paddy had an assured future. This makes the tragedy of his loss in a helicopter accident in the South Atlantic all the more poignant. He will be most sorely missed by his Squadron and many friends.

24386053 Corporal John Newton
(Royal Electrical and Mechanical Engineers)

John Newton joined the Infantry Junior Leader's Battalion at Shorncliffe in 1975. His intention had always been to become a member of the Parachute Regiment. However, because of an injury sustained during his Para Selection Course, this was not to be and in 1977 he transferred to the Royal Electrical and Mechanical Engineers. The excellent grounding provided by the IJLB had served to increase his interest in weapons and so his choice of REME was most natural giving ample opportunity for him to exercise his instructional flair as well as becoming master of their maintenance and repair.

In 1980 he joined 22 SAS and soon became an invaluable member of the team of armourers who support the Regiment. His good humour, discretion and above all his professional expertise confirmed for him a position of deep respect with those Sabre Squadrons with whom he worked. Exercises in Greece and Kenya tested his skills of improvisation to the complete satisfaction of those he was supporting. Just prior to the Falkland Crisis he qualified as a Parachutist.

His time at Hereford allowed him full rein for a variety of sporting activities, including rock climbing, free-fall parachuting, cricket, squash and regular turn-outs for the Regimental and local rugby teams. He was a founder member of the Hereford Army Gun Club.

On the night of 19 May during a routine cross deck operation in the South Atlantic, the Sea King helicopter in which he was travelling crashed. His loss, with all his potential, zest for life and excellent prospects for the future was the cruellest of blows. He will be sorely missed by his great many friends in 22 SAS and throughout the Army.

24369281 Corporal Rab Burns

Rab joined the Army Apprentice College at Harrogate as a Radio Telegraphist in September 1975. He completed his training in August 1977 after a successful two years during which he was promoted to A/T L/Cpl. In September of that year he was posted to 244 Signal Squadron (Air Support) at RAF Brize Norton. He volunteered to serve in Hereford in March 1979, and successfully completed the Signals

Selection Course. After a short period he was then posted to G Squadron and during his time with the SAS was awarded the GSM for service in Northern Ireland. Rab was a quiet but happy person with a passion for the bagpipes and was a gifted piper. He will be much missed by his friends.

24256419 Corporal Steve Sykes

Steve enlisted originally into the RAC Junior Leader's Regiment in September 1972 where he served for a year. During this period he became interested in communications and at his own request was transferred to the Army Apprentice College, Harrogate, in May 1973. In 1975 he completed his training as a Radio Telegraphist and immediately volunteered for service with the Parachute Brigade. Unfortunately at this time the Army was being reorganized and after service with his new unit, for only two months, 216 (Parachute) Signal Squadron, was disbanded and he was posted to BAOR to serve with 604 Signal Troop in Munster. Steve still hankered after parachute training however and in February 1978 was accepted into the Signal Squadron after undergoing Signals selection. Steve was awarded the GSM for service in Northern Ireland and gained the distinction of being top student on his RTG A1 course in January this year. He was a keen parachutist, a cross-country skier and runner and ran in the SAS Regimental Marathon in September 1981. He much deserved his recent promotion and as a cheerful steady worker will be much missed by his friends and contemporaries.

24442111 L Corporal Paul Lightfoot

Paul enlisted in August 1977 and followed in his father's footsteps when he chose both the Army Apprentice College at Harrogate and the trade of Radio Telegraphist. After completing his apprenticeship in August 1979 he was posted to 11 Signal Regiment where he volunteered for 264 SAS Signal Squadron, successfully completed the signals selection course in October 1979. During his time with G Squadron he gained the GSM for service in Northern Ireland.

Paul was a cheerful and popular young man who enjoyed his job and was keen to pass the SAS Selection, towards which goal he was training hard physically.

24398223 Corporal Michael McHugh

Michael enlisted in the Army in August 1976, when he was sixteen. He joined the Royal Signals Junior Leader's Regiment at Warcop and after a year's training was posted to 8 Signal Regiment at Catterick and completed trade training as a Radio Telegraphist in February 1978. He volunteered for service with 264 SAS Signal Squadron and completed the Signals Selection Course in June 1978. During his time with G Squadron he was awarded the GSM with Clasp for Northern Ireland. Michael was a very fit young man and an excellent down-hill skier. He had a cheerful personality, was popular with his Squadron and will be sadly missed by all who knew him.

Flight-Lieutenant Garth Hawkins, RAF

Garth first worked with the Regiment in Canada in 1979. By 1982 he had served with all Squadrons, both in UK and Overseas, and had extended his considerable influence to the TA as well.

Instinctively one knew that his genial bulk, infectious grin and unkempt appearance suited him well for work with Special Forces. What may not have been so apparent for those who worked alongside him, was that in addition to being a brilliant expert in his own field, and a patient but exacting instructor, he was also a keen and gifted cricketer and footballer, who was always the last to leave the clubhouse after any party. Somehow he also found time to be a pub owner, property dealer, dog lover, car enthusiast, gardener, builder and musician. He was also an intensely devoted family man.

Garth was a larger than life character who commands all our respect for what he gave to the Regiment. He will be sorely missed both professionally and personally.

Corporal Douglas McCormack (Royal Signals)

Doug McCormack was Garth Hawkins' signaller and partner. Wherever Garth's hatless figure appeared the faithful
Doug would not be far behind, driving the Land-Rover,
operating the radio set, cooking the meal, taking Dougal or
Biggles for a walk, or paying for the next beer. The two were
inseparable and had intense loyalty and respect for each
other, and were perhaps a supreme example of a special
forces team in action.

Doug was also an intensely devoted family man and
private individual with many hidden talents. Few of his rank
or age group for example are German linguists.

His life's ambition was to join 264 (SAS) Signal Squadron,
and ultimately the Regiment. Tragically he died alongside
members of both, having volunteered yet again to be with
Garth.

Bibliography

Books

Banks, J. *The Wages of War*. Leo Cooper, London, 1977

Barthrop, M. *Crater to the Creggan: The Royal Anglian Regiment, 1964–74*. Leo Cooper, London, 1976

Barzilay, D. *The British Army in Ulster*, Vols. 2 and 3. Century Services, Belfast, 1973, 1978; Beekman Publications, New York, 1976

Beaumont, R. A. *Military Elites: Special Fighting Units in the Modern World*. Robert Hale, London, 1976; Bobbs-Merrill, Indianapolis, 1974

Blaxland, G. *The Regiments Depart: The British Army, 1945–70*. William Kimber, London, 1971

Burchett, W. and Roebuck, D. *The Whores of War*. Penguin, London and New York, 1977

Clutterbuck, R. *Guerrillas and Terrorists*. Faber and Faber, London, 1977

Colvin, I. *The Rise and Fall of Moise Tshombe*. Leslie Frewin, London, 1968

Cowles, V. *The Phantom Major*. Collins, London, 1958; Harper and Row, New York, 1958

Darby, P. *British Defence Policy East of Suez, 1947–1968*. Oxford University Press, Oxford and New York, 1973

Dempster, C. and Tomkins, D. *Fire Power*. Corgi, London, 1978

Devlin, P. *The Fall of the Northern Ireland Executive*. Paddy Devlin, Belfast, 1975

Dillon, M. and Lehane, D. *Political Murder in Northern Ireland*. Penguin, London and New York, 1973

Dobson, C. and Payne, R. *The Weapons of Terror: International Terrorism at Work*. Macmillan, London, 1979

Farran, R. *Winged Dagger*. Collins, London, 1948

Fleming, J. and Faux, R. *Soldiers on Everest*. HMSO, London, 1977

Fox, Robert. *Eyewitness Falklands: A Personal Account of the Falklands Campaign.* Methuen London Ltd, London, 1982

Greenwood, C. *Police Tactics in Armed Operations.* Arms and Armour Press, London, 1980

Halliday, F. *Arabia Without Sultans.* Penguin, London and New York, 1974, 1975

– *Armed Struggle in Arabia: Counter Insurgency in Oman.* The Gulf Committee, 1976

Harper, S. *Last Sunset.* Collins, London, 1978

Harris, Robert. *Gotcha! The Media, The Government and The Falklands Crisis.* Faber and Faber, London, 1983

Hart, Sir Basil H. Liddell. *The Sword and the Pen: A Collection of the World's Greatest Military Writings.* Cassell, London, 1978; T. Y. Crowell, New York, 1976

Hastings, Max and Jenkins, Simon. *The Battle For The Falklands.* Michael Joseph, London, 1983

Hoare, M. *Congo Mercenary.* Robert Hale, London, 1967; Walker and Co., New York, 1967

James, H. D. and Sheil-Small, D. *A Pride of Gurkhas.* Leo Cooper, London, 1975

Kitson, F. *Bunch of Five.* Faber and Faber, London, 1977

Maclean, F. *Eastern Approaches.* Jonathan Cape, London, 1949; US title: *Escape to Adventure.* Little Brown, Boston, 1950

Mockler, A. *Mercenaries.* Macdonald, London, 1970

Paget, J. *Last Post: Aden 1964–67.* Faber and Faber, London, 1969; Faber and Faber, Salem, 1969

Pocock, T. *Fighting General – The Public and Private Campaigns of General Sir Walter Walker.* Collins, London, 1973

Seale, P. and McConville, M. *The Hilton Assignment.* Temple Smith, London, 1973; Praeger, New York, 1973

Smiley, D. and Kemp, P. *Arabian Assignment.* Leo Cooper, London, 1975

Smith, E. D. *East of Katmandu* (7th Duke of Edinburgh's Own Gurkha Rifles). Leo Cooper, London, 1976

Stirling, D. 'The Special Air Service' (from *The World History of Paratroopers* by Pierre Sergent). Soc. de Prod. Litteraire, Paris, 1974

Sunday Express Magazine team. *War In The Falklands.* Weidenfeld and Nicolson Ltd, London, 1982

Sunday Times Insight Team. *Ulster.* Penguin, London and New York, 1972

– *The Falklands War: The Full Story.* André Deutsch, London; Sphere Books, London, 1982

Swearengen, T. F. *The World's Fighting Shotguns.* Arms and Armour Press, London, 1979; T.B.N. Enterprise, Alexandria, 1978

Taber, R. *The War of the Flea: A Study of Guerrilla Warfare, Theory and Practice.* Paladin, London, 1970; Citadel Press, Secaucus, 1970

Ten Years of Terrorism: Collected Views. Royal United Services Institute, London, 1979; Crane Russak, New York, 1979

Townsend, J. *Oman: The Making of the Modern State.* Croom Helm, London, 1977; St Martin's Press, New York, 1977

Walker, General Sir Walter. *The Bear at the Back Door.* Foreign Affairs Publishing Co., London, 1978

Warner, P. *The Special Air Service.* William Kimber, London, 1971

Watson, P. *War on the Mind: The Military Uses and Abuses of Psychology.* Hutchinson, London, 1978; Basic Books, New York, 1978

Young, D. *Four Five: 45 Commando, Royal Marines, 1943–71.* Leo Cooper, London, 1972

Periodicals

Daily Express, 13 January 1976; *Daily Mail,* 17 September 1977; *Daily Mirror,* 19 December 1977; *Daily Telegraph,* 4 February 1970; *Guardian,* 11 December 1976 and 3 August 1979; *Mars & Minerva* (Journal of the SAS Regiment); *Republican News,* 24 June 1978; *Sunday Dispatch* (series), September 1959; *Sunday People,* 6 August 1967; *Sunday Times,* 18 January 1970, 9 May 1976, 10 July 1977, 17 July 1977 and 27 November 1977; *The Times,* 9 April 1959; *Time Out,* 21–27 July 1978 and 8–14 December 1978; *Wire* (The Journal of the Royal Corps of Signals).

Index